INTR

MARINE INSURANCE

Training Notes for Brokers

Second Edition

Author of

Dictionary of Marine Insurance Terms & Clauses
Marine Insurance Principles & Basic Practice
Marine Insurance Cargo Practice
Marine Insurance Hull Practice
The Insurance of Merchant Ships & Shipowners' Interests
Marine Reinsurance Terms & Abbreviations
Marine Insurance and Re-Insurance Abbreviations in Practice
Co-author of
Marine Reinsurance (Brown & Reed)
Lloyd's Market Practice (Brown & Wormell)
Handbook to Marine Insurance (Dover & Brown)

British Library Cataloguing in Publication Data
Brown, Robert H
Introduction to Marine Insurance
Training Notes for Brokers
Insurance – Second Edition
1 Title

ISBN 1 85609 079 5

Introduction
to
Marine Insurance

Training Notes for Brokers

Second Edition

Robert H Brown,
F.Inst. A.M.

London

Witherby & Co. Ltd.
32-36 Aylesbury Street
London EC1R 0ET

First Edition 1987
Second Edition 1995

WITHERBY

PUBLISHERS

Printed and Published by
Witherby & Co. Ltd.
32-36 Aylesbury Street
London EC1R 0ET
Tel No. 0171 251 5341
Fax No. 0171 251 1296

INTRODUCTION TO MARINE INSURANCE

SECOND EDITION

This is the first in a series of reading courses written by R. H. Brown to cover technical marine insurance. It is based largely on the practice of insurance broking in the London market; but provides useful instruction for all who have newly joined the practice of marine insurance. These notes may be used also as a refresher for those practitioners who have not previously enjoyed formal instruction in the subject. Anyone intending to follow the subsequent courses in this series is advised to study the introductory course first.

Training officers giving verbal instruction based on this course should allow approximately one and half hours for each section. It is advisable that instruction be supported by OHP illustration and further examples to illustrate the text.

In this, the second, edition the text of the earlier edition has been updated, restructured and rewritten. This edition of the course book embraces, amongst other things, an introduction to the single market at Lloyd's and, insofar as they affect the scope of this course, other changes in London market practices and procedures. However, during the rewriting process further changes in London market practice and procedures have been proposed and some of these have been adopted. Trainees and practitioners reading these notes must appreciate that marine insurance practice adapts to meet the demands of progress in worldwide commercial practices and it is advisable for one to keep abreast of market changes; updating these notes further, as necessary. When the text is revised for a new printing the revised page heading will indicate the date and/or year when the text on the page was revised.

CONTENTS

SECTION ONE

INTRODUCTION TO MARINE INSURANCE

1. The History and Development of Marine Insurance Practice
2. Trade in Relation to Marine Insurance and the Documentary Credits System
3. Export Credit Guarantee Insurance
4. Customary Methods for Sale of Goods and the Need for Insurance
5. The Importance of Marine Insurance in Trade and Commerce
6. The Insurance of Ships

SECTION ONE

1. The History and Development of Marine Insurance Practice

Marine insurance is the earliest form of insurance to be practised. It is believed that a form of mutual insurance was practised in China around 4000 BC but there is no evidence of private underwriters offering insurance protection at that time. Early records indicate that marine insurance underwriting was practised in Genoa, Pisa and Florence during the 14th century. It is believed that a Florentine policy issued in 1523 formed the basis of the SG form of policy that was adopted by Lloyd`s in the 18th century.

Whilst the introduction of marine insurance into London is still somewhat obscure it seems to have co-incided with the arrival of the Lombards from Italy. This family of merchants and financiers settled in the City of London and it was from these influential people that Lombard Street derived its name and reputation as the financial centre of London.

It was in the coffee houses located in the area around Lombard Street that private financiers would operate as merchant underwriters writing risks offered to them by brokers acting as intermediaries for merchant adventurers trading with overseas markets. It is interesting to note that there was no sharp division between brokers and underwriters in those early days. A merchant might well act as a broker or underwriter for other merchants and, from time to time, an underwriter might act as a broker in negotiating risks with other underwriters. John Julius Angerstein, one of the leading characters in the London market during the 18th century, acted as both a broker and an underwriter in Lloyd`s coffee house. Today, of course, no Lloyd`s broker is permitted to accept risks as an underwriter in the Room at Lloyd`s, nor to act as an underwriting agent (other than as a members` agent); although this does not restrict a broker from being a "name" in a Lloyd`s syndicate.

It was common practice for a merchant to have his own ship to carry his goods; although some merchants entrusted their goods to others to carry. A ship laden with goods and exposed to risk was termed a "marine adventure" (MIA, 1906, sect. 3). To finance an adventure the merchant would borrow money from a financier (the Lombards and Jewry often providing the finance for the adventure). The security for the loan was usually vested in the ship and goods at risk. This security was constantly exposed to risk from marine perils throughout the voyage so, as additional security, the lender would insist that the borrower should effect an insurance contract from which the financial loss could be recovered if the security was lost or diminished by an insured peril. This practice created a need for insurance protection and an insurance market developed from this need.

Details of the insurance cover were set out in a contract by which the insurer would "underwrite" the risk; that is to say he would undertake (ie guarantee) to make good the loss. It was from this practice that the term "underwriter" was given to the guarantor. The contract became known as a "policy of insurance". As a matter of interest Samuel Johnson`s dictionary of 1790 states that the word "policy" comes from the Spanish word "polica" which is based on latin and means "a warrant for money" (the word "warrant" in this context meaning "promise"). The underwriter would be acceptable to the lender as security for the loan only if he was a person of considerable financial standing who was prepared to back policies written by him to the full extent of his personal fortune.

Private underwriters would make themselves available for business in the various coffee houses to be found at that time in the City of London; probably the most famous of these establishments being Edward Lloyd's coffee house in Lombard Street. Edward Lloyd had been master of an earlier coffee house located in Salutation Precinct, off Tower Street, but there is no evidence to indicate that insurance business was conducted there. He moved to the Lombard Street coffee house in 1691; so the name *Lloyd's* was not associated with insurance practice until the latter part of the 17th century.

The risks entailed in private underwriting were all too apparent in a world disturbed by political upheaval and many private underwriters suffered severely from war losses. Perhaps the biggest blow to the developing market came in 1693 when the, so called, Smyrna Fleet suffered tremendous losses in the Bay of Lagos, off the coast of Portugal.

The Smyrna Fleet, which comprised a convoy of some 400 ships (mainly Dutch and British), was attacked by a French force which completely overwhelmed the 24 escorting men of war; resulting in the loss or capture of nearly 100 merchantmen. The overall loss of ships and cargo was estimated at over £1,000,000. Although the risk was spread over many underwriters only the richest of these were able to survive this catastrophe and many underwriters faced ruin with the complete loss of their personal fortunes. The Smyrna Fleet disaster had far reaching effects, because it caused merchants and money lenders to doubt the security offered by private underwriting. Further, the remaining underwriters began to consider the desirability of excluding war risks cover from policies of marine insurance; thereby giving merchants, shipowners and financiers further cause for concern.

Attempts were made by merchants to discourage private underwriting and some private underwriters suggested this be countered by offering consolidated facilities in the formation of insurance corporations. The suggestion met with little success at the time and would, in any case, have been thwarted by the introduction of the "Bubble Act" in June, 1721. It is a matter of historic record that, during the latter part of the 17th century and the early part of the 18th century, a number of very speculative "wild cat" schemes appeared in the City of London which resulted in ruin to many small speculators. This state of affairs came to a head with the collapse of the "South Sea Trading Company" (commonly referred to as the "South Sea Bubble"); following which the British Government introduced the "Bubble Act". The Act prohibited underwriting in partnerships and curbed the formation of insurance companies. The Act, also, prohibited the practice of reinsurance in the UK; which probably stifled the development of the London marine insurance market for over 100 years. Two insurance organisations continued to operate in the London company market throughout this period of restraint because they had been granted Royal Charters on the 22 June, 1720, and were exempt from the restrictions of the Bubble Act regarding formation of companies. These were the "Royal Exchange Assurance Corporation" (which had been writing marine insurance risks since 1515) and the "London Assurance". Between them these organisations held a monopoly of the company insurance market until the Bubble Act was repealed in 1824.

2. Trade in Relation to Marine Insurance and the Documentary Credits System

Whilst it might be desirable, from the point of view of public policy, for ships and goods to be always insured when at risk there is no compulsion, in English law, for either of these interests to be insured. A shipowner is at liberty to expose his ship to risk without insurance and a cargo owner has the same rights regarding the goods at risk. In practice, a party with an uninsured interest at risk is termed a "self insurer" and a party who insures only part of his interest in a particular risk is termed a "co-insurer".

Circumstances usually determine the need for insurance protection. In the case of a ship a mortgagee may make it a condition of the loan that the ship be insured to protect his security. As we have seen earlier, a lender of money to finance a cargo adventure would require the shipper to effect an insurance contract to protect his security. A similar system to the latter operates today where a bank discounts a letter of credit. In any event, to be self insured, a shipowner or merchant would need to set aside a substantial sum of money to protect his business from the effect of losses. Insurance provides these reserves and frees the assured`s capital for use as cash flow if needed. Thus, marine insurance has become a practical necessity for sound business protection; growing from need rather than from persuasion.

Although it is not directly connected with insurance practice the cargo insurance trainee should be aware of the basics of the documentary credits system for payment of goods exported abroad. This system relates to insurance when one of the documents used in the system is an insurance policy or an insurance certificate; in practice it is most likely to be the latter (eg a certificate issued off a cargo open cover). The system is designed to protect the interests of both seller and buyer. It seeks to protect the seller from non-payment for goods which have been forwarded before payment therefor has been received; and to protect the buyer from loss of money paid in advance where goods fail to arrive. The system operates on the understanding that payment for the goods is guaranteed once the goods have arrived at the port or place of discharge from the overseas vessel; but no payment is made if the consignment fails to arrive at the port or place of discharge.

The documentary credits system is so called because everything depends on the documents involved. These are as follows:

1 - A letter of credit
2 - An export invoice
3 - A bill of lading

Where the buyer includes the insurance premium in the letter of credit (eg the goods are purchased on CIF terms) a policy or certificate of insurance will be added to the documents listed above . The export invoice and the bill of lading are termed "documents of title" because they are evidence that the holder has title to the goods specified therein. The procedure operates in stages as follows:

Stage 1 - The seller issues an export invoice for the price of the goods, but does not send it to the buyer. The export invoice is retained by the seller until the goods are shipped.

Stage 2 - The buyer, having agreed the purchase contract, arranges for his bank to send a letter of credit to the seller. This document is irrevocable but will not be honoured by the issuing bank until it has been confirmed by the buyer.

Stage 3 - The seller places the goods in the hands of the overseas carrier and receives a bill of lading from the carrier. The bill of lading incorporates the conditions of carriage and is deemed to be a receipt for the goods described therein. Initially it is a "received for shipment" bill which does not guarantee the goods have been shipped on the overseas vessel. When the goods are shipped the bill of lading is either endorsed "shipped" or is replaced with a "shipped" bill of lading. The documentary credits system demands that the bill of lading be "clean". A clean bill of lading is one which is not qualified in any way to show the goods were other than as described therein and were in a sound condition when received by the carrier. A bill of lading that bears any qualification regarding the condition and/or quantity of the goods is termed a "dirty" or "foul" bill.

Stage 4 - The seller now holds the letter of credit, the export invoice and the bill of lading. Where the conditions of sale so demand the seller must provide, also, evidence of insurance (a policy or certificate). The seller forwards these documents to the bank that is to represent his interests in the system. The bank may be prepared to "discount the letter of credit" by advancing the amount due thereon, less a commission for the service, to the seller. In such case the bank will insist on a certificate of insurance or a policy being incorporated with the documents, irrespective of whether or not the terms of sale demand such evidence of insurance. A bank will often dictate the conditions on which such insurance be effected.

Stage 5 - Where the seller`s bank has discounted the letter of credit the bank forwards the documents to the buyer`s bank; retaining the insurance document except where this is demanded by the conditions of sale. Where the seller`s bank has not discounted the letter of credit the bank forwards all the documents to the buyer`s bank. The buyer`s bank retains the documents until the buyer confirms the letter of credit.

Stage 6 - When the overseas carrying vessel arrives at the port or place of discharge the goods are placed in the care of a warehouseman by the carrier; the carrier retaining a maritime lien on the goods until the consignee produces the bill of lading as evidence of title and takes delivery. The consignee is advised of the location of the discharged goods but cannot take delivery without production of the bill of lading.

Stage 7 - The buyer (the consignee) goes to his bank and confirms the letter of credit; in exchange for which he receives the documents held by his bank. The buyer`s bank arranges for transfer of the amount specified in the letter of credit to the seller`s bank who, if the letter of credit has not been already discounted, credits the seller`s account with this amount.

Stage 8 - The consignee presents the bill of lading to the warehouseman, signs a receipt for the goods, and takes delivery.

With development of international computerised communication networks the documents in the above system will be almost certainly be replaced with electronic messages when satisfactory security safeguards can be incorporated in networks. To accommodate such changes it will probably be necessary to introduce a new procedure whereby shippers and forwarders will be responsible for delivery of the goods to the named destination (often up country from the discharge port). Cargo insurance practitioners are advised to watch developments in this respect.

3. Export Credit Guarantee Insurance

Export credit guarantee insurance is intended to protect the assured from financial loss suffered following non-payment for goods he has exported on trust. The cover does not protect the assured from the consequences of unscrupulous clients who take delivery of goods but refuse to pay for them. A seller who has doubts about the integrity of a buyer should use the documentary credits system to ensure payment. The export credit guarantee insurance would be used, for example, in circumstances where the seller has, rightly, placed trust in the buyer but the latter is prevented from paying by some national currency control or, perhaps, due to insolvency of the buyer.

The existence of an ECG insurance contract encourages the assured to trade with buyers in countries to which he might, otherwise, be less inclined to export. To encourage trade, particularly with developing countries, the British Government formed the Export Credits Guarantee Department (ECGD) which offered both long term and short term insurance protection against non-payment for goods supplied by British exporters. The ECGD cover was not designed to embrace inevitable loss. Until changes took place in 1990 ECGD cover was available, at the discretion of the Department, for individual consignments or for the seller`s whole export account in respect of exports to specific areas. But, during 1990, the ECGD`s short term portfolio was privatised; leaving the Department with only the long term portfolio.

4. Customary Methods for Sale of Goods and the Need for Insurance

There are many ways in which goods can be sold, depending on the agreement between the parties; and, often, the need to effect insurance for seller and/or buyer becomes apparent from the terms of sale. Below are listed some of the more common abbreviations used for terms of sale with comments on the seller`s and buyer`s interest and responsibilities regarding the goods; and the extent to which each party should arrange insurance protection.

CIF (Cost, insurance and freight) - This is a very common term of sale used in respect of goods sold to an overseas buyer who is prepared to leave all arrangements and provision of insurance protection to the seller. The parties agree a price for the goods which incorporates the cost of the goods (ie the prime cost plus a profit margin) plus the insurance premium plus the cost of shipping the goods to the overseas discharge port (the latter cost being termed "freight") The seller has effected the insurance contract and assigns the policy (or certificate of insurance in most cases) to the buyer. The seller is responsible for all expense incurred in connection with carriage of the goods to the point where the goods are delivered to the consignee at the port of discharge.

The seller retains the insurable interest in the goods until title is passed to the buyer; which is usually at the point when the buyer pays for the goods by confirming the letter of credit. The assignee`s insurable interest in the goods does not attach until title for the goods passes to him; but, because the insurance document has been assigned to him, he acquires all rights of the assignor and can claim on the policy or certificate, as the case may be, as though he held an insurable interest throughout the period of cover.

Although the seller`s insurable interest will cease when transfer of title takes place it is customary for the seller to effect the insurance contract to cover the goods on a "warehouse to warehouse" basis so that insurance cover does not terminate on transfer of title, nor (unless this be the final warehouse) on delivery of the goods to the consignee at the port of discharge, but to continue until delivery at the final destination warehouse at the end of transit.

In the case of a CIF sale valuation of the goods for insurance purposes is usually expressed as CIF + ...% (prime cost of the goods, plus the premium, plus freight charges, plus a percentage to allow for profit on the prime cost). In this respect attention is directed to policy valuation in section 4 of these notes. It is not normally necessary for a separate seller`s interest insurance contract to be effected; although a seller might consider effecting a policy to cover the goods awaiting disposal at the place of discharge in the event that the buyer fails to confirm the letter of credit. Such seller`s interest policy should make provision to insure the goods during their disposal or return to the seller; but is unlikely to cover costs incurred by the seller in regard to the disposal or return transit.

C & F (Cost and freight) - This is the same as a CIF sale contract but with the difference that the seller does not effect insurance protection for the buyer and does not incorporate an insurance premium in the price of the goods. The responsibility of the seller to meet transport expenses is the same as for a CIF contract and the seller retains an insurable interest in the goods until passage of title when the letter of credit is confirmed. It is expected that the buyer will arrange his own insurance cover which he usually does on a "warehouse to warehouse" basis despite the fact that he enjoys no insurable interest in the goods until passage of title. C & F sale contracts are usually arranged where circumstances dictate that the buyer must effect the insurance on imports within his own country or where the buyer has an open cover insurance under which he is obliged to insure the goods.

In the case of a C & F contract of sale it is advisable for the seller to effect a seller`s interest "warehouse to warehouse" insurance contract on a contingency basis to protect him from dispatching the goods uninsured should the buyer failed to effect an insurance contract of his own. A "contingency" policy comes into effect only where the named contingency arises. In this case, one would arrange for the insurance to come into effect in circumstances where the insurable interest remained with the seller because, say, the buyer failed to pay for the goods.

FOB (Free on board) - This type of contract is customarily used for the sale of bulk cargoes (eg coal, ores, grain, etc.) where the purchaser buys the goods at the port of shipment. The seller is responsible for all expenses up to the time the goods are loaded on board the overseas vessel. The buyer provides the vessel and becomes responsible for the goods as they are loaded on board. In the absence of any definition expressed in the contract disputes often arise in defining the exact point at which responsibility passes from seller to buyer; so it is preferable that the point of transfer be made clear in the contract. Nonetheless, there is a general opinion that, in the absence of agreement to the contrary, responsibility transfers as the goods pass over the ship`s rail. There are variations to the FOB type of sale whereby the contract specifies the point at which the seller`s responsibility ceases somewhere within the loading port area; as in the case of an FAS contract (see below).

With FOB sales each party arranges their own insurance protection. The wording of the seller`s interest insurance contract should make it clear that cover is only "to FOB at......", that is to say cover terminates as the goods are loaded on board the overseas vessel. Conversely, the buyer`s interest policy should be effected "from FOB at......" and specify the place of termination. In theory, passage of title takes place at the so called "FOB" point, but in practice this is dependent on payment for the goods having been made in accordance with the terms of the contract.

FOR (Free on rail) - This is the same as FOB but relating to loading onto rail transport instead of carriage by an overseas vessel. If no marine transit is involved the parties will each arrange their own insurance contracts in accordance with non-marine practice and procedures. If marine transit is involved the buyer`s interest insurance would attach "from FOR to the named destination". One may see the term "FIW - Free in wagons" used for this type of contract. Variations relate to carriage by craft or barge and carriage by road (the latter often being termed "FOT" - free on truck). In cases of doubt one should qualify the abbreviation and its intention.

FAS (Free alongside ship) - The comments above, regarding FOB sale contracts, apply equally to this type of sale; except that the seller is not responsible for loading the goods on the overseas vessel. His responsibility ceases once the goods have been delivered alongside the vessel. One sees the term used in respect of goods that are delivered to the ship by barge or lighter and in ports where the goods are loaded by means of the ship`s lifting gear rather than by port installations. Sometimes the abbreviation is loosely used for contracts whereby the seller delivers the goods to a port warehouse and leaves the buyer to collect them therefrom, but this should be made clear in the contract terms. An example relates to oil FAS sales whereby the buyer customarily collects the oil by pipeline from shore tanks. The marine (buyer`s interest) policy should be clearly worded to indicate the point of attachment.

FFA (Free from alongside) - This operates in the same way as a CIF or C & F sale contract (which of these applies depends on the contractual insurance arrangements) except that the seller`s responsibility for the goods ceases when the goods have been discharged from the overseas vessel. The buyer is responsible for moving the goods from the dock and for their storage and care from then onwards. No insurance premium is incorporated in the invoice so the seller needs to effect insurance to cover his interest in the goods until, at least, delivery to the buyer at the port of discharge.

FOA (Free on board at airport) - This is an FOB type of sale contract but is used in connection with tranport by air. Basically, it operates in the same way as as an FOB contract and the comments for FOB (see above) apply.

FOQ (Free on quay) - This abbreviation is usually applied in the same way as an FAS sale contract; the comments above on the latter also applying here.

EXQ (Ex quay) - This abbreviation is applied to a sale contract which operates in the same way as an FFA contract (see comments above).

EXS (Ex ship) - This is another term for an FAS sale contract (see comments above).

5. The Importance of Marine Insurance in Trade and Commerce

One should not underestimate the importance of insurance in modern trade and commerce. The following list draws attention to a number of factors that illustrate this importance. The course leader invites trainees to comment on these:

1 - Insurance protects the assured from financial loss
2 - Insurance encourages trade
3 - Insurance releases cash which, otherwise, would be reserved to meet potential losses
4 - Insurance provides a reserve pool from which the assured can recover his losses
5 - Insurance allows the assured to trade in security, knowing that an insured disaster will not ruin his business
6 - To support the above the onus is on the insurer to maintain an adequate reserve pool to meet all possible claim demands from policy holders; such reserve being backed by ample and properly structured reinsurance protection

6. The Insurance of Ships

In this context the term "ship" is applied to all types of vessel that may be exposed to to the perils of the seas or any other navigable waters. This would range from small boats to very large ocean going vessels. The insurance of small craft operating independently from a large vessel (eg lighters, barges, yachts, tugs etc.) is a specialist subject which is not embraced within the notes of this introductory course. The notes concentrate on the insurance of large ocean going ships.

One usually thinks of the owner as the assured but, where the owner engages a shipping manager to operate his vessel, the manager is responsible for insuring the ship. It is customary to refer to the insurance of the ship itself as a hull & machinery insurance; the abbreviation H & M being commonly used in the marine market for this purpose. The same abbreviation, when used for the insurance of a large sailing vessel, is deemed to mean hull and materials. More information on hull and machinery interest can be found in Section 6. An ocean going vessel is registered and classed when she is being built. The registration establishes her "flag" and the classification determines the standard which she must maintain to remain in her class; the classification society also determines the ship's loadline for cargo carrying purposes. The class of a ship, and maintainance of that class, is particularly important to hull underwriters for it gives some indication regarding the condition of the vessel and the way in which the proposer cares for the ship. It is also important to cargo underwriters because they know the cargo will be safer when carried by a good class vessel than might be the case if the vessel is of a lower class. More information on the structure, etc. of ships can be found in "Training Notes for Brokers - The Insurance of Merchant Ships" (Witherby 1990) and in "Marine Insurance - Volume Three - Hull Practice" by Brown (Witherby 1993).

It is customary for an H & M policy to be effected on full conditions, as expressed in the main set of the ITC (Institute Time Clauses), or a similar set of hull conditions, for a period of 12 months. Other sets of standard insurance conditions are available to cover the hull & machinery of the ship on limited terms (eg Total Loss Only). Shipowners and ship managers also insure interests related to the operation of the ship (eg anticipated freight); these being termed "hull interest" insurances. Throughout the notes comment will be made, as applicable to the text, to the various types of insurance for ships but, for more detail, practitioners are advised to consult the books recommended above.

SELF STUDY QUESTIONS

Before moving on to the next section satisfy yourself that you have absorbed the subject matter in Section One. The following questions should be answered without reference to the text:

1. Where was marine insurance practice in evidence prior to its introduction to London?

2. What is a "marine adventure"?

3. Who was Edward Lloyd? What was his connection with marine insurance?

4. What event, in 1693, caused merchants to doubt the security of insurances offered by private underwriters?

5. How did the "Bubble Act" (1720) affect the marine insurance and reinsurance markets in London and when were these restrictions lifted?

6. How does the "documentary credits" system operate?

7. Which are the "documents of title" in the documentary credits system?

8. What is export credit guarantee insurance?

9. Define the abbreviations "CIF", "C & F" and "FOB". To what do they relate and how do they affect attachment and termination of a marine insurance contract?

10. Summarise the importance of marine insurance in trade and commerce.

11. What is the purpose of ship classification?

12. What is a "hull interest" policy?

SECTION TWO

MARINE INSURANCE MARKETS & ASSOCIATIONS

1. Introduction to Lloyd`s Marine Insurance Market
2. Lloyd`s Underwriting Members
3. Lloyd`s Corporate Membership
4. Lloyd`s Underwriting Agents and Syndication
5. Lloyd`s Council, Committee and Regulatory Boards
6. The Corporation of Lloyd`s
7. Security in a Lloyd`s Policy
8. Lloyd`s Underwriters` Association
9. Lloyd`s Agents and the Intelligence Service
10. Lloyd`s Single Market
11. The London Marine Insurance Company Market
12. The Institute of London Underwriters
13. Marine Insurance Markets Outside London
14. Insurance Brokers and Brokers` Associations
15. Conclusion

SECTION TWO

1. Introduction to Lloyd`s Marine Insurance Market

Although a large part of the insurance business placed in the London market today is written by insurance companies Lloyd`s market, despite its recent setbacks, continues to play an important role in the development of the London market scene. Lloyd`s is steeped in some 300 years of tradition and many of the practices introduced during this market`s development form the basis of worldwide marine insurance practice today. It follows that a study of Lloyd`s would be incomplete without, at least, an outline of its historic development.

In Section one comment was made about Edward Lloyd`s coffee house from which the modern Lloyd`s took its title. Whilst Edward Lloyd was neither underwriter nor broker and took no part in the conduct of marine insurance in his coffee house such conduct was surely influenced by the respectability of his establishment and the moral integrity of the man himself.

Edward Lloyd`s integrity and respectability (in a London that was rife with sharp business practices) soon became a byword in the City when he set up as a coffeeman in Salutation Precinct, off Tower Street, in the late 17th century. Lloyd, son of a Hainault (Essex) hosiery manufacturer, was a family man with three children and was in his late forties when he first became a coffeeman. City businessmen found the Tower Street coffee house, with its proximity to the Pool of London (the main anchorage for ships visiting London), a convenient and satisfactory place to meet their contempories and to transact shipping business. The financial centre was Lombard Street and, when (in 1691) Edward Lloyd moved his coffee business to new premises in Number 16, Lombard Street it became recognised as the main centre for the transaction of marine insurance contracts. His appointment to churchwarden at the church of St Mary Woolnuth, located at the end of Lombard Street, further advanced Edward Lloyd`s moral reputation. He guarded this with great care and restricted his patrons to only those who reflected his own high standards of business ethics; providing these with writing materials, a waiter service and shipping information. The standard of high morality created by Edward Lloyd was to follow Lloyd`s over the centuries, influencing the conduct of business and leading to the high regard with which Lloyd`s has been held by world wide business communities.

The influence the master of the coffee house had on the conduct of business became markedly apparent after Edward Lloyd died on 15 February, 1713. Successive masters did not display the same moral rectitude as Edward Lloyd and a decline in standards soon developed. This decline, based largely on the presence of gambling elements, disturbed the serious underwriters and brokers of the day to such an extent that they encouraged, and financed, one Thomas Fielding (a waiter at Lloyd`s) to set up a rival coffee house at number 5, Pope`s Head alley (this alley being off Lombard Street and almost opposite Lloyd`s coffee house); calling this "The New Lloyd`s". The majority of underwriters and brokers seceded to the new Lloyd`s coffee house and a period of rivalry between the coffee house masters broke out. Disputes over the publication of "Lloyd`s List" by both establishments and arguments over the use of the name Lloyd`s (sullied by the activities in the Lombard Street house) brought unsavoury publicity which prompted those who frequented the new Lloyd`s coffee house to seek more formal premises elsewhere, ostensibly because the Pope`s Head Alley premises were "extremely inauspicious to health and inconvenient in respect to business".

To implement this decision a group of 79 merchants, underwriters and brokers met on 13 December, 1771, and decided each to subscribe £100 to a fund to be set up at the Bank of England to provide for the "building of a new coffee house" and, in January, 1772, the first Committee of Lloyd`s, comprising nine members, was elected by the subscribers to administer the fund and to find the new premises. A "subscribers` list" was created and each person on the list was required to pay a lump sum call of £20 towards administration costs; each new subscriber on being added to the list paid a similar amount..

It was essential that the new premises be located within the confines of the financial centre of the City of London, but vacant space therein was practically unobtainable during the 18th century. Several other coffee houses were put forward as options but were rejected by the Committee since they offered no better facilities than No.5 Pope`s Head alley. The search continued for several years during which time the subscribers were forced to suffer the increasing disadvantages at No.5 whilst the list of subscribers steadily increased to add to the congestion.

It was largely due to the intervention of John Julius Angerstein, a broker/underwriter, who though not a member of the original Committee was an influential and prominent figure in the market and later became Chairman of Lloyd`s, that the lease of a suite of rooms in the Royal Exchange was eventually signed in November, 1773. The lease on No. 5 Pope`s Head alley was terminated on Saturday 5 March 1774 and, on Monday 7 March 1774, the "subscribers to New Lloyd`s", as they styled themselves, commenced business in the rooms at the Royal Exchange. Historians might care to note that No.5 Popes` Head alley was destroyed along with 17 other houses in the great Cornhill fire of 1779. Not all underwriters and shipping patrons had deserted from the old Lloyd`s coffee house at No. 16, Lombard Street and it continued to operate for many years; nonetheless, by 1785, records show that these premises were standing empty.

Although the Royal Exchange rooms were not spacious or well appointed by modern standards they were infinitely preferable to the premises recently vacated. The new premises comprised three rooms, one of which was relatively small compared with the others, and a kitchen. The small room was set aside as a Committee room. The largest of the other two (some 55ft x 15ft) was a "public" room which was intended as a coffee house for the use of clients seeking business with subscribers; although it was not there for this purpose many contracts were actually negotiated in the public room. The second, inner, room (some 48ft x 20ft) was intended for use of subscribers and their associates only and was called the Great Room. Tradition was difficult to break in the conservative atmosphere of underwriting so it is, perhaps, not surprising, that the coffee house image was retained and one would see underwriters seated in coffee house style boxes with waiters, in addition to supplying writing materials to underwriters and brokers, serving coffee to both subscribers and their customers from the adjacent kitchen.

By April, 1774, the list of subscribers had increased to 179 and these, combined with members of the public who strayed into the Great Room to carry out transactions often not of an underwriting nature, caused "a crowded and disordered state" in that Room; so, in January 1778, the Committee ordered a board to be affixed to the door of the Great Room with the following displayed thereon "Subscribers and their Connections only are to be admitted into the within Room". A waiter was stationed at the door to enforce the restriction and all personnel desirous of entering the Room were required to pay £15 each for life membership. Eventually, the title of this Room was changed to the "Subscribers` Room", more familiarly known today as "The Room" in practice, and entrance was allowed only to persons bearing a Room ticket. This, effectively, barred the public from approaching underwriters directly although it must be admitted that many direct transactions still took place in the Public room; a practice which was to be prohibited in later years.

It was in the Royal Exchange that many of the practices and procedures operating in Lloyd`s today were introduced and developed. Restriction of entry to the Room is still practised; but subscribers are permitted to appoint "substitutes" to transact business therein on their behalf. The modern Room practitioner must pass a Lloyd`s introductory examination to be permitted to hold a full "Permit of Entry" (commonly termed a "Room ticket"); no such requirement being demanded of Room practitioners in the Royal Exchange. Syndication (see Part 4, below) also started during the days in the Royal Exchange and the slip placing procedure (see Section 3) was developed in the Royal Exchange.

Underwriters and brokers practised the business of negotiating insurance contracts at the Royal Exchange for 154 years; apart from a period whilst the Royal Exchange was being rebuilt following a disastrous fire in January 1838. For a while after the fire underwriters and brokers continued their business transactions in a number of coffee houses and taverns in the City; but eventually accepted the offer of three rooms in the London Tavern. This accommodation was not satisfactory for a permanent home and nine years later the Society of underwriters and subscribers moved into the newly built Royal Exchange.

Thoughout the Royal Exchange era the principles of private underwriting, trust and integrity established in Edward Lloyd`s coffee house were maintained; perpetuated by the honesty in business dealings practised by John Julius Angerstein, Sir Brook Watson (a member of the original 1772 Committee and Chairman of Lloyd`s in 1796) and other leading figures in the market. Each underwriting member wrote for his own account, pledged the whole of his personal fortune to the risks he wrote and accepted unlimited liability. As the Society developed many changes in its structure took place. An Act of incorporation in 1811 embraced both underwriting and non-underwriting members with the power to vote at elections, etc. in a Corporate self regulating body which upheld the principles of unlimited liability; although, at that time, there was no central fund to protect policyholders in the event that an insurer became insolvent. Additionally, access to the Room was granted to annual Subscribers and Associates; the latter comprising claims adjusters, accountants and others not directly concerned with underwriting. At that time the activities of an insurance broker were not restricted, as they are today, to representation of his client`s interests and many brokers also acted as underwriters in their own names and as agents for proposers; a practice which inevitably led to a conflict of interests.

For many years each underwriting member continued to write business solely for his own account but the demand for expansion of capital to accommodate increasing values and the growth of potential liabilities could not be met by the capacity of underwriters` private means. In fact, it soon became apparent that proposers treated with scepticism contracts for large amounts where only one underwriter accepted the whole risk. This was illustrated when a young broker showed a slip to Mr. Richard Thornton to cover £250,000 on a shipment of gold to Russia, expecting him to write a substantial lead line. Instead, Mr Thornton wrote a line for the full amount and, when the broker protested that his client would not accept such a heavy commitment from one underwriter, the underwriter offered to deposit

Exchequer bills for the amount written until the risk had run off. This was, however, a "one off" and, in general, brokers found that underwriters who had previously written 100% lines followed an underwriting policy of writing only proportionate lines; the leading underwriter negotiating the contract and premium rate with the broker and writing a fairly large lead line with following underwriters taking up the outstanding balance on the same placing slip. This turned out to be not a bad practice because it encouraged "spread of risk" which became an important feature of sound underwriting practice.

Still further capital was needed to increase underwriting capacity but it was not practical to invite more active underwriters to an already overcrowded market; even if some could be found with the necessary underwriting skills and experience. The problem was resolved by introducing syndication whereby the active underwriter in the Room would represent a number of underwriting members who took no active part in the business but committed their personal wealth to cover the risks written by the active underwriter in return for a relative proportion of the profits accruing from the performance of those contracts. For more detail concerning syndication see Part 4, below.

Eventually, continued growth made it apparent that the activities of Lloyd`s could not be confined to the accommodation at the Royal Exchange and, as the Society has grown larger and larger Lloyd`s have moved the Room on several occasions since the Royal Exchange days. We shall not dwell on these moves except to comment, for the record, that they took place in 1928, 1956 and 1986; the last being to the "space age" building occupied by Lloyd`s today in Lime Street, London.

Whilst Lloyd`s remained predominantly a marine market for most of its early history, non-marine business was introduced in the Royal Exchange in the latter part of the 19th century. Non-marine business (including aviation and motor classes) developed to become a major part of the 20th century market; the premium income generated thereby exceeding that generated by the marine market.

A spate of adverse years since 1980 resulted in heavy calls on the wealth of an unusually high number of underwriting members, many of whom had to cease underwriting; whilst others, disenchanted with the results of their accounts and dubious of the future, withdrew from their syndicate participations. As a result, the lists of registered members (see Part 2, below) which stood at 26,500 (comprising 350 syndicates and including some 5,000 working members) in 1991 had decreased dramatically to 19,537 (228 syndicates) by 1993. The introduction of a "single" market in 1991 (see Section 3) makes it difficult to maintain statistics regarding separate classes of business; so one cannot say to what extent these changes have affected the balance between non-marine and marine business in the current Lloyd`s market. So far as these notes are concerned such balance is of academic interest only except to say that the marine market still has an important part to play in the present and future roles of Lloyd`s.

2. Lloyd`s Underwriting Members

Since the introduction of syndication at the Royal Exchange, during the 19th century, the term "underwriting member" at Lloyd`s has referred to an individual who satisfied the Committee of Lloyd`s, regarding personal wealth and other matters, as being a suitable person to underwrite business at Lloyd`s through the medium of an underwriting agent. From 1 January, 1994, a new form of membership was introduced;

being *Corporate membership*. Comment on this form of membership appears in Part 3, below.

During the development of Lloyd`s membership was restricted to male subscribers but the "men only" rule was rescinded in 1970. Today a large part of the community is made up of female members; and female brokers transacting business in the Room as well as female assistants sitting in underwriting boxes are very much in evidence.

An applicant for underwriting membership must, first, choose a Lloyd`s underwriting agent (see Part 4, below) with whom to register. The applicant must be not less than 21 years of age and be able to satisfy Lloyd`s that he/she is a fit person to be elected to membership. The agent will ensure that certain criteria are met and obtain agreement from two existing members, to support the application, before submitting the name of the applicant to Lloyd`s. The applicant`s personal financial affairs will be subjected to a stringent "means" test to ensure financial stability. Subject to the show of wealth indicating a satisfactory financial status the applicant will be called to appear before the, so termed, "Rota Committee". This Committee, the members of which are approved by the Committee of Lloyd`s, meets when necessary specifically for the purpose of vetting applicants for election to membership. If the Rota Committee is satisfied with the outcome of the interview the applicant`s name and details are currently circulated to all members of the Committee of Lloyd`s for consideration (trainees should note that this role of the Committee might be taken over by the new Regulatory Board or Marketing Board). Periodically, the Committee of Lloyd`s, or relative Board, will meet to vote on new applications for election to membership. If any Committee or Board member, as the case may be, votes against the application it will be rejected without explanation (ie a majority vote is not entertained). Underwriting years run from 1st January to 31st December in any one year and no member is permitted to commence trading during an underwriting year; so new members cannot commence trading until the first day of January following their election.

Lloyd`s Act, 1982, demands that the ruling body at Lloyd`s (ie the Council of Lloyd`s) shall maintain a register of underwriting members. Underwriting members are classified in two main groups; these being "vocational" members (termed "working" members, in practice) and "external" members. The register is in two parts; working and external members being shown in separate lists. The ratio of working members to the whole underwriting membership is probably less than 20%; so the capacity of Lloyd`s market lies mainly with external members. Corporate members are recorded separately in a third register.

In practice, each member listed in the register is termed a "name" (see "syndication" on Part 4). A working member who retires from active work in the Room, but maintains the role of an underwriting member, continues to be registered as a "working" member. The difference between these two types of underwriting member is important to the understanding of how Lloyd`s is structured.

Vocational (Working) member - A member who is principally concerned with the practice of underwriting in the Room. The term would embrace any underwriting member who holds a full valid permit of entry to the Room with the right to transact business therein. (eg active underwriters and their "box" staff and practising Lloyd`s brokers and their substitutes).

External member - A member who plays no active part in the day to day activities of the Room. Such member has no control over underwriting policy or the active underwriter and would not hold a Room entry permit. His/her membership status does not carry the right to demand entry to the Room and any request to visit the Room must be generated through the medium of the member`s agent in the underwriting agency with which he/she is registered.

Lloyd`s maintains a "central fund" (see Part 4, below) to meet commitments of Lloyd`s policies. Every name must contribute to the fund, on a scale which is determined annually, but this fund is for the benefit of policyholders only and is not available to reimburse names for losses they suffer; nor can the fund be used to "bail out" names who become insolvent. Except in the case of corporate membership (for which special rules apply - See Part 3), a name commits the whole of his/her personal fortune to meet liabilities incurred on his/her behalf by the active underwriter and, although they can effect reinsurance contracts to effectively limit their liability (see PSL, below), names are not permitted to directly limit liability incurred in the performance of contracts written by the active underwriter on their behalf. Such liability is "several"; which is to say that each name is responsible only for liabilities attaching to his/her individual name and accepts no responsibility for liabilities attaching to other names in the same syndicate or policy [Ref. Lloyd`s Act, 1982, sect.8(2)]. One would expect the underwriting agency with whom the name is registered to arrange a PSL (personal stop loss) reinsurance contract to protect the name from excessive liabilities.

The potential liability of a name is restricted by imposing a limit on the amount of premium that can be accepted by the active underwriter for that name`s account in any one underwriting year (termed the "year of account"). The PIL (premium income limit) is agreed with the member`s underwriting agent within parameters pre-determined by the Council of Lloyd`s. The parameters are set out in categories which may change annually so trainees should update the information herein as necessary.

Lloyd`s business plan for 1995 introduced a new class of membership for *high liquidity* members. These are members who have high liquidity assets and income above a specified level. Members in this class are allowed to participate in the market at a lower ratio of funds to their overall premium limit; subject to a high maximum deposit and the need to reconfirm their assets annually. Special arrangements exist, also, for individual members under "members` agents` pooling arrangements" (termed *MAPA*, in practice). A MAPA is an arrangement whereby a members` agent (see Part 4) pools underwriting capacity and each member participating therein shares rateably in participations across a spread of syndicates. This system enables members of a MAPA to further implement the "spread of risk" underwriting principle by writing smaller lines on a number of risks across a large range of syndicates. Membership of a MAPA is not compulsory; individual members having the option to continue underwriting on the traditional basis if they so wish; or to underwrite partly traditionally and partly within the structure of a MAPA. Corporate members, who appoint a members` agent to represent their interests, can participate in a MAPA; otherwise this method of underwriting is not open to the member. Subject to separate regulatory guidelines, Lloyd`s business plan requires that each MAPA shall have a diversification of syndicate participants and that there is an accurate description of the risk composition.

There are six categories of underwriting membership which apply to both new members and existing members. An applicant for membership, in consultation with the member`s underwriting agent, selects the category which shall apply. The member must show the means required by that category and deposit with Lloyd`s the sum demanded by that category in accordance with the show of wealth and the agreed premium income limit (PIL).

The following notes regarding membership requirements and the structure of Lloyd`s are for guidance only. Many changes are taking place in the Lloyd`s market at the time of this revision; so trainees, particularly those studying for insurance examinations or for entry to Lloyd`s, are advised to update the following information as necessary.

From January 1995 the categories for underwriting membership at Lloyd`s are as follows:

Category 1 - New members who wish to commence underwriting from 1 January 1995 (see table below for minimum means required for this category) and existing members who have shown means of £250,000 or more;

Category 2 - Existing members who have shown minimum means of at least £100,000 but less than £250,000;

Category 3 - Existing members who have shown means of less than £100,000; also new vocational, connected or associated members who have been admitted in this category with effect from 1 January, 1995, and who are allowed to show means lower than £100,000;

Category 4 - Vocational, connected or associated members who have been admitted with only a nominal show of means;

Category 5 - Members wishing to underwrite as high liquidity names;

Category 6 - Members who wish to underwrite as a participant in a MAPA. Although these members are placed in category 6 the limits in the following table are shown with categories 1 to 4, as appropriate to assets, etc.

Each member must deposit funds with Lloyd`s which are held as immediate security against future liabilities. The deposit is based on the member`s agreed PIL but, for categories 1 to 4, is subject to a minimum deposit of £25,000. In the case of category 5 the minimum deposit is £200,000.

As they arise the member must pay claims out of premium income. If Lloyd`s finds it necessary to draw on the deposit to meet claims the name must immediately deposit further funds with Lloyd`s to restore the deposit to its former level or retire from underwriting. If a name retires from underwriting the deposit is retained for a further two years under the three year accounting system (see Part 7); after which the deposit (or the balance remaining thereof if the deposit has been called upon by Lloyd`s to settle claims) is returned to the retiring member.

For information, a table of categories appears below which illustrates the relationship between the underwriting member`s means, PIL and deposits at Lloyd`s. This table is based on information published by Lloyd`s for membership as from 1 January, 1995, and should be updated by trainees as necessary:

(Text continues on Page 9)

Lloyd`s Membership - Financial Requirements (1995)

Note - In each case the minimum deposit for categories 1 to 4 is £25,000 which allows the underwriting member to earn an annual premium of up to £50,000. A maximum PIL (premium income limit) is determined which may not be exceeded during any one underwriting year. Where an underwriting member opts for a PIL that is higher than the PIL agreed he/she must show a correspondingly higher level of means and must deposit with Lloyd`s the percentage specified of the selected PIL; the table below giving some guidance in this respect. Any increase in PIL is subject to £5,000 increments. The term "bespoke" in the table refers to any form of underwriting other than within a MAPA. The symbol + means that increases in PIL are permissible, in £5,000 increments, subject to a corresponding increase in deposit and an acceptable level of means.

Category	**Means (£)**	**Overall PIL (£)**	**Deposit (£)** (min 25,000)
1 (bespoke)	250,000+	50,000+	30% of PIL (min 25,000)
1 (MAPA)	250,000+	50,000+	25% of PIL (min 25,000)
2 (bespoke)	100,000 - 249,999	50,000 - 620,000	40% of PIL (min 25,000 max 248,000)
2 (MAPA)	100,000 - 249,999	50,000 - 992,000	25% of PIL (min 25,000 max 248,000)
3 (bespoke)	less than 100,000	50,000 - 195,000	50% of PIL (min 25,000 max 97,500)
3 (MAPA)	less than 100,000	50,000 - 243,750	40% of PIL (min 25,000 max 97,500)
4 (bespoke)	Not applicable	50,000 - 100,000	50% of PIL (min 25,000 max 50,000)
4 (MAPA)	Not applicable	50,000 - 125,000	40% of PIL (min 25,000 max 50,000)
5 (high liquidity)	500,000 or, if higher, 50% of funds at Lloyd`s	1,000,000 (min)+	20% of PIL (min 200,000)
6 (MAPA)	Depending on "means" level, see categories 1 to 4 above		

An underwriting member must sign an agreement to the effect that the required means for the category will be maintained and must apply for re-categorising or retire from underwriting, as the case may be, if the required level of means is not maintained. Lloyd`s reserves the right to call upon a name to reaffirm his/her financial status at any time and to demand that the name shall retire from underwriting if the required status is not maintained. An underwriting member may be a name on more than one syndicate; subject to the overall PIL in the above table.

3. Lloyd`s Corporate Membership

Breaking with tradition, the Council of Lloyd`s invited the formation of trust funds to commence underwriting at Lloyd`s in the 1994 year of account. The liability of each trust fund is limited to its share capital; on a similar basis to the limitation of liability enjoyed by shareholders in a British insurance company. Thus, a shareholder registered in the trust fund has no liability beyond the value of his/her shareholding. This category is intended to provide new capital for Lloyd`s market, rather than to replace the traditional unlimited liability system of capacity, but there has been much speculation regarding its effect and one must await developments to see if the intention is fulfilled in fact.

The trust fund, representing its registered shareholders jointly, is termed a "corporate member" and is referred to as such in the following comments. Where a corporate member joins a syndicate it is termed an "incorporated name". The Rules for corporate membership require, amongst other things, that the member must be dedictated exclusively to underwriting business at Lloyd`s, including directly ancillary business, and must not have investments in other corporate members, Lloyd`s agencies or Lloyd`s brokers.

Except where it can display appropriate syndicate analysis skills, a corporate member must retain one or more Lloyd`s advisers to provide syndicate analysis and to negotiate syndicate participation; all Lloyd`s members` agents are qualified to undertake this role. Special provisions apply regarding assets held by a corporate member and a PIL is fixed by agreement. But, in any case, the corporate member must deposit with Lloyd`s an amount equal to 50% of its PIL; with a minimum of £1,500,000.

4. Lloyd`s Underwriting Agents and Syndication

As an underwriting member a person has no direct contact with business conducted on his/her behalf in the Room. Lloyd`s Acts require that an underwriting member may transact business at Lloyd`s only through the medium of an underwriting agent. The underwriting affairs of a name are conducted on his/her behalf by a registered Lloyd`s underwriting agency. There are, of course, names on syndicates who practise in the Room (eg brokers and active underwriters) but when they do so they are not "wearing an underwriting member`s hat" so to speak.

An underwriting member is registered with an underwriting agency which invites the member to become a name in a syndicate. There are three types of Lloyd`s underwriting agent; these being (1) a members` agent, (2) a co-ordinating agent and (3) a managing agent. The difference between these will be come clear in the following notes; but, first, let us define the term "Lloyd`s syndicate".

A Lloyd`s syndicate is a group of underwriting members who offer a consolidated capacity; but with each name being a separate entity therein. An "active underwriter" is appointed by the managing agent, as a salaried official, to represent the syndicate in the Room. The active underwriter transacts business on behalf of the names in the syndicate who are committed to honour his acceptances. A name has no control over the active underwriter; so names must be aware that they are placing their entire wealth at the disposal of the active underwriter and have faith in his judgement and ability. At one time the active underwriter was always the head of the syndicate and was writing in his own name for a large part of the risk. Then came a period when many active underwriters were only salaried officials, with no personal commitment for the risks they wrote. Today, whilst active underwriters are still salaried officials appointed by the managing agent, regulations demand that each active underwriter be a name on the syndicate/s for which he writes; so that he has a personal interest in the outcome of risks he writes. An active underwriter may not write business for a name in excess of the PIL permitted to that name. It should be noted that, whilst the appointment of an active underwriter at Lloyd`s is at the discretion of the relevant Lloyd`s underwriting agency, no person may be newly appointed to this post (with effect from 1 January 1995) unless such person is a Chartered Insurer; the minimum qualification by examination being ACII - Associate of the Chartered Insurance Institute.

Joining a syndicate does not relieve a name from any of the liabilities attaching to that name. The name remains liable to the full extent of his/her personal fortune and may not rely on other names in the syndicate to come to his/her rescue in times of trouble. Further, the name is not responsible for liabilities incurred by other names in the syndicate.

The underwriting agency might act solely as a members` agent, solely as a managing agent or embrace both roles, operating separately, within one agency.

*Members` Agent* - A members` agent looks after the affairs of each name registered with the agency but plays no part in active underwriting. There are four types of members` agent; these being:

(1) An independent members` agent
(2) A members` agent who is associated with Lloyd`s brokers
(3) A members` agent who is associated with a managing agent
(4) A combined agent

Let us consider the roles of each of these members` agents in more detail:

(1) An independent members` agent is involved solely in the underwriting affairs of members. Such agent is not connected, by way of ownership or control, with any managing agent, any syndicate or any Lloyd`s broker. The agent advises a candidate for membership on the prospects regarding various managing agencies and the desirability of joining a particular syndicate or not, as the case may be. Once the member becomes a name on a syndicate the independent members` agent liaises with the managing agent of the relevant syndicate to ensure his principal`s affairs are properly conducted and safeguarded.

(2) Lloyd`s Act, 1982, in order to avoid a conflict of interests, prohibits Lloyd`s brokers from acting as managing agents. The Act does not prohibit a broker from acting as a members` agent; but such members` agent is placed in a separate category from an independent members` agent. Nonetheless, such agent has the same responsibilities as an independent members` agent and must not be connected, by way of ownership or control, with the activities of a managing agent.

(3) This type of members` agent is one, who, although not himself a managing agent, operates in association with a managing agent. Because the operation of the agency incorporates the activities of a managing agent it must not be associated with any Lloyd`s brokers. The responsibilities of the members` agent in this type of agency are the same as those for an independent members` agent; but members do not join syndicates other than those controlled by the managing side of the agency.

(4) This type of agent combines the role of members` agent with the role of a managing agent. The agency operates in much the same way as in (3), above, with the responsibilities to members being the same, but the agent is also subject to Council of Lloyd`s regulations regarding the conduct of managing agents. A combined agent must not be associated with Lloyd`s brokers.

Managing Agent - The managing agent`s role is to deal with the formation and general underwriting policy of syndicates, to appoint the active underwriter/s and staff and to deal with all matters relating to the underwriting of risks (eg administrative support, communication and advice systems, liaison with Corporation departments, preparation of financial reports, etc.). The managing agent delegates much of his responsibility regarding the actual risks to the active underwriter; leaving the latter to make all decisions concerning acceptance of risks and validity of claims, to maintain underwriting records, etc. and to arrange an effective reinsurance programme to protect the syndicate's acceptances.

Lloyd's Act, 1982, prohibits Lloyd's brokers from acting as managing agents, but places no such restriction on the role of members' agents. Should a managing agent need to contact an underwriting member such contact must be arranged through the medium of the relevant members' agent.

Lloyd's underwriting agencies have their own representative body in the LUAA (Lloyd's Underwriting Agents' Association). The LUAA provides a forum for discussion on matters of common interest both to the agents and the names they represent on Lloyd's syndicates. The LUAA plays an important part in representing its members in discussion with the Council of Lloyd's and in keeping members informed on matters affecting them (eg changes in taxation legislation, etc.)

5. Lloyd's Council, Committee and Regulatory Boards

The first Committee of Lloyd's was elected in January, 1772. It comprised nine members. For the benefit of trainees who are interested in the history of Lloyd's it might be noted that the first Committee members were Martin Kuyk Van Meirop (chair), John Wilkinson, John Townson, Joshua Readshaw, James Black, John Ewer, James Bourdieu, John Witmore and Brook Watson.

For over two hundred years underwriting practices at Lloyd's were regulated by the Committee of Lloyd's. This situation pertained until self regulation was curbed by Lloyd's Act, 1982. This Act reduced the controlling influence of the Committee of Lloyd's when Section 3 of the Act demanded the formation of the Council of Lloyd's. The Act required that there should be 27 members in the Council; comprising the elected 16 members of the Committee of Lloyd's (all "working" members), plus 8 members elected from the names in the external register and 3 persons (other than underwriting members at Lloyd's) to be nominated by the Council and approved by the Governor of the Bank of England.

The Act gave powers to the Council of Lloyd's to increase or decrease the number of Council members, provided that not more than two thirds of the Council were working members. Shortly after its formation the Council exercised these powers to increase the number of Council members to 28 and to reduce the Committee of Lloyd's to 12 working members. In 1992 the structure of the Council comprised the 12 members elected to the Committee of Lloyd's from the working members' register, the 8 members elected from the external members' register and 8 persons, not otherwise connected with Lloyd's who were nominated by the Council. This structure, whilst allowing the Committee of Lloyd's considerable influence in the decisions made by the Council, afforded the external members and the nominated members, jointly, the opportunity to outvote the Committee members on issues of serious contention. The Council retained overall authority on all matters regarding conduct of the Society; making byelaws, dealing with major financial matters, disciplinary procedures, etc., but, generally, left the day to day running of the market to the Committee of Lloyd's. The Chief Executive of Lloyd's (see Part 6) is a Deputy Chairman of both the Council and Committee. In recent years further changes to the structure of the regulating bodies controlling Lloyd`s market have been introduced.

*Council of Lloyd`s (1993)* - The Council of Lloyd`s, at the time of writing, comprises 19 members; this being made up of 7 working members, 5 external members and 7 nominated members (the latter including the Chief Executive). The 7 working members are the Committee of Lloyd`s. The Chairman of the Council and his two Deputy Chairmen also occupy these roles in the Committee of Lloyd`s.

Council of Lloyd`s (1994, 1995) - There are proposals to reduce the number of Council members to 17 in 1994 (6 working, 4 external and 8 nominated) and to further reduce the Council in 1995 to 16 members (6 working, 4 external and 6 nominated). Trainees are advised to confirm the changes if and as they occur and, where necessary, amend these notes accordingly.

*Lloyd`s Regulatory and Market Boards* - During 1992 plans were formulated to change the self regulation structure at Lloyd`s by introducing a new Regulatory board and a Market Board, these two bodies to co-operate to bring more regulation to the marketplace with particular emphasis on client needs. It is probable that some of the Council`s responsibilities (eg disciplinary procedures, etc.) can be more effectively carried out by these Boards and their duties could affect the future role of the Committee of Lloyd`s; but this remains to be seen. For the present, the structure of these Boards will be of interest.

Lloyd`s Regulatory Board (1993) - The Regulatory Board comprises 16 members. All the Council members, other than working members, are on the Regulatory Board. Since there are only 12 such members on the present Council, the other four members of the Board are persons with special skills, and who are not working members, appointed by the Council.

Lloyd`s Market Board (1993) - The Market Board comprises 17 members, which include the 7 working members on the Council, the Chairman of the Council, the Deputy Chairmen of the Council, the Chief Executive and other persons co-opted from the market. Both the Regulatory Board and the Marketing Board report to the Council of Lloyd`s.

6. The Corporation of Lloyd`s

Lloyd`s was incorporated by the Lloyd`s Act, 1871, and became a "body corporate with common seal, with power to purchase, take, hold and dispose of, lands and other property". Thus was born the Corporation of Lloyd`s. The Corporation is purely a representative body and has no powers to underwrite risks; these powers being vested, solely, in the underwriting members and their underwriting agents. Nevertheless, the Corporation has been delegated with the duty to issue policies on behalf of names; binding the latter by policy seal to the performance of the contracts evidenced by the policies. The Corporation conducts and administers the affairs of the Society of Lloyd`s and provides the premises, administrative staff and services necessary for the conduct of insurance business at Lloyd`s. It is financed by subscription from the underwriting members.

The Corporation provides a variety of services for the benefit of the Society, many of which will be considered in subsequent notes insofar as they relate to marine insurance. Amongst these services are the policy signing and accounting services, claims settlement services, the intelligence service and various financial and advisory services. Lloyd`s of London Press, which also comes within the ambit of the

Corporation, is responsible for many publications that are of considerable assistance to marine underwriters and the shipping world generally. Prominent amongst these is Lloyd`s List which has the distinction of developing from a news sheet published by Edward Lloyd in his Lombard Street coffee house during the 18th century. The head of each Corporation department reports to the Chief Executive who is a nominated member on the Council of Lloyd`s where he serves as a Deputy Chairman; exercising the same role in the Committee of Lloyd`s.

7. Security in a Lloyd`s Policy

The worldwide reputation enjoyed by Lloyd`s is very much due to its impeccable security system for the protection of policyholders. Apart from the stringent means test applied to applicants for underwriting membership, and the deposits demanded from members, an exacting annual audit is conducted into the affairs of each syndicate and, if deemed necessary, the financial status of names. The audit is intended to reveal, at an early stage, any circumstance which might lead to eventual insolvency so that, if possible, steps can be taken to remedy the situation. Names will be asked to increase their deposits to meet the threat and any name that does not co-operate will be requested to retire immediately from underwriting further risks. Names are also requested, at intervals, to confirm the required wealth status. Failure in this respect will result in the name being re-categorised with a correspondingly reduced PIL (see Part 2, above) or requested to retire from underwriting.

The, so called, "Bubble" Act, 1720, prohibited a private underwriter from taking profit from his underwriting activities during the year of account. The Act also made the underwriter wait for his profits until a period of time had elapsed after completion of the year of account. This was to allow time for any outstanding and late claims to be taken into account. The Bubble Act was repealed in 1824, but Lloyd`s continued to maintain a principle whereby premiums are retained in a trust fund for a further two years from the end of the relevant year of account; only claims and expenses being paid out of the account. This is termed the "three year accounting" system and can be illustrated by the following figures which relate to a 1993 year of account:

Premium income (1993)		£1,800,000
Claims paid in 1993	£900,000	
Claims paid in 1994	£200,000	
Claims paid in 1995	£100,000	£1,200,000
Profit for 1993		£ 600,000

The account can now be closed for 1993, with provision for any future demands on the year being protected by a "stop loss" reinsurance contract; the premium therefor being a deduction from the profit figure. The Council of Lloyd`s imposes restrictions on managing agents regarding reinsurances to close. Trainees and practitioners involved in this type of reinsurance contract should check on the current position before proceeding.

In addition to the above security protections, the Corporation of Lloyd`s maintains a Central Fund for the protection of policy holders with valid claims that cannot be met by underwriting members. This fund is maintained by compulsory subscription. Each member contributes an amount set by the Council of Lloyd`s. It is proposed that for 1994, 1995 and 1996 the contribution will not exceed 1.5% of the allocated limit for corporate members and 0.6% of the premium limit for individual members. It is important to appreciate that this fund operates at the discretion of the Council of Lloyd`s and is not available to help names who get into difficulty.

8. Lloyd`s Underwriters` Association

Towards the end of the 19th century the active underwriters at Lloyd`s found it was becoming more and more difficult to spare time from their underwriting duties to attend meetings to resolve matters of common interest. It was felt that a small group of active underwriters could be appointed to represent the majority in small meetings which could concentrate on the matters in hand and, probably, be more efficient than would be the case where all active underwriters had to attend every meeting. Membership of the Association was voluntary and, in its early days, the LUA (as it became known) represented the interests of all active underwriters who chose to join the Association. With the development of non-marine business, in the 20th century, the market gradually separated into syndicates who wrote the different classes of business (subsequently determined by audit classification) and other underwriters` Associations were formed (ie Lloyd`s Non-marine Association - the NMA, Lloyd`s Motor Underwriters Association - the LMUA and Lloyd`s Aviation Underwriters` Association - the LAUA). Nevertheless, the Association representing marine interests continued to retain its title as the LUA, without reference to its marine connotations.

Membership of the LUA continued, in theory, to be voluntary but in fact, prior to the introduction of the "single" market at Lloyd`s in 1991 (see part 9), every active underwriter writing marine business was a member of the Association. Within the structure of the single market the clear cut divisions between marine and non-marine syndicates, as designated by audit classification, no longer exist so a decision needed to be made regarding membership of the LUA. The underwriters` Associations of today offer two classes of membership; being "full" membership and "associate" membership. A full member enjoys all the rights of membership, including election to the Committee, full voting rights, receipt of all bulletins, information and the benefit of advice, etc. An associate member is entitled to receive bulletins and information published by the LUA. He can, also, seek advice from the administration but can take no personal part in LUA activities.

Active underwriters are, in theory, still free to abstain from membership but, where 15% or more of the syndicate`s gross annual income is marine business one would expect the active underwriter to apply for full membership of the LUA. Active underwriters representing syndicates which cover marine business, but where the gross annual income is less than 15%, might consider the annual fee for full membership (particularly if the active underwriter is a member of one or more of the other underwriters` Associations) to be excessive, but such underwriters are encouraged to apply for associate membership of the LUA so that they keep in touch with market developments and the outcome of liaison between the LUA and other bodies outside Lloyd`s.

Although the Committee of the LUA is composed entirely of active underwriters in the Room the LUA does not take any part in the underwriting activities of its members, nor in the processing of marine insurance contracts. The Committee is supported by a salaried staff which deals with all administrative matters under the direction of the Secretary of the LUA; providing advice when requested and producing and distributing bulletins and other information documents to members. Members of the LUA are serve on a number of Committees representing various market interests and liaising with other market Associations (eg members of the LUA join members of the ILU to serve on the Technical & Clauses Committee, which is concerned with marine insurance clauses; particularly the Institute clauses). The LUA also maintains a close liaison with such bodies as the ILU (Institute of London Underwriters), the LIBC (Lloyd`s Insurance Brokers` Committee) and the IUMI (International Union of Marine Insurers).

9. Lloyd`s Agents and the Intelligence Service

In 1811 a ship ran aground at Dover and became prey to anyone who sought to appropriate her cargo, etc. A local businessman showed great public spirit by arranging to safeguard the ship and cargo; thereby earning the gratitude of the insurers whose claims would have been almost certainly enhanced without such action. As a gesture of recognition Lloyd`s made the businessman an honorary agent, to represent them in the area should any similar circumstance arise in the future. This was the first appointment of a Lloyd`s agent and formed the basis for all future appointments.

Lloyd`s agents are appointed by the Corporation of Lloyd`s and, today, there is a Lloyd`s agent located in most of the world`s major ports and in many of the smaller ports. The agent receives no remuneration for holding this post but, such is the local business prestige gained from being appointed as a Lloyd`s agent, that the Corporation experiences no difficulty in finding suitable businessmen to fill vacant posts. The integrity associated with Lloyd`s is reflected in their agents and evidenced by the agents` conduct towards all who seek their help. The Corporation have no powers to write insurance business so their agents are similarly restricted in their activities. This is not always immediately apparent because the person appointed as a Lloyd`s agent will have other business activities (usually connected with shipping) amongst which could be an underwriting agency for one or more insuramce companies; but this does not alter the fact that as a Lloyd`s agent he cannot accept business on behalf of Lloyd`s underwriters.

The prime duty of a Lloyd`s agent is to collect information in his area (eg shipping movements, casualties, etc.) which might be of interest to Lloyd`s underwriters and to transmit this, by the fastest means available to him, to the Corporation of Lloyd`s in London. Modern Lloyd`s agents are located in most areas where there is a constant movement of traffic, including major airports as well as seaports, and provide intelligence on both marine and non-marine matters. The agent receives no fee or reimbursement of expenses regarding the information he transmits.

The agent holds himself available to assist anyone who requires his services; particularly, though not specifically, those with an interest in a Lloyd`s policy. He arranges surveys of damaged ships and goods and arranges for the issue of survey reports in connection therewith. He may be called upon to keep a watching brief on activities regarding damaged ships and cargoes and to look after underwriters` interests in connection with these. Within the SCA (Settlement of claims abroad) system a Lloyd`s agent may be empowered to settle claims on cargo policies and certificates; receiving an appropriate fee from underwriters for this service. It is common for a settling agent to act for the ILU as well as for Lloyd`s in cargo claim settlement; particularly in the case of lost or damaged goods insured by a joint cargo certificate. For all services other than the provision of information the agent is entitled to a fee from the party giving him instructions.

Lloyd`s Agency Department, under the auspices of the Corporation of Lloyd`s, deals with all matters concerning the appointment and conduct of Lloyd`s agents. This department, under the direction of the controller of agencies, liaises between the Corporation and the network of Lloyd`s agents.

The information transmitted to Lloyd`s by agents is received in the Corporation department that deals with the intelligence service. The intelligence service provides a very important link between the London insurance and shipping community and the rest of the world. Any information of immediate concern to underwriters is displayed, without delay, on a notice board in the Room; this board being updated as necessary throughout the working day. Other information is relayed to the appropriate Corporation department for action. The editors of Lloyd`s list, a daily newspaper, are particularly interested in information regarding shipping movements and casualties received from agents and keep in close touch with the intelligence service; as do the editors of other Lloyd`s publications.

10. Lloyd`s Single Market

In recent years moves have been made to remove internal market barriers which, it was contended, were stifling the smooth transaction of business in the past. One of these barriers was the restriction which placed syndicates into underwriting classes and prohibited a, so termed, non-marine underwriter from writing marine business. Defenders of the barriers would propound the defence that no underwriter should accept a risk that he does not fully understand and to remove the barrier would allow the uninformed to participate in such risks by merely "following the leader". Upholders of the removal contended that it would provide a more open market and make much needed greater capacity available to brokers seeking cover for high values and high potential liabilities. Whatever the merit of the arguments for and against the proposals, a decision was made to change Lloyd`s to a single market for all risks commencing from the 1 January, 1991. The change will certainly encourage "spread of risk" which is a basic philosophy of sound underwriting.

So the practice of grouping syndicates into classes of business ceased to operate at the end of 1990 and active underwriters are now allowed, with some exceptions regarding excess of loss business and personal stop loss reinsurances, to write a line on any slip presented to them, irrespective of the class of business.

It is still early days to see how the Single market will develop for such development has many factors which need to be considered if future difficulties are to be avoided. One important factor is the requirement for underwriting agents to disclose to names the class of business the active underwriter is writing on their behalf and any changes to this underwriting policy that take place. For example, a name who joined a previously classed marine syndicate may not be prepared to accept liability for, say, aviation risks and may withdraw his participation in a syndicate where the underwriting policy was not to his/her liking.

In the Room itself there is a, more or less, standard practice whereby active underwriters follow an established lead in the relevant class of business; believing that the lead`s long experience in this particular class has made his judgement sound and worth following. Working in Lloyd`s single market following underwriters will continue to respect such experience in leaders and it is incumbent on marine brokers to offer the slip first to an active underwriter who predominantly writes marine hull or cargo business, as the case may be, before approaching the remainder of the market to obtain lines to complete the placing. Once he has obtained a "marine" lead, appropriate to the risk, the broker is no longer restricted to, what was, the "marine" market and may offer the slip to any active Lloyd`s underwriter who is prepared to write a line thereon.

Previously LPSO kept a watching brief on signed lines to ensure that active Lloyd`s underwriters did not write business in any class other than that permitted by the agency agreement. This was done by allocating "audit codes" to risks. Lifting the restriction by introducing a single Lloyd`s market made it no longer necessary for the LPSO to monitor signed lines; so the audit classification system was withdrawn for all risks commencing on or after 1 January, 1991. Nevertheless, administratively, it remains necessary to classify risks for statistical and advice purposes. To implement this lettered "risk codes" were introduced. The relevant risk code is entered in the broker`s slip and, provided it is entered at an early stage during the placing procedure, additionally assists following underwriters to recognise and record for themselves the classes of risk they write; thereby enabling them to keep within guidelines, if any, established by the syndicate`s underwriting agency.

11. The London Marine Insurance Company Market

The "Bubble" Act, 1720, prohibited groups of people from joining together to form insurance companies. The Society of Lloyd`s, being an association of private underwriters writing as individuals, was not affected by the prohibition but small companies existing at that time were forced to cease trading. Two exceptions, the London Assurance and the Royal Exchange Assurance Corporation, were granted Royal charters to allow them to continue trading and these two companies held a monopoly of the company market for over 100 years until the Bubble Act was repealed in 1824. After this repeal a number of insurance companies began to appear in the London market and, following introduction of the Joint Stock Act, 1844, this market grew steadily to provide an influential part of the London insurance scene.

A British insurance company must be authorised by the Secretary of State for Trade and Industry. The Insurance Companies Act, 1982, places restrictions on the conduct of any company that carries on the business of insurance. The Act requires the company to declare its assets on application and authorisation will be granted only if the company can show and maintain the assets at the level required by the authorisation. The administrative office of the Department of Trade and Industry is required to monitor the company`s accounts to ensure continuance of a satisfactory financial status. Further, the Act provides that a company can trade only in its designated class of business. British insurance companies cannot co-operate with Lloyd`s by offering a "single market" system without a change in the Act, so brokers continue to place marine business with companies that specialise in that class of business or, in the case of composite companies, with the marine branch of the company. In fact, brokers probably find that the unchanged face of the company market provides them with a group of underwriting managers who are well known to underwriters at Lloyd`s, for their expertise in marine insurance, and who will write large lead lines which are readily followed by the single market active underwriters at Lloyd`s.

The insurance company will have limited liability in relation to its assets; this being unlike the current position of a name in a Lloyd`s syndicate. Thus a company shareholder cannot be called upon to surrender his or her personal fortune to meet liabilities incurred by the company. It should be noted that there is no company equivalent to the central fund held at Lloyd`s so a company policyholder has no other source from which to recover any loss he is unable to recover from an insurance company that is in liquidation. The Institute of London Underwriters (see Part 12) issues policies on behalf of its members but does not guarantee claims or premium returns attaching to such policies.

Lloyd`s syndicates are subject to an annual audit (see above) but, under the current rules, are not required to publish annual accounts. Conversely, a British insurance company must, in addition to submitting to an independent annual audit, publish annual accounts. At least once every five years the company must prepare a long term account which is made available for investigation to determine the continued solvency of the company. Statements of account must be deposited with the office of the Secretary of State for Trade and Industry in accordance with the requirements of Section 18 of the Insurance Companies Act, 1982. The company is required by law to maintain a margin of solvency which is usually based on a PIL (premium income limit) similar to the system used for the names in a Lloyd`s syndicate (See Part 2), but related to the company`s assets. In the case of the large marine insurance companies their assets are so huge that the the PIL limitation seldom presents capacity problems for the underwriting manager. It is customary for marine insurance companies to conduct a three year accounting system, similar to that illustrated in Part 7 for Lloyd`s syndicates, to determine its profits.

The manager appointed by the Board of Directors to accept marine risks on behalf of the company is a salaried official of the company. In practice, he is referred to as the "underwriter" in a marine insurance company or as the "marine underwriter" in a composite company. He reports to the Board of Directors and is responsible for maintaining the underwriting policy directed by the Board but he undertakes no personal liability for risks he writes on behalf of his company.

12. The Institute of London Underwriters

The ILU was founded in 1884 to represent the interests of marine insurance companies based in London. Since its formation the ambit of the Institute has been extended to embrace aviation business; although it is still mainly concerned with marine insurance. It must not be assumed that all London based companies writing marine and/or aviation business are members of the ILU; nor that the current structure of the ILU is restricted to London based companies. Since Britain became a partner in the European Economic Community several companies based in EEC countries have been admitted to membership of the Institute. It is not the intention of these introductory notes to give details of the current structure of the membership, which is determined at the discretion of the Board of the ILU. Trainees and practitioners seeking such detail are advised to contact the administration department at the ILU.

The ILU holds a very influential position in the London marine insurance scene. Members of the ILU are invited to serve on joint committees along with members of the LUA (Lloyd`s Underwriters` Association - see Part 8); thereby helping to serve the marine insurance market as a whole. The "Technical & Clauses Committee" is one such joint committee. This committee meets regularly to discuss and make recommendations to the London market on various technical matters of common interest and, in particular, the structure of the Institute clauses. These sets of clauses are the standard marine insurance clauses used in the London market and are adopted by many insurers, worldwide, as a basis for marine insurance contracts.

Since the 1939/45 war the ILU has operated a policy signing office which was developed on similar lines to the LPSO; the latter having commenced operation in 1924 as Lloyd`s policy signing bureau. It is of passing interest to note that current practitioners` reference to both policy signing offices as the "bureau" stems from the old LPSB days. Although the ILU issues signed and sealed combined company policies on behalf of its members it assumes no responsibility for losses attaching to such policies. It is mandatory for all Lloyd`s marine policies to be signed and sealed at the LPSO; but such policy signing restriction is not imposed on the Institute companies. The Institute companies are free to issue and sign their own policies if they so desire; but, generally, they find it more convenient, when sharing a risk with other ILU members, to have the ILU PSO check, sign and seal combined policies on their behalf.

The ILU operates a central accounting system and advisory services similar to Lloyd`s and communicates electronically with its members who are users of LIMNET.

13. Marine Insurance Markets Outside London

Although it can be said that the majority of UK marine insurance business is conducted in the London market one must not forget that other markets exist in the UK. A thriving market operates in Liverpool and one finds representatives of Lloyd`s brokers and marine companies in other cities with a maritime connection.

Whilst there is no direct equivalent to Lloyd`s market elsewhere in the world marine insurance company markets can be found in most countries with a sufficient demand from commercial interests to support such a market. Sometime foreign Government restrictions on insurance activities create the demand for a local marine insurance market which, whilst writing risks relating to that country`s trade, often reinsure those risks in the London market thereby involving the London market (both Lloyd`s and companies) in an international reinsurance network.

13. Insurance Brokers and Brokers` Associations

An insurance broker is an agent whose services are engaged by the proposer of an insurance contract to negotiate, on behalf of his principal, the terms and conditions of the proposed contract with the intended insurer. The activities of the broker are governed by the law of agency under which he must, at all times when acting as agent for his principal, conduct himself in a manner that will not prejudice the interests of his principal. An insurance broker is not obliged to accept an order; nor, if he does so, does he guarantee to place the insurance contract on the terms and conditions requested by his client. However, if the broker does accept the order, he undertakes to use all his skill and endeavours to place the insurance on the best terms and conditions available to him. A broker who is guilty of negligence whereby his client is prejudiced lays himself open to service of suit by his client to claim damages under the law of agency. A broker is neither an insured nor an insurer; he is an intermediary between the insured and the insurer. On occasions, the broker might find himself acting on behalf of the insurer (eg when he is authorised to accept risks on behalf of the insurer in a broker`s cover) but, when he does so, he is acting as an agent for his principal who, in such case, is the insurer and is still bound by the law of agency to represent the insurer`s interests in binding him to the risk accepted; but the broker has no responsibility for claims attaching to the risks so accepted.

The duties of insurance brokers are mainly carried out by employees; some (placing and claims personnel) holding entry permits to the Room as substitutes for their employers. So far as the law is concerned the actions of an employee in carrying out the duties of the broker are the responsibility of the employer. Thus, any negligence on the part of an employee, which prejudices the broker`s principal, is deemed to be negligence of the broker, his employer, who must bear the consequencies of such negligence.

The conduct of Lloyd`s brokers is subject to a Code of Practice which was introduced by Lloyd`s in November, 1988. Strict adherence to this code is required by the Council of Lloyd`s who have powers to discipline any broker and/or broker`s substitute who is in breach of the code. *All trainees and practitioners who work with or for a Lloyd`s broker are strongly advised to obtain a copy of this code and ensure their conduct complies with its requirements.*

The Brokers` Registration Act, 1977, requires all British insurance brokers to be registered with the Insurance Brokers` Registration Council (IBRC). The Act prohibits any person from styling himself as an "insurance broker" except when he is so registered. To obtain registration the applicant must satisfy the Council with regard to his competence, experience and financial stability to carry out the duties and comply with the responsibilities of an insurance broker. Prior to the introduction of the Act therc were several respresentative brokers` organisations. To bring these together under one umbrella the British Insurance Brokers` Association (BIBA) was formed. Since its formation the structure of the Association has changed, to absorb investment brokers; becoming the British Insurance and Investment Brokers` Association (BIIBA). Although, administratively, the IBRC operates under the auspices of the BIIBA it is not compulsory for a registered broker to be a member of BIIBA. In fact, many Lloyd`s brokers, whilst being registered with the IBRC, prefer to be represented, solely, by Lloyd`s Insurance Brokers` Committee and are not members of the BIIBA.

About the same time as the LUA (see Part 8) was being formed at the Royal Exchange brokers operating in the Room formed their own Lloyd`s Brokers` Association. The title was later changed to Lloyd`s Insurance Brokers` Association (LIBA) and remained as such for some 80 years. All Lloyd`s brokers were members of the LIBA which became a major source of information and assistance to brokers throughout its existence. With formation of the BIBA (later the BIIBA) in 1978 the LIBA was replaced with Lloyd`s Insurance Brokers` Committee (LIBC) which now operates autonomously within the BIIBA.

Lloyd`s Insurance Brokers` Committee comprises 16 members elected from among the Board directors of practising Lloyd`s brokers. Each year the committee elect three of their number to the roles of Chairman and two Deputy Chairmen. Sub-committees are formed, as necessary to deal with matters of common interest to the broking community; practitioners from members` offices often being co-opted to serve on a sub-committee to contribute their experience to its deliberations. A sub-committee has no powers other than to make recommendations on its findings. LIBC maintains an administration staff which implements the communication procedures and other activities concerning the committee and sub-committees. Representatives of the LIBC serve on various market joint committees; thereby bring the brokers` point of view to the drafting of standard wordings and clauses and to matters concerning the brokers` role in the London market. The LIBC circulars are particularly important in keeping brokers informed on current developments in market practice and changes in procedures as well as other matters that affect brokers.

15. Conclusion

This set of course notes has been prepared during an atmosphere of great change in Lloyd`s market structure. In recent years adverse results have caused much dissatisfaction amongst underwriting members and the desirability of continuing with the principle of unlimited liability has been in question. A wholesale withdrawal of names from Lloyd`s market could have serious consequences, for the very existence of the market depends on continuance of the capacity provided by the names whose wealth lies behind the risks written by the active underwriters. Loss of a large part of this capacity would make it difficult for active underwriters to write the large risks currently being absorbed by the market.

To resolve these problems the Council of Lloyd`s looked at, amongst other things, ways to replace any lost capacity; also to provide a, much needed, increase of capacity for the future. The introduction of capital with limited liability (see corporate membership in Part 3) strikes at the heart of Lloyd`s traditional underwriting principle of unlimited liability. The upholding of this principle was one of the main reasons why Lloyd`s underwriters were exempt from the restrictions of the Bubble Act, from 1720 to 1824, and the principle has remained enshrined in 300 years of successful practice. At an extraordinary general meeting on 20 October, 1993, the Council of Lloyd`s put the proposal for corporate membership to the vote. Around 13,500 members voted at the meeting, with less than 600 opposing the motion; hence its introduction in 1994.

Further, to support the future of Lloyd`s, applications were invited for individuals to register as high liquidity underwriting members (see Part 2, above); and members` agents are now permitted to group members, who wish to avail themselves of this facility, into a "Members` Agents` Pooling Arrangement", termed a MAPA in practice (see Part 2, above).

By implementing the proposals above, as well as amending some of the rules for membership, introducing a number of cost cutting measures and introducing more efficient procedural changes during the period 1994 to 1996, it is expected that Lloyd`s market will be set for a target capacity of between £10 billion and £12 billion by 1997.

Every effort has been made to incorporate the latest changes in London market practice in these notes but one cannot over-emphasise the need for trainees and practitioners to watch market developments and update the notes as necessary.

SEE FOLLOWING PAGE FOR SELF STUDY QUESTIONAIRE

SELF STUDY QUESTIONS

Before moving on to the next section satisfy yourself that you have absorbed the subject matter in Sections One & Two. The following questions should be answered without reference to the text:

1. When was the first Committee of Lloyd`s formed and what was the main purpose for its formation?

2. There are four types of members` agent dealing with the affairs of underwriting members at Lloyd`s. What is the difference between these?

3. Why does Lloyd`s Act 1982 prohibit a Lloyd`s broker from acting as a managing agent representing the interests of names in a syndicate?

4. Membership and the role of "names" at Lloyd`s -
(a) What are the requirements for an individual to be elected to underwriting membership Lloyd`s?
(b) What is the difference between an "external" member and a "working" member?
(c) What is a "name" in a Lloyd`s syndicate and to what extent is the liability of a name in a syndicate limited?
(d) What is an "incorporated name" at Lloyd`s?
(e) What is a "high liquidity name" at Lloyd`s?
(f) What is a MAPA?

5. What are the roles and structure of the Council of Lloyd`s, the Committee of Lloyd`s and Lloyd`s Regulatory and Market Boards?

6. What are the roles of the Corporation of Lloyd`s, the LUA and the LIBC?

7. How is the security in a Lloyd`s policy protected and how does this compare with the security offered in a policy issued by, or on behalf of, a British insurance company?

8. What is the role of a Lloyd`s agent?

9. Why has Lloyd`s changed its structure to a "single" market and how does this new structure compare with the previous market structure?

10. Who are the members of the ILU and how does this organisation operate?

This page is left blank for Trainees` notes

SECTION THREE

EFFECTING MARINE INSURANCE CONTRACTS

1. Introduction
2. The Broker`s Role in Relation to the Proposer
3. The Lloyd`s Broker in Relation to the London Market
4. Introduction to Facultative and Obligatory Contracts
5. The Slip as the Basis of the Marine Insurance Contract
6. The Format of a Placing Slip
7. Selecting the Market and the Leading Underwriter
8. Obligations of Underwriters in Regard to Written Lines
9. Overplacing and Signing Down
10. Use of the Broker`s Covernote
11. Agreements and Amendments after Placing
12. Held covered agreements
13. Effecting Open Cover Contracts
14. Effecting Renewals on Term Contracts
15. Electronic Placing

SECTION THREE

1. Introduction

Except where otherwise specified herein, the comments in these notes are based on English law and practice. References to the "MIA, 1906" relate to the Marine Insurance Act, 1906, which codified English law as at 21st December, 1906. The legal position established by this Act is accepted as law in connection with marine insurance contracts effected in many countries; some of whom have incorporated the British Act into their own statutes. Undoubtedly, there are countries that have not adopted the MIA, 1906, relying on their own common law to settle disputes in court, and there have been legal decisions both in the UK and elsewhere since December, 1906, which one must take into account in disputes. Recognising this, the ILU (Institute of London Underwriters) incorporates the "English Law & Practice" clause in all relevant sets of marine insurance clauses published by them; thereby ensuring that disputes in respect of contracts bearing these clauses are not prejudiced by variances between English law and practice and foreign law and practice.

The placing procedure outlined in this section relates to "face to face" negotiations between the broker and the underwriter as practised at Lloyd`s and in the in the London marine insurance company market. A similar procedure has been adopted in many overseas markets; although there is, probably, more telephone placing in such markets than one sees in the London marine insurance market. Even in countries where the London market slip placing system operates there are probably local market procedures not embraced within these notes, so instructors, trainees and practitioners operating in markets outside London should amend the notes, as necessary, to comply with local market practice. As LIMNET (London Insurance Market Network) develops it is anticipated that electronic placing procedures will be introduced and, at the time of writing, a pilot scheme is being implemented to test the viability of this type of placing. For the time being, at least, these notes embrace only limited comment on electronic placing; further information being available to interested practitioners through market manuals which are published by the authoritative bodies concerned (eg Lloyd`s Policy Signing and Central Acounting Manual).

All insurance brokers practising in the United Kingdom must be registered with the Insurance Brokers` Registration Council (IBRC) and are subject to a Code of Practice set down by the IBRC. Nevertheless, the Council of Lloyd`s considered it desirable to publish their own Code of Practice for Lloyd`s brokers under Paragraph 20 of Lloyd`s Brokers` Byelaw (No.5 of 1988). The code was published on 6th July 1988 and all brokers (including their substitutes and employees) must comply with the rules established by the code or be subject to disciplinary procedures imposed by the Council of Lloyd`s. The code is based on the IBRC code but is specifically designed to establish a recognised standard of professional conduct in the Lloyd`s community; in particular to ensure Lloyd`s brokers discharge their duties in accordance with the intention and spirit of the codes. Lloyd`s Code of Practice came into force on 1st November, 1988. Although reference is made herein to the duties of brokers in connection with the code, all personnel reading these notes are advised to obtain and study a copy of this code to supplement, were necessary, the information herein.

2. The Broker`s Role in Relation to the Proposer

There are two parties to a marine insurance contract; the proposer and the accepter. The former is, normally, termed the "assured" in marine insurance practice; although, technically, he remains the proposer until the contract between the parties has been concluded. The latter is the underwriter who accepts the contract (ie an underwriting member at Lloyd`s or an insurance company, as the case may be). The contract is *concluded* when the active underwriter (Lloyd`s) or underwriting manager (company) indicates acceptance of the risk on the broker`s slip or on any other document used to indicate acceptance (MIA, 1906, sec.21).

A broker whose services are involved in the negotiations leading up to conclusion of contract is **not** a party to the insurance contract. The btroker is merely an intermediary who represents the proposer in offering the risk to the underwriter and in negotiating the terms and conditions of the contract. Thus, the broker has no rights in the insurance contract; other than a lien on the policy which he may exercise in event of non-payment of premium (MIA, 1906, sec.53 sub.2). In practice, it is possible for a broker to be nominated by the assured to represent him as his agent in the policy. For example, one might see the name of the broker expressed as agent for the named assured in a facultative reinsurance policy. An assured in a direct policy for a very large amount is unlikely to allow the broker to be named in the policy as his agent because it would negate his right to take the policy to another broker for claim collection in cases where he is dissatisfied with the claims service offered by the placing broker.

In general, an assured is not obliged to avail himself of the services of a broker. If he is confident in his knowledge of marine insurance conditions and his ability to negotiate a contract to his best advantage the proposer he may approach an insurance company without recourse to a broker`s services. However, a proposer who wishes to conclude a marine insurance contract with a Lloyd`s underwriter can do so only through the medium of a Lloyd`s broker. Proposers in the London market recognise the value of using the wide experience of a Lloyd`s broker and most marine insurance contracts placed in this market are negotiated through the medium of a Lloyd`s broker. Perhaps encouraged by the spread of risk offered by the broker operation, proposers in some overseas markets use the services of brokers, agents or consultants operating in the same way as brokers operate in the London market, but one frequently encounters the direct approach in overseas markets where the value of spread of risk over a group of insurers may not be so readily recognised by the proposer.

The long experience of a well established broker with his expert knowledge of markets, insurance conditions and premium rating over a wide range of marine risks is invaluable to a proposer for it is unlikely that the proposer will have the same experience and knowledge, even within his own scope of business. By conducting a risk management exercise a broker can pinpoint areas of potential hazard and be able to advise his client on ways of reducing the risks and/or arranging adequate insurance protection. The broker`s knowledge of insurance markets makes it less likely that the risk will be placed with poor security. Where there is a large risk to place it is the broker who has the experience to spread the risk over a wide market; thereby saving the proposer from the task of finding an insurer with the capacity to cover the whole risk and providing a broader security base.

Under the current system in the London market the placing and advice service provided by the marine insurance broker is free to the proposer. The broker is remunerated by commission paid by the underwriters. This is termed "brokerage" and is deducted by the broker from the premium paid by the assured before the net premium is paid to the underwriter. The brokerage system, which is outlined in Section four, is frequently criticised by various sections of the underwriting community and is often under review but the London market is pre-occupied with other matters, for the time being, so there appears to be no move, at present, to change the brokerage system.

A broking firm is a financial organisation which seeks, through its business dealings, to make money for itself, its partners or its shareholders, as the case may be. The broker`s prime objective is to obtain profitable orders and to place the business generated by those orders speedily and efficiently. To achieve this objective the broker may be faced with temptations to take short cuts and other measures to attain profitability at all costs. Regrettably, there have been brokers who have failed to maintain the high standards demanded by the insurance community and society generally resulting in prejudice to their clients` interests.

When carrying out transactions a broker should always -

(1) Observe market rules of behaviour
(2) Be honest in dealings with both client and underwriter
(3) Observe the principle of good faith when placing or renewing a contract
(4) Remember he represents the interests of his principal only
(5) Use all his skill and experience to obtain the best cover for his client and at the most reasonable rate
(6) Remember that an underwriter will always regard the broker as the assured in matters where there is a breach of good faith

In regard to (4), above, the term "principal" means the party whom the broker is representing in a particular transaction. Generally, one thinks of the transaction as the placing of a risk; in which case the broker is acting for the proposer (his client) who then becomes his principal. It sometimes happens that the broker accepts instructions from the underwriter (eg to arrange a survey or to accept risks on behalf of the underwriter under a binding authority) in which case he is acting for the underwriter who, so far as the instruction is concerned, is his principal. Where a broker finds himself with a conflict of interests (eg where to carry out the instructions of one party could be prejudicial to the other party) he should seriously consider whether it is prudent for him to accept instructions from both parties.

The instruction given to the broker by the proposer is termed the *order*. The broker is not obliged to accept the order and, if he feels that to accept the order would create a conflict of interests (eg materially affect his obligations to another party) he should seriously consider his position before accepting the order. Further, the Code of Practice for Lloyd`s brokers states that a broker should not accept an order when he is not competent to handle that order efficiently. Other brokers might consider this to be good advice for them also. A broker should also reject an order where he has doubts about the credibility of the proposer. When accepting an order the broker should take care to ensure he is "as one" with the proposer. In other words, the broker must be absolutely clear on the substance of the order and be sure that the proposer understands his own instructions. In this respect the broker`s experience should enable him to know what information the underwriter will require to assess the risk. If this information is not complete the broker should clarify the position with the proposer. Cases of doubt should be clarified before the broker proceeds further. Verbal instructions should always be confirmed in writing. Although these responsibilities rest on the broker it is doubtful that an action for damages against the broker would succeed if he fails to elicit information from his client; particularly where the client withheld the information from the broker.

The broker is an agent of his client and is bound by the law of agency. In cases where the broker`s negligence has prejudiced his client the latter may have grounds to sue the broker in a court of law for damages. The broker must remember that the law regards an insurance broker as an expert in his field with full knowledge of the technicalities of the insurance contract he is handling. Any incompetence or lack of the necessary knowledge may well be considered as negligence by the court. Under English law, to protect the public at large, an insurance broker is required to maintain an adequate professional indemnity insurance policy; often referred to, in practice, as an "errors & omissions" policy. This is to ensure that sufficient funds are available to meet negligence awards made against the broker.

On acceptance of the order the broker is expected to act with diligence in complying with the proposer`s instructions. The broker should advise his client when he has completed the placing but, irrespective of the circumstances or pressures he is under, the broker should never confirm the placing until it is completed. The broker is not obliged to complete a placing simply because he has accepted the order. Provided he has used all his skill and experience to effect the placing he cannot be held accountable for his failure. Nevertheless, if he is unable to complete a placing he must advise his principal of this without delay.

Particular attention should be directed to application of the principle of good faith (see Section 7).

There appear to be no legal precedents for circumstances where brokers (ie broking firms) act jointly in placing a risk; but the following practical guidelines might be useful to trainees and practitioners. In general, in the absence of any agreement to the contrary, where a broker acts jointly with another broker in placing a risk, he is deemed to be directly responsible the proposer, as his principal, and his responsiblities are the same as though he were acting as a sole agent for the proposer. An exception can occur where a producing broker appoints a joint broker to represent him in placing the risk, or part thereof, in another market (see below).

A joint broker involved in placing a risk should ensure that both he and the other broker are "as one" in understanding the insurance contract and should clearly understand their joint roles in regard to the transaction. In cases of dispute between the joint brokers the client`s interests must take precedence; the brokers taking instructions from the client, if necessary, to resolve the dispute.

It is customary for the principal broker to prepare the placing slip and other documentation. Where the placing slip and/or covernote is issued in their joint names, the other broker is responsible for checking the documentation to ensure that it is correctly prepared, complies with the proposer`s instructions, accurately reflects the intentions of the parties to the contract and, in the case of the covernote, correctly shows the detail regarding the placing.

Where a producing broker appoints another broker to act as a joint broker in placing part, or the whole, of a risk in another market the producing broker is acting as principal to the joint broker and is responsible for keeping him advised of all matters pertaining to the transaction.

3. The Lloyd`s Broker in Relation to the London Market

The term "Lloyd`s broker" can apply to an individual who conducts business in his own name or a firm which specialises in the business of insurance broking. The following comments regarding a Lloyd`s broker apply equally to individuals and broking firms. A Lloyd`s broker is one who has satisfied the Committee of Lloyd`s regarding his experience, integrity and financial standing, as being a fit and proper person to negotiate contracts at Lloyd`s. Having been admitted to the Lloyd`s community he becomes a member of the LIBC (see Section 2). Provided he holds a valid entry permit (referred to as a Room ticket, in practice) the broker may enter the Underwriting Room at Lloyd`s to transact business. Further he may obtain Room tickets for employees (termed "substitutes") to represent him in the Room. Whilst a Lloyd`s broker may be expected to place a reasonable amount of business at Lloyd`s there is no compulsion in this respect and he is free to place business in any market that provides his client with the best deal.

Although most marine insurance business in the UK is placed through the medium of Lloyd`s brokers only a small proportion of British registered brokers are Lloyd`s brokers. Thus, most UK brokers find their activities restricted to the company market. However, it is not uncommon for a non-Lloyd`s broker to make an arrangement with a Lloyd`s broker to allow him the opportunity to offer a Lloyd`s policy to his clients. Trainees should watch developments in this respect because, every now and again, the restrictions of access to the Room are reviewed in an attempt to allow more freedom of access and so to broaden the scope of business conducted at Lloyd`s.

Comment was made in part 2, above, to the Code of Practice for Lloyd`s Brokers. The Council of Lloyd`s is ever conscious of its responsibility for the conduct of those who practise in Lloyd`s market and requires all Lloyd`s brokers to comply with the rules set down in the Code of Practice. Further, the Council of Lloyd`s reviews, as deemed necessary, the position of brokers operating in the Marketplace. One such review is taking place at the time of writing, so brokers and other practitioners who use these notes should watch local develoments and amend these notes as necessary.

4. Introduction to Facultative and Obligatory Contracts

The term "facultative" implies "choice" or "option", as opposed to compulsion. In marine insurance practice a contract may be effected for a single voyage, for a series of voyages or for a period of time. A contract to cover a ship is usually a time contract, but may be for a voyage or series of voyages. In each case the hull insurance contract is insured facultatively; the underwriter exercising a free choice whether or not to accept the proposal. A contract to cover cargo is normally effected on a "voyage" basis but few cargo insurance contracts are effected facultatively for a specific voyage. It is more customary for the underwriter to accept a proposal for a long term time contract (called an "open cover" in practice) which will cover an unspecified number of voyages. In this case each voyage or sending will be declared as it takes place and, provided it comes within the scope and limits of the contract, the underwriter is obliged to accept each declaration. This is termed an "obligatory" contract. In this introductory course it is not intended to go into detail concerning the operation of open covers. For such detail the trainee should consult a course on marine cargo practice.

5. The Slip as the Basis of the Marine Insurance Contract

Records do not indicate exactly when the slip placing system was first introduced to the marine insurance scene. It is believed to have stemmed from a practice, exercised in London coffee houses (note - Lloyd`s was not the only coffee house where marine insurance contracts were made during the 18th century), where the broker would have to wait for each underwriter to signify his acceptance on a formal policy document. To speed up the procedure the broker would obtain agreement to accept the risk, or part thereof in the case of large risks, from each underwriter before the formal policy was issued. Acceptance by the underwriter was indicated on a slip of paper and constituted a promise to issue a policy, in due course, to cover the risk. Such pieces of paper became known as "promissory slips".

During the French wars of William III stamp duty on all marine insurance policies was introduced. For the record it can be noted that stamp duty on marine insurance policies issued in the UK continued to be enforced until it was abolished on 1st August, 1970. In those early days all marine insurance contracts were on a "voyage" basis and many risks ran off without incident before a policy could be issued. This encouraged underwriters and brokers to save effort and expense by waiving the issue of formal policies and to rely on the promissory slip as the only evidence of the existence of a contract. In such cases no stamp duty was paid and the Government of the day considered this practice to be an abuse of the stamp laws. The threat of heavy stamp duty during the early part of the 18th century created an increase in the abuse so, in 1724, the Government introduced an Act which prohibited the "giving of Promissory Notes instead of Policies". This Act also required the underwriter to issue a duly stamped policy within three days from the time he accepted the risk; thereby, effectively, acknowledging the existence of placing slips prior to the issue of a policy, provided such slips were not issued in place of a policy.

In practice, many underwriters and brokers ignored the provisions of the 1724 Act and continued to proceed as they had always done. This went on for many years undisturbed until the year 1795 when the 1724 Act was strengthened with a penalty of £500 to be awarded against anyone who effected a marine insurance contract without a policy bearing the requisite stamp duty. Even this did not deter practitioners who continued to ignore the statutory requirements but, eventually, in 1807 the Government brought a successful prosecution against one underwriting member (a Mr Pearson Walton) for tax evasion in connection with the use of an unstamped document of insurance. This caused consternation in the market and the Committee of Lloyd`s appealed to the Commissioners for Taxes to relieve the pressure on the market but with little success until a compromise was reached in 1810. The compromise seems to have relied heavily on evidence to the effect that slips presented at Lloyd`s were only a temporary measure and the underwriter`s promised acceptance was entered thereon by the broker who also added the underwriter`s initials. Further, the Commissioners were assured that, under no circumstances, did the underwriter`s name appear on the slip. It is doubtful that this evidence was true in fact because it seems inconceivable that a broker would be satisfied with a slip that had not been, at least, initialled by the underwriter or that an underwriter could be relied upon to honour a contract which was based on a slip on which he had not personally written his acceptance of the risk. Nevertheless, the Commissioners for Taxes appear to have accepted this evidence and allowed the slip system to continue; on condition that every slip used at Lloyd`s was presented only until a policy could be issued the next morning (the stamp due thereon being taken that day).

Whatever the truth of the evidence submitted at the appeal, one cannot imagine the slip system continuing as presented to the Commissioners for Taxes. Certainly, there is plenty of evidence to show that, as the slip system developed both at Lloyd`s and subsequently in the company market, initialling of the slip by underwriters became the standard practice. Probably realising that stamped policies were not forthcoming as agreed in the compromise the Government made one final attempt to force the issue. By an Act of Parliament, in 1814, all slips were required to bear the stamp duty attaching to the risk. The stamp duty was, then, to be refunded against the issue of a stamped policy. Compliance with the 1814 Act became so cumbersome that, eventually, it proved unworkable and the requirement was largely ignored (with the blessing of the overworked stamp office) so that, by 1817, there appear to have been no slips which bore stamp duty. After this failure the Government seems to have given up on the matter for no further statutory action was taken to restrict the use of slips in the London market.

The London market slip placing system has survived criticism for some three hundred years and continues to be the primary procedure for concluding contracts of marine insurance at Lloyd`s and in the London company market. The slip remains a promissory document. When the onerous stamp duty on English marine insurance policies was reduced to a simple 6d head charge there was some speculation on the possibility of giving the slip legal status by attaching a 6d stamp thereto and one saw the, newly introduced, "slip policy" (see Section 4) submitted to the bureaux so stamped. However, legal opinion inclined to the view that a slip policy was no more acceptable as legal evidence in a court of law, whether or not it be stamped, than any other broker`s slip. With the 1970 abolition of stamp duty on marine insurance policies the argument became a matter of academic interest only.

Today, the position of the broker`s slip in relation to the contract is established by the MIA, 1906 (secs. 21 & 22). Section 21 acknowledges the use of a slip in negotiating a marine insurance contract and provides that the *contract is concluded* between the parties when the insurer indicates his acceptance of the proposal on the slip or covering note or other customary memorandum of the contract. It is for this reason that every acceptance on a slip must show the date the line was written. Section 22 provides that a contract of marine insurance is inadmissible as evidence in law unless it is embodied in a marine policy. It follows that, despite the belief of some practitioners to the contrary, no legal action can be taken in any court that is subject to English jurisdiction against the underwriter on the evidence of the slip alone; although the slip can be called for, in support of the policy, to show evidence of intent. It has been known for a court to order a policy to be redrafted and resubmitted to the court where its terms are contrary to the intention expressed in the slip.

So the broker`s slip is binding in honour only but, despite its legal invalidity, the slip is too valuable in the process of placing marine insurance contracts for its use to be discontinued. One might add that the slip is so enshrined in London market practice that its format will continue to be used when electronic placing becomes the norm, as it undoubtedly will, in the London market with the passage of time.

In modern practice the broker uses a slip to effect contracts both at Lloyd's and in the company market. When so doing he obtains acceptances from many underwriters on the same slip. Thus, a slip might have listed thereon acceptances from various Lloyd's syndicates and acceptances from various London based marine insurance companies. Where part of the risk is placed outside the London market the broker might consider it expedient to send a copy of the slip to insurers who have agreed to accept a line asking them to confirm their acceptance thereon and return the slip to the broker. On receipt of this confirmation the broker might find it convenient to note these acceptances on the original slip so that he can refer thereto to see all lines written to cover the risk.

When he commences placing a risk the broker approaches the underwriter he has selected to lead the slip (see part 6). He negotiates the terms and conditions of the contract with the leader; following underwriters accepting the terms and conditions agreed with the leader. Each underwriter writes the amount he will accept; indicating this as a percentage of the amount to be placed. This acceptance is termed the underwriter's *line*. Although each line is a proportion of the whole it constitutes a separate contract between the relevant underwriter and the assured; the provisions of the MIA, 1906, sec.24 sub.2, regarding combined policies, applying equally to placing slips. Similarly, where an active underwriter at Lloyd's writes a line on a slip, this line is shared, as a separate contract with the assured, between the names in the syndicate being represented by the active underwriter.

6. The Format of a Placing Slip

There are several types of broker's slip used in the London marine insurance market. In this set of notes we shall concern ourselves solely with slips used for placing risks facultatively; the basic format for such slips being amended, as appropriate, for obligatory contracts. Before considering the format of a facultative placing slip, the use of other slips connected with these needs to be defined.

Original slip - This is the placing slip referred to above. It is so termed to identify it in comparison with any copy slip that might be used in practice.

Off slip - This is a typed copy of the original slip. A photocopy of the original slip might be acceptable as a copy slip; but, if it is to be used for signing and accounting purposes it will need to be backed by a letter of indemnity, lodged with the bureau, whereby the broker undertakes responsibility for any difference between the copy and the original; otherwise a photocopy is unlikely to be accepted by the bureau unless it is authenticated by the leading underwriter on the slip for the market concerned.

Signing slip - This can be the original slip or an off slip, as above defined. It is used in the London market policy signing and accounting procedures. It is seldom that the original slip will be used for signing and accounting purposes because, where there are lines on the slip from both Lloyd's and the company market, the broker would have to delay the procedure for one market whilst awaiting return of the slip from the other market. To avoid this, it is customary for the broker to type a separate signing slip for each market, so that he can submit the signing and accounting documents to each market at the same time. It is customary for a signing slip to be intialled by the underwriter leading the relevant market to authenticate it for the bureau.

Closing slip - Another term for a signing slip; customarily applied only when the slip is used in the accounting procedure.

Standard slip - The standard format for a marine signing slip was introduced to the London market in 1970 in an effort to reduce the number of clerical errors and errors of omission caused, mainly it was thought, by the wide variety in the formats of broker`s slips. For many years it was mandatory for the broker`s slip to be restricted to a document that comprised three or more panels, each of which was 4.75 inches wide. This format was adopted both by Lloyd`s and by member companies of the ILU. To accommodate this joint adoption the standard format was designed, not only for LPSO needs, but to provide for entries that related only to the Institute PSO procedures. The growing use of word processers encouraged the London market to adopt an A4 size of slip which is in common use today. The A4 slip comprises a set of consecutively numbered sheets of A4 paper which are bound into a folder. Although the original purpose of the standardisation was to facilitate more accurate signing and accounting it soon became apparent that the same design and format should be used in original slips and, today, London underwriters will not entertain a facultative risk that is proposed to them on any document other than in the standard slip format. The comments that follow herein regarding detail to be entered in a placing slip relate to both the old type of standard slip and the A4 type of slip.

An important part in the structure of a standard slip is the printed grid in which administrative detail is entered. This is of interest solely to practitioners in the London market, so only passing comment concerning these entries appears in these notes. The purpose of the grid is to set out in a standard format all the information that needs to be picked up by the bureau when processing the risk for accounting, records and statistical purposes. Many of the entries are in code; these being taken from code lists supplied to practitioners via various market information sources. The coding system is not for secrecy but is a convenient method for entering information in the small space provided by the grid boxes. Some of the codes are entered by the broker, whilst others are entered by the leading underwriter. Practitioners submitting a signing slip or closing slip to a bureau should ensure that all necessary codes have been correctly entered. Incorrect codes will result in wrong records and statistics being prepared and omission of an entry will probably result in a slip being rejected by the bureau until the matter has been remedied.

Modern practice in the London market demands the use of computerisation; the computer operators being specialists in their area and seldom with knowledge of the technicalities of insurance contracts. The coding system, referred to above, provides for accurate computer entries of administrative data, but does not lend itself to such easy entry or recording of placing detail. When the standard slip format was being designed it was realised that this provided an opportunity to standardise the format of placing data on the broker`s slip. Such standardisation assists brokers to prepare slips in a way that important detail is not omitted and, if the same format appears on the original slip, helps underwriters to understand the placing data more readily. It also makes it easier for non-insurance technicians to enter placing data in computers and recorded advices. It is interesting to note that the original instructions on the use of the standard slip did not require a marine broker to *type* the detail in an *original* slip; nor was he required to follow the standard format when entering the placing data on the original slip. However, if he entered placing data on the original slip in any other format the rules demanded that he must prepare a separate, typed, signing slip for submission to the bureau and the placing data thereon had to be in the standard format. In practice, today, it is unlikely one would see an original slip written by hand and it is customary for the placing data to be in the standard format in the original slip.

Placing data varies, depending on the type of risk being placed and the form of contract. It would be burdensome for the newcomer to the marine insurance industry to try to master all the formats available so we shall confine ourselves to the basic headings as shown below; leaving trainees to relate these to practice as their experience develops.

In a slip prepared for a facultative placing the data must be entered in the following order:

1. Type of insurance
2. Type of policy
3. Name of assured
4. Name of ship
5. Period of insurance or the voyage covered, as appropriate
6. Insured interest
7. Sum insured and insured value
8. Trading limits &/or warranties
9. Conditions of insurance
10. Rate of premium
11. Any additional information concerning the risk that the broker wants recorded as having been advised to the underwriter
12. Deductions (including brokerage)

If one is using the early form of standard slip the placing data must be shown on the *face* of the slip (none of it appearing on the reverse of a panel); the slip comprising a sufficient number of panels to ensure this. The structure of an A4 slip must show the placing detail on the sheet immediately following the sheet with the administrative grid thereon; if there is insufficient room on this sheet the data should continue on the next consecutively numbered sheet so that sheets reserved for underwriters` lines do not intercede with placing data.

Before comment is made in respect of the above list it would be appropriate to consider the use of abbreviations. To make the best use of the limited space available on the old form of broker`s slip it became the practice for brokers to use abbreviations in placing detail. Although there is much more space available in the revelant sheet of the slip in the A4 format brokers continue to use abbreviations as a matter of expediency. There is nothing wrong with this practice provided only standard abbreviations are used; so that both broker and underwriter know the meaning of an abbreviation. One should avoid using an abbreviation that has more than one meaning or an abbreviation that is unfamiliar to the market. Trainees and practitioners seeking information on marine insurance abbreviations might find it convenient to consult "Abbreviations used in Marine Insurance & Reinsurance Practice" (Brown - Witherby

1993). The following brief comments on the entries to be made against the headings listed above might prove useful.

1. *Type of insurance* - This determines the class of insurance (eg Marine hull, Marine cargo, Marine liability, etc.). It supports the risk code shown in the relevant box in the administrative grid and makes the class of risk immediately apparent to any underwriter who normally restricts his acceptances to a certain class or certain classes of insurance.

2. *Type of policy* - This information was important in the early days of standardisation (1970) because, whilst the marine market mainly used the SG form of policy, there were other types of policy available for various incidental non-marine risks which were written in the marine market. During the transitional period, following introduction of the MAR form of policy, it was necessary to determine to which form of policy it was intended the Institute clauses (entered as an abbreviation under placing heading 8) would apply. Today the entry would, almost certainly, be "MAR form"; but practitioners should note that any broker who enters "SG form" (assuming he can find an underwriter in the London market who continues to write marine insurance contracts on this form) must **not** use any of the current Institute clauses headed "for use only with the new policy" in the slip conditions; nor enter, under placing heading 8, abbreviations for standard clauses (eg ICC or ITC) because the latter no longer exist for use with the SG form of policy.

3. *Name of assured* - No comment necessary.

4. *Name of ship* - In the case of a hull insurance or a hull interest insurance this will be the name of the ship that is the subject matter of the insurance contract; often, in the case of an H & M proposal, with the type of ship and its tonnage shown to give the underwriter some idea of its likely exposure to risk and its size. In the case of a cargo insurance or a cargo interest insurance this will be the name of the overseas carrying vessel. In some cases the name of the carrying vessel may not be known at the time of placing; in which case the broker enters "TBA L/U". This means that the name of the carrying vessel will be advised to the leading underwriter on the slip when it is known. The leading underwriter may qualify this with a condition requiring the carrying vessel to be an "approved" vessel (ie of not less than an acceptable minimum class) with the provision that carriage on vessels that are not approved will be held covered on payment of an additional premium.

Accuracy in the name of the ship is important. Until the introduction of the ICC (1982) a cargo policy would hold the assured covered in the case of an error in the description of the carrying vessel; but no such provision appears in the current ICC. Further, there is no provision in the standard insurance conditions used for hull insurances which holds the assured covered in the case of misdescription of the insured vessel.

5. *Period of insurance* - This entry depends on whether the insurance contract is to be effected on a *time* basis or on a *voyage* basis. Most ships are insured on a time basis whilst it is customary to insure goods in transit by sea on a voyage basis.

Time insurances - In the case of a time insurance contract covering a ship one should show clearly the exact time and date of attachment and termination which it is intended shall be agreed in the contract. The time zone should be shown. In practice, it is customary for hull underwriters to restrict cover to 12 months, but the standard ITC (Institute time clauses - Hulls) will hold the assured covered if the ship is at sea or in a port of refuge or of call at the time of natural expiry; provided the assured invokes the "continuation clause" before the natural expiry time expressed in the policy. It is customary for standard hull time clauses to incorporate an automatic termination clause which comes into effect in event of certain specified circumstances arising (eg the vessel is sold). Although one sometimes sees time contracts insuring goods in warehouses, or in other land based locations, most cargo time insurance contracts are open covers (ie obligatory contracts) and are seldom effected for a fixed period of time. They are customarily agreed as attaching from a specified date (or a date to be agreed with the leading underwriter) on an "always open" basis and are subject to the terms of an agreed cancellation clause.

Voyage insurances - When a hull voyage insurance contract is proposed the broker must indicate in the slip whether the risk shall attach *"from"* the specified place or *"at & from"* such place. The difference between these two terms can be found in the "Rules for Construction of the Policy" (numbers 2 & 3) in the First Schedule to the MIA, 1906. All insurance contracts proposed to cover goods in transit by sea are effected on a "voyage" basis and the points of attachment and termination are determined by the conditions specified under placing heading number 8 so it is necessary for only outline detail (eg name of place for commencement of transit and the intended final destination) to be entered under placing heading number 5 on the slip.

Continuation of cover under a voyage insurance contract (for both hull and cargo) during commencement and prosecution of an insured voyage is subject to the MIA, 1906, Secs.42 to 49; but practitioners should examine the insurance conditions to see how these matters are dealt with in practice.

Accuracy in description of the voyage is important. Until the introduction of the ICC (1982) a cargo policy would hold the assured covered in the case of an error or omission in the description of the voyage; but no such provision appears in the current ICC. Further, there is no provision in the standard insurance conditions used for hull insurances which holds the assured covered in the case of misdescription of the insured voyage.

6. *Insured interest* - One should refer to Section 6 (Insurable interest) to understand the difference between the subject matter insured and the insured interest. Entered here is the interest to which the subject matter insured relates. For example, in the case of an insurance relating to the ship itself the insured interest could be the hull & machinery of the ship or, perhaps, an insurance to cover liabilities incurred by the assured in connection with operation of the ship; the latter being referred to as a "hull interest". Thus, where the contract is proposed to cover loss of or damage to the ship one would enter "H & M" (hull & machinery); but, where the contract is proposed to cover the liabilities that might be incurred in connection with operating the ship, one would enter "Shipowner's liability". Variations to these might occur. For example, a slip prepared to cover a ship under construction would indicate this with, say, "Construction risks".

Where the slip relates to cargo in transit it is customary to describe the cargo under this heading, with its quantity or weight. For example, "....... cases of agricultural machinery". Care should be exercised when making this entry because, unlike earlier sets of the ICC, cargo insurance conditions designed for use with the MAR form of policy do **not** hold the assured covered in the event of any omission or misdescription of the insured interest.

7. *Sum insured/Insured value* - This entry relates to both the sum insured and the insured value.

Sum insured - The sum insured for a hull & machinery policy or a cargo policy is the total amount proposed to be insured. This may be the full value or it may be a proportion thereof. If it is for an amount less than the insured value it is important that the broker makes this clear and completes the box at the foot of the administrative grid sheet in the A4 slip (a similar box is printed at the foot of panel 2 in the old standard slip format). By completing this box the broker shows the relationship between the sum insured and the broker's order as a guide to both underwriters and the relevant policy signing office. Where the insured interest relates to liabilities the amount entered is the limit of liability recoverable. If the liability limit applies to successive losses (see Section 14) one should add "any one occurrence" or similar wording, as appropriate to the circumstances. It is not necessary to so qualify the sum insured for hull & machinery insurances or cargo insurance because, where applicable to the interest, the principle of successive losses is automatically applied to these (MIA, 1906, scc.77). Each underwriter subscribing the slip will expect his written line to apply as a percentage of the sum insured or the limit of liability, as the case may be.

Insured value - This applies only to the insurance of property (eg the hull & machinery of a ship or cargo in transit). By agreeing to the insured value the underwriter is accepting that the property is so valued and, except in a case of fraud, he cannot object at the time of claim that the insured value is incorrect (MIA, 1906, sec.27). If the broker &/or underwriter fails to enter the insured value in the slip the policy, when issued, will be an *unvalued* policy and all claims will be based on the insurable value (see Sections 4 & 12). Liability insurances are not subject to valuation so, for such policies, no insured value is expressed in the slip; the limit of indemnity being as indicated for the sum insured.

8. *Trading limits and warranties* - If no trading limits or location warranties (see Section 8) are incorporated in an H & M policy the premium rate will assume the ship to be trading worldwide. If the proposer agrees to limited trading the broker will indicate the limits here and the premium rate will be reduced in proportion to the reduced hazard potential. Whether the proposal relates to a hull or cargo policy any warranties imposed by underwriters will be entered here by the leader. Where an entry is made under this heading the broker should satisfy himself that, should the assured require it and the underwriter agree, provision is made, either here or in the insurance conditions, to hold covered breaches of warranty, etc.

9. *Conditions of insurance* - Great care must be exercised to ensure that both broker and underwriter fully understand the cover provided by the conditions proposed and accepted. Abbreviations may be used for standard clauses and conditions (eg ITC for Institute time clauses, ICC A for Institute cargo clauses on A conditions, etc.). Showing the relevant clause number and date (eg ITC CL.280 1.10.83) helps in this respect and avoids later misunderstandings; particularly in cases where a new clause has been issued recently or where there are two sets of standard clauses with the same title but different reference numbers. Where the insurance conditions are other than

standard, or are the leading underwriter's own conditions for the type of risk, the broker usually enters the reference "as attached" under the placing heading and affixes a copy of the conditions to the slip. Except where they are his own conditions, the broker must expect the leading underwriter to devote time to the study of the non-standard conditions before writing a line on the slip. Those responsible for preparing covernotes and policies should not use a copy of the non-standard conditions, even though they are commonly used by the broker, without checking the slip to ensure that the leading underwriter has not qualified the conditions somewhere in the slip (eg inserted a warranty); amending the conditions if necessary before inserting them in the covernote or policy.

10. *Rate of premium* - Where the broker's experience makes him confident that the premium rate he proposes will be acceptable to the leading underwriter he may insert this here. If he is not confident about the rate he should leave this space blank for the leader's attention. The rate will be shown as a percentage which, in cases of hull & machinery policies and policies covering goods in transit, will be applied to the sum insured to arrive at the premium. In other cases the basis of calculation should be shown (eg a minimum flat rate or an adjustable rate for liability cover, etc.). Where applicable, the basis of payment (eg deferred account) must be shown here; otherwise the premium becomes due without an extension of the standard period of credit allowed. For the London market the period of credit will be determined by the "settlement due date" entered in the relevant box in the administrative data grid. For insurances effected outside the London market, and in the absence of premium settlement credit arrangements, the full premium is payable on or before the date the policy is issued and, in any case, before inception of risk.

11. *Additional information* - No comment necessary.

12. *Deductions (including brokerage)* - Many years ago it was agreed that London market underwriters would allow standard deductions to be applied to the premium due on marine insurance policies. These permitted the broker to enjoy a fixed percentage deduction as his commission (termed "brokerage") and to pass on to the assured a discount against early "cash" payment of the premium. Attention is directed to Section 5 for details in this respect. Market practices vary but if the broker is seeking deductions which allow him to pass on a higher percentage of discount to his client he must agree this concession with the leading underwriter and have the special deductions inserted in the slip; otherwise, by leaving this space blank, the broker is permitted to apply only the standard deductions to the gross premium.

13. Several Liability Notice - During recent years a number of insurance companies have become insolvent and have been unable to meet their liabilities in respect of lines written on slips which bore acceptances from co-insurers (eg other insurance companies and Lloyd's syndicates). In English law and practice the "several" liability nature of each transaction has always been recognised; but this has not always been the case in some foreign jurisdictions and less informed assured contend that insurers who subscribe to the same risk should contribute to make good insured losses not recoverable from insolvent companies with lines on the same slip. To make it clear to assured and others that each line on a slip, covernote, policy or other insurance document is a separate contract with the assured the London market has published a "several liabilities notice". With effect from 1st August, 1994, this clause must appear in all brokers` slips, covernotes, policies and other documents issued in support of the insurance contract. The clause is issued in two formats; one for direct insurance contracts and the other for reinsurance contracts. It is intended that it will eventually be printed in the MAR form of policy but, in the meantime, trainees can probably obtain a copy from their London market Association.

7. Selecting the Market and the Leading Underwriter

Once the broker clearly understands the risk to be proposed to the underwriter he prepares the placing slip. Information on the slip need not be detailed but it must be sufficiently clear to identify the risk and to indicate the intentions of the parties to the contract. Attention is directed to comments in part 6 above regarding slip preparation; particularly in the use of abbreviations.

Having completed preparation of the slip and, if appropriate, a slip registration form the broker selects the markets he will approach with the proposal. A Lloyd`s broker, despite his designation, is not obliged to use Lloyd`s market. He will concentrate on this market when his client has requested it or, if not so requested, where to do so would be in his client`s best interests. However, the Lloyd`s broker is free, as is any other broker, to approach any market outside Lloyd`s where he feels he will obtain the best cover for his client at the most reasonable rate. In selecting a market, and the underwriters in that market, the broker would do well to observe the following guidelines:

Capacity - This term refers to the maximum amount an insurer can accept within his underwriting strategy and the amount of capital that lies behind the risks he writes. Brokers learn from experience the capacity to be expected from various markets and underwriters in those markets. The broker should be satisfied that the market he approaches has sufficient capacity to absorb the size of the risk, or the part thereof, being offered to that market. In cases of exceptionally high values or limits of liability the broker will probably find it necessary to extend the proposal over several markets. Sometimes the broker finds it impossible to attract sufficient acceptances in his regular markets to complete the placing but he may be able to place the balance in markets with which he is not so familiar. Nevertheless, when spreading the risk over a wide area of markets, it is very important for the broker to avoid prejudice to his client`s interests by approaching markets with a poor security record. Early anticipation of the size of lines the broker can expect will save him a lot of time and effort in placing a risk.

Claim collection experience - The broker would do well to anticipate, and avoid, markets where difficulties might arise in claim collection. In some overseas markets national restrictions and financial controls prejudice the collection of claims. The broker learns from adverse experience suffered by himself and other broker colleagues/associates which markets to avoid for this reason.

Security - This term relates to the ability of an underwriter to meet his liabilities. It is of prime importance that the cover be as secure as possible and, although he does not guarantee the solvency of the underwriters with whom he places the risk, the marine insurance broker should take care to avoid placing the risk in any market where questions of inadequate security have been raised or with any underwriter whose solvency he has reason to doubt.

The Leader - Where a proposal is likely to demand acceptances from a number of insurers, as is normally the case for all contracts other than those for minor amounts, the proposal is submitted to a leading underwriter (termed the "Leader" in practice) who negotiates the terms and conditions of the contract and signifies his acceptance by writing a *line* on the slip. For more detail on the obligations of underwriters in regard to written lines attention is directed to the notes in part 8. In the London market the leader may be the active underwriter representing a Lloyd`s syndicate or the marine underwriting manager representing an insurance company. When selecting his leader the broker should be reasonably certain that other underwriters will follow without questioning the terms and conditions agreed with the leader. Only experience can teach a broker which underwriters make suitable leaders and newcomers to Lloyd`s new "single" market will need to be guided in this respect by more experienced brokers.

Following underwriters - Technically, underwriters who follow the leader on the original slip (termed "followers" in practice) are entitled to question the terms and conditions of the contract even though these have been already agreed with the leader; but, ideally, the broker would prefer followers who do not raise such questions, accepting the proposal on a "take it or leave it" basis. It is customary for a follower to write a lower line than the leader but there is no hard and fast rule on the matter. In practice, recognising that followers tend to write lower lines, the broker will find it beneficial to encourage the leader to write as large a line as possible; thereby making completion much easier.

8. Obligations of Underwriters in Regard to Written Lines

The term *written line* relates to the amount the underwriter writes on a slip to indicate the amount he will accept of the risk. He confirms his acceptance by initialling the slip and entering the date of the acceptance and his reference. In the London market the line is written as a percentage which could cause confusion if the broker or leading underwriter does not make clear on the slip the amount to which the percentage is to be applied. Completion of the box at the foot of the sheet in the A4 slip which incorporates the administrative grid will serve this purpose (a similar box appears at the foot of panel two in the old standard slip format).

When the underwriter writes his line on the original slip and initials it he concludes a contract with the assured, on the date stated by his initial, for the percentage of the risk indicated by his written line. Although it is common practice to sign down lines (see part 9, below) if the broker does not sign down the line (eg because he is unable to obtain sufficient lines for him so to do), or signs down for by less than intimated to the underwriter, the underwriter is bound to honour the written line. Any underwriter in the London market who is not happy with this position should consider the amount he writes more carefully. The contract concluded in the original slip is not enforcable in an English court of law until it is embodied in a formal policy document; but the underwriter has given his word to abide by the terms of the contract and is, therefore, bound in honour to observe the terms of the contract. The latter point is particularly important in regard to PPI policies (see Section 4) which are not acceptable as evidence in a court that is subject to English jurisdiction and/or English law and practice.

Although London market practice allows a broker to reduce a written line where he has overplaced the risk (see part 9, below) in no other circumstances may the broker alter the written line without the express permission of the underwriter who wrote the line. Thus, if the broker has been unable to complete the placing he must not increase any written line on the slip; although he is at liberty to approach any underwriter subscribing the slip to ask him, at his option, to increase his line. A "leading underwriter agreement" on a slip gives no authority to the leader to alter the written lines of followers.

An assured is not obliged to accept the security offered and, at his option, can reject any lines shown on the broker's covernote (see part 10, below). In such event the broker must not simply delete the acceptance shown on the slip; even where he has overplaced the risk; which might make him think he could simply ignore the rejected line and re-calculate the lines in the signing down procedure. The underwriter who wrote the rejected line will have recorded his acceptance, so the broker must re-approach him with the original slip for the rejected line to be deleted. The broker should then attempt to replace the rejected line. If the broker has overplaced the risk he can re-adjust the signed lines; but, if these have been already advised to the underwriters or their representatives, he must obtain approval for the re-adjustment.

A large lead line helps the broker to complete a placing and there have been occasions when a broker has persuaded a reluctant underwriter to write a large line on condition that the broker arranges reinsurance protection. A broker making such an arrangement with an underwriter should consider his position carefully. It could be considered that the arrangement is a "material fact" when proposing the risk to following underwriters; in which case failure to disclose the arrangement to a follower would consitute a breach of good faith (See consequences of such breach in Section 7).

9. Overplacing and Signing Down

As commented earlier, it is commonplace in the London market for the broker to overplace the risk (ie to accept written lines which aggregate more than 100% in total). In fact, when considering a proposal, an underwriter might well ask the broker how much the slip will sign down and gauge his written line accordingly. There are many practical reasons for overplacing a risk. A broker may have a proposal which is particularly good business for an underwriter, so that cover is completed on the slip with only a few written lines. Without freedom to overplace the broker would find that the major underwriters (ie the potential leaders) would take the cream of the business and followers would see nothing but mediocre and poor business. The broker who has freedom to overplace can accept large lead lines, which take up a good part of the proposal, but still be able to offer the slip to a followers in a wider market. The practice of overplacing also allows the broker to offer particlarly good business, even though it is already fully covered on the slip, to an underwriter who has helped him in the past with an "oblige" line. Further, by supporting this practice the market encourages "spread of risk"; a fundamental principle of sound underwriting which lightens the burden of a large claims on individual underwriters. The practice of overplacing for the above reasons is not recognised in regard to risks that are placed directly with insurance companies (ie other than through the medium of a broker).

When the broker overplaces he must, once he has finished placing the risk, reduce each written line proportionately so that the total of the lines is reduced to

100% of the risk. This practice is termed *signing down*. In no circumstances may the broker "sign up" a slip by increasing written lines without written approval from the underwriters subscribing the slip.

The process of signing down is simple as is illustrated below:

	Written line	*Signed line*
Lloyd`s syndicate (leader)	25.00%	20%
Lloyd`s syndicate	25.00%	20%
Lloyd`s syndicate	25.00%	20%
ILU Company	25.00%	20%
ILU Company	12.50%	10%
Non-Inst Company	12.50%	10%
	125.00%	100%

Whilst the practice of overplacing and signing down written lines is acceptable in the London market one must appreciate that markets outside London may not recognise it. Thus, brokers placing part of the risk with an underwriter located outside London might find they are bound to retain the written line when signing the risk and should take this into account in their calculations.

The term "signing down" may be used for a different purpose; such as a circumstance where a provisional value is placed in a facultative cargo insurance contract. The written lines will be signed down in the customary manner; but, additionally, the sum insured and value will be reduced to reflect the true value when the goods are shipped. Completion of the box at the foot of the administrative grid sheet in the A4 slip is particularly important in such case.

10. Use of the Broker`s Covernote

On completion of a placing the broker should advise his principal without delay. In the case of a facultative placing it is customary for the broker to send written confirmation in the form of a covernote to his principal. There is no standard wording for a covernote; each broking firm devising its own format. A typical covernote issued by the Lloyd`s broker would commence with "In accordance with your instructions we have effected an insurance contract on your behalf as follows:-" or some similar wording.

In English law the broker`s covernote is no more than a communication from an agent to his principal. It will be noted that, at no time, does a London broker state that he has "insured" the risk; indicating, by the above words, that he has merely carried out the instructions of his principal. To emphasise this the broker incorporates a list of the "security" with whom the risk is insured. The term "security", when used in relation to a covernote, means the insurers who have accepted the proposal. Except in the case of covernotes issued to clients in the USA (see below), the broker can show the Lloyd`s participation in the same covernote as other security. The broker indicates the "Lloyd`s" participation as one item on the covernote; showing only the total of all lines to be signed (ie the signed lines) on behalf of Lloyd`s syndicates subscribing the risk. But, in all cases where insurance companies are concerned (even those for whom a combined policy will be issued by the ILU), the broker must show the name of each company separately on the covernote with the company`s signed line. Naturally, practitioners will check to see that all the signed lines shown on the covernote total 100% of the amount placed before signing the covernote. Under US law a separate covernote must be issued for Lloyd`s participation in US business; even where there is a company participation in the same slip. Generally, only the total Lloyd`s participation needs to be shown on such covernotes, but the laws of certain States in the USA require that the signed line of each Lloyd`s syndicate be shown on the broker`s covernote. French law also requires that the signed line of each participating Lloyd`s syndicate be shown separately on the covernote. Interested trainees and practitioners might find it convenient to check with Lloyd`s Legislation Department for advice when issuing covernotes relating to contracts that are subject to jurisdiction of other countries.

In English law the broker`s covernote has no value as an instrument for use as evidence in a court of law where no formal policy has been submitted to the court as evidence of contract. Any action against the underwriters, or any of them, must be pursued with the formal policy document as evidence of contract. The broker`s covernote may be admitted as evidence in a legal action against the broker for breach of contract (eg in a case of broker`s negligence that has prejudiced the assured`s right to claim under the policy). Nevertheless, one must not assume that courts outside English jurisdiction will view the legal value of a broker`s covernote in the same way as an English court in claims against insurers; even when that covernote has been issued by a British broker and the risk is placed at Lloyd`s and/or with UK based companies. For example, where a contract covering US business is written by insurers licensed by the US Government to write such business the policy must be made subject to US jurisdiction. In such cases the insurer is subject to US law which provides, amongst other things, that the insurer is bound by the first evidence of the insurance contract received by the assured; which may well be the broker`s covernote. Further, US law does not recognise the principle of "several" liability and considers that all the insurers in a combined contract are jointly liable for performance of the contract irrespective of each party`s separate contribution to the contract.

The broker`s client is under no legal obligation to read the covernote. It is, therefore, particularly important for the broker to check the covernote for accuracy before signing it. It is no defence for a negligent broker facing an action for damages to allege that the assured was aware of a discrepancy because he had acknowledged receipt of the covernote and the covernote clearly showed the discrepancy. Further, although the contract between proposer and underwriter was concluded when the underwriter initialled the original slip it is still subject to ratification by the assured; and the assured can ratify it even after he is aware of a loss (MIA, 1906, sec.86). As commented earlier, the assured is not obliged to accept any security written in the covernote; although an exception might apply where the assured requested the security and later, having changed his mind, expresses dissatisfaction with that security. He can request the broker to replace a line with a more acceptable security. The broker does not guarantee success in replacing the line but he must use his best endeavours to comply with his principal`s request and he must advise his client of any failure to replace the line without delay.

During recent years a number of insurance companies have become insolvent and have been unable to meet their liabilities in respect of lines written on slips which bore acceptances from co-insurers (eg other insurance companies and Lloyd`s syndicates). In English law and practice the "several" liability nature of each transaction has always been recognised; but this has not always been the case in some foreign jurisdictions and less informed assured contend that insurers who subscribe to the same risk should contribute to make good insured losses not recoverable from insolvent companies with lines on the same slip. To make it clear to assured and others that each line on a slip, covernote, policy or other insurance document is a separate contract with the assured the London market has published a "several liabilities notice". With effect from 1st August, 1994, this clause must appear in all brokers` slips, covernotes, policies and other documents issued in support of the insurance contract. The clause is issued in two formats; one for direct insurance contracts and the other for reinsurance contracts. It is intended that it will eventually be printed in the MAR form of policy but, in the meantime, trainees can probably obtain a copy from their London market Association.

11. Agreements and Amendments after Placing

In theory, the broker should approach every underwriter who has written a line on the slip to obtain agreement to any change in the cover after the placing has been completed. In practice, however, various schemes have been introduced in the London market to save time and effort where the change does not materially affect the risk. Such arrangements are termed "leading underwriter agreements". Over the years London market brokers have devised a variety of wordings for this purpose, mostly to their advantage it must be said, but not all such wordings have received underwriters` approval. The trainee should be aware that, in the absence of any specific definition to the contrary, the following definitions regarding leading underwriters, which vary depending on the circumstances, shall apply -

Leading underwriter - This term means:

(1) Lloyd`s only slip - The active underwriter representing the Lloyd`s syndicate with whom the broker has negotiated the contract and whose written line is the first to appear on the original slip, or

(2) ILU companies only slip - The underwriting manager representing the insurance company with whom the broker has negotiated the contract on the original slip, or

(3) Combined slip - The active underwriter representing the syndicate which heads all other syndicate lines on the same original slip, plus the underwriting manager representing the ILU company that heads the other companies on the original slip.

Three leaders - This term means:

(a) Lloyd`s only slip - The first active underwriter, as in (1) above, plus the active underwriters representing the next two syndicates on the slip, or

(b) ILU companies only slip - The underwriting manager representing the first ILU company, as in (2) above, plus the underwriting managers representing the next two ILU companies on the slip, or

(c) Combined slip - The first active underwriter, as in (1) above, plus the active underwriter representing the next syndicate on the slip *and* the underwriting manager, as in (2) above, plus the underwriting manager representing the next ILU company on the slip.

One might see leading underwriter agreements as part of the printed format in a placing slip; but one should bear in mind that any underwriter (leader or follower) is at liberty to delete or amend such wording before he writes his line on the slip.

Nevertheless, where a leading underwriter agreement was in the original slip at the time a following underwriter wrote his line on the slip the follower is honour bound to follow the leader in acceptance of anything approved by the leader in conformity with the terms of the agreement. It is for this reason that the London market has published rules as guidelines for leaders in this respect. All London market brokers must be aware of these rules:

A leading underwriter may **not** agree on behalf of following underwriters -

1. Any agreement to amend or alter the risk where there is no leading underwriter agreement already expressed in the original slip.
2. An increase in any underwriter's line, other than his own.
3. Anything which materially alters the risk; even where the slip incorporates wording that allows the leader this freedom.
4. Any extension or continuation of cover where the slip or insurance conditions do not incorporate a relevant "held covered" agreement.
5. Any increase in the insured value or amount on which percentage lines are based; except where special provision therefor has been made in the slip or insurance conditions.

In general, and subject to any restriction expressed in the slip (see "Standard London Market Agreements" below) or a restrictive market understanding, the leading underwriter/s may agree, on behalf of and without reference to, the following underwriters -

1. A date of attachment of risk or cover, or a date of sailing where appropriate.
2. Additional premiums and amended terms, if appropriate, for breach of warranty where the breach is held covered by the insurance conditions.
3. Advice of a ship's name or a change of name.
4. Advice of the name of a carrying overseas vessel.
5. Additional premiums for cargo carried by overage, etc. vessels.
6. Continuation of cover where held covered by the policy conditions.
7. Cancellation of cover and, relevant return premiums due, where the policy terms so provide due to change in circumstances (eg sale of the insured vessel).
8. Return premiums earned in accordance with the policy conditions.
9. New &/or acquired vessels added to a hull fleet, where these are held covered by the insurance conditions.
10. Any other circumstance which comes within the terms of a "held covered" agreement specially expressed in the slip or in the policy conditions.
11. Declarations under open cover, where appropriate.

Standard London Market Agreements - In the past London brokers have experienced difficulty in deciding whether or not they need to advise, or obtain agreements from, following underwriters. To assist them, and the London market generally, three special forms of agreement are used in the London marine insurance market; whereby leading underwriters instruct the broker in this respect. These are as follows :-

LUAMH (Leading Underwriter Agreement Marine Hull) - This is used in slips that cover the hull & machinery of ships and slips covering hull interests.

LUAMC (Leading Underwriter Agreement Marine Cargo) - This is used in slips that cover cargo and slips that cover cargo interests.

LUAGM (Leading Underwriter Agreement General Marine) - This is available for use in either hull or cargo slips. It is used where the insured interest is different from the normal marine insurance business (eg a hull construction risk which embraces an element of non-marine interests).

These introductory notes are not intended for market procedural training and it is left to the trainee to follow up market practice and procedures regarding the specific use, completion and application of these agreements; but some general observations might prove useful. The relevant agreement stamp is expressed in the broker's original slip as required. The agreement stamp is is in a "box" format; the leader/s initialling the agreement and indicating, in the appropriate boxes, the procedure to be followed by the broker in obtaining approval from, or in advising, following underwriters. These are "three leader" agreements and are subject to approval as in the above definition. Where the broker has been instructed only to advise following underwriters it is customary for him to be allowed five working days for this purpose.

12. Held Covered Agreements

The term "held covered" relates to circumstances where the the insurer is prepared to extend the insurance contract to embrace a risk that is not already covered thereby. There are two types of held covered agreement. One is expressed in the policy conditions, whilst the other can be seen in a broker's original slip.

Held covered agreements in policy conditions - The premium payable in consideration of the insurance protection provided by the policy conditions is due from inception of risk; although, in some cases (see "deferred account" in Section 5) arrangements might be made for premium to be paid in instalments. Irrespective of the method of premium payment, the policy embraces only those risks and circumstances that are expressed in the insurance conditions as being covered thereby and, in the case of a time policy, only for the period of time expressed therein. However, the assured may be aware of the possibility of exposure to risk not contemplated by the policy premium and, whilst preferring to pay only the basic premium at the outset, would be happy to bear an additional premium to cover the, unlikely but possible, additional risks should they arise. For example, consider a fishing vessel that is insured at a premium of £X per annum provided she operates only up to 3 miles offshore; the restriction being expressed as a warranty (see Section 8). The assured would like to be covered if the vessel strayed outside the warranty restricted area but, to have the warranty deleted the premium would be £X+Y per annum. Rather than pay the higher premium to cover a circumstance that might not occur, the assured accepts the basic conditions with the warranty therein and, to accommodate the assured, the underwriters incorporate a provision in the policy conditions which, subject to payment of an additional premium (payable only if the provision is invoked), holds the assured covered in event of a breach of the warranty.

It is common for standard policy conditions to specify certain circumstances in respect of which there is no cover (eg a hull & machinery policy might exclude contractual towage and/or restrict navigation in certain areas, or a cargo policy might terminate the insurance contract upon termination of the contract of carriage at an intermediate port). Further, there might be statutory requirements that terminate cover during the currency of the policy (eg the MIA, 1906, discharges the underwriters covering a ship for a specific voyage from all further liability in event of unreasonable delay in prosecution of the voyage). In practice, however, underwriters recognise that these matters are often outside control of the assured and incorporate clauses in the policy conditions whereby, subject to compliance by the assured with specified requirements, the underwriters hold the assured covered in such eventualities.

A "held covered" agreement might be incorporated in a policy to allow the assured to continue a time policy after natural expiry. As an example of this consider a policy that has been effected to insure the hull & machinery of a ship for a fixed period of time, say 12 months. Once the risk attaches the insurance will continue, subject to any termination clause incorporated therein not coming into operation, until the expiry time and date specified in the policy. Cover will then terminate automatically unless the assured has taken steps to renew the insurance contract *before* the policy lapses. Imagine the difficulty the assured would face if the ship was in danger at sea when the policy lapsed! The underwriters would be loth to accept the proposal for renewal in such circumstances. A similar problem would arise if the ship had run aground or was in a damaged condition in a port of refuge when renewal was requested. Hopefully, the assured's broker would anticipate the problems and suggest the assured proposes renewal *before* the policy expires; but what if the ship is on her last voyage? Perhaps the assured would not wish to pay the full premium for a further 12 months when he only requires cover until the ship reaches her destination.

In practice, the above situation is anticipated in the standard policy conditions for H & M insurance contracts. For example, the ITC, 1983, incorporate a "continuation" clause which can be invoked by the assured in the above circumstances. Unlike some other h/c agreements this requires the assured to invoke the clause *before* the policy expires, so it does not protect an apathetic assured who overlooks the imminent expiry of his policy. However, provided the assured notifies underwriters of his intention to invoke the clause before the policy expires and pays a pro rata monthly additional premium, the cover continues until the ship reaches her planned destination as specified in the clause.

The requirement to give prior notice, as in the hull time policy continuation clause, is an exception to the general rule. In most cases, underwriters recognise that an assured, particularly in cargo insurance contracts, is seldom aware of the occurrence to which the h/c agreement relates until after the event. So, in both hull and cargo policies, one sees h/c provisions which require the assured only to notify the underwriters immediately he is aware of the occurrence. Of course, when agreeing to such a clause, underwriters are trusting the assured not to abuse the concession by trying to avoid payment of the additional premium where no loss has occurred during the extension of cover. There are so many variations to these clauses that practitioners need to read the relevant clause carefully, in every case, to determine its application. This is particularly important where the clause allows underwriters to change the insurance conditions in addition to charging an additional premium; as often happens in regard to h/c provisions in H & M policies. Practitioners should be aware, also, that a h/c provision in a policy is usually limited to only such circumstances as are specified in the clause. For example, whilst the breach of warranty clause in the ITC, 1983, holds the assured covered for breach of certain specified warranties (eg the "towage" warranty), breach of other warranties in a hull & machinery policy, unspecified in the clause, (eg the "disbursements" warranty) is not embraced by the clause.

Held covered agreements in a broker's slip - These agreements do not fall in the same category as the above, in that they are not concerned with change of circumstances. An example appears in a slip used to negotiate a hull fleet insurance contract with the term "new &/or acquired vessels held covered". The original slip already shows a list of the vessels covered with their agreed insured values; underwriters' lines being based on the top value in the fleet. By this agreement underwriters allow the leading underwriter/s to accept, on their behalf, additions to the fleet provided the value of each added vessel does not exceed the top value in the list already attached to the slip; the broker usually being instructed by the leader to advise all followers within 5 working days of the addition. Except where an arrangement to the contrary has been agreed, where the vessel to be added has a value in excess of the fleet top value, the broker must obtain approval for the addition from all underwriters subscribing the slip.

Another example of a slip h/c agreement occurs where the broker asks the underwriter/s to hold covered a particular risk or renewal of an expiring time policy; pending confirmation by his client. Such agreement requires approval from all underwriters subscribing the slip. It has been known for such provisional arrangements to left outstanding for an unreasonable period of time. However, in the London market, there is an understanding that the risk or renewal, as the case may be, will be held covered for no more than 14 days unless the assured's confirmation is conveyed to the underwriters before the expiry of this period.

13. Effecting Open Cover Contracts

The term "open cover" is generic in that it can be used for any form of contract wherein the underwriters have undertaken an obligation to accept declarations of individual insurances, which fall within the scope of the cover, without further negotiation of the contract. They are, therefore, "obligatory" contracts. The first form of obligatory contract to be introduced to the marine insurance market was the "floating policy". This comprised a policy form which covered each cargo declaration coming within its scope up to an agreed limit per overseas carrying vessel. An overall limit for the policy was agreed and, as each declaration was made, the overall limit would be reduced until it was extinguished, the policy then lapsing automatically. In theory, the arrangement could have been made more flexible in the London market by embodying the contract in a broker's slip; although underwriters preferred the floating policy system because they received the full premium, based on the overall limit, in advance and only adjusted it when the policy lapsed. In any case, UK stamp duty laws required the existence of a policy form, effected from the outset, bearing "voyage" stamp duty for the overall limit. For example, a floating policy effected in 1950 for an overall limit of £500,000 would bear £25 stamp duty none of which was refundable if the policy lapsed before the limit had been exhausted. The abolition, in 1959, of voyage based stamp duty for cargo policies might have revived the flagging demand for this type of cover had it not been for the concern of many assured that they would be left uninsured if they, or their broker, forgot to effect a succeeding policy as the old one began to run out of cover. The fact is that London brokers had taken steps, long before the abolition of voyage based stamp duty, to effect long term open cover slip contracts to protect the assured; with floating policies issued off these to satisfy the stamp duty laws. Floating policies continued to be used, as formal contracts issued off broker's slip based open covers, until marine policy stamp duty was finally abolished altogether, in 1970, when the market gradually absorbed the slip based open cover as the norm with policies issued only when required for legal purposes. Accordingly, it is unlikely that one will see a cargo floating policy used in today`s London market; although they are still used in other markets where contracts are negotiated, without the medium of a broker, directly between the proposer and the insurer. Comment on the structure of a floating policy is not necessary here because this type of contract incorporates, as far as applicable thereto, all the main ingredients of an open cover.

Open covers may be used for any marine insurance or marine reinsurance contract where multiple declarations can be absorbed by a single contract. The main purpose of open cover is to save time and effort in negotiating a separate insurance contract to cover each subject matter where the basic cover can be negotiated in a single contract to embrace all the subject matters to be insured. It is also advantageous to a cargo assured who enjoys advance cover at agreed rates of premium; thereby enabling him to cost his goods more accurately when quoting prices to buyers.

The marine open cover can take a variety of forms but there are two basic types; the first being a contract between the proposer and the underwriter, whilst the second is a contract between the broker and the underwriter. In marine insurance practice the latter is termed a "broker`s cover". An underwriter seldom knows the identity of the proposed assureds when negotiating a broker`s cover. This information will not be available until declarations are made on the cover. The underwriter is dealing entirely with the broker and is authorising the latter to accept business on his behalf, therefore, in this respect the broker is an agent of the underwriter. This can create a conflict of interests for the broker who is declaring risks under the contract as an agent for the assured, whilst acting as agent for the underwriter in accepting those risks. Brokers operating such covers should bear this in mind and take steps to ensure that one principal is not prejudiced in favour of the other.

Some, though not all, brokers` covers allow the broker to issue an insurance certificate for each declaration; the certificates being supplied in blank, with the underwriter`s signature thereon. The broker completes the detail of the risk in the certificate and countersigns it before sending it to his client. The underwriter`s claims representatives will honour the certificate as though it had been issued directly to the assured by the underwriter. Because the broker is being given considerable freedom to bind the underwriter the wording of the contract will limit the authority given to the broker. The, perhaps more descriptive, term "binding authority" is often used in respect of such contracts; particularly in non-marine markets. In the London market these authorities are subject to many rules regarding their use. It is intended only to outline the use and structure of open covers in these notes, so interested practitioners are advised to study the rules separately rather than to rely on the introductory notes for information on the operation of brokers` covers.

In theory, the open cover system can be used for hull insurance contracts but the nature of these interests lends itself more to facultative placing; although one sometimes sees brokers` covers used in the hull market, particularly brokers` covers for hull TLO reinsurance contracts. The most common form of open cover is a cargo "term" contract. A cargo term contract is one which is effected for a period of time rather than for a specific voyage or series of voyages; the latter, where appropriate, being insured by an "open slip". Section 25(2) of the MIA, 1906, states that a policy issued for a period exceeding 12 months is invalid in a court of law; so, until this section of the Act was repealed in 1959, cargo open covers were restricted to a period 12 months, with the broker negotiating a new open cover annually to succeed the expiring cover. Although one might still see such limited term cargo covers in use today, particularly in circumstances where the subscribing insurers wish to maintain a watching brief on the progress of the cover, the vast majority of cargo open covers are effected to attach from a specified date and to continue "always open" until one of the parties to the contract gives notice to cancel the cover.

Negotiating a cargo open cover contract is a major broking task; the leader often taking several days to study the cover wording, the insurance conditions and the rating schedule before agreeing to conclude the contract. In the case of a large contract it may be some weeks before the placing can be completed so, instead of showing an attachment date the broker types "TBA L/U" in the slip. This means that the broker will submit the attachment date later to the leader, for agreement, and will advise the date to the following underwriters.

Once the cover attaches it continues indefinitely until one of the parties gives notice to cancel the contract. It is important, therefore, that a specific cancellation clause be expressed in the wording. There are many forms of cancellation clause. A common version allows either party to give 30 days notice to cancel the contract and 7 days notice to cancel only war & strikes risks. On receipt of the notice the assured can still declare shipments which commence transit before the expiry of the notice period; such shipments continuing to be covered after the notice has expired until the cover on these lapses in accordance with the insurance conditions for each risk. Once the notice period expires no further declarations can be made.

As in the case of a floating policy a limit is expressed in the open cover for each declaration or each sending or each shipment, or other limit in accordance with the cover wording. But, unlike the floating policy, there is no aggregate limit in the open cover. The assured is expected to declare each sending consecutively as it takes place. He may not insure elsewhere any risk that should be declared under the cover. Even where a sending is for an amount which is more than the cover limit he must still declare that portion of it which comes within the scope of the cover. It is customary for occasional declarations of larger amounts to be accepted by special agreement but, if the underwriter refuses to accept this the broker will need to seek additional, facultative, cover for the excess amount. If individual requests for an increase in the limit occur frequently it is customary for the broker to make a proposal to the underwriter to increase the cover limit for all declarations.

Premium rates are specified in a schedule to the cover. In London market practice it is customary for the assured to receive pads of printed, consecutively numbered and pre-signed, certificates in blank with a number of copies to each certificate number. As he sends forward each shipment the assured completes a certificate and countersigns it; the original normally being used in the documentary credit system. The assured sends one copy of the certificate to the broker as a declaration. Periodically, the broker calculates the premium for a batch of certificates, debits the assured and closes this amount in the appropriate market signing and accounting procedures.

The procedure for effecting a cargo open cover depends on the relevant market practice. Where such covers are negotiated directly between proposer and insurer no placing slip is involved so the legal restrictions regarding slips do not apply and different procedural arrangements might be agreed. The same would apply to a contract that is negotiated by a broker but outside the slip placing procedure (eg in an overseas market). In the London market it is customary for a cargo open cover to be negotiated within the slip placing system so the contract suffers the same disadvantages as outlined in part 5, above. It cannot be recognised legally until it is embodied in a formal marine insurance contract. Nonetheless, it is not customary for formal policies to be issued off cargo open covers until a court case is being contemplated; all parties usually being satisfied with the insurance certificate arrangement.

14. Effecting Renewals on Term Contracts

As commented above, marine insurance contracts based on time are no longer restricted to 12 months; section 25(2) of the MIA, 1906, having been repealed in August, 1959. Nevertheless, for a variety of reasons, hull underwriters have, with some exceptions, continued to restrict time policies to a period of no more than 12 months. Thus, the assured needs to renew his hull & machinery, and any ancillary policies relating thereto, annually.

The procedure for effecting a renewal is the same as outlined earlier for a facultative H & M contract. The assured and his client are still bound by the principle of good faith (see Section 7). Unless it is reasonable to assume the underwriter is already aware of it they must disclose and truly represent every circumstance that is material to the risk. This particularly applies to outstanding claims, concerning which the underwriter has not yet been advised, attaching to the expiring contract.

Renewals of H & M policies in the London market are subject to a joint understanding whereby premium increases will apply automatically if justified by the loss ratio indicated in the expiring contract. Premium rating on H & M policies is partly based on the insured value so, where applicable, rating adjustments are applied on renewal to reflect any increase or decrease in the insured value.

London market brokers usually seek renewal of H & M contracts some time before the policy expires but, if the negotiations commence too early, there is a possibility that underwriters could not take into account losses occurring late in the policy year when deciding whether or not to renew or write their lines on the succeeding policy. To reduce the chance of exceptionally early renewing of the contract there is a market understanding that no renewal may be presented to a leader for consideration more than two months before the commencement date of the new policy. In practice, brokers often request that the renewal be held covered subject to the assured's approval or subject to receipt of instructions from the assured, as the case may be. Nevertheless, it will be recalled that any agreement obtained by the broker to hold covered renewal is recognised by London market underwriters for no more than 14 days after such agreement has been obtained; irrespective of whether or not the expiring policy lapses during the held covered period.

15. Electronic Placing

During the development of electronic communication in the London market many procedures are changing. The primary object of electronic communication is to replace, where practical, manually prepared paper documentation with electronic messages; thereby increasing efficiency, speeding up the various processes within the market and increasing profitability. In time, electronic communication links will be established worldwide. LIMNET (London Insurance Market Network) is the centre of the London market operation and those closely involved with the development of LIMNET have concentrated, in the first instance, on accounting procedures (eg premium advices, claims advices, settlements, etc.).

When considering electronic placing one might have regard for the words of the Chairman of the LIMNET board, at a seminar in October, 1993, when he said "What we are talking about is Electronic Data Interchange (EDI). We cannot trade without EDI - we may be able to today but we will not be able to in the future. Electronic placing support is the first natural application for EDI. It takes the starting point for the negotiation and the transaction from which everything else is driven".

Although forward planning envisages a procedure whereby contracts can be negotiated by electronic messages this will not take place until the pilot schemes, already in operation, have tested the viability of electronic placing. Accordingly, trainees should consider the observations below on the operation of electronic placing with this in mind and watch market developments for practical detail.

It is probable that, in the first instance, an electronic placing scheme will apply solely to standardised placing packages. Certain types of non-marine risk are based on standard policy wordings which vary little in the final contract; so these lend themselves more readily to electronic placing packages. But the diversity of marine insurance contracts, particularly cargo open covers, might make the necessary standardisation impractical in the short term and one suspects that it will be a long time before electronic placing becomes the norm in the marine insurance market. It is suggested that, for the time being, trainees should study face to face broking and placing documentation appropriate thereto, as covered by the preceding comments in this Section; although it can be noted that Lloyd's business plan expects all business placed at Lloyd's to be supported by a full electronic version of the contract by January, 1996.

SEE OVERPAGE FOR SELF STUDY QUESTIONAIRE

SELF STUDY QUESTIONS

Before moving on to the next section satisfy yourself that you have absorbed the subject matter in Section Three. The following questions should be answered without reference to the text.

1. The broker is an agent:-
   (a) Who is the broker`s "principal"?
   (b) In what circumstances can the broker find himself with a conflict of interests when acting for his principal?
   (c) In what circumstances can the broker be sued by his principal for damages?
   (d) The notes recommend guideline rules for the broker when placing business. What are these rules?

2. What is the difference between a facultative contract and an obligatory contract? Can you give an example of an obligatory contract frequently used in the marine insurance market?

3. Lloyd`s brokers use placing slips to negotiate and conclude marine insurance contracts in the London market:-
   (a) What is the legal value of a placing slip?
   (b) When is the insurance contract deemed to be concluded?
   (c) Define the term "original slip".

4. When selecting markets and insurers:-
   (a) What factors should the broker bear in mind when selecting a market?
   (b) What is the difference between a "leader" and a "follower"?
   (c) With whom does the broker negotiate the contract?
   (d) To what extent is an underwriter obliged to honour his written line?

5. Having completed the placing the broker issues a covernote to the assured:-
   (a) What is the purpose of the broker`s covernote?
   (b) Under English law does the broker`s covernote have any legal value in binding the underwriters listed therein to the contract?
   (c) Does the answer to (b) apply equally to contracts that are subject to foreign jurisdiction?

6. Do you understand the application of "leading underwriter" agreements, "three leader" agreements and "held covered" agreements; and restrictions applied to the use of these agreements in London market practice?

7. What are the essential elements of a cargo open cover?

8. Must the assured and broker observe the principle of good faith when negotiating renewal of a term contract?

9. Why is it essential for the "several liability notice" to appear in all brokers` slips, covernotes, policies and certificates?

SECTION FOUR

POLICIES, CLAUSES, FRANCHISES AND DEDUCTIBLES

1. Introduction to the Marine Insurance Policy
2. The Insurance Policy as a Contract
3. Lloyd`s SG Policy and Insurance Company Equivalents
4. The London Market MAR Policy Form
5. Marine Insurance Clauses
6. Gambling Policies and PPI Policies
7. Jurisdiction and Law & Practice Clauses
8. Valued and Unvalued Policies
9. Policy Assignment
10. Policy Franchises, Deductibles and Excesses
11. Combined Policies
12. Duplicate and Copy Policies
13. Renewal Policies
14. Slip Policies
15. Cargo Insurance Certificates
16. Several Liability Notice

SECTION FOUR

1. Introduction to the Marine Insurance Policy

From the early days of marine insurance practice many forms of marine insurance policy have been devised. These early policy wordings were drafted by the underwriter issuing the policy to suit the risks as he saw them. The policy would be structured to cover the hazards to which the ship and/or cargo would be exposed during a specified voyage and the extent to which the underwriter would indemnify the assured for losses suffered during the voyage. The variations in the approach to drafting early policy forms can be seen in archive copies of Italian policies produced during the 11th century; before marine insurance was introduced in the London market.

From these early policy documents there emerged three forms of standard document which were in fairly common use in London during the 15th/16th centuries. These were the *SG* policy form covering ship and goods in one policy, the *S* policy form covering only the ship and the *G* policy form covering, solely, the goods carried by an overseas vessel. No time policies existed at that time so the subject matter insured was covered during a sea voyage only; any land risk to goods in transit being left for the owner's account.

It is commonly believed that only the SG form of policy survived but, although this is true where the Lloyd's market is concerned, the company market, when insuring ship and goods separately, continued to use the S form of policy for the insurance of ships and the G policy form for the insurance of goods in transit, as appropriate thereto. To London market practitioners the difference between these policy forms may be academic but experience will show that, at least for the time being, some overseas markets continue to base their contracts on the old (pre 1982 for cargo and pre October 1983 for hull) clauses and conditions. Such markets must continue to use the old forms of policy for this purpose.

2. The Insurance Policy as a Contract

The broker's placing slip is the most important document used in London market practice. This is also the case in other markets where the slip system is used and insurance contracts are based on English law & practice. Nevertheless, it will be recalled from earlier comment that the broker's slip is not recognised by English courts as a formal contract of insurance. It might be argued that, since the refusal to recognise the contract in the slip was based on the desire of successive Governments to maintain the revenue received from marine policy stamp duty, abolition of such duty in 1970 would make the slip a legally recognised document. The argument fails when one studies Section 22 of the MIA, 1906. It is unlikely this section of the Act will be repealed while the brevity of slip structure continues because courts of law would require full clausing on slips which is not practical. Knowledge that the slip will not form the legal contract enables practitioners to limit the placing detail thereon to only sufficient information to identify the risk and to give a brief outline of the insurance conditions; often with no more than an abbreviated reference to standard marine insurance clauses. Experienced underwriters understand the intentions of the broker when proposing the risk on the slip in this abbreviated format and are content to conclude the contract on this basis. Nonetheless, translation of abbreviations is always subject to human error so a court of law, in attempting to settle a dispute over unclear wording in the policy form, may call upon the slip as evidence to support the formal policy and to clarify the intentions of the parties to the contract.

Although an English court will not recognise the contract, when only the broker's slip is offered as evidence, section 21 of the MIA, 1906, provides that the conract is deemed to be *concluded* (ie agreed between underwriter and proposer) when the underwriter indicates his acceptance on the slip; such acceptance being expressed by the underwriter's written line supported by his initials.

Until the introduction of the MAR form of policy (see part 4) in the London market the perils covered by the insurance contract were expressed, amongst other things, in the policy form itself. With the passage of time underwriters began to agree clauses, conditions and perils which were not expressed in the policy form and it became necessary for clauses to be attached to the form to give effect to these differences. Further, although the standard policy form provided spaces for insertion of identifying information, it became customary for a schedule to be attached to the policy form for this purpose. The result was a mixture of conditions which often confused the parties to the contract and frequently led to disputes, both in and out of court, on the actual meaning of the contract. In later years underwriters were to insert "paramount" clauses in hull policies to make it clear that specified exclusions should take precedence over anything in the policy with which they were inconsistent but, prior to this practice, there were many cases of ambiguity which required direction from a court of law to determine whether or not a disputed claim was collectable under the policy. In fact, it was once commented "it is well known in the Courts of England that the Lloyd's marine insurance policy is a most incomprehensible document!". Despite the use of paramount clauses there are still disputes over the interpretation of policies and it should not be assumed that all these are necessarily resolved in favour of underwriters.

To be fair, underwriters do their best to avoid confusion but whilst they see the meaning of a clause one way a court of law might take an opposite view. For example, in the case of "Martin - v - Russell (1960)" the insured goods were covered until they were delivered at the final warehouse at the destination named in the policy (ie anywhere in the UK). A loss occurred whilst the goods were in a distribution warehouse following discharge from the overseas vessel. The cargo underwriters denied liability, contending that a distribution warehouse was the "final" warehouse within the meaning of the policy wording. The court held that the wording of the relevant clause did not make this clear and that underwriters were liable for the claim because, in the court's opinion, the final warehouse was the place where transit finally ended after the goods were distributed to the various destinations. The decision in this case led to a revision of warehouse to warehouse cover in cargo policies and introduction of the first form of the "transit clause", this clause being a common feature in cargo policies today.

Ambiguity may arise, also, in the way in which a policy is constructed. The way in which clauses are inserted in and/or attached to the policy together with different forms of printing can cause ambiguity in interpreting the meaning of the contract. A court will always apply ordinary commonsense in making a decision but may resort to the, so called, Rules of Interpretation (sometimes called the Rules of Precedence) in coming to a conclusion. The Rules apply to the form of wording, the clausing of the policy and the insurance conditions. The court gives precedence, as below, in ascending order (ie typed wording takes precedence over printed wording):-

Policy wording	Policy clauses/conditions
1. Underwriter`s handwriting	1. Attached clauses
2. Typed wording	2. Clauses in policy margin
3. Printed wording	3. Conditions in body of policy

No precedence is given to different typefaces in printing (ie **bold** type and *italics* are for emphasis only); nor does highlighting with coloured print make any difference in law. If ambiguity still remains after applying these Rules the court determines which party to the contract shall derive benefit from the ambiguity. Where the insurer has prepared and signed the policy (signature by a policy signing office is deemed to be the signature of the insurer) the court will almost certainly construe ambiguity in favour of the assured. On the other hand, where the broker submits the policy to the insurer or to the appropriate signing office for signature, the court will take the fact that the broker has prepared the policy document into account in coming to a decision; although the court might still favour the assured since the insurer`s representatives have had the opportunity to examine the policy before it was signed.

When the MAR policy form (see part 4) was introduced the practice of expressing insured perils and certain clauses in the printed policy form was discontinued. Further, although the original format of the MAR policy provided spaces in which information could be typed a practice has developed whereby such information is expressed in a schedule which is attached to the policy form. This change in format has gone a long way towards reducing the ambiguity previously created by adding inconsistent clauses and conditions to a policy form with insured perils, etc. printed therein. Nevertheless, so far, it has not been made clear whether a court will treat wording that has been reproduced on a modern word processer or in a computer print-out as "typing" in relation to the rules of interpretation, to which reference was made earlier; so one might still encounter problems in this respect.

3. Lloyd`s SG Policy and Insurance Company Equivalents

Because Lloyd`s market no longer uses the SG form of policy there is no such document today as *Lloyd`s* SG form and London market practitioners may consider a study of Lloyd`s SG policy form to be of academic interest only. Nevertheless, trainees should know something about this type of document because marine insurance contracts effected in some overseas markets continue to be based on policies similar in structure and format to Lloyd`s SG policy form. It is more than ten years since the London market abrogated the Lloyd`s SG policy form and policies of a similar format issued by London marine insurance companies in favour of a new form of contract based on the MAR form of policy. For many years, prior to this, it had been customary for overseas insurers and their clients to adopt London market marine insurance policies and the Institute clauses for use therewith; but, on this occasion, some overseas markets and their clients were loth to change to the MAR form of policy and to accept the new clauses published by the ILU for use with the MAR form of policy. These notes on the SG policy and similar policy formats are for the benefit of these markets and for reference by London market practitioners who are concerned with reinsurances of contracts that incorporate conditions expressed in the old Institute clauses. For the record the term *old* Institute clauses means those sets of conditions withdrawn by the ILU at the time the SG form of policy was abbrogated in the London market (see parts 4 & 5).

The abbreviation SG means "ship and goods". By studying the wording of the SG policy as reproduced in the first schedule to the MIA, 1906, one can see this cover expressed in the following wording:

> "upon any kind of goods and merchandises, and **also** upon the body, tackle, apparel, ordance, munition, artillery, boat, and other furniture, of and in the good ship or vessel called the ...."

In an attempt to standardise the wordings of policy forms Lloyd`s adopted the SG form, in 1779, and all Lloyd`s underwriters undertook to use this policy for every marine insurance contract written by them. In those days underwriters offered insurance protection only for a specific voyage and there was nothing wrong with the undertaking to insure both ship and goods in one policy where the proposer owned both the ship and the cargo or, if carrying cargo for another, was arranging to insure that cargo together with the ship. Further, it will be noted that, unless certain goods were specified in the policy, the insurance contract embraced all cargo carried during the voyage and on board at the time of the accident. Thus the undertaking given by Lloyd`s underwriters was broad in its concept and later proved to be impractical when ships became insured separately from cargo interests.

Despite its impracticability hull underwriters at Lloyd`s continued to use the SG policy for the insurance of a ship alone, without amending the above quoted wording and, for time policies, without deleting the "voyage" wording in the policy form. Similarly, cargo underwriters at Lloyd`s continued to use the SG policy for goods in transit by sea without deleting the policy wording which embraced the ship as part of the subject matter insured by the contract. When questioned on this in later years hull practitioners would dismiss the arguments of critics by alleging that they were merely academic and everyone knew that a hull policy covered only the ship because the subject matter insured was expressed by the words "hull & machinery" or, in the case of a sailing ship, "hull & materials". Similar arguments against critics were expressed by cargo practitioners; so the confusing practice continued, despite constant criticism in courts of law, throughout the life of Lloyd`s SG policy.

The London insurance company market was small during the 18th century and there was no organisation, such as the ILU, to jointly represent company insurers` interests and to liaise with Lloyd`s underwriters. Each company devised its own form of policy and, no doubt, used the SG format for insurances where the shipowner wanted to insure both ship and goods for a particular voyage. However, none of the marine insurance companies of the day followed Lloyd`s, in 1779, by adopting the SG policy as a standard contract form. It was not until 1795 that companies decided to use common policy forms for marine insurance. For circumstances where the ship and cargo were insured by one policy they used the SG format; but for circumstances where cargo was insured separately the companies used the "G" policy and, similarly, for circumstances where the ship was insured separately they used the "S" form of policy. The "G" policy was the same as an SG policy but the above quoted wording was amended to omit reference to the ship as a subject matter insured; naming the vessel only to identify it as a carrier. The "S" policy was the same as an SG policy but the above quoted wording was amended to omit all reference to the goods carried on board the insured ship. Overseas practioners intending to use the old Institute clauses will probably attach these to a "cargo" policy or a "hull" policy, in the format printed by the ILU for use with these clauses. Although the "Reference Book of Marine Insurance Clauses" (Witherby) currently incorporates a copy of the hull policy form (based on the old "S" policy) used by the ILU prior to introduction of the MAR policy form to the hull market the ILU policy signing department does not actually sign or seal this form when a contract (eg an insurance which is subject to the Institute builders` risks clauses, 1972) is based thereon. In such case the old policy form is incorporated, with the broker`s clauses, in a MAR form of policy with a bridging clause to ensure that the English law & practice clause applies to the contract.

References below to the SG form apply to the S and G forms of policy, as appropriate thereto.

4. The London Market MAR Policy Form

As commented earlier, over the years, considerable criticism was directed to the continued use of the SG form of cover for marine insurance contracts. The confusion referred to above only added to the grounds for criticism of confusion created by trying to equate modern practice with redundant phraseology. In the middle of the 19th century an abortive attempt was made by Lloyd`s to revise the policy form. After two and half years the committee charged with the task recomended that the SG policy wording be retained because any change would invite protracted, and expensive, litigation to establish the meanings of new terms introduced by the revision. In other words, they were afraid of the repercussions that change might raise. Further developments in practice made the SG form of cover even more redundant during the 100 years or so following the first attempt to revise Lloyd`s policy wording. The SG form had been designed with only "voyage" insurances in mind but cargo practice had extended cover to embrace land risks in "warehouse to warehouse" cover and hull practice had gone over mainly to the insurance of ships for periods of time.

During the 1960`s the maritime nations of the world were looking at ways in which long held traditions, based on voluminous paper transactions and inefficient procedures, could be revised to simplify documentation and to make international commercial practice less cumbersome and more efficient. All shipping organisations began to examine ways in which redundant wording could be removed from documents and the remaining wording clarified to equate with modern practice. Within this framework the London marine insurance market set up a joint committee to examine the SG policy format and the way clauses were used to amend it to arrive at the agreed contract. This committee ignored the previous concept of retaining but revising the SG form and decided to scrap it altogether in favour of a contract based almost entirely on the Institute clauses. Because the MIA, 1906, requires the existence of a formal policy document for legal purposes a new "plain" policy form was designed. This form omitted all the policy "conditions" and all the printed clauses that appeared in the SG form. These embraced the "policy perils" (see Section 10), the "sue & labour clause" (see Section 13) and the "waiver clause" (see Section 11); the substance of these, as appropriate to the cover, being transferred to the relevant Institute clauses. Lloyd`s printed this new form as the MAR form; whilst the ILU printed their version as the new Marine Policy. In practice the new form of policy is known as the MAR form whether the contract is placed at Lloyd`s or with marine insurance companies.

The MAR form is a simple document. It might be described as a "policy folder" since it is intended to enclose the policy conditions in the form of attachments and clauses. The issuing authority is printed on the face of the form. The face of a MAR policy subscribed by Lloyd`s underwriters bears, at its head, Lloyd`s crest followed by "Lloyd`s Marine Policy" and, at its foot, the abbreviation MAR. The face of a MAR policy subscribed by member companies, who have authorised the ILU to issue policies on their behalf, bears, at its head, "The Institute of London Underwriters" followed by the Institute crest, followed by "Companies Marine Policy". MAR forms issued by other insurance companies (ie members who have not authorised the ILU to issue policies on their behalf and non-Institute companies, including companies outside the London market who have adopted the new Institute clauses) follow the pattern of the ILU marine policy but with appropriate variations to the face of the policy.

The MAR form incorporates an "attestation" clause whereby the insurers specified therein undertake to insure against loss, damage, liability or expense, insofar as these are covered by the policy conditions, up to the amount of indemnity agreed in the policy. The MAR form used by Lloyd`s and the ILU bears an "English jurisdiction" clause (see part 8). Lloyd`s MAR form, also, bears a "survey" clause which applies only to cargo insurances and the ILU form bears a statement that the policy must be signed by the party in whose name it is drawn when submitted to support a claim or request for premium return; assigned policies (see part 9) to bear the signature of the assignee.

5. Marine Insurance Clauses

From the time it became apparent that the perils and conditions expressed in the SG form of policy needed amendment to meet the demands of proposers it has been necessary to clause marine insurance policies. Some clauses were printed in the policy wording (eg - the "memorandum", see part 10; the "sue & labour" clause, see Section 13; the "waiver" clause, see Section 11; and the "free of capture and seizure" clause, see Section 10). Some of these, with other clauses, were inserted in the margin of the policy form. As time progressed so did the volume of clauses initiated by various underwriters and brokers. Rather than continually altering the policy wording these clauses were attached to the face of the policy. There were so many variations in clauses that their attachment to the policy often created a cumbersome, confusing and untidy document. Matters came to a head towards the end of the 19th century and a decision was taken to standardise all hull insurance clauses to be used for attachment to the policy form.

Institute Hull Clauses (SG Policy) - A Technical & Clauses Committee, a joint Committee comprising members of the LUA (see Section 2) and representatives from the London company market, designed the first sets of Institute clauses for use with the SG form of policy. These were for hull insurance contracts and were published by the Institute of London Underwriters. They were titled the "Institute Time Clauses - Hulls" (ITC). A similar set of clauses was published for hull voyage contracts; being termed the "Institute Voyage Clauses - Hulls" (IVC). The last sets of these ITC and IVC conditions to be published were dated October 1970. They provided a comprehensive form of cover; adding perils not contemplated by the SG form of policy and embracing both total and partial loss. The clauses further extended the SG policy to embrace limited collision liability. No doubt because of the wide scope of cover the ITC and IVC were referred to, incorrectly, in practice as "all risks" conditions. In fact, they covered only specified perils but the misnomer has persisted amongst practitioners and is still in common use when reference is made to the current ITC and IVC published for use with the MAR form of policy.

Over the years various other sets of hull and hull interest clauses, based on the ITC or IVC as appropriate, were published. Clauses were published by the ILU to cover ships on "limited" terms (ie on conditions less wide than the, so called, "all risks" conditions). These included clauses for use in contracts where the assured was prepared to bear partial losses, either partly or fully (eg FPA clauses and FOD clauses); also clauses covering total loss only. Various ancillary hull interest clauses were also published as required. All these sets of clauses have been withdrawn by the ILU (see below) but interested practitioners can find information concerning these in "Marine Insurance - Volume 3 - Hull Practice - Second Edition" by Brown (Witherby, 1993).

Institute Cargo Clauses (SG Policy) - The Technical & Clauses Committee did not carry out a similar exercise for the cargo insurance market during the 19th century. It was not until 1912 that standard cargo clauses were introduced. Two sets of cargo clauses were published in the first instance. These were the "Institute Cargo Clauses with Average" (ICC WA) and the "Institute Cargo Clauses - Free of Particular Average" (ICC - FPA). Both sets of clauses covered the goods during the specified voyage and relied heavily on the cover provided by the SG form of policy as the basis of the contract. In fact, a contract which relied on the ICC conditions would be incomprehensible unless they were combined with the wording of the SG policy to which the ICC were attached because, apart from the absence of the clauses printed in the policy form (eg the "sue & labour" clause), there would be no perils expressed in the contract.

The ICC WA covered both total and partial loss as did the SG policy form but supplemented the cover with standard clauses which amended, extended or reduced the SG policy cover, as appropriate thereto. The ICC FPA provided the same cover as the ICC WA, but restricted cover for particular average losses. Many years later, in compliance with popular demand, the Technical & Clauses Committee designed a new set of clauses which were based on the ICC WA, but extended the perils expressed in the policy (see Section 10) to embrace "all risks", subject to the exclusion of war etc. risks. In practice, the ICC "All Risks" became the most commonly used set of cargo clauses. Later, various sets of "trade clauses" (ie special conditions agreed between the ILU and certain Trade Associations), based on the ICC, were published by the ILU for use with the SG form of policy.

None of the above sets of cargo clauses is currently published by the ILU but information on the cover provided by the old cargo clauses can be found in "Marine Insurance - Volume Two - Cargo Practice - Fourth Edition" by Brown (Witherby 1985).

Institute Cargo Clauses (MAR Policy) - The SG form of policy was abrogated for all cargo insurance contracts, effected in the London market, attaching on and after 1st January, 1982. A transitional period (18 months) was allowed to give brokers and assureds the opportunity to run off open cover contracts, or to cancel these at a convenient time, and to effect new contracts based on conditions designed for use with the new MAR form of policy. The last sets of the old ICC to be published by the ILU were dated 1963 and these remained available for use with open covers during the transitional period. When the transitional period expired the ILU withdrew the ICC WA, the ICC FPA and the ICC "All Risks" conditions.

Prior to abbrogation of the SG form of policy new sets of standard cargo clauses had been designed by the Technical & Clauses Committee. These offered a different concept in cargo insurance conditions and were published by the ILU, with the effective date 1st January, 1982, for use with the MAR form of policy for all new business based on the standard cargo conditions and attaching as and from that date. There are three basic sets of the ICC (1982), being A, B and C. None of these equates with the old clauses; the London cargo insurance market no longer writing business on WA or FPA terms. All three sets of the ICC (1982) cover both total and partial loss; the only difference between them lying in the perils covered. The ICC A cover "all risks", subject to expressed exclusions. The ICC B cover only specified perils, subject to expressed exclusions. The ICC C, also, cover only specified perils, subject to expressed exclusions, but do not provide as wide a cover as the B clauses. The Institute trade clauses published for use with the SG form of policy remained in force for some time after the standard ICC (1982) were adopted. This was to allow time for Trade Associations to consider the new types of cover being offered. Some could not come to agreement and the clauses relating to these trades were withdrawn with no alternatives offered. For those Associations (the majority) who came to an agreement new trade clauses have been published based on whichever set of the new ICC is appropriate; the old trade clauses being withdrawn.

Information concerning the cargo clauses published for use with the MAR form of policy can be found in "Marine Insurance - Volume Two - Cargo Practice" by Brown (Witherby 1985) and in "Analysis of Marine Insurance Clauses - Book One - The Institute Cargo Clauses 1982" by Brown (Witherby 1983).

Institute Hull Clauses (MAR Policy) - The MAR form of policy was not adopted by the London hull insurance market until late in 1983, when hull underwriters undertook to write all new contracts attaching on or after the 1st October, 1983, only on conditions based on the new MAR form of policy. The Technical & Clauses Committee drafted new hull clauses (ITC, IVC, etc.) for this purpose and these were published by the ILU for use in the new types of contract. A transitional period (much shorter than had been allowed in the cargo market) was allowed for old type contracts to run off but, when this expired, the ILU withdrew the old style hull clauses. Whilst drafting the new hull clauses the Technical & Clauses Committee took the opportunity to update the policy perils. Some of the perils expressed in the SG policy form (see Section 10) were retained and incorporated in the new clauses. Outdated perils printed in the SG policy form were ignored. Perils added to the SG form by the old ITC and IVC were reconsidered and restructured to convey more clearly the intentions of the underwriters. Similarly, some clauses from the old ITC and IVC, albeit restructured in some cases, were retained and some new clauses were added. The 1983 standard ITC and IVC follow the old (1970) ITC and IVC in covering total loss, partial loss and limited collision liability. New hull TLO clauses were introduced to replace the old clauses. No equivalent set of clauses to equate with the old hull FOD cover exists today; but the old hull FPA type of cover was replaced with a new set of conditions which provides similar cover but in a format that is less confusing than the old clauses. Practitioners seeking more information regarding the 1983 hull clauses should refer to "Marine Insurance - Volume Three - Hull Practice" by Brown (Witherby 1993) and to "Analysis of Marine Insurance Clauses - Book Two - Institute Time Clauses - Hulls" by Brown (Witherby 1983).

Institute Time Clauses (1995) - Reference herein to the ITC used with the MAR form of policy (particularly to individual clause numbers therein) relates solely to the hull clauses published by the ILU in 1983 because these clauses are current during the revision. Nevertheless, trainees and practitioners should note that, during the revision of these introductory notes, a working party of the London market Joint Hull Committee (see Section 2) have completed a review of the ITC (1983) in the light of modern practice. As a result of this review drafts of new hull time clauses have been put to the London market for consideration. Two new versions of the ITC, A and B versions, are under consideration and, if these are acceptable to the London market, will probably be published in 1995.

Once these new hull clauses are published they will replace the basic ITC (1983); the latter being withdrawn by the ILU from a date to be advised. However, since the 1995 clauses have yet to be been published at the time of revision, it is not practical to incorporate detailed information in any set of course notes. For the time being, however, it might be useful to note that both sets of the proposed 1995 clauses follow the pattern of the ITC (1983). There are several variations from the 1983 coverage and both sets of the proposed 1995 clauses incorporate new clauses (eg a "classification" clause and a "radioactive contamination exclusion" clause); but the B conditions provide a narrower coverage than the A conditions. It is to be expected that, once the new ITC have been successfully launched, attention will be given to revision of the other sets of hull and hull interest clauses published by the ILU for use with the MAR form of policy. Trainees and practitioners referring to the recommended hull practice book ("Marine Insurance - Volume 3 - Hull Practice" by Brown) for a more advanced study should bear the above comments in mind.

Other Marine Insurance Clauses - Over the years the ILU published, as required, a number of ancillary clauses for use with contracts based on the SG form of policy. Those inapplicable to the new form of cover were withdrawn at the appropriate time, but those that were not directly associated with the cover provided by the SG form of policy have been retained and are available for use with contracts based on the MAR form of cover. Copies of the latter can be found, with copies of all Institute clauses published for use with the MAR form of policy, in a current edition of "The Reference Book of Marine Insurance Clauses" (Witherby).

Various special clauses are prepared by underwriters and brokers. These are referred to, in practice, as Market clauses, Brokers' clauses, Underwriters' clauses or Owners' clauses, as the case may be. Trainees must learn from experience when to use these clauses. Further clauses and conditions are introduced to the market by overseas authorities. Some of these (eg the American Hull Form) are still based on the old SG form of cover; whilst others (eg the Standard Dutch Hull Form) are based on the new type of cover. Care must be exercised when using any of these sets of conditions to ensure that the correct policy form applies.

Copyright of Institute Clauses - Trainees and practitioners should note that the Institute of London Underwriters hold the copyright on all sets of "Institute" clauses. Thus, except where the ILU has so authorised, the reproduction of Institute clauses by any party is prohibited. This does not restrict the use of Institute clauses in any marine insurance contract but practitioners must not print their own sets of Institute clauses for use in these contracts and/or policies and/or certificates. Practitioners may purchase copies of the relevant clauses from the authorised printers and distributers; these being Witherby & Co. Ltd. 32-36, Aylesbury St., London, EC1R 0ET, England.

6. Gambling Policies and PPI Policies

Marine insurance practice is very much based on trust. In the past unscrupulous proposers have often attempted to exploit the vulnerability of marine underwriters by proposing policies of insurance where they had no interest in the subject matter insured and no reasonable expectation of acquiring such interest. Although they stood to lose nothing if an accident should befall the subject matter insured they sought to make a profit from the accident by claiming on the policy. Marine insurance exists so that the losses suffered by the unfortunate individual shall be borne by underwriters. It does not exist to provide a medium for making a profit out of a loss. Over the years certain protections for underwriters were introduced in common law and were subsequently codified in the Marine Insurance Act, 1906. The MIA, 1906, made no attempt to prohibit contracts where the assured had no insurable interest but it made it clear that the courts of England would not entertain any action brought on a contract that was inconsistent with the requirements of a marine insurance policy as set out section 4 of the Act.

Section 4 of the MIA, 1906, provides that "Every contract of marine insurance by way of gaming or wagering is void". This means that an English court will not recognise a gambling policy. To determine whether or not a policy falls within this category one must have regard for the principle of insurable interest, as defined in the Act, and for the definition of a gaming or wagering policy as expressed in section 4(2) of the MIA, 1906. The Act provides that a contract of marine insurance is deemed to be a gaming or wagering policy where the assured has no insurable interest therein and where the contract is entered into without any expectation of acquiring an insurable interest. Notes on hull and cargo interests can be found in Section 6.

Further, a policy is deemed to be a gaming or wagering contract where it incorporates any condition as follows, or a similar condion:

(1) Interest or no interest; or
(2) Without further proof of interest than the policy itself; or
(3) Without benefit of salvage to the insurer (except where there is no possibility of salvage)

Despite these restictions some abuses continued and it was deemed necessary to introduce further legislation to strengthen the above restrictions in the MIA, 1906. The Marine Insurance (Gambling Policies) Act, 1909, provides that any person (ie proposer, broker or underwriter) who knowingly effects a gaming or wagering contract is guilty of an offence under the Act and is liable to prosecution. Conviction for an offence under the 1909 Act can result in forfeiture, to the Crown, of all proceeds from the contract and the offender can be, at the discretion of the court, fined or awarded a prison sentence of six months with or without hard labour.

The Gambling Policies Act seems to have achieved its purpose for there appears to be no record of any prosecutions being pursued under the Act. In any event, although a contract falling within the category covered by the Act would not be admitted as evidence in an English court, the assured could avoid prosecution if he could prove, despite the wording of the policy, that he actually did have an insurable interest at the time of loss. It will be noted that the assured need not have an insurable interest in a marine policy at the time the contract is negotiated. Provided he had at that time a reasonable expectation of acquiring an insurable interest this is sufficient;

even if the insurable interest does not in fact materialise. For example, a shipowner buys a new ship to which he will acquire title when it is delivered to him at a specified port. He can effect a policy in advance to cover the ship (or add it to his existing fleet policy if agreed with his underwriters) before delivery takes place; the insurance to attach from the time the ship is delivered to him. If the ship is lost before delivery no claim attaches to the policy and the proposer is not guilty of an offence under the Gambling Policies Act.

One must not forget that, although there may be no offence under the Gambling Policies Act, the restrictions listed above in regard to the MIA, 1906, still apply. A policy which contains any clause whereby underwriters waive their subrogation rights would not be recognised by an English court; nor would a policy which contains a condition that proof of interest is waived.

PPI Policies - The abbreviation *PPI* is frequently used in marine insurance practice. It mean "policy proof of interest" and, when it appears in a policy, the underwriter undertakes not to demand proof of insurable interest at the time of loss. In the absence of this condition the claims adjuster representing the underwriter is entitled to demand proof that the assured had a insurable interest at the time of loss. However, underwriters recognise that there are certain types of interest that are difficult to define or, even if their existence can be proved, it is difficult for the assured to prove the extent of his loss. In such cases the underwriter may be prepared to waive proof of interest but, conscious of their vulnerability in this respect underwriters limit this concession to only a few interests. For example, an experienced underwriter when negotiating a contract to cover the hull and machinery of a ship would never agree to a PPI clause in the policy; neither would a cargo underwriter accept ordinary cargo in transit subject to this condition.

One is unlikely to see a PPI policy used for a contract which covers partial loss. The nature of the arrangement lends itself only to circumstances where the ship becomes a total loss. For example, one might see goods insured by a policy which covers "increased value" of the goods. The policy would be for a fixed amount, and probably on a TLVO (Total loss of vessel only) basis or subject to some similar condition. One would expect to see the words "To pay as cargo" expressed in the slip and policy. This means that the assured only has to show that a total loss of the cargo insured by an underlying (linked) policy was settled, and to produce the PPI policy, for the claim to be settled on the latter.

PPI policies are more commonly found in the hull market where ship operators have several nebulous interests related to the insured ship and which are not embraced by his H & M policy. Examples are increased value of hull and machinery, anticipated freight and disbursements incurred in ship operation (for more information on these see Section 6). It is customary for a shipowner to insure these interests on a TLO (Total loss only) basis in a PPI policy wherein the underwriters admit the assured has a full interest up to the sum insured without demanding proof of this. As in the earlier example, the assured only has to show a claim for total loss was settled on the (linked) hull & machinery policy to claim the full sum insured by the PPI policy.

It is not an offence to effect a PPI provided there is no contravention of the Gambling Policies Act, 1909. Any person who effects a PPI policy knowing the proposer does not have a relevant insurable interest, and has no reasonable expectation of acquiring such insurable interest, in relation to the subject matter insured (ie ship or cargo) to which the the PPI policy is linked would be guilty of an offence under the Act.

The assured and his broker should always remember that a PPI policy is an "honour" contract. If an underwriter refuses to pay a claim under the contract there is no legal remedy available to the assured to force the underwriter to honour his obligations. It was thought, at one time (and some practitioners still labour under this misconception) that one could avoid the legal disadvantages of such a contract by omitting any reference to the PPI undertaking from the policy document. To this end the PPI agreement was confined to the slip and a separate PPI clause was printed for use with the policy. This clause incorporated words to the effect that, at the assured's option, it could be removed from the policy. To facilitate such removal the clause would be "pinned" to the policy document (the format of some later versions incorporated a perforated line which allowed the clause to be affixed to the policy by the upper margin yet still be removable by tearing it off). The futility of this practice was illustrated in the case of "Edwards -v- Motor Union (1922)" when the court declared a marine insurance PPI policy void despite the fact that the PPI clause had been removed.

Hull underwriters are particularly aware that too much freedom in the use of PPI policies could encourage abuse of the system. It would be impractical for each underwriter to examine every proposal in detail so an express warranty (see Section 8) is incorporated in all H & M policies. This warranty appears in the "disbursements clause" which lists those interests that may be insured in addition to the H & M policy. Any breach of this warranty discharges the underwriters subscribing the *H & M* policy from all liability and, effectively, also renders the PPI policies inactive.

7. Jurisdiction and Law & Practice Clauses

The term "jurisdiction", in this context, means the authority empowered to make legal decisions in cases of dispute between the parties to a marine insurance contract. When considering a policy issued in London one would assume this to be subject to "English" jurisdiction. Over the years it became apparent that this assumption was not founded in fact and many cases came to light where the assured had pursued an action in a foreign court in the belief that the relevant court would make a decision to his advantage.

London underwriters decided that, when designing the new MAR policy, they would take steps to ensure underwriters' rights could be challenged only in a court which is subject to English jurisdiction. To this end a clause is printed in the MAR policy form which states *This insurance is subject to English jurisdiction*.

London practitioners refer to any jurisdiction other than English as "Foreign jurisdiction" and to any condition in the contract whereby the underwriter agrees to comply with directions of a court located outside the UK as a "foreign jurisdiction clause". Unless the underwriters subscribing a MAR policy issued in the UK agree to a foreign jurisdiction clause in the contract the English jurisdiction clause must not be deleted. It is expected that overseas markets adopting the MAR form of policy will incorporate their own form of jurisdiction clause.

Most contracts effected in the London market do not incorporate a foreign jurisdiction clause but there are no market restrictions on London underwriters regarding foreign jurisdiction clauses. Where the proposer is domiciled in another country, or operates his business in another country, it is common for him to request that a foreign jurisdiction clause be incorporated in the contract and rarely do underwriters refuse this request. One is unlikely to see an "open" clause (ie one whereby the underwriter undertakes to recognise *any* jurisdiction) agreed in practice. Experience shows that each foreign jurisdiction clause used in the London market specifies the name of the country concerned. For example, one often sees a US (United States of America) jurisdiction clause in a hull policy issued in the London market for a US assured.

English law & practice clauses - Interpretation of the SG form of policy was determined by applying English law and practice. That is to say the contract was deemed to be subject to the Rules of precedence (see part 2), to English statutes (eg MIA, 1906), to precedents established in English law and to practices established in the London market. The clauses published by the ILU for use with the SG form of policy were drafted with this in mind but it did not seem necessary to incorporate a clause to this effect in either hull or cargo policies because most court decisions were based on English law and practice.

In recent years there has been a proliferation in contracts which incorporate a foreign jurisdiction clause and the London market became concerned that foreign courts would interpret the conditions expressed in the Institute hull and cargo clauses in a way that was never intended when the relevant clauses were drafted. Further, it has become common for overseas practitioners to use Institute clauses. The London market assumed this practice would continue when the new clauses were introduced for use with the MAR form of policy and feared that foreign jurisdiction would mis-interpret the new clauses if decisions were based on local law and practice.

Accordingly, the Technical & Clauses Committee took the opportunity to incorporate an "English law & practice" clause in each main set of clauses published for use with the MAR form of policy. Since its introduction many practitioners have failed to recognise the purpose of this clause and have asked underwriters to delete it when a foreign jurisdiction clause is agreed. In fact, this is precisely the sort of contract for which the English law & practice clause was introduced. The English law & practice clause must **not be deleted** in any circumstances. The existence of this clause in the contract ensures that a court in a foreign jurisdiction will base its decision on English law and practice rather than on the law and practice of the foreign jurisdiction and, thereby, interpret the Institute clauses as intended by the Technical & Clauses Committee. Practitioners in markets outside London should refrain from using the Institute clauses if they are not prepared to accept English law and practice in disputes.

8. Valued and Unvalued Policies

A marine insurance policy may be "valued" or "unvalued". Section 27(2) of the MIA, 1906, defines a "valued" policy as one "which specifies the agreed value of the subject matter insured". Thus, the word "value" or "valued" must appear in the policy for it to be treated as a valued policy. In modern practice it is customary to express the value and sum insured separately in slip and policy; whether or not both figures are the same.

Specifying the sum insured (ie the total of the signed lines) in a policy does not make it a valued policy. Any policy which does not express the agreed value, as such, is an "unvalued" policy, even though it specifies the sum insured by the policy, and is subject to the restrictions applicable to unvalued policies on which comment is made later in these notes.

Valued policies are used for policies covering property at risk (eg hull & machinery of a ship, goods in transit, etc.). Policies covering ancillary interests relating to property at risk (eg anticipated freight, ship's disbursements, managers' commissions, etc.) are effected on an unvalued basis and specify a sum insured but no insured value. Contracts covering liabilities in addition to physical loss or damage (eg a contract subject to the ITC) are effected on valued policies; the insured value being treated as the measure of indemnity (see Sections 11 and 12) for physical damage and the basis on which liability claims are calculated. Contracts covering liabilities only are effected on unvalued policies and specify a limit of liability instead of an insured value.

In the absence of fraud, the value agreed in a valued policy is conclusive of the insurable value of the subject matter insured whether the loss be total or partial (MIA, 1906, sec. 27 sub.3). Accordingly, relevant claims will be based on the agreed value even though, at the time of loss, the actual value of the subject matter insured may have increased or decreased.

Total loss claims - A total loss can be an *actual* total loss or a *constructive* total loss (see Section 11). Unless the policy otherwise provides the insured value is not conclusive in establishing whether or not the property is a constructive total loss (MIA, 1906, sec.27 sub.4).

Example 1 (Hulls) - A ship has a market value of £4,000,000. The underwriter agrees to insure the ship for a period of 12 months for her full value. The sum insured is £4,000,000 and the insured value is expressed in the policy as £4,000,000. During the currency of the policy the market value of the ship decreases and, at the time of loss, is only £3,200,000. In example (*a*), below, the ship was totally lost by an insured peril. In examples (*b*) and (*c*), below, the ship was badly damaged by an insured peril and the estimated cost of repairs was so high that a constructive total loss settlement was considered.

(*a*) Actual total loss - The decrease in value makes no difference. The claim under the policy is £4,000,000.

(*b*) Where there is no CTL clause in policy the insured value would be ignored until the assured's right to claim a claim a constructive total loss had been proved. For this purpose the cost of repairs (in this case estimated at £3,300,000) would be compared with the actual repaired value of the ship. In this case a CTL would be agreed and the claim under the policy would be £4,000,000.

(*c*) Where there is a CTL clause in policy the assured's right to claim a constructive total loss would be tested by comparing the estimated cost of repairs (ie £3,300,000) with the insured value, instead of the repaired value, so no CTL would be allowed. The assured could still claim for a partial loss (see Section 12) and would be entitled to reimbursement of the actual cost of repairs less the policy deductible.

Example 2 (Hulls) - A ship has a market value of £4,000,000. The underwriter agrees to insure the ship for a period of 12 months, with the insured value expressed in the policy as £4,000,000, but for a sum insured of £3,000,000. During the currency of the policy the market value of the ship decreases and, at the time of loss, is only £3,200,000. In example (*a*), below, the ship was totally lost by an insured peril. In examples (*b*) and (*c*), below, the ship was badly damaged by an insured peril and the estimated cost of repairs was so high that a constructive total loss settlement was considered.

(*a*) Actual total loss - The decrease in value makes no difference. The claim under the policy is for the full sum insured of £3,000,000.

(*b*) Constructive total loss - There is no CTL clause in the policy so whether or not there are grounds for a constructive total loss is determined as in the MIA, 1906, (see Section 11) by comparing the cost of repairs, estimated at £3,300,000, with the repaired value of the ship (ie £3,200,000). A CTL would be allowed. The claim under the policy is for the full sum insured of £3,000,000.

(*c*) Constructive total loss - The policy incorporates a CTL clause so whether or not a CTL will be allowed is determined as provided by the MIA, 1906 (see Section 11) but with the "insured" value replacing the "repaired" value in the calculation. No CTL would be allowed but the assured would still be entitled to claim for the cost of repairs as a partial loss (see Section 12) and would be reimbursed for 3/4ths of the cost of repairs less the policy deductible.

Example 3 (Cargo) - The goods are insured by a voyage policy for £10,000 so valued. In example (*a*), below, the cargo was totally lost by an insured peril during transit. In example (*b*), below, the cargo was discharged short of destination because it had been badly damaged by an insured peril during the earlier part of the voyage. Unlike the CTL clause in a hull policy the CTL clause in a cargo policy does not alter the provisions of the MIA, 1906, regarding the basis for determining whether or not there is a CTL (see Section 11). So the estimated costs of recovering and reconditioning the goods (if necessary) are totalled. To this total one adds the probable cost of forwarding the goods to the planned destination. The result is then compared with the estimated value of the goods on arrival at the planned destination. If the costs so calculated exceed the probable arrived value of the goods the assured can claim a CTL.

(a) Actual total loss - The sound market value of the goods at the time of loss was estimated at £9,800 but no regard is had for the diminution in value and the claim payable under the policy would be £10,000.

(b) Constructive total loss - The actual value of the goods in their damaged condition on arrival at the planned destination was estimated at £5,000. The probable total costs of recovery, reconditioning and forwarding was estimated to be £5,200. A CTL claim would be allowed. Other than for determining whether or not a CTL would be allowed the above valuations are disregarded and the claim under the policy would be for the full insured value of £10,000.

Damage claims (ship) - Where the hull & machinery of a ship is insured for her full insured value the cost of repairs is recoverable up to the insured value in any one accident, less the policy deductible (see Section 12). No regard is had for the market value at the time of loss. If the sum insured is less than the insured value the claim is reduced proportionately.

Damage claims (cargo) - Arrived values are taken into account only for determining the percentage of depreciation (see Section 12). The percentage of depreciation is then applied to the the insured value to determine the claim under the policy. If the sum insured is less than the insured value the claim is reduced proportionately.

When the risk is shared by a group of underwriters, and more than one policy is issued to cover the risk, the full insured value must be expressed in each policy together with the sum insured by that policy. For example, the policies issued in respect of a slip, with an insured value of £100,000, written 60% at Lloyd`s and 40% by ILU companies would express the sums insured and insured value as follows:

Lloyd`s policy	Sum insured £60,000	Insured value £100,000
Institute combined policy	Sum insured £40,000	Insured value £100,000

An unvalued policy is one which does not specify the insured value of the subject matter insured but, subject to the limit of the sum insured, leaves the insurable value to be subsequently ascertained (MIA, 1906, sec. 28).

In the case of a ship this would be the actual value of the ship at the time she commences the risk. The definition in the MIA, 1906, contemplated only voyage insurances. If unvalued policies were used for hull time policies today one would interpret the term "commencement of the risk" as meaning commencement of the voyage during which the accident occurs. It is indeed fortunate that such valuation is unlikely to be necessary in modern practice because it is notoriously difficult to value a ship accurately; and to have to do so at the commencement of each voyage in case an accident might occur would place an intolerable burden on the shipowner or ship operator. Nonetheless, if a claim did fall on an unvalued policy covering a ship the insurable value would become the amount on which the measure of indemnity would be based. The disadvantage of an unvalued hull policy becomes apparent if one considers a situation where the ship is insured for, say, £3,000,000 (which is the sum insured) and a total loss occurs during a voyage at the commencement of which the insurable value of the vessel was only £2,800,000. The claim allowed would be for the latter figure and any contention by the assured that he should be entitled to £3,000,000 because he had paid premium for the larger amount would fail in a court of law.

In the case of an unvalued cargo policy the insurable value is the prime cost of the goods, plus shipping costs and the insurance premium. Where an exporter insures goods in transit overseas to his buyer the measure of indemnity allowed by the MIA, 1906, for a claim on an unvalued policy places the assured in the position as though he had never shipped the goods because the valuation assessed in accordance with the Act does not include any profit the shipper (ie the seller) expects to earn for selling the goods. A valued policy would redress this position by allowing the assured to propose his own valuation to the underwriter; which valuation would include a percentage to cover the expected profit on the sale, to be agreed as the insured value.

From the above, it should be clear that the assured has much better cover where the policy incorporates an insured valued in addition to a sum insured. The practice of agreeing insured values is peculiar to the marine market (ie it is not customary for non-marine underwriters to issue valued policies). However, brokers should remember that it is market practice to use a valued policy for all insurance contracts covering ships against physical loss or damage and for all marine insurance contracts covering goods against physical loss or damage. It should not be necessary for the proposer to request a valued policy where it is customary for a valued policy to be used and a broker who failed to incorporate an insured value in the above circumstances could, if the assured was prejudiced by the broker's negligence, find himself being sued for damages under the law of agency.

When proposing an open cover or any other form of long term marine insurance contract to insure physical loss or damage to ship or goods the broker must ensure that provision is made therein for policies, etc. issued off the contract to be on a "valued" basis. Further, practitioners should note that it is customary for underwriters to incorporate a "basis of valuation" clause in cargo open covers to provide for circumstances where no insured value has been declared for a particular cargo shipment at the time of loss.

When proposing a contract to reinsure underwriters who have written lines on a marine insurance contract covering physical loss of or damage to ship or physical loss of or damage to goods in transit by sea the broker must ensure that the reinsurance follows the insured value in the original policy. This is done by adding "VOP" (valued as original policy or policies) to the reinsurance slip so that the reinsurance is based on a valued policy. Failure to do this will entitle the reinsuring underwriters to treat the reinsurance policy as an unvalued policy.

Before leaving the subject of valuation in policies claims practitioners should note that it is wise to check the clauses attached to a marine insurance contract to see if there is any condition therein which relates to the insured value. An example would be a clause in the ITC (1983) whereby the insured value is automatically reduced if the ship proceeds on a "break up" voyage without prior notification to the underwriters regarding the nature of the voyage.

9. Policy Assignment

In the absence of any agreement expressed or implied in the contract that the policy shall be assigned, or in the absence of any legal direction requiring the policy to be assigned, where the assured parts with his insurable interest during the currency of the the policy a marine insurance contract lapses immediately. Beneficial interest in the policy does not automatically follow the passage of insurable interest to another party (MIA, 1906, sec. 15). For example, unless the conditions of the policy provide otherwise, when a hull assured sells or otherwise disposes of the ship during the currency of the policy, the insurance cover terminates automatically upon such transfer of title. In practice, hull policies incorporate a termination clause which has the same effect but, even if this clause were to be deleted, the situation would not change. The underwriter would no longer be on risk; unless the deletion was qualified to the contrary with appropriate wording in the policy.

Cargo policies do not incorporate an automatic termination clause of the type one sees in hull policies. It is common for cargo insurance contracts to be effected by the seller (the premium being included in the insured value and in the price paid for the goods) which implies that the cargo policies and/or cargo certificates will be assigned to the buyer. This practice is recognised by the law which accepts that such policies and certificates automatically follow transfer of title to the goods. Nonetheless, it must be recognised that this relaxation applies only to goods sold on terms (eg CIF - see Section 1) where the premium is included in the price paid for the goods. Where the terms of sale are otherwise (eg C&F) the insurance contract lapses, as above, on transfer of title to the goods to the buyer.

Unless the policy expressly provides therefor, no premium is returnable to the assured by reason of the policy lapsing on transfer of insurable interest. Hull time policies usually allow a pro rata return of premium if the policy is cancelled; but it is not customary for return premiums to be allowed in a hull voyage policy nor in a cargo policy.

Although assignment does not automatically follow transfer of insurable interest in the subject matter insured Section 50 (1) of the MIA, 1906, provides that, except where it incorporates a condition prohibiting or restricting assignment, a marine insurance policy is freely assignable by the assured to another party and it may be assigned either before or after loss. Assignment may be implemented by endorsement to the insurance document. Cargo claims practitioners will recognise the signature of the assignor on the policy or certificate as evidence of assignment of the policy or certificate to the holder thereof. Hull underwriters will recognise assignment only when they have agreed to it in writing and where it is expressed in a dated endorsement, signed by the assured (and, where applicable, any subsequent assignee) which is affixed to the hull policy.

When a marine insurance policy is assigned to another party the assignee takes over all the beneficial rights in the policy that the assignor enjoyed. The assignee can sue in his own name but the the underwriter is entitled to raise any defence arising out of the contract which he would have been entitled to make if the action had been brought against him by the party in whose name the policy was effected. Thus, where the proposer or his broker was guilty of a breach of good faith in negotiating the contract (see Section 7) the underwriter can reject the claim made by the assignee even though the assignee was innocent, and indeed unaware, of the breach. In such event the assignee may be entitled to take action against the assignor, but in no circumstances does he have any rights against the underwriter. The assignee must abide by any conditions by which the assignor is bound and, for example, must comply with any express or implied warranties attaching to the contract. Where the assignor committed a breach of warranty (see Section 8) prior to assignment of the policy such breach still affects claims made by the assignee even where the assignee was innocent of the breach. Concerning the latter an exception is made in hull insurance practice where breach of the "disbursements" warranty (see Section 8) is waived in regard to a claim from a mortgagee who has accepted the policy, in good faith, as security for a loan and was unaware of the breach of warranty. This is the only concession hull underwriters will make to mortgagees who accept the mortgagor`s policy to protect their security for the loan. No concessions are allowed regarding breaches of good faith or other breaches of warranty by the named assured in the policy and brokers might consider it desirable to advise mortgagees to effect their own insurance contracts to cover the loan. Recognising this need the ILU published special mortgagees interest clauses, in 1986, for use with the MAR form of policy.

10. Policy Franchises, Deductibles and Excesses

A Florentine ordinance of 1526 decreed that certain specified types of commodity were not embraced by the general term "all kinds of goods and merchandises" in a marine insurance policy; such policy being in the SG format. To be covered such goods had to be specified as the subject matter insured in the policy. In practice underwriters, when covering these goods in transit by sea, excluded particular average losses. Although English jurisdiction was not subject to the Florentine ordinance private underwriters in London were using the same SG form of policy and followed Italian practice.

In the year 1749 the "memorandum" was added, by general consent of underwriters, to the various policy forms based on the SG format. This memorandum, albeit with variations to the original wording, appeared at the foot of the SG policy form adopted by Lloyd`s, in 1779, as the standard marine insurance policy. It can be seen in the sample of that policy in the first schedule to the MIA, 1906. Company policies based on the SG format also incorporated a memorandum with varied wording depending on whether the insurance covered a ship or goods in transit.

The following comments on the memorandum are for the benefit of practitioners who continue to use the SG form of policy and clauses designed for attachment thereto. The comments refer to the form of memorandum as it was reproduced in the MIA, 1906 (ie they apply, as appropriate thereto, to both hull and cargo insurances). For the sake of simplicity in the comments below we refer to the term "free of average unless general", which appeared in the memorandum, as "free of particular average".

Before examining the memorandum let us consider the cover provided by an SG form of policy. In the absence of any provision to the contrary, and subject to the operation of an insured peril, an SG policy form covered the following types of loss:

1. **Total loss (actual and constructive)**
2. **Particular average damage to the subject matter insured**
3. **General average sacrifice of the subject matter insured**
4. **General average contributions**
5. **Salvage charges and salvage contributions**
6. **Sue & labour charges**
7. **Particular charges (eg survey fees, reconditioning costs, etc.)**

FPA conditions - Although the ILU does not publish marine insurance conditions on an FPA (free of particular average) basis for use with the MAR form of policy the term FPA was commonly used in the London market during the reign of the SG form of policy. It was used when insuring certain types of cargo, in some limited terms H&M insurances and for limited terms cargo reinsurance contracts. Practitioners wishing to effect an insurance or reinsurance on FPA terms, and based on the MAR form of policy, will need to draft their own wording for this purpose.

Contrary to uninformed opinion at the time the term FPA did *not* mean "total loss only". Except where the term was otherwise qualified by the policy conditions an FPA policy covered all the types of loss listed above except item 2. Because item 2 was not covered the listed expenses and charges would be covered under an FPA insurance only insofar as they did not relate to particular average. The first part of the memorandum, relating only to cargo, warranted that corn, fish, salt, fruit, flour and seed were free of particular average unless the ship was stranded. It should be appreciated that the particular average did not have to be caused by the stranding. It was sufficient for the claimant to show that the ship had stranded at some time during the voyage, with the insured cargo on board at the time, for the particular average claim to attach to the policy.

Franchises - The second part of the memorandum also related only to cargo and warranted that sugar, tobacco, hemp, flax, hides and skins were free of particular average under 5% unless the ship was stranded. Such insurances would cover all the items listed above but, except for goods on board a ship that had stranded, claims for particular average would be subject to a 5% franchise.

Practitioners referred to the percentage specified in the memorandum as the "policy franchise" (loosely adopted from the French word "franchise", which means "free from"). It was only particular average loss *under* the franchise that was excluded from the policy. Thus, by way of definition, a marine insurance franchise is a percentage expressed in the policy which must be attained before a particular average loss is recoverable but, once it is attained, the particular average loss is recoverable in full. The following simple illustration will clarify any doubt:

Value of goods	*Loss*	*Franchise*	*Claim*
£10,000	2%	3%	nil
£10,000	3%	3%	3% = £300
£10,000	4%	3%	4% = £400

The third part of the memorandum related to insurances covering any cargo not specified in parts one and two and to ship and freight policies. It warranted that the policy was free of particular average under 3% unless the ship was stranded. Cargo insurances would cover all the items types of loss listed above but, except for goods on board a ship that had stranded, claims for particular average would be subject to a 3% franchise.

Franchise in cargo insurance - The term "unless stranded" meant that the warranty did not apply to the insured cargo if, at any time during the voyage, the ship was stranded provided the insured goods were on board at the time of the stranding (For a definition of the term "stranded" see Section 10 and Rule 14 of the "Rules for Construction of the Policy" in the first schedule to the MIA, 1906). It is important for concerned practitioners to appreciate that the loss of or damage to the goods did not have to be *caused by* the stranding for the franchise to be waived.

From the time they were first introduced (1912) to the time they were withdrawn by the ILU at the end of 1981 the ICC WA covered particular average subject to the restrictions applied by the memorandum. Nevertheless, the "average" clause in the ICC WA reduced the effect of the policy memorandum by extending the exemption "stranding" to embrace craft carrying the goods between ship and shore and, also, exempted from the memorandum provisions particular average incurred in circumstances where the insured goods were on board a ship or craft which was sunk, on fire, in collision or in contact with any external substance (other than water, but including ice) at any time during the period of transit.

By applying the FPA clause in the ICC FPA underwriters agreed to extend the cover in the SG form of policy to embrace particular average suffered by the insured goods provided the goods were on board the ship or craft when such vessel stranded or was sunk, on fire, in collision or in contact with any external substance (other than water but including ice) at any time during the period of transit. If none of these extenuating circumstances applied no claim for particular average would be entertained.

During the last years of the ICC WA conditions cargo underwriters frequently agreed to cover the goods "iop" (irrespective of percentage). This agreement had the effect of deleting the memorandum so that, where any of the items in the above list of types of loss were covered, the FPA condition in the memorandum did not apply and no franchise was applied to particular average claims. In practice cargo underwriters when writing insurances covering "all risks" always agreed these on an iop basis. The ICC "All risks" designed for use with the SG form of policy were iop conditions.

The memorandum does not appear in contracts based on the MAR form of policy and neither the "average" clause nor the "FPA" clause appears in any of the ICC (1982) conditions.

Franchise in H & M insurance - The 3% franchise expressed in the last part of the memorandum applied to hull & machinery policies effected on full conditions. However, in practice, although the memorandum still appeared in hull policies based on the SG format, its provisions were over-ridden by a clause in the ITC and in other relevant sets of hull clauses.

This clause, whilst still applying a 3% franchise to the aggregate of particular average claims incurred in any one round voyage, qualified this condition by agreeing to pay, irrespective of the franchise percentage, for damage to the ship *caused by* the insured ship being stranded, sunk, on fire or in collision with another ship or vessel. Unlike cargo insurance conditions, the hull insurance conditions still applied the 3% franchise to "contact" damage. Incidentally, it should be noted that insurers writing hull & machinery risks on the SG form of policy regarded damage caused to the ship by grounding in certain areas (eg Suez canal, Panama canal, etc.) as "contact" damage rather than "stranding" damage and applied the 3% franchise to such damage. The costs of a survey incurred specially to examine the bottom of the ship for damage following a stranding were recoverable even where no damage was found. But this latter concession did not apply to survey costs incurred to examine the ship`s bottom following grounding, in respect of which underwriters did not pay for the survey if no damage was found. Where particular average damage to the ship`s bottom was found following a grounding the survey costs were aggregated with the reasonable cost of repairing the particular average damage and the 3% franchise applied.

The 3% franchise (sometimes changed to a fixed amount in practice) continued to be incorporated in H & M insurances written on Institute hull clauses until October 1969 when the relevant clause in the ITC and the IVC, designed for attachment to the SG form of policy, was removed from the conditions in favour of a new clause which replaced the franchise provision with a policy deductible.

Franchise in freight at risk policies - It will be recalled that the 3% franchise expressed in the memorandum applied to freight insurances. The SG policy was referring to freight at risk insurances; not to policies covering anticipated freight. A freight at risk policy is one which insures freight payable to the carrier on safe discharge of the cargo to which it relates. The carrier has the insurable interest in a freight at risk policy (see Section 6). Where the cargo, in respect of which the freight is at risk of the carrier, suffers a particular average loss the freight paid to the carrier on delivery of the goods is reduced proportionately and, if he has insured the freight a particular average loss is recoverable under his freight at risk policy. The memorandum in the SG form of policy provided that particular average recoverable on freight should, except where the ship had stranded with the relevant cargo on board, be subject to the 3% franchise which was applied to the sum insured by the policy. Where the freight was insured by an SG form of policy for a period of time the 3% franchise applied, subject to any provision in clauses attached to the policy, to the insured freight attaching to the cargo that had suffered the particular average loss.

The SG policy contemplated only freight relating to overseas carriage but the Institute freight time and voyage clauses used with the SG form of policy extended the cover to embrace freight at the assured's risk whilst the goods were being carried in craft between ship and shore. These clauses also provided that the franchise be applied separately to the freight attaching to each craftload. The Institute freight clauses, used with the SG form of policy, incorporated a clause (called the "franchise" clause) which replaced the memorandum conditions. This clause, whilst still applying a 3% franchise to particular average claims replaced the memorandum exemption (stranding) with circumstances where the ship or craft had "been stranded, sunk or on fire". This had the effect of waiving the franchise if, during transit of the goods, any of these specified circumstances occurred irrespective of the proximate cause of the loss; provided, of course, the loss was caused by an insured peril. The term "on fire" could cause problems in defining how big a fire needed to be before one could say a vessel was actually "on fire". The franchise clause in the Institute freight clauses avoided this problem by agreeing to pay particular average actually caused by fire without reference to the franchise. Particular average caused by collision was treated in the same way but it should be noted that particular average caused by contact of the ship or craft with any external substance remained subject to the franchise.

As commented earlier, there is no memorandum printed in the MAR form of policy and the franchise system is not used in connection with hull and cargo insurances effected on this form of contract. Nevertheless, the Institute freight clauses (both time and voyage) published for use with the MAR form of policy incorporate a 3% franchise clause.

Application of this clause is different from the old application of a franchise in that it is relates to *all* partial losses, other than general average. This means that only freight attaching to cargo which was totally lost in the overseas vessel or, where applicable, in a craft and general average losses escape application of the 3% franchise. The freight attaching to each craftload, where applicable, is treated as a separate insurance and the 3% franchise is applied to partial loss in respect of the freight relating to the goods carried by that particular craft. More information concerning application of the franchise in freight policies can be found in "Marine Insurance - Volume 3 - Hull Practice" by Brown (Witherby 1993).

Deductibles - A "deductible" is an amount or a percentage specified in a policy which is deducted from any claim to which it relates. The term is seldom used in cargo insurance contracts but is common to any H & M insurance that covers partial loss. The deductible system had replaced the franchise system for hull insurances in the American market for many years before it was introduced to the Institute hull clauses; the latter taking place when the ITC/IVC were published by the ILU in 1969 with a deductible clause replacing the old franchise clause. To avoid confusion many practitioners deleted the memorandum from H & M policies based on the SG format when they used the, then new type of, ITC/IVC. The deductible clause appeared in the ITC (1970) and in the IVC (1970), which were the last sets of hull clauses to be published by the ILU for use with the SG form of policy. The deductible clause in the ITC/IVC (1970) made no cross reference to the memorandum which continued to be printed in the SG form of policy to which the 1970 hull clauses were attached so, as commented above, many practitioners deleted the memorandum when preparing this type of policy; a practice which practitioners who continue to use the SG format for hull policies might find it expedient to follow.

Where there is a deductible in a policy the assured becomes a co-insurer for that part of a loss to which it applies but, under English law, the insurer is entitled to the whole of any recovery up to the claim paid; the assured enjoying no recovery rights in regard to the amount of the deductible. The laws of other countries might not apply the same rule of law so, to ensure that it continued to apply when Institute hull clauses were used in hull insurance contracts based on the SG form of policy but subject to foreign jurisdiction, the ITC/IVC (1970) incorporated a provision by which a contractual undertaking entitled underwriters to recoveries as provided by English law.

The basis for applying the policy deductible, which was set out in the Institute hull clauses published for use with the SG form of policy, has remained the same where the Institute hull clauses are used with the MAR form of policy. Except where otherwise stated, the following comments relate to either form of hull contract.

In practice, the policy deductible is usually in the form of a fixed amount which is agreed between the proposer and the insurer at the time the contract is being negotiated. The amount so agreed is specified in a space provided therefor in the "deductible" clause printed in the relevant set of hull clauses when it is attached to the policy. An example of a hull deductible clause can be found in the ITC, 1983 (ref. CL.280 cl.12).

In every case where the hull policy covers the types of loss listed earlier in this Section (ie it is not a TLO policy) the deductible is applied, except as provided below, to all insured partial losses incurred in each separate accident. In other words, the deductible (unlike a franchise) is not restricted to particular average. It is applied to *all* partial losses (including collision liability and sue & labour charges), with the exception of sue & labour charges associated with a total loss and the costs of surveying the bottom of the ship to determine whether any damage has been caused by a stranding.

When applying the hull policy deductible to a claim one aggregates all losses (other than those excepted) incurred in each separate accident and applies the deductible to the total. It follows that, where repairs relating to several accidents are carried out at one time, the deductible may be applied more than once in the final calculations. Difficulties in determining a "separate accident" in cases of heavy weather damage are resolved by a section of the deductible clause which provides that all heavy weather damage occurring during a single passage between two ports shall be aggregated and be deemed as being caused by one accident.

The comments above regarding recovery rights enjoyed by hull underwriters under the ITC/IVC (1970) apply equally to underwriters' rights under a MAR policy with the ITC (1983) or the IVC (1983) attached thereto.

Many complications can arise in the application of hull policy deductibles but the text herein is necessarily brief because these notes are intended only as an introduction to marine insurance principles and practice. Practitioners seeking more detailed information on the application of hull policy deductibles are recommended to refer to "Marine Insurance - Volume Three - Hull Practice" by Brown (Witherby 1993). However, trainees should note that a hull policy may be subject to more than one deductible. In the hull practice book recommended above one can find detail on the application of "machinery damage additional deductibles" and on the implementauion of "annual aggregate deductibles", both of which feature frequently in hull and machinery insurance contracts.

Excesses - The term "excess", as used in this Section, must not be confused with the hull interest term "excess liabilities" nor with "excess reinsurance" contracts. The text herein is concerned with an "excess" which is an amount expressed in a contract that insures property against marine risks and which must be exceeded before a partial loss claim becomes payable. Once this amount is exceeded the claim is paid but only insofar as it exceeds the stated excess. It will be recalled that, in the franchise system, the loss only had to *attain* the franchise amount for a claim to attach to the policy and the underwriter paid the claim *in full* once the franchise had been attained.

The term "excess" was commonly used in hull insurance practice when the franchise system (see above) prevailed. Its application was, effectively, the same as a deductible. With abrogation of the franchise system in hull policies, and introduction of the deductible system, the use of excesses in hull insurance was phased out in the London market. At one time the ILU published clauses to provide for hull policies which incorporated an excess but no similar Institute clauses are published today.

The ICC (1963) FPA and WA were designed with the FPA warranty and franchise provision in the memorandum in mind but took no account of any excess provision cargo underwriters might incorporate in the contract where certain types of cargo were concerned; such underwriters drafting their own wordings to implement the excess provision. The ICC (1982) A, B and C, designed for use with the MAR form of policy, incorporate neither a franchise nor an excess provision. The London market leaves cargo underwriters to decide whether or not some such restriction should be applied to claims and to devise their own wording to implement the provision.

11. Combined Policies

A "combined" policy is a document that incorporates the commitments of more than one insurer in a single policy. It will be recalled that syndication does not affect the, so called, several liability of a name in the syndicate (see Section Two). Similarly, the joint signing of several syndicates in one policy does not affect the individual liability of a syndicate in respect of claims under the policy.

In practice it is common for a risk to be shared between a number of syndicates; the active underwriter for each syndicate writing his line on the slip. When the risk is submitted to LPSO (Lloyd`s Policy Signing Office) the signing office enters the details of each subscribing syndicate in a computer. When LPSO is satisfied that the policy is in order a "signing table" is printed by the computer. The signing table lists the signed lines of all the subscribing syndicates, with their references, etc. The signing table is attached to the policy; but, as commented above, each syndicate`s liability is separate. When serving suit under the policy action is taken against only one syndicate, usually the leader. If this action succeeds it does not legally bind the other syndicates to pay the claim but, in practice, there is nothing to be gained by defending a further action so following underwriters follow the court`s decision and agree the settlement.

The combined policy is executed by the LPSO (a Department of the Corporation of Lloyd`s) but the Corporation does not accept any responsibility for claims attaching to the policy. Only the participating syndicates are liable for claims under the policy and, although the laws of other countries might not take the same view, English law provides that each individual syndicate is deemed to have effected a separate contract with the assured and is liable only for its proportion of any claim attaching to the policy; no syndicate being responsible for the liabilities of other syndicates whose lines appear in the policy (MIA, 1906, sec. 24 sub. 2).

Where Institute companies share the same risk a combined policy is executed on their behalf by the ILU policy signing office. This policy also incorporates a signing table and English law treats each company`s liability in exactly the same way as it does the liabilities of syndicates in a Lloyd`s combined policy.

Where a risk is written in the London market by several non-Institute companies on a broker's slip the broker might, with the companies' approval, prepare a single combined company policy for their participarion in the risk. In such case the the policy is executed by the leading company specified therein on behalf of the other subscribing non-Institute companies. As above, English law treats each company's participation as a separate contract in this type of combined policy.

When a claim is rejected on behalf of all the subscribing underwriters and the assured decides to take the matter to court he sues only one of the underwriters participating in the policy; this usually being the first syndicate or the first company, as the case may be, to appear in the policy. Should the court find in the assured's favour following underwriters accept this decision; thereby avoiding expensive legal action against each underwriter, the result of which would be the same. The claim is then settled by all the participating underwriters.

Because a combined policy represents a separate contract between the assured and each subscribing insurer any individual insurer has the right to reject a claim even though all the others have agreed to settle. In such event the assured can use the combined policy in evidence to take legal action against the rejecting underwriter without involving the other underwriters in the case. Should an individual insurer become insolvent and be unable to meet his liabilities no action can be pursued, under English law, against the other insurers expressed in the policy to recover the loss suffered by the assured by reason of the insolvency. However, it is important to appreciate that the latter position might not pertain under some foreign jurisdictions.

12. Duplicate and Copy Policies

Where a policy has been lost or mislaid, and it is required for claims or for other purposes, the assured may request the issue of a *duplicate* policy. In London market practice the broker will need to give a satisfactory explanation of the reason for requesting the duplicate policy and to submit a letter of indemnity to the signing authority. By this letter the assured undertakes to refund to the underwriters any claim or premium return that is subsequently collected more than once by reason of two policies being in existence for the same risk.

A duplicate policy is an exact copy of the original policy and, where applicable, bears the seal that is normally impressed on an original document; but is marked to indicate that it is a duplicate, rather than an original policy. A duplicate policy might not be acceptable by a bank in the documentary credits system but, so far as underwriters are concerned, it is treated as though it were the original policy.

A *copy* policy is a copy of the original policy which is issued at the request of the assured. Except where some restriction is imposed by the signing authority the assured may request as many copies of the policy as he likes. In London market practice the copies must accompany the original policy when this is submitted by the broker to the signing authority for approval, signature and seal. It is customary for the copy policy to be so marked to indicate its status but, in any case, only a paper "copy" seal is affixed where the normal policy seal would be impressed; so the document can be recognised as being only a copy of the original without further examination. This recognition is important because, unless a special agreement has been obtained to the contrary, underwriters will not accept the copy policy to support a claim attaching to the insurance contract; nor will they return any premium due to the assured without presentation of the original policy.

13. Renewal Policies

Section 25(2) of the MIA, 1906, states that any marine insurance policy effected for a period exceeding 12 months is invalid. This section of the Act was repealed in August 1959 but, in practice, hull underwriters in the London market and in many overseas markets continued to restrict time policies to a period of 12 months. This practice continues today and, unless provision has been made to hold covered renewal, the contract will automatically terminate at the time and date specified in the policy for expiry. London market practitioners should note that a slip agreement to hold covered renewal of a time policy is valid for no more than 14 days.

For many years most hull policies were effected for a period of 12 months commencing from January the first. This practice created a "renewal period" during the last quarter of the year which was fraught with anxiety amongst brokers, who were all attempting to place renewals at the same time, and problems for underwriters in coping with the demand. To relieve the pressure most brokers managed to stagger renewals over the year; thereby spreading the workload more evenly and avoiding an end-of-year rush in placing renewals, but this only partly relieved the pressure on those concerned with policy preparation and signing; aggravated by the need for a new policy document (complete in all respects and fully claused) to be prepared and executed, even where there were no changes in conditions, insured value, sum insured or the security.

Between 1970 and 1983 many changes were made in London market procedures in addition to the changes in insurance conditions commented upon earlier. Amid these changes practitioners found time to consider the position of renewal policies. Little could be done where there were major changes in conditions or changes in security but it was felt that a more practical approach could be applied to circumstances where there were no major changes and the security in the expiring policy remained the same in the renewal. To this end Lloyd`s and the ILU introduced a new form of policy for London market renewals. Lloyd`s policy is termed the MAREN form and the ILU policy is termed "Companies Renewal Policy". Both are simple documents whereby underwriters agree to renew the policy on the expiring terms and conditions; subject, sometimes, to minor changes which are endorsed as such on the renewal form. Use of the renewal form is restricted to circumstances where there is no change in the security, no change in the insured value or sum insured and no major change in conditions. Further, the maximum period to be covered by a renewal policy is still restricted to 12 months.

14. Slip Policies

After the second world war Lloyd`s brokers realised they were incurring considerable unnecessary expense in preparing insurance policies which were of no practical use to their clients. The mountain of unwanted policies stored in brokers` vaults was growing and taking up costly space. To reduce the amount of paper work and to save storage space non-marine brokers suggested the slip policy scheme to underwriters.

At that time English law insisted that a properly stamped policy be issued for every marine insurance contract. Brokers prepared the policies and submitted them, with the accounting documents, to the relevant policy signing office. It was the responsibility of underwriters to ensure the policy bore the correct stamp duty and the policy signing office would reject any policy which was not in the standard format and properly stamped.

With abolition of English marine policy stamp duty on a scale basis (1 Aug 1959) the London market examined the feasibility of introducing a slip policy scheme to the marine market; particularly for use where hull TLO reinsurances were concerned. However, they were faced with two problems. The first of these was the fact that, although scale stamp duty had been abolished, there still remained a requirement for a 6d (old sixpenny) head charge per policy to be paid. It was suggested that this could be resolved by attaching an ordinary 6d postage stamp to the policy. Eventually, complete abolition of English marine policy stamp duty (1970) made this practice unnecessary.

The second problem was a different matter. Section 22 of the MIA, 1906, refused to recognise a marine insurance contract that was not embodied in a formal policy document. Legal opinion inclined to the view that there was no breach of law in treating the marine signing slip as a policy for practical purposes (eg for premium accounting, claim settlement, etc.) provided it bore the necessary stamp duty but, without a change in the MIA, 1906, the slip, even though it be stamped, would not be recognised as a marine insurance contract in a court of law.

The savings to be achieved in time, costs and storage space were too great for marine practitioners to abandon the scheme on a legal technicality and the marine market considered that the undertaking to isue a formal policy on request, as practised in the non-marine market, would satisfy dissidents. So a decision was made to adopt the same procedure as the non-marine market by attaching a slip policy sticker to the signing slip with an undertaking expressed therein whereby the subscribing underwriters would issue a formal policy at any time the assured requested it. Marine underwriters were still dubious about the legal position and restricted the early slip policies to hull TLO reinsurance contracts.

Over the years the scope of the marine slip policy scheme has been extended to embrace all types of marine business for which the parties concerned do not require a full policy to be issued; but limitations have been applied where the business emanates from certain foreign countries and business under binding authorities is outside the scope of the scheme.

Some practitioners have argued that the undertaking to issue a formal policy on demand might not be honoured by an official receiver who is handling the affairs of an insurance company in liquidation; but, in support of the scheme, it must be said that no problems in this respect appear to have been encountered so far.

Both Lloyd`s and the ILU publish similar slip policy forms for the use of practitioners. Both forms are, effectively, the same. For reference, London practitioners can find a copy of the Lloyd`s form (LPO 212A) in Lloyd`s Policy Signing & Central Accounting Manual; whilst other interested practitioners can find a copy of SP2, the ILU form, in the "Reference Book of Marine Insurance Clauses" (Witherby). The document incorporates an "attestation" clause in the format one sees in a formal policy document; plus an undertaking whereby the subscribing underwriters will issue a formal policy at the request of the assured.

15. Cargo Insurance Certificates

An insurance certificate is a document issued by, or on behalf of, an insurer to certify the existence of an insurance contract. It evidences the existence of a contract between the insurer and the assured; the broker's covernote, which only confirms that the broker has complied with his principal's instructions, is not an insurance certificate.

Under English law, the insurance certificate is not a legally binding contract and, in the absence of a properly executed policy the certificate is not acceptable as evidence in an English court. However, practitioners should be aware that this situation may not pertain in other jurisdictions. For example, a US court may accept an insurance certificate to indicate the existence of a contract without production of the policy.

In practice, a marine underwriter will honour a cargo insurance certificate as though it were the policy provided it bears the underwriter's signature (or the signature of a person authorised to represent the underwriter); settling claims thereon. A certificate issued on behalf of an underwriter by a broker and countersigned by a broker against the authorised underwriter's signature thereon is honoured by the underwriter as though it had been issued by the underwriter. Similarly, a cargo insurance certificate issued by an assured to an assignee and countersigned by the assured against the underwriter's signature thereon is honoured by the underwriter as though it had been issued by the underwriter.

Where the assured holds a policy there is unlikely to be a need for a certificate to be issued. In such case, should the assured require further evidence of insurance to satisfy a third party, a copy of the policy will often suffice. This is the case with hull insurance contracts effected to cover mortgaged vessels. In such circumstances the mortgagee might insist on holding the original policy; the assured retaining copies of the policy for practical purposes.

In cargo insurance London market practice there are few facultative insurance contracts; and correspondingly few formal cargo policies are issued. In the majority of cases the broker effects an open cover contract on behalf of the assured under which the assured declares each shipment, coming within the scope of the cover, as it goes forward. It would be impractical to issue a policy for each shipment so LPSO or the ILU, as the case may be, supplies, on request from the broker, a set of consecutively numbered certificates printed with the conditions of the cover and with blank spaces for insertion of details of the risk. It is customary for an original and (say) two copies of each numbered certificate (in blank) to be supplied. Each certificate bears the authorisation of the issuing body (eg LPSO) but will not be honoured by the underwriters unless it is countersigned by the assured. As each shipment goes forward the assured completes the next numbered certificate with details of the shipment and countersigns it. The assured may retain the original for claims purposes or assign it to a bank or buyer in the documentary credits system; such assignment conveying the same rights to the assignee as an assigned policy (see Part 9). Provided the certificate so permits the assignee may present it to an overseas agent (eg a Lloyd's agent) for claim settlement but, where the certificate is marked CPL (claims payable London) it may be presented only in the London market claims procedure for settlement.

In London market practice certificates may be used, also, in the implementation of brokers' covers. A broker's cover is an open cover which has been effected between the broker and the subscribing underwriters with no named assured. Such cover can take a variety of forms depending on the business involved. A common one is the contract which a broker effects to take a variety of cargo insurances from different clients; often covering a particular commodity. For example, a "Nicaraguan cotton" cover. This is designed to insure all cargoes of cotton shipped from Nicaragua for various clients of the broker thereby saving the broker from the task of negotiating many individual contracts with the same group of underwriters. The underwriters agree to accept every shipment coming within the scope of the cover and issue the broker with pre-printed consecutively numbered certificates (similar to those above); thereby enabling the broker to issue a certificate of insurance to his client..

Brokers` certificates are usually coded to indicate that they are issued by a broker (eg the code LB appearing on the certificate indicates that the certificate has been issued by a Lloyd`s broker). A broker`s cover may be termed a "binding authority", in practice, because it binds the subscribing underwriters to acceptance of the risks the broker declares under the cover. When accepting a risk on behalf of the underwriters the broker completes a certificate, countersigns it and forwards it to the assured. The assured may retain this certificate for presentation to underwriters in connection with a claim (even a claim made through the intermediary of a different broker) or assign it to a buyer or other party (eg a bank) as evidence of insurance in the documentary credits system. It may be used, where appropriate, in the settlement of claims abroad system.

Practitioners seeking more detailed information on cargo insurance certificates are advised to consult "Marine Insurance Vol. 2 - Cargo Practice" - 4th Edition, 1985, by Brown (Witherby).

16. Several Liability Notice

During recent years a number of insurance companies have become insolvent and have been unable to meet their liabilities in respect of lines written on slips which bore acceptances from co-insurers (eg other insurance companies and Lloyd`s syndicates). In English law and practice the "several" liability nature of each transaction has always been recognised; but this has not always been the case in some foreign jurisdictions and less informed assured contend that insurers who subscribe to the same risk should contribute to make good insured losses not recoverable from insolvent companies with lines on the same slip. To make it clear to assured and others that each line on a slip, covernote, policy or other insurance document is a separate contract with the assured the London market has published a "several liabilities notice".

With effect from 1st August, 1994, this clause must appear in all brokers` slips, covernotes, policies and other documents issued in support of the insurance contract. The clause is issued in two formats; one for direct insurance contracts and the other for reinsurance contracts. It is intended that it will eventually be printed in the MAR form of policy but, in the meantime, trainees can probably obtain a copy from their relevant London market Association.

SEE OVERPAGE FOR SELF STUDY QUESTIONAIRE

SELF STUDY QUESTIONS

Before moving on to the next section satisfy yourself that you have absorbed the subject matter in the previous Sections. The following questions should be answered without reference to the text:

1. Although the MIA, 1906, accepts that the broker's slip is the basis of the contract an English court will not accept the slip as evidence unless its terms are embodied in a formal marine insurance policy. Why is this?

2. In what manner, and in whose favour, does English law construe the terms of a marine insurance policy in which the conditions are ambiguous?

3. What is an SG policy form and how does it differ from the MAR form of policy?

4. Why is it impractical to use Institute clauses designed for use with the MAR form of policy in an SG policy form?

5. What is a PPI policy and for what types of insurable interest is such a policy used in practice? Although the PPI policy is not acceptable in a court of law it is not necessarily an illegal contract; comment on this statement.

6. Why do London underwriters insist on the English law & practice clause appearing in all MAR policies with the Institute clauses incorporated therein?

7. What is the difference between a "valued" policy and an "unvalued" policy?

8. What is the effect of assigning a marine insurance policy and in which type of policy do underwriters restrict assignment?

9. Can you explain the difference in application of a policy franchise as opposed to a policy deductible?

10. What is the difference between a "duplicate" policy and a "copy" policy?

11. What is a "slip" policy? Comment on its legal validity.

12. For what purpose are cargo insurance certificates used?

This page is left blank for Trainees` notes

SECTION FIVE

PREMIUMS, RETURNS, POLICY PREPARATION, SIGNING & ACCOUNTING

1. Responsibilities of Assured and Broker regarding Premium Payment
2. Introduction to London Market Accounting Procedures
3. Introduction to Lloyd`s Market Terms of Trade
4. Customary Deductions from Gross Premium allowed to Broker
5. Insurance Premium Tax
6. Additional Premiums and "Held Covered" Agreements
7. Returnable Premiums
8. Policy Preparation and Signing
9. Introduction to London Market Policy Signing and Accounting Procedures
10. Insolvency of Insurance Companies regarding Premiums, Returns and Claims

SECTION FIVE

1. Responsibilities of Assured and Broker regarding Premium Payment

Premium is the money paid by the assured to the underwriter in order to bind the underwriter to performance of the contract of insurance. In principle, if the underwriter has not received the premium he is not obliged to honour the contract. However, until the introduction of the MAR policy (January 1982 for cargo and October 1983 for hull) Lloyd`s market used the SG form of policy for marine insurance contracts; the SG form incorporating an acknowledgement of receipt for the premium from the assured.

Acknowledgement of receipt for the premium from the assured reflected the 18th century practice whereby claims had to be paid within one month of settlement (ie agreement with underwriters) whilst premiums due from brokers were not collectible until the end of the year. Although this practice changed over the years the premium receipt remained in Lloyd`s SG policy. Retention of the premium receipt in the policy placed the broker in an onerous position because the broker remained responsible for the premium, whether or not he had received from the assured, but his client who held the policy could claim on it from the underwriters even where he had not paid the premium to the broker. Admitted, as we shall see later, the broker was afforded some protection by the lien he has on the policy; but it was not always expedient for the broker to exercise this right. Practitioners should note that policy forms in the SG format used by insurance companies did not incorporate a receipt for the premium and it is suggested that underwriters who continue to write risks based on the SG format of policy follow the insurance companies in this respect, rather than copy Lloyd`s SG policy form.

At one time it was common for the slip and policy to show a fixed amount as the premium for the risk but, in modern practice, a premium percentage rate appears in both slip and policy. The following simple calculation illustrates the application of the premium rate to arrive at the gross premium payable:

A slip covers a sum insured of £100,000 which is shared between Lloyd`s (60%) and ILU companies (40%). The premium rate is 4%

	Signed line total	*Sum insured*	*Rate*	*Premium*
Lloyd`s policy	60%	£60000	4%	£2400
ILU policy	40%	£40000	4%	£1600

Section 52 of the MIA, 1906, requires that the premium be paid to the underwriter either at the time the policy is issued or before the policy is issued. In cases where a person proposes a facultative insurance contract directly (ie other than via the medium of a broker) it is customary for the underwriter to insist on advance payment of the premium. Where an open cover contract has been concluded directly with the underwriter it is customary for the underwriter to agree premium settlement on, say, a monthly basis.

Where the contract of insurance, whether it be facultative or on an open cover basis, is effected via the medium of a broker it is customary for the underwriter to allow the broker a period of credit (see Part 3 below) for premium settlement. Records do not indicate when the practice of allowing credit to brokers commenced but, as commented above, it was certainly common practice during the 18th century.

Because the broker is allowed a period of credit he is held, in English law, to be responsible for payment of the premium to the underwriter. This legal position stemmed from a Lloyd's practice (now obsolete) of issuing a policy with a receipt for the premium printed thereon whether or not the premium had been actually paid to the underwriter. The authority for this position in law is established by section 53 of the MIA, 1906.

To protect the broker, to some extent, the same section of the Act allows the broker to exercise a lien on any policy in respect of which the assured has not paid the premium. The lien allows the broker to retain possession of the policy until the premium has been settled and may be applied to a policy where premium remains outstanding on earlier policies; except, in the latter case, where the premium on the earlier policies has been held back by an agent of the assured and not by the assured. Exercising the lien on the policy does not give the broker any rights in the insurance contract itself. It does not permit him to make a claim on the policy without instructions from his client; nor does it give him the right to retain any part of a claim to reimburse himself for outstanding premium.

Although marine insurers no longer incorporate a receipt for the premium in the policy document the broker still retains the right to exercise his lien on the policy. In theory, the lien is a useful asset but, in practice, it is of doubtful value; particularly in cargo insurance where certificates are issued, in lieu of policies, off open covers and where premium settlement takes place periodically for all risks attaching to the cover. A broker might be able to exercise his lien in the hull insurance market but, in practice, the procedural nature of arranging the insurance contracts on ships and on hull interests makes such action impractical in most cases.

Hull underwriters often agree to accept the premium attaching to a term policy (eg a policy effected for 12 months) on a "deferred account" basis. The dates for premium settlement are agreed during negotiations to conclude the contract; each instalment becoming due at the commencement of the period to which it relates.

Example -

Policy period 12 months from 1 January. Annual premium £240,000, payable in four instalments.

Instalment 1	£60,000 payable at inception
Instalment 2	£60,000 payable at 1 April
Instalment 3	£60,000 payable at 1 June
Instalment 4	£60,000 payable at 1 October

It is customary for the slip to incorporate the abbreviation FPIL (Full premium if lost). This means that, should the ship become a total loss (actual or constructive) from any cause during the currency of the policy, all outstanding premium instalments become immediately due for settlement; the policy lapsing with the total loss

The premium on a policy covering the hull & machinery of a ship for a period of time is calculated on an annual rate; even when the policy period is for a shorter term. Thus, a premium rate of 2% on a six months H & M insurance contract would be expressed in the slip as - "Rate 2% pro rata of 4% PA."

In such case the premium (calculated at 2%) would be paid at inception of the contract. When the broker negotiates the contract with the leader it is customary for the underwriter to qualify the short term rate in the slip with FPIL; as in the case of deferred account. Hence, the full annual premium falls due under the contract if the ship becomes a total loss (from any cause) during the currency of the policy. This means that, in the event of a total loss before the policy`s natural expiry date, the assured will be required to pay the balance of the annual premium.

It is a matter for the broker to decide any period of credit he allows his client for premium payment; but a broker in the London market is still bound by the market terms of trade agreement (see Part 3, below) to settle the premium with underwriters on the due date, whether or not his client has paid.

2. Introduction to London Market Accounting Procedures

Until 1962 Lloyd`s brokers were required to settle premiums directly with Lloyd`s syndicates; usually on a monthly basis. The broker would prepare the accounting document (termed a "bureau sheet") which would be sent to LPSO, along with a signing slip and the prepared policy document. Agreed premium returns were dealt with in the same way. After checking the accuracy of the accounting information LPSO would produce an advice card for each relevant syndicate. Each month the broker would send a cheque to each syndicate, as appropriate, to settle his net premium account with that syndicate.

This cumbersome procedure came to an end, in the Lloyd`s market, in 1962 when the introduction of a, computer based, scheme made it possible for LPSO to monitor settlements within a centralised accounting system (referred to hereinafter as C/A). This system encompassed all credits and debits (premiums, returns, claims and refunds) and allowed each broker &/or syndicate to remit a single payment each month to C/A to cover all debits due in the Lloyd`s underwriting and broking market. C/A would, then, remit a single payment to each syndicate or broker to cover all credits due to the relevant party. The C/A system continued to allow the broker to submit details on a bureau sheet to LPSO and LPSO continued to send advice cards to the syndicates; but, additionally, the information was fed into Lloyd`s C/A computer.

In April, 1970, the bureau sheet was replaced with the PAN (Premium advice note) but, basically, the system continued to operate as previously. Generally, the advice card procedure was operated on a weekly basis and, with each batch of advice cards, a syndicate would receive a tabulation sheet listing the items indicated on the accompanying advice cards. A separate batch of advice cards and an accompanying tabulation sheet was provided for each "settlement" currency (these being £, US$ and Can$). Advice cards were punched with holes through which the syndicate`s computer could read the information on the card. Where so requested LPSO would supply the information on magnetic tape for use in syndicates` computers. Confirmation of C/A entries was provided for each broker on a BDS (Broker`s daily statement). Such statement was updated daily by the C/A computer but the broker`s copy was, in most cases, made available only on a weekly basis. At the end of each month C/A would produce settlement statements which showed the items due for settlement, in accordance with the TOC (Terms of credit) agreement, in that month; one for each settlement currency. At first each broker and syndicate would submit a cheque or similar document to settle their accounts, but this practice gave way to settlements by direct debit in due course through the banking systems.

It was many years after Lloyd`s adopted central accounting that the ILU followed suit; although the ILU PSO did maintain an advice system for members whose policies were checked and signed through the ILU PSO. Nevertheless, by the time the PAN was introduced the ILU had adopted a similar central accounting system to Lloyd`s and the PAN soon became known as the London premium advice note (LPAN).

With the introduction of LIMNET (London Insurance Market Network) in 1987 changes began to take place in London market accounting procedures. LIMNET is not a central computer, as some practitioners think; it is an electronic communication system supplied by IBM. By using one single electronic connection a user can obtain connection to all other LIMNET members. It was reported in 1990 that more than 500 organisations had connected themselves to LIMNET; including all company members of the ILU and, today, most firms of Lloyd`s brokers are connected to LIMNET.

These introductory notes do not offer detailed information on the operation of LIMNET but some comment is necessary because this is probably the most important development in accounting and communication to take place in the London market this century. The intention of LIMNET is to allow all transactions that, previously (and currently, in some cases), were carried out by using paper documentation to be communicated electronically, at the touch of a button. Because proposed users need to adapt their own computer systems to link into LIMNET development of a fully integrated system is taking time. Abolition of the Lloyd`s advice card procedure, see above, was an early indication of the practicality of the new system. Certain areas of centralised accounting, regarding claims and premiums, are mostly transacted via LIMNET and, in time, one expects to see all accounting documentation dealt with by this modern method.

Eventually LIMNET will link with other electronic comunication systems on a worldwide basis; involving practitioners in most insurance markets in learning standardised codes which can be recognised internationally. An example would be acceptance of a standard code for dates, showing the year/month/day in this order and as two digits for each (eg 94/07/21 would mean July 21, 1994).

3. Introduction to London Market Terms of Trade

It is recorded that, in 1748, brokers collected premiums for risks they placed and retained these for payment to underwriters on an annual settlement date. On the other hand underwriters were required to settle claims within one month of approving the claim. It is not clear when matters changed but, during the early part of the 19th century brokers were settling premiums on a quarterly basis whilst still collecting claims on a monthly basis. By the middle of the 20th century underwriters and brokers were settling their accounts mostly, on a monthly basis; but with 3 months credit allowed to brokers for premium settlement. Despite these generous terms brokers were often accused of late settlement.

Whilst the C/A system smoothed the procedure for settlement it did nothing to encourage early payment of premium by brokers. The problem of late settlement had concerned underwriters for years and various suggestions had been made to resolve the problem. In principle, underwriters were content to allow brokers a reasonable period of credit to settle premiums; but, prior to the introduction of terms of credit in 1970, the settlement procedure was linked only to the date of the "signing number", which number was not allocated until the broker submitted documents to the signing authority in the accounting procedure. There was no control requiring brokers to submit accounting documents at any particular time which meant that brokers could determine their own settlement date by simply deferring submission of documents to the signing authority.

To monitor settlement Lloyd's introduced two new measures in 1970. One of these was the "separation procedure" (see Part 9). The other was introduction of the TOC (Terms of credit) scheme. The TOC scheme required the broker to ensure that an entry was made in the TOC box in the signing slip. It was intended that the leader would make this entry (being the month and year of settlement) in the original slip when writing his line; allowance being made for late or early settlement where so agreed. When documents were submitted to LPSO the C/A computer would interpret the entry and ensure that the item appeared in the correct monthly settlement statement for both underwriters and broker. The ILU adopted the same system and, for a while, matters seemed to improve.

Nevertheless, despite the care taken in devising the TOC system its value still relied on the broker submitting his accounting documents in time for the correct settlement date to be implemented, and late signings continued to plague underwriters. In an effort to remedy this situation the "slip registration" scheme (see Part 9) was introduced.

Although the TOC scheme was ingenious it proved to be unworkable in practice; mainly because it relied on full co-operation from all the parties involved which was not forthcoming. So, in January 1987, the TOC scheme was replaced with a simpler, but much more workable scheme which took the title of TOT (Terms of Trade) to differentiate it from the old scheme. Under the TOT procedure the leading underwriter enters the "settlement due" date in the placing slip; the broker reproducing this in the signing slip. The broker is required to submit the accounting information to the relevant authority in time for C/A to enter it in the correct settlement statement as indicated by the settlement due date.

4 Customary Deductions from Gross Premium Allowed to Broker

Since the days when marine insurance contracts were concluded in london coffee houses brokers have been permitted to make a deduction, from the premium they collected from their clients, as remuneration for producing the business for underwriters; paying only the net premium when settling underwriters' accounts. This practice continues today and, although the broker receives his remuneration from the underwriters, the broker remains agent of the proposer and to whom he is responsible under the law of agency. The amount so deducted is termed "brokerage" in practice and should not be confused with other deductions or discounts allowed by underwriters. Records of the 18th century indicate that the customary brokerage was 5% of the gross premium agreed in the contract. When drawing up his annual account the 18th century broker would balance the net premium income with claims paid by the underwriter. If the balance was a credit in favour of the underwriter the broker would receive 10% of the credit balance, as a form of profit commission, in addition to his normal brokerage; thereby encouraging the broker to offer good business to the underwriter. This system of broker remuneration persisted with brokerage remaining at 5% but with an increase in the profit commission to 12% by the middle of the 19th century.

With the passage of time underwriters demanded earlier settlement of premiums, as we have seen in Part 3 above. Brokers` profit commission disappeared, leaving the broker with only the basic 5% brokerage as remuneration for producing business. Despite protests from brokers the basic brokerage for producing direct marine business has remained as 5% to this day. However, during the early part of the 20th century underwriters agreed to allow a discount to the assured for "cash" settlement of premiums at a rate of 10% of the gross premium less the brokerage (ie 9.5% of the gross premium). Later requests for an increase in brokerage were strongly resisted. Eventually underwriters relented but with a difference of opinion between hull and cargo underwriters regarding the extra brokerage to be allowed. Hull underwriters agreed to allow an additional deduction of 0.50% on the gross premium; whilst cargo underwriters allowed 2.5% on the premium net of brokerage and the client`s discount. For the record, the agreed calculations were as follows:

	Hull		*Cargo*
Gross	100.00		100.00
Brokerage 5%	5.00		5.00
Net	95.00		95.00
Client discount 10%	9.50		9.50
Net	85.50		85.50
Allowance 0.5% o.g.	.50	2.5% o.n.	2.14
Net	85.00		83.36
Total discount	15.00%		16.64%

Where no specific discounts or deductions are agreed and expressed in the broker`s placing slip the standard deductions, as above, still apply. In cargo practice, today, it is customary for underwriters to agree a total deduction (often 22% or more) and to leave the disposal of the deduction at the broker`s discretion. The attitude of hull underwriters is not uniform. In today`s hardening market it is not easy to persuade a hull underwriter to allow more than the standard hull deductions, as above, although one has seen deductions of around 20% allowed in some hull contracts.

It should be noted that the proportion of a hull premium deduction that relates to the assured`s commission for "cash" is reduced by half where the premium is paid by deferred account.

5. Insurance Premium Tax

It will be recalled that stamp duty (see Section 4) was, at one time, levied on all marine insurance policies effected in the United Kingdom and on any marine insurance policy received in the UK; though it be effected in an overseas market. Stamp duty on marine insurance contracts was abolished in the UK in 1970; and, from 1st of August that year, no stamp duty was levied on marine insurance contracts effected in UK markets or received from abroad. Suggestions were made regarding the introduction of a tax on premium, to be paid by the assured, but it was feared that the proposed tax would prejudice income derived from business emanating from overseas; so nothing came of the suggestion.

Other countries levy tax on premiums paid in respect of marine insurance contracts; which tax often applies to business placed wholly or partly in the UK. These introductory notes do not offer details in this respect but, generally, the countries concerned make it the responsibility of the assured to pay this tax. One only sees the foreign tax referred to when underwriters have agreed to reimburse the assured for tax paid. Such agreement is negotiated at the time of placing and appears on the broker's slip as UPT (underwriters pay tax). In such case the broker may include the tax with the agreed deductions when settling the premium. However, it should be noted that underwriters are entitled to demand proof that the tax has been paid before allowing a tax deduction.

It is proposed that the Finance Act, 1994, shall come into force with effect from 1 October 1994. By this Act IPT (Insurance premium tax) will be levied on premiums for most general insurance contracts effected in the UK. The primary liability to account for the tax will rest with the appropriate insurance company; special provisions being made where premium tax attaches to a contract placed at Lloyd's. IPT will apply to the premium paid in respect of any "taxable insurance contract". Section 70 of the Act defines a "taxable insurance contract" and, amongst other things, specifies those contracts to which IPT shall not apply. Subject to certain qualifications, the exemptions include:

(a) - A contract of reinsurance;
(b) - A contract relating to a commercial ship;
(c) - A contract relating to one risk which is situated outside the United Kingdom;
(d) - A contract relating to two or more risks, each of which is situated outside the United Kingdom;
(e) - A contract relating to loss of or damage to goods in foreign or international transit where the assured enters into the contract in the course of business carried out by him. However, it should be noted that premium paid to cover a seller's interest in an FOB contract is <u>not</u> exempt from IPT.

It follows that it is probable most marine insurance contracts will be exempt from IPT; but trainees and practitioners are advised to keep a watching brief on developments and, if in doubt, they should check with the relevant authorities.

6. Additional Premiums and "Held Covered" Agreements

An AP (additional premium) is a sum of money paid by the assured to the underwriter in consideration of cover for some increase in risk not contemplated by the policy premium.

A "held covered" agreement is a condition in the insurance contract whereby the underwriter undertakes to cover a certain specified risk should the subject matter insured be exposed to such risk. "Held covered" agreements can take a variety of forms; the nature of the agreement being recognised by its wording. The agreement may be expressed in a broker's slip and not be part of the formal contract (eg an agreement to hold covered a renewal, see below, or an agreement to hold covered a particular interest or risk, subject to ratification by the assured). Agreements expressed in the formal contract are usually subject to payment of an AP; without which the additional risk is not covered.

Except where the contract otherwise provides, where the h/c agreement is subject to payment of an AP the assured *must* notify the underwriter immediately he is aware that the subject matter insured has been exposed to the risk contemplated by the h/c agreement; this condition applying irrespective of whether or not the exposure has already terminated and irrespective of whether or not any loss or damage has been suffered. In some cases (as, for example, may be provided in the contract concerning breach of a particular warranty) the contract may require notice to the underwriter *before* the subject matter insured is exposed to the additional risk. The wording of the agreement may permit the underwriter to amend the terms of the contract so far as the held covered risk is concerned; but, in any case, the assured must pay the agreed AP. If no AP amount or rate has been agreed a *reasonable* AP becomes payable (MIA, 1906, sect. 31). An example of such a situation can be seen in the "continuation" clause in the ITC (1983). This clause holds the assured covered in the event that the ship is on a voyage at the time the policy is due to expire and, subject to prior notice and payment of an AP to be agreed, allows the assured to extend the period of cover until the ship reaches her planned destination.

Not all h/c agreements relate to premium matters. For example, a broker may ask the underwriter to hold covered renewal of a term contract, which is due to expire, to allow him time to obtain renewal instructions from his client. In London marine market practice such agreements are valid for no more than 14 days.

7. Returnable Premiums

Sections 83 to 84 of the MIA, 1906, provide that premium is returnable in the following circumstances:

1. Where the contract is void from inception;
2. Where the contract is avoided by the insurer from inception, and the contract had not already attached at the time of such avoidance;
3. Where the subject matter insured, or part thereof, has not been imperilled;
4. Where the assured has no insurable interest in the subject matter insured; and no reasonable expectation of acquiring such interest;
5. In respect of any amount overinsured by a unvalued policy;
6. In respect of any amount over-insured by a valued policy due to innocent double insurance;
7. Where the contract provides for a return of premium, by agreement, and a circumstance relating to the agreement arises.

Irrespective of the above, no premium return is payable if there has been fraud or illegality on the part of the assured in connection with the insurance contract.

Unless the policy otherwise provides all returnable premiums are subject to any deductions allowed against the premium before payment to the underwriter:

Example - 12 months H & M policy. Cancelled by mutual agreement on expiry of 6 months; underwriters agreeing a pro rata return of premium.

Annual gross premium	£140,000
Deductions 15%	21,000
Net annual premium	£119,000

RP £119,000 x 50% = £59,500

The following comments on the above list might be useful.

Item 1. *Void contracts* - An insurance contract can be void for a variety of reasons. By way of definition a *void* contract is one which a court of law will not recognise. Since no claim can be legally enforced under a void contract the MIA, 1906, does not recognise the existence of the contract and assumes any premium paid to be returnable. However, although the Act does not recognise a PPI (policy proof of interest) policy and, in fact, declares such policies to be void (MIA, 1906, Sect.4-2b) these policies are frequently used in marine insurance practice and claims thereunder are strictly honoured by underwriters. Accordingly, item 1 in the list is not recognised in practice where PPI policies ae concerned.

Item 2. *Avoidance of contract* - The underwriter may avoid the contract from inception-

(a) in a voyage policy, where the voyage does not commence within a reasonable period of time after the underwriter wrote the risk; or

(b) in any policy, where the assured or his broker was guilty of a breach of good faith (see Section 7) when negotiating the contract.

Nevertheless, no return of premium is allowed in the above circumstances where the risk has already attached when the underwriter avoids the contract (MIA, 1906, Sect.84-3a).

The following examples will help one to understand the application of return premiums in relation to (a), above:

Example 1 - A ship is insured for a particular voyage "from" a specified port. The risk will not attach until the ship actually sails from the departure port; no cover attaching whilst the ship remains at the port. Following unreasonable delay in departure the underwriter avoids the contract which, accordingly, does not attach. No premium is payable and, if the premium has been already paid, it must be returned to the assured.

Example 2 - A ship is insured for a particular voyage "at and from" a specified port. Provided the ship is lying at the named port of departure at that time, the risk attaches as soon as the underwriter concludes the contract on the broker's slip. If the ship is not at the port of departure at the time the underwriter concludes the contract the risk does not attach until the ship arrives at such port. Following unreasonable delay in commencing the insured voyage the underwriter avoids the contract. Such avoidance is effective from inception of the risk but *no* return premium is payable because the risk had already attached.

When considering (b), above, experience shows that such circumstances usually arise when claim investigations are being carried out so one would expect the risk to have attached before the underwriter discovered the breach of good faith. Thus, it is unlikely that the assured would be entitled to a return of premium in these circumstances.

Item 3. *Not imperilled* - As an example consider circumstances where the merchant arranges an insurance contract, in advance, to cover goods in transit by sea to a specified destination; but the goods are not actually forwarded (eg the sale contract is cancelled before transit commences). The assured would not be liable for the premium or, if it had been already paid, the assured would be entitled to return of the premium.

Similarly, where 1000 cases of merchandise were insured and only 800 cases were forwarded the assured would be entitled to return of the relevant part of the premium.

However, it should be noted that, where a specific voyage is insured by the policy and the adventure is terminated short of the destination expressed in the policy (for *any* reason), such termination does not entitle the assured to a return of any part of the premium unless the contract expressly states that a return premium is payable in such event.

Item 4. *No insurable interest* - Section 6 of these notes outlines the principle of insurable interest; which interest must exist at the time of loss for a claim to attach to the policy. Where it transpires that the assured had no insurable interest *throughout* the period covered by the insurance contract no claim is recoverable under the policy and the assured is entitled to a return of any premium he has paid in respect of the contract. Where an insurable interest has existed during the currency of the policy, even where that interest did not attach until some time after the policy cover commenced (eg a "contingent interest") or terminated at some time during the currency of the policy, none of the premium is returnable; except where a condition in the contract (eg the "returns" clause in the ITC) allows for a return of part of the premium.

Particular attention is directed to the notes above concerning fraud and illegality. A proposer of an insurance contract who, knowing he has no insurable interest in the subject matter insured and no reasonable expectation of acquiring such interest, effects such contract would be guilty of an offence under the Marine Insurance (Gambling Policies) Act, 1909. In such case, the offender forfeits any right to a return of premium when the contract is declared void.

Item 5. *Over-insurance (unvalued policy)* - In practice today it is customary to effect a marine insurance contract, covering property, on an agreed value basis; the value expressed in the policy being termed the "insured value". In the unlikely event that no insured value is expressed in the policy the insurance cover is limited to the market value of the property at the time of loss. Where the sum insured in an unvalued policy exceeds the market value of the property the excess amount is uninsured; so any premium paid in respect of this excess amount is returnable to the assured.

Liability policies are effected on an unvalued basis and incorporate a limit of liability. There is no limit to the amount one may insure by a liability policy and where the risk has attached, unless provision is made therefor in the insurance conditions, no return premium is recoverable under a liability policy.

Item 6. - *Over-insurance (valued policy)* - In marine insurance law (MIA, 1906, Sect. 27) the insured value expressed in the policy is deemed to be the value of the property for insurance purposes. Where the proposer agrees an insured value with the insurer this is deemed to be conclusive of the value of the property, even where it subsequently transpires that the market value of the property is less than the insured value, and no return premium can be recovered where the property is thereby overinsured. It should be noted that, notwithstanding the foregoing, the underwriter might be entitled to challenge the insured value where he has been misled by the proposer and a breach of good faith in this respect can be proved (see notes in Section 7 regarding a breach of good faith) and can deny liability under the policy where such has been proved without returning the premium or any part thereof. The same would apply where a declaration of value was made fraudulently by the assured.

However, where, due to an administrative error or a misunderstanding, more than one insurance contract is effected to cover the same risk, whereby more than the insured value is insured, there is deemed to be a "double" insurance. In a case of double insurance arrangements must be made to cancel the amount by which the property is over-insured (MIA, 1906, Sect. 32) and the premium relating thereto must be returned to the assured. It should be noted that where one of the policies has borne the entire risk, or a claim has been paid under one of the policies, no premium is returnable under such policy. Further, where the proposer knowingly effects a double insurance no premium is returnable under any of the policies.

Item 7. *Return by Agreement* - Although there may be exceptions in practice, it is not customary for one to see an agreement in a cargo insurance contract providing for any part of the premium to be returned. Thus, one is unlikely to see a "returns" clause in a cargo policy and no "returns" clause appears in any of the standard sets of cargo clauses; nor, except where war &/or strikes risks are insured, does one see a returns clause in a hull voyage policy.

It is customary for policies covering the hull & machinery of a ship for a period of time to incorporate a clause allowing for return of part of the annual premium in the event that the policy is cancelled before its natural expiry date. H & M policies also incorporate a provision agreeing to return part of the premium in the event that the ship is laid up during the currency of the policy. For details regarding return premiums in a hull policy trainees and practitioners ae advised to consult "Marine Insurance - Volume 3 - Hull Practice" by R H Brown (Witherby 1994). The following brief notes are based, where appropriate, on the Institute Time Clauses (1983), the Institute War & Strikes clauses, Hulls, (1983) for both time and voyage and the relevant Institute Freight clauses.

Mutual Cancellation - The ITC (1983) incorporate a mutual cancellation clause whereby a net premium return shall be allowed for each unexpired calendar month. The return is forfeit if the ship becomes a total loss from any cause (insured or not) before the cancellation becomes effective. A similar condition appears in freight time clauses.

Automatic Cancellation - The ITC (1983) and similar sets of hull time clauses incorporate a "termination" clause which comes into effect when a change of circumstances (as specified in the clause) comes into effect. An example would be automatic termination because the ship had been sold. In such event the net premium for the unexpired period of the policy is returnable to the assured. This is calculated on a pro rata daily basis.

Hull war & strikes policies do not incorporate the same termination clause as the ITC, but both time and voyage policies incorporate a clause which allows the assured to claim a pro rata daily return of the net premium paid in event of the time policy being cancelled due to sale of vessel; or an agreed return in regard to the cancelled voyage policy, as the case may be. Further, both time and voyage policies incorporate a clause which terminates the policy automatically upon the outbreak of a major war or upon the hostile detonation of a nuclear weapon anywhere in the world; the assured being entitled under the time policy to a pro rata daily return of premium for the unexpired period of the policy; or to an agreed return in regard to the cancelled voyage policy, as the case may be. Hull war & strikes policies, both time and voyage, incorporate a clause which allows the underwriter to give 7 days notice to cancel the policy in order to agree new conditions and/or a new premium rate. If the notice is not withdrawn the assured is entitled to a pro rata daily premium return for the unexpired period of the time policy or to an agreed return in respect of the cancelled voyage policy, as the case may be.

Lay up returns - H & M and freight *time* policies also incorporate a clause which allows the assured to claim return of part of the premium if the ship is laid up during the currency of the policy. The underwriter retains such part of the premium as relates to the reduced risk whilst the ship is laid up and returns the balance to the assured. The amount retained is termed a "port risk retention" and the amount returned is termed a "lay up return". In the ITC (1983) the assured is entitled to a lay up return only when the ship has been laid up in approved waters for a period of not less than 30 consecutive days. In principle, a period of lay up entitles the assured to a return of one twefth of the annual net premium less the appropriate port risks retention; but he cannot collect his earned returns until the policy expires. Should the insured vessel become a total loss (from any cause) before the policy expires all earned lay up returns are forfeit. It should be noted that an assured can effect an insurance contract to cover loss of earned lay up returns.

Where a total loss is paid on a voyage policy the insurance cover is terminated from the time of the total loss irrespective of whether or not the voyage was completed; and, where a total loss is paid on a time policy the insurance cover is terminated from the time of the total loss, irrespective of any unexpired period remaining under the policy. No part of the premium is returnable in either case.

It should be noted that, whilst no cancellation or agreed returns clauses appear in standard cargo policy wordings, it is customary for cancellation clauses to appear on cargo open covers. Nevertheless, there is no provision in an open cover allowing for premium returns because the insurance on risks that have already attached when cancellation becomes effective is allowed to continue until completion of transit.

8. Policy Preparation and Signing

One should never forget that the policy is a legal document which binds the parties to the performance of the marine insurance contract. Generally, a legal contract is drafted by a person who is versed in the law of contract and competent to draft a contract that clearly sets out the legal responsibilities of the parties concerned. The marine insurance policy is the exception to the rule in this respect. It is, often, prepared by office staff who have little, if any, formal training in legal matters. Nevertheless, despite much criticism from courts of law, particularly regarding ambiguity, the marine insurance policy seems to have stood the test of time in many legal actions which have proved that a detailed knowledge of the law is not essential for preparing policies in practice. The most important concern when preparing a policy is a complete understanding of the intentions of the parties in concluding the contract; particularly where wording other than standard clauses and conditions apply. One would expect the trainee to receive formal "desk top" instruction in policy preparation, with examples, before being allowed to prepare and submit documents for signing and sealing; so these notes provide only general guidelines, as follows:

(1) Ensure that the correct policy form, as specified in the broker`s slip, is used;
(2) Data entered in the policy form, if any, must be typewritten;
(3) Where data is detailed it is customary to enter "as attached" in the appropriate space/s in the policy form and to attach the (typed or printed) wording to the form;
(4) Interpret the placing slip correctly and make every effort to avoid ambiguity in the construction of the policy (see Section 4). In cases of doubt consult the placing broker to discover the intentions of the parties;
(5) All clauses and/or wordings must be firmly adhered to the policy form in such a way that removal of the clause or wording would be apparent;
(6) Where the contract is subject to standard clauses (eg Institute hull clauses), ensure the correct set of *current* clauses is attached to the policy, with particular attention to the title, reference number and date;
(7) Ensure that only those clauses specified in the broker`s slip are used in the policy;
(8) In cases of doubt (eg the wrong clause is shown in, or a clause or customary condition is missing from, the broker`s slip) refer the matter to the broker before preparing the policy;
(9) The completed policy should present a clean neat document which is clear, unambiguous and correctly interprets the conditions expressed in the broker`s placing slip.

The issue of a formal policy document is the responsibility of the underwriter who accepted the line on the original slip. During the days when Lloyd`s was located at the Royal Exchange, London, each underwriter operating for his own account, or each active underwriter representing a syndicate, would issue a separate policy to cover his line on a slip. With increases in values the number of lines on a single slip grew and brokers found themselves coping with many policies to cover one risk. The procedure of policy preparation and policy issue became so cumbersome that unacceptable delays occurred whilst brokers waited for Lloyd`s policies to be issued. To combat this situation brokers began preparing the policy documents themselves; submitting the policy to the appropriate underwriter for approval and signature. This system worked satisfactorily for a while but it was soon recognised that it was time consuming and expensive for a broker to prepare a separate policy document for each line on the slip; further, there was evidence that errors in preparation were causing differences between the policy wordings and construction.

Eventually Lloyd`s market agreed that a "combined" policy document could be prepared by the broker to encompass all the lines on a brokers slip covering the same risk. The combined policy system was operated in the Room at Lloyd`s for many years but it was far from satisfactory. The broker`s boy would place the prepared policy document, with the original slip, in a wire basket at one side of the leading underwriter`s box in the Room. The leader would check the accuracy of the policy document and enter therein his line, signature and reference at the head of the column space provided in the policy for that purpose. He would then place the document in a wire tray at the other side of his box for collection by the broker. The broker`s boy would collect the document and carry out the same procedure with each of the following underwriters; returning with it to his office when all appropriate underwriters had inserted their lines, signatures and references.

Losses of, disfigurations to and, dare we suggest, alterations to original slips during the signing procedure caused brokers to replace the original slip with a copy thereof for policy signing purposes; retaining the original slip safely in the broker`s office (see Section 3 for notes on signing slips). Further, the condition of the policy form, after passing through so many hands, was hardly indicative of the quality one would expect from an organisation such as Lloyd`s.

Perhaps more important to underwriters was the congestion in the Room, encouraged mainly by masses of brokers` boys milling around delivering, collecting and carrying policy signing documents between boxes. So, in 1914, a proposal was made to set up a separate policy signing bureau to which combined policy forms could be submitted by brokers for checking and signing. However, there was much opposition from underwriters who did not want to delegate control of policy signing to a bureau. Intervention of the first world war postponed the proposal and it was not until 1918 it was reintroduced to the market for consideration. Loss of manpower during the war years had made Room policy signing very difficult to operate; so the proposal was accepted with more enthusiasm than had, previously, been the case. Lloyd`s Policy Signing Bureau was established in 1918 on a voluntary basis and, although the majority of underwriters were in favour of the new system, there were still those who insisted on Room signings. This left brokers with the task of operating two systems with obvious disadvantages.

Following the discovery of fraudulent practices regarding policies intimating that they had been issued at Lloyd`s, whereas they had not been so issued, the Corporation of Lloyd`s published a notice in 1924 to the effect that no policy would be recognised by Lloyd`s unless it bore the seal of Lloyd`s Policy Signing Bureau (LPSB). Effectively, this made it mandatory for all policies to be submitted to the Bureau for sealing. Nevertheless, for a while, Room signings continued; the broker preparing the policy, submitting it to the appropriate underwriter/s in the Room for signature and, then, taking it to LPSB for the seal to be impressed in the document.

Gradually, all marine underwriters at Lloyd`s accepted the competence of the personnel at LPSB to approve policy documents on their behalf and, by the time LPSB changed its title to Lloyd`s Policy Signing Office (LPSO as it is so known today), only policies with a very low premium continued to be signed in the Room; the premium income from these not justifying the minimum processing charge each subscribing underwriter had to pay for an LPSO signing. Eventually, the scope of the activities at LPSO embraced premium advices to underwriters and the broker would submit a "bureau sheet" (today the LPAN, London premium advice note, fulfils a similar purpose) to LPSO with the policy document (see Part 9, below).

During the time that the above policy signing procedures were developing at Lloyd`s each insurance company with a line on a broker`s slip would issue its own policy document. To initiate the procedure the broker would submit a "closing advice" to each relevant company; the closing advice showing details of the risk, conditions, rate, etc. Although the ILU was established towards the end of the 19th century this organisation did not set up a Policy Signing Office until towards the end of the second world war. The ILU PSO adopted the same procedure as LPSO. In fact, the early staff of the ILU PSO, recruited from policy personnel in member companies, worked at first alongside LPSO staff at Pinewood during the early days of the formation of the ILU PSO. The ILU published a company version of the "combined" policy form (see Section 4) which the broker would prepare and submit to the ILU PSO. Companies who were not members of the ILU continued to issue their own policies, individually against closing advices from brokers; although a practice did develop whereby the leading non-Institute company subscribing a slip would sign a combined policy on behalf of the other non-Institute companies on the slip.

From the foregoing it can be seen that, for many years, it has been the practice for brokers to prepare the policy document and to submit it to underwriters or the relevant PSO for checking, signing and, where appropriate, sealing. But, it will be recalled that, primarily, the responsibility for issuing a marine insurance policy lies on the underwriter. Over the years suggestions have been made for LPSO to prepare their own policy documents but, whilst the SG form (see Section 4) was the basis of the marine insurance contract there was some reluctance to change an established practice, which had successfully produced satisfactory policies in a modern world from a complicated and often misunderstood policy form. Abrogation of the SG form of policy and its replacement with the MAR policy form has produced a much simpler marine insurance contract; particularly when the contract is based on a standard set of clauses.

Since January, 1994, LPSO PPS (the Policy Production Service operated by LPSO in connection with LPG - Lloyd`s Processing Group) have undertaken responsiblity for preparing certain types of policy on behalf of risks placed at Lloyd`s. So far as marine insurance is concerned this service has been limited to relatively uncomplicated contracts; based mainly on the clauses published by the ILU. At first, the LPSO service has been offered on a voluntary basis; Lloyd`s brokers continuing to prepare their own policy documents if they so desire. Where the contract is not subject to mandatory (see below) conditions brokers requiring a policy from LPSO PPS complete a standard request form specifying their requirements. It is not necessary for the broker to request LPSO policy production for a mandated service because, for mandatory conditions, LPSO PPS undertakes to issue the relevant policy automatically within 10 days of receiving the Stage One documentation or, where communications regarding policy signing and accounting are conducted via LIMNET, from confirmation of the relevant electronic message implementing Stage One of the London market policy signing and accounting procedure (see Part 9, below, regarding the latter).

During 1994 it is becoming compulsory for marine insurance contracts, based on, so called, "mandated" Institute clauses, and placed at Lloyd`s, to be evidenced by policy documents prepared by LPSO PPS. Where these are concerned a request form is not, normally, necessary. The following brief comments on mandated clauses are based on information available at the time of writing and are for guidance only. Trainees and practitioners in the London market who find it necessary to update this information should consult the relevant Service Guide (and supplements thereto) published by LPSO; also the periodic bulletin "Matters", published by Lloyd`s Processing Group.

Effective from 1st May, 1994, the standard Institute clauses for use in contracts covering hull & machinery are mandated (ie ITC, Hulls; IVC, Hulls and Port Risks conditions). The AHF (American Hull Form) and the Institute Mortgagees Interest, Hulls, clauses are also mandated from 1st May,1994. Effective from 1st July, 1994, the standard cargo clauses (ie ICC A, B and C and ICC air sendings) are mandated. Also effective from 1st July, 1994, the Institute Yacht clauses and the American yacht clauses are mandated. Where reinsurance is concerned marine excess of loss contracts were mandated effective from 1st January, 1994. It is probable that other sets of Institute clauses will not be mandated until the scheme has been proved satisfactory;

but it is expected that, by 1st January, 1996, all standard marine clauses used in the London market will be mandated and that LPSO PPS will be preparing policies for all marine insurance contracts placed at Lloyd`s that are subject to standard (Institute, etc.) conditions.

Trainees and practitioners interested in the preparation and signing of FDO (for declaration purposes only) policies and slip policies should consult LPSO PPS for information on the procedure to be adopted for these.

For the time being, at least, the ILU have no plans to follow Lloyd`s in the preparation of marine insurance policies. In fact, it is not compulsory for Institute companies to avail themselves of the policy signing and accounting services offered by the ILU. Accordingly policy preparation by brokers for submission of documents to the ILU PSO continues; as does the procedure for policy preparation, etc. for lines written by non-Institute companies.

Trainees and practitioners in markets outside London should bear the above information in mind, when dealing with the London market, but will, of course, continue to follow the policy preparation and signing procedures established in their own markets.

In all cases where the marine insurance policy is prepared by the underwriter or the underwriter`s representative it is incumbent upon the broker to examine the policy to ensure that it complies with the terms and conditions of contract expressed in the broker`s placing slip. If the broker is not satisfied with the policy it should be returned to the issuing authority for clarification and/or correction.

9. Introduction to London Market Signing and Accounting Procedures

There are many procedures that could come under this heading but the following notes, being solely of an introductory nature, relate only to the development of the Separation procedure and the S & A procedure practised in the London market today. In this connection one might find it convenient to refer, also, to the comments on terms of trade, central accounting and premium settlement procedures which appear in Parts 2 and 3 of this Section; also to the comments in Part 8, above, regarding the development and current implementation of procedures for policy preparation and signing in the London market. Further, it must be emphasised that, as LIMNET procedures develop, much of the information in the Separation procedure and in the S & A procedure may be communicated by electronic message. Trainees and practitioners studying the procedures outlined herein are advised to consider these notes in relation to the current practices in their offices regarding the operation of LIMNET and, where necessary, to update these notes accordingly. The ILU PSO adopted the same procedures for signing and premium accounting advices as LPSO, so an understanding of the LPSO procedure is all that is needed for the trainee to comprehend the procedure for the ILU PSO; although one should note that for policies based on mandated conditions only stage one of the Separation procedure will operate at Lloyd`s.

As we know, LPSB (later to become LPSO) was introduced to handle policy checking, signing and sealing on behalf of syndicates at Lloyd`s. However, as time passed, LPSO extended their functions to embrace the processing of premium advices. A system developed whereby premium advice and policy signing were linked in one procedure, to become known as the "policy signing and accounting procedure"; this being the S & A procedure, as it known today. The "Separation procedure" (see below) was not introduced until 1970; prior to which only the S & A procedure existed in the London market where Lloyd`s and ILU companies were concerned.

The S & A procedure required the broker to submit a "bureau sheet" (incorporating the premium accounting advice) with the prepared policy document and a signing slip to LPSO. No premium advice was sent to syndicates by the broker when he implemented the S & A procedure and no premium accounting or settlement procedure could be operated until the bureau sheet had been processed at LPSO and the information thereon forwarded to the appropriate syndicate/s. Prior to the introduction of central accounting at Lloyd`s, in 1962, although premium advices were dealt with in the S & A procedure, a Lloyd`s broker would settle his premium liability with each syndicate individually in accordance with credit, etc. arrangements with the syndicate concerned. It should be noted that, whereas all Lloyd`s syndicates receive their premiums via central accounting today, not all ILU companies subscribe to the ILU central accounting system and London brokers find themselves still settling directly with some ILU companies.

During the 1960`s it was recognised that there were lengthy delays between the time a risk attached and the date of premium settlement. Brokers protested that the delay in premium settlement was unavoidable because they encountered difficulties in policy preparation; such preparation being an integral part of the S & A procedure which they were unable to initiate without production of the policy. To circumvent this underwriters introduced the "Separation procedure". At the same time the PAN (premium advice note) was introduced to replace the old bureau sheet. Modern practitioners may refer to the PAN as the LPAN (London premium advice note) but, for the purpose of these notes we shall continue to use the abbreviation PAN. Trainees should note that, for many years, the operation of advising premium details to underwriters has been referred to as "closing" the risk.

The Separation procedure demands that the broker must not delay accounting merely to wait for production of the policy document. If he cannot produce the policy without delay he must use the Separation procedure which is carried out in two stages.

Stage One - In good time to allow for settlement to be made by the appropriate date under the terms of trade scheme, the broker must submit the signing slip and PAN to LPSO for processing (for mandated contracts - see above regarding policy preparation - the broker must also supply any special wording necessary for use in policy preparation by LPSO). LPSO allocates a signing number and date to the item; impressing this on the PAN and signing slip, enters the data in the computer and advises underwriters of the closing by electronic message via LIMNET. The PAN is retained by LPSO and the referenced signing slip is returned to the broker. Where the contract relates to mandated conditions no further action is required of the broker; the Lloyd`s policy being prepared automatically by LPSO PPS from the information supplied in stage one

Stage Two - Where the item relates to a non-mandated contract (or is within the ILU procedure) the broker must, within a reasonable period of time after receiving the referenced signing slip, submit the prepared policy document with the signing slip to the signing office; where it is checked, signed and sealed before both policy and signing slip are returned to the broker. When preparing a policy for submission to either LPSO or the ILU PSO it is not necessary for the broker to enter the lines, syndicates or references in the policy document. The PSO will raise a signing list by referring to the allocated policy number in its computer; such list being affixed to the policy by the PSO.

In the "S & A procedure" the broker carries out both stage one and stage two at one time. This procedure may be used by the broker, in place of the Separation procedure, only where its use creates no delay in premium settlement. In practice, one sees the S & A procedure used only where the policy is required urgently by the broker`s client.

Where the risk is placed with a non-Institute company, or an Institute company that has not authorised the ILU to sign policies on their behalf , the broker submits a "closing advice" to the insurance company who will issue the policy in due course, invoicing the broker for the premium. Most marine insurance companies in London, who have not authorised the ILU to represent them in policy signing and accounting, are signatories to the CCSA (combined company signing agreement). For such companies the broker prepares a combined policy form which is similar in structure to the ILU combined company policy form (see Witherby`s reference book of marine insurance clauses), but omitting, of course, the ILU title and all references to the ILU. Retaining the policy form, for the time being, the broker sends a closing advice to each company, other than the leader, with a line on the placing slip. These companies will not issue a policy but will invoice the broker for the premium. The broker waits for two weeks to see if any objections are raised regarding the insurance conditions expressed in the closing advices. If no objections are received the broker submits the combined company form with a closing advice to the leading company. The leading company will check and sign the combined policy on behalf of all the relevant companies, which the boker has listed therein, and will return the signed policy to the broker; invoicing him for the premium due to the leading company.

10. Insolvency of Insurance Companies regarding Premiums, Returns and Claims

Insolvency s not a matter of concern where the insurance contract is evidenced by a Lloyd`s policy because the central fund and securities maintained at Lloyd`s guarantee payment of valid claims even if an underwriting member becomes insolvent. However, there is no central fund, even for ILU companies, which guarantees payment of claims in the event that an insurance company becomes insolvent.

Where a policy has been issued by a company that becomes insolvent the broker remains responsible for the premium due in respect of the policy (MIA, 1906, sect.53-1). Similarly, the assured is responsible for payment of the premium to the broker; although, in practice, the broker might find it difficult to collect the premium once the assured becomes aware of the company`s insolvency. In such circumstances the broker`s lien on the policy (see Part 1, above) has little effect to enforce payment of the premium by the assured.

The insolvent company`s liability for claims and earned premium returns is direct to the assured (MIA, 1906, sect.53-1). Thus, in event of insolvency of the insurance company, the assured who holds the policy becomes a creditor against any assets available to the company for settlement of its liabilities. It follows that, except where the assured can prove negligence on the part of the broker during negotiations to conclude the contract with the insurance company, there is no liability on the part of the broker to make good losses suffered by the assured as a result of the insurance company`s insolvency.

Where the insurance contract has been concluded on a broker`s slip in the Lloyd`s market insolvency of one of the syndicates on the slip does not prejudice the policy signing procedure, which continues in the normal manner, because Lloyd`s guarantees the cover and is still empowered to sign the policy. Nonetheless, where the contract has been concluded with an Institute company that becomes insolvent before the policy is issued, the ILU has no powers to sign the policy on behalf of the insolvent company; so the contract becomes non-effective and the potential assured has no claim on the assets of the insolvent company. The latter position applies equally to a contract, evidenced only by the broker`s slip, which is effected with a non-Institute company; it being beyond the powers of the official handling the liquidation of the company to ratify the contract or to issue a policy. Attention is directed to the London market "Several Liability Notice" in Part 16 of Section 4.

SELF STUDY QUESTIONS

Before moving on to the next section satisfy yourself that you have absorbed the subject matter in the previous Sections. The following questions should be answered without reference to the text:

1. Where a broker negotiates a marine insurance contract, in respect of which a policy is issued before premium is paid to the underwriter, is the broker responsible for payment of the premium when he has not received the premium from his client?

2. What is "deferred account" and how does it operate in London market practice?

3. How does the C/A system operate in Lloyd`s market?

4. What is LIMNET and why was this system introduced?

5. Premium payments are usually subject to deductions, including brokerage. Where no special deductions are agreed what are the "customary" deductions to be applied to the premium for (a) a hull contract and (b) a cargo contract?

6. What do you know about IPT?

7. What does the abbreviation "h/c" mean in a broker`s marine slip. In what circumstances are such slip agreements used and what restrictions are normally applied to their implementation?

8. What are "lay up" returns? To what type of marine insurance contract do they apply and under what circumstances can the assured claim a lay up return?

9. What is the "Separation procedure" and how does it operate? When does LPSO PPS prepare the policy in this procedure? Who prepares an ILU policy in this procedure?

10. How does insolvency of the insurer affect the assured`s position when (a) he holds a Lloyd`s policy; (b) he holds a policy issued by the ILU; or (c) he holds a policy issued by a non-Institute company?

SECTION SIX

PRINCIPLE OF INSURABLE INTEREST

1. Provisions of the MIA, 1906 Regarding the Proposer`s Right to Effect a Marine Insurance Contract

2. Void Contracts and the MIA, 1909.

3. Effecting a Marine Insurance Contract Without Insurable Interest

4. Practical Examples of Cargo and Hull Interests

5. Insurer`s Right to Reinsure

6. Marine Insurance Contracts that are Invalid in Relation to Insurable Interest

7. The Use of PPI Policies in Marine Insurance Principles and Practice

8. Co-insurance, Underinsurance and Overinsurance

9. Effect of Assignment of Rights in a Marine Insurance Policy

SECTION SIX

1. Provisions of the MIA, 1906, Regarding the Proposer`s Right to Effect a Marine Insurance Contract

The principle of insurable interest is fundamental to all insurance contracts. It is based on the theory that a person who proposes an insurance contract is seeking protection from loss, rather than seeking a profit from the existence of the policy.

The Marine Insurance Act, 1906, codifies English law on marine insurance contracts as at 21st December, 1906. This Act repealed earlier Acts relating to marine insurance when it came into force on 1st January, 1907. No similar Statute applies to disputes relating to non-marine insurance contracts but courts tend to follow the MIA, 1906, in practice, where appropriate to the circumstances; otherwise precedents are taken from case law not embraced by the MIA, 1906. In the following notes comments are made regarding various sections of the MIA, 1906, which relate to insurable interest and subjects connected therewith.

Section 5 - *Definition of insurable interest*

This section of the Act confers an insurable interest on any person interested in a marine adventure. Although section 5 of the Act refers to a "person", in this respect, the law, in practice, extends this term to embrace any party or organisation (eg a shipping company, exporting company, etc.) that proposes a marine insurance contract.

The term "marine adventure" relates to property exposed to maritime risks. Cross reference to Section 2 of the Act will show that a marine adventure can embrace property exposed to risk on inland waters and any land risk which may be incidental to a sea voyage; also ship construction and launching can constitute a marine adventure.

Section 5(2) defines insurable interest for legal purposes and examination students are advised to study this detail. For these introductory notes it can be said that, to have an insurable interest, the person must be interested in the adventure to the extent that he can suffer a loss should an accident befall the adventure or the subject matter insured therein, or whereby he may incur a legal liability in respect of the adventure.

Section 6 - *Attachment of interest*

In other classes of insurance one may need to have an insurable interest at the time the contract is concluded to legally effect an insurance contract but marine insurance law does not demand that the proposer shall have an insurable interest at the time the contract is concluded. It will be recalled, that a contract is deemed to have been concluded when the underwriter signifies his acceptance of the risk on the broker`s slip or other document used for placing the risk (MIA, 1906, sect. 21). The proposer needs only to have a *reasonable expectation of acquiring* an insurable interest to legally effect a marine insurance contract. For example, a merchant can conclude an open cover contract to embrace shipments to be declared as they take place; thereby covering insurable interests that do not exist at the time of placing.

Section 6 of the Act provides that an assured, who effects a marine insurance contract in anticipation of acquiring an insurable interest, may not claim under the contract if no insurable interest exists at the time of loss. As an example consider the position of a ship operator who effected a policy to cover a new ship for 12 months from 1st March; the contract being concluded on 2nd February. Insurable interest would remain with the previous owner until delivery to the buyer. The assured expected delivery by 1st March but delivery was delayed and the policy inception date passed before the ship commenced the delivery voyage. On 8th March the ship was on her delivery voyage when she was totally lost by an insured peril. Although, chronologically, cover had attached before the loss occurred no claim would attach to the policy because the assured had not acquired an insurable interest at the time of loss.

Further, where the assured loses his insurable interest before a loss occurs he cannot recover the loss under the policy. As an example consider the position where the assured has effected a policy to cover the insured ship for a period of 12 months. Cover attaches and continues but, during the period of cover, the assured disposes of the ship and, thereby, loses title to it. His insurable interest in the ship ceases to exist on passage of title and he cannot claim under the policy for any loss occurring after he loses title to the ship. In this respect, see, also, comments in Part 9, below, regarding transfer of interest and assignment of policies. Section 6 of the Act, also, provides that, where an assured has no interest at the time of loss, he cannot acquire interest by any act or election after he is aware of the loss.

It is interesting to note that hull underwriters are content with the protections provided by the MIA, 1906, regarding circumstances where the assured has no insurable interest at the time of loss; relying, no doubt, on the "sale of vessel" clause which appears in hull time policies. On the other hand, probably bearing in mind the common practice whereby cargo policies and certificates are frequently assigned to buyers of the insured goods (see notes on assignment in Part 9, below), cargo underwriters make their position clear to cargo assureds and assignees by incorporating an "insurable interest" clause in the Institute cargo clauses published by the ILU for use with the MAR form of policy. This clause states that no claim will attach to the policy where the assured has no insurable interest at the time of loss.

Before we leave Section 6 of the Act it would be useful to comment on the "lost or not lost" clause, to which reference is made in this section of the Act. This clause is embraced by the wording of the SG form of policy. It relates to a situation where the proposer effects a facultative contract retrospectively (ie the risk has already attached when the contract is proposed to the underwriter). By the "lost or not lost" clause the underwriter agrees, conditionally, to accept the risk from inception including claims for losses that occurred prior to the date of conclusion of contract. Although the underwriter agrees to pay claims for insured losses that occurred before he wrote the risk the acceptance is conditional upon the assured not being aware of any loss, or accident that might result in a loss, at the time he concluded the contract with the underwriter. If the proposer is aware of such loss or accident and has communicated this knowledge to the underwriter before concluding the contract he can claim the loss under the policy.

The "lost or not lost" clause was designed for use in voyage policies and it should be noted that this clause does not appear in the MAR form of policy. This plain policy form is intended for use with both time and voyage insurance contracts; whereas the SG form (though it was used in practice for both time and voyage contracts) was designed with only voyage contracts in mind. Although one would not expect to see a "lost or not lost" clauses in the ITC or any similar set of hull time clauses, it would seem reasonable for this clause to appear in the IVC (Institute voyage clauses).

Nevertheless, this is not the case, so brokers would be well advised to keep this omission in mind when instructed to effect a hull & machinery policy to cover the insured ship for a specific voyage after the voyage has commenced and to add the "lost or not lost" clause to the conditions expressed in the placing slip.

This precaution is not necessary in cargo insurance practice based on the Institute cargo clauses because these standard conditions incorporate the clause in the same format that it appeared in the SG form of policy.

Section 7 - *Defeasible and Contingent Interests*

A defeasible interest is one which exists at the commencement of the risk but ceases to exist during the period covered by the insurance. An example would be where an importer enters into a sales contract which allows him to reject the goods and treat them as at the seller`s risk if delivery is overdue. The buyer insures the goods on a "warehouse to warehouse" basis for his own account as a defeasible interest; the buyer`s insurance cover terminating if and when he rejects the goods. It should be noted that, should the insurance cover terminate during transit, the assured is not entitled to a return of any part of the premium unless provision has been made for such return in the insurance conditions.

A contingent interest is one which attaches after the adventure has commenced. If the seller, in the above example, effected a policy to cover the goods in the event that the buyer exercised his rejection rights such policy would be based on a contingent interest and would not come into effect except where the buyer rejected the goods. As a further example, consider a "freight contingency" policy. It is common practice for timber to be carried on condition that freight (ie the remuneration paid for carriage of the goods) is paid when the timber is discharged from the overseas vessel. A freight voyage policy would cover the freight payable on discharge of the timber from the overseas vessel against loss of freight from marine perils. Where the timber is to continue transit by, say, barge to its final destination a separate insurance would be effected to cover losses that might occur during the onward leg of the transit. This additional insurance is a "freight contingency" insurance because the insurable interest therein is contingent on whether or not the timber has been lost during the overseas transit.

Section 8 - *Partial Interest*

In theory, a person may effect an insurance contract to cover only part of the property exposed to risk. Thus, where property is owned by two parties either party can effect an insurance contract to cover his part of the property, irrespective of whether or not the other party effects insurance cover for his part of the risk or effects it with different insurers. In ship insurance it is impractical to effect an insurance to cover only part of a ship when the whole is at risk. It might be possible for a part owner of goods to insure his part of the cargo provided he made it clear which part of the cargo was covered by the policy and which part was not insured; but this is not a common practice.

2. Void Contracts and the MIA, 1909

By way of definition a *void* contract is one that is of no value or effect. A contract may be declared as void by a court of law or it may be a contract that comes within the provisions of a Statute which holds it as void. Where a contract is void no claim is collectible thereunder. One should refer to the notes in Section 5 regarding return of premiums in respect of void contracts.

Section 4 of the MIA, 1906, is concerned with "gaming and wagering" contracts. A gaming and wagering contract is one in respect of which the assured has no insurable interest and has no expectation of acquiring such interest. The term embraces, also, any contract that is made "interest or no interest" or "without further proof of interest than the policy itself" (ie a PPI policy) or "without benefit of salvage to the insurer", or any like term. Section 4 of the Act declares such policies as void.

The MIA, 1906, does not impose a penalty on any person who effects a marine insurance contract by way of gaming or wagering; but it does ensure that courts of law will not recognise such contracts by declaring them as void. Accordingly, the underwriter is at liberty to waive proof of interest when he writes a PPI policy; but he is not permitted to write a contract in respect of which he knows no insurable interest exists nor is likely to exist. To do so would be an offence under the Marine Insurance (Gambling Policies) Act, 1909. In later notes comment will be made on the use of PPI policies in practice as, also, comment will be made on the waiver of subrogation rights in connection with the term "without benefit of salvage" in section 4 of the Act.

The Marine Insurance (Gambling Policies) Act was introduced on 20th October, 1909, to prohibit "gambling on loss by maritime perils". The Act makes it an offence for:

(a) Any person to effect a marine insurance contract where that person has no insurable interest in the subject matter insured, nor any *bona fide* expectation of acquiring such interest;

(b) Any person who is in the employment of a shipowner (other than a part owner of the ship) to effect a marine insurance contract on a ship, which is owned by his employer, on a PPI basis or without benefit of salvage or any like term;

(c) Any broker, or agent, to effect any of the contracts under (a) or (b) where he does so knowing about the unacceptable circumstances;

(d) Any underwriter to write any of the contracts under (a) or (b) where he does so knowing about the unacceptable circumstances.

Note - Comment (b) above is not intended to apply to an employee who, on instructions from his employer, effects a PPI policy, etc. on behalf of his employer; although such policy would still be void in a court of law. Further, it should be noted that no prosecutions have been pursued under this section of the MIA, 1909.

The penalty for an offence under the Gambling Policies Act, 1909, is at the discretion of the court which, upon conviction, may impose imprisonment, with or without hard labour, for a period not exceeding 6 months; or a fine not exceeding £100. Any money made in respect of the contract is forfeit to the Crown.

3. Effecting a Marine Insurance Contract Without Insurable Interest

As can be seen from the preceding comments the need for insurable interest is vital to a marine insurance contract. On no accasion does an underwriter waive the need for existence of insurable interest in the subject matter insured; even when effecting a contract in respect of which proof of insurable interest is waived. Before we move on to examples of insurable interest let us summarise the provisions covered by the preceding comments.

(1) The proposer need not have an insurable interest at the time he negotiates the contract with the insurer; but he must have a *bona fide* expectation of acquiring an insurable interest.
(2) The assured must have an insurable interest at the time of loss. This applies also to a PPI policy.
(3) Any policy that comes within the legal definition of a gaming or wagering contract is void in a court of law. This includes a PPI policy.
(4) Any proposer who effects a contract in contravention of the MIA, 1909, can, upon conviction, be fined or sent to prison.
(5) Any broker who, knowingly, effects a contract in contravention of the MIA, 1909, can, upon conviction, be fined or sent to prison.
(6) Any underwriter who, knowingly, effects a contract in contravention of the MIA, 1909, can, upon conviction, be fined or sent to prison.

4. Practical Examples of Cargo and Hull Interests

The following examples will assist one in recognising the existence of insurable interest in practice.

Cargo Interests

(1) *Proprietary interest* - This is where the proposer actually owns the goods. The subject matter of the insurance is the goods themselves. The insurable interest is the relationship of the assured to the goods as the owner thereof; this being the actual value of the goods at risk to the proposer. The insured value can include other interests (eg shipping charges and premium paid by the assured, also expected profit from sale and delivery of the goods).

(2) *Freight (ref MIA, 1906, sect. 12)* - Although the term freight is defined in the first schedule to the MIA, 1906, as the remuneration paid to the shipowner or charterer, as the case may be, for carrying the goods (and includes profit derived by the shipowner from the carriage of his own goods) the term in relation to insurable interest can embrace all charges incidental to the cost of shipping the goods. The cargo owner has an insurable interest in the freight only when he has paid it to the carrier in advance on a non-returnable basis. By custom the cargo owner`s interest in freight is not insured separately but is included in the insured value expressed in a valued policy or certificate.

Where freight is not payable until outturn (ie it is not paid until the goods are discharged from the overseas vessel) the freight is not at risk of the cargo owner during the voyage so he has no insurable interest therein. The insurable interest in freight payable on discharge at destination is vested in the carrier; not the cargo owner.

(3) *Premium (MIA, 1906, sect. 13)* - Once the risk has attached the premium is deemed to have been earned by the underwriter. Accordingly, the cargo owner has an insurable interest in the premium he has paid in advance and which is at risk during the voyage. By custom the premium is not insured separately but is included in the insured value expressed in the policy or certificate.

(4) *Profit* - No provision is made for this in the MIA, 1906, b market practice (unchallenged by law) for the cargo assured to be allowed to a reasonable percentage to the insurable value (ie cost, freight and insurance premi when determining the insured value to be expressed in a valued policy (see notes in Section 4, above) to cover the profit he expects to derive from safe arrival of the goods.

(5) *Defeasible and Contingent interests (MIA, 1906, sect. 7)* - See notes in Part 1, above.

(6) *Respondentia (MIA, 1906, sect. 10)* - Probably obsolete in practice. This related to an insurance effected by a lender of money to cover his loan against marine risks whilst the borrower completed the insured voyage to the planned destination. One saw this type of insurable interest in practice when it was common for shipowners to carry their own goods for speculative sale anywhere that a market could be found. The shipowner, finding himself in a foreign port and needing funds to continue the voyage, would approach a local bank or person who was prepared to advance a loan to finance the remainder of the voyage. Sometimes the security for the loan was vested solely in the cargo; but, on other occasions, it was vested in both ship and cargo. The policy would be effected in the name of the lender and would cover marine perils. It is probable that cover would be restricted to total loss only of the subject matter insured. The "subject matter insured" would be the cargo or the ship and cargo, as the case may be, and the insurable interest would be the loan and interest accruing thereto.

During the 17th century it was not unusual for a financier, when approached by a speculative shipowner at an intermediate port, to invest in the adventure, rather than to lend money to the shipowner. The reward for his investment was a share in the profits enjoyed by the outcome of the adventure rather than repayment of a loan with interest. The new investor would become a party to the adventure and, although he did not have an interest in ownership of the goods, he would be prejudiced by failure of the ship to complete the adventure or by loss of or damage to the goods. Thus, the new investor would have a respondentia interest in the safe arrival of the ship and goods for the money he had invested in the adventure.

(7) *Consignee's interest (MIA, 1906, Sect. 14-2)* - Where a consignee pays in advance for goods to be forwarded to him the payment he has made is at his risk during the transit of the goods. In such case, the consignee has an insurable interest in the amount at risk and he is entitled to effect a policy to cover this. Where such a policy has been effected the subject matter insured thereby is the goods at risk and the policy would pay only when an insured peril had caused a loss of the subject matter insured.

As in the case of a mortgagor (see "hull interests", below) the consignor retains a proprietary interest in the goods and can effect his own policy to cover the goods until they are delivered to the consignee. Where both parties each have an insurable interest to cover the same subject matter insured this is termed a "quantum of interest".

(8) *Cargo liabilities (MIA, 1906, sect. 5-2)* - Although one does not see marine insurance contracts effected to cover many of the legal liabilities a cargo owner can incur one must not assume that a cargo owner has no insurable interest in legal liabilities. As is the case with any other commercial practitioner, the cargo owner can incur contractual and/or third party liabilities in connection with the marine transit of goods and he has an insurable interest in certain of these liabilities.

xhaustive, the following examples give some indication of the ner's potential legal liabilities; most of which are **not** insured by o policies:

al liability to -
- (a) Carriers, by land and/or air and/or sea
- (b) Warehousemen
- (c) Container operators
- (d) Cargo handlers
- (e) Lighterers, barge operators, etc.
- (f) Port and/or harbour authorities
- (g) Waterways authorities

(2) *Third party liability in connection with -*
- (a) Loss of or damage to other cargo (eg taint)
- (b) Some circumstances involving collision of carrying vessels
- (c) Pollution and/or contamination
- (d) Removal of obstructions and/or hazardous wreck

(3) *Liability under contract or otherwise in connection with -*
- (a) Salvage operations
- (b) Services in the nature of salvage
- (c) General average

Hull Interests

(1) *Proprietary Interest* - This arises where the proposer actually owns the ship to be insured. Provided the insurance is expressed in a "valued" policy (see notes in Section 4) a proprietary insurable interest allows the shipowner to insure the hull and machinery of the ship against maritime perils for any amount that is acceptable to the underwriter. In the unlikely event that the contract is evidenced by an "unvalued" policy the insurable interest is limited to the market value of the ship at the time she commences the insured voyage. Where the insured vessel is operated and/or managed by a shipping company the insurable interest is vested in the company; shareholders in the company having **no** insurable interest in the ship.

The party with a proprietary interest may have certain "ancillary" insurable interests in connection with the operation of the ship; but it should be noted that the conditions of a hull & machinery policy will restrict the amount that may be insured in respect of certain ancillary insurances. For details concerning these restrictions interested practitioners and trainees are advised to consult "Marine Insurance - Volume 3 - Hull Practice" by Brown (Witherby - 2nd edition 1993). Introductory notes on ancillary hull interests appear separately below.

(2) *Premium (MIA, 1906, sect. 13)* - The ship operator has an insurable interest in the premium paid for insurance of the ship. Where the premium relates to a voyage insurance the whole premium paid may be insured. It is customary for a hull & machinery policy to be effected for a period of 12 months. The whole premium relating to such a policy may be insured (even where it is to be paid in instalments) for the same 12 months period. However, the ITC (1983) incorporate a restriction which demands that the premium policy shall incorporate a condition whereby the sum insured reduces by one twelfth each month. The policy is termed a "premium reducing policy", in

practice, and is effected on a TLO basis, to follow a total loss paid on the underlying H & M policy.

(3) *Charterer's interest* - A charterer is a person (or company) who hires a ship from the shipowner, shipping company or ship manager, as the case may be. A charterhire contract (termed a "charterparty") details the conditions of hire. Where the charterer hires the ship, with the intention of supplying his own crew and running the ship himself as though he were the owner of the ship, he undertakes to care for the ship and to return it, as provided by the charterparty, in the same condition as it was when he took delivery. In this case the charterer has the same insurable interests as the shipowner regarding loss of or damage to the ship and may insure the vessel as though he had a proprietary interest therein. The charterer also has an insurable interest in any of the ancillary interests (see below) insofar as they relate to his operation of the ship.

Where the shipowner, manager, etc. continues to operate the ship whilst it is under charter the proprietary insurable interest remains with the owner, manager, etc.; as do any ancillary interests relating thereto. The charterer's insurable interest would be restricted to any contractual or third party liabilities he might incur within the terms of the charterparty.

(4) *Freight* - As defined above, this is the remuneration paid to an overseas carrier for loading, caring for, conveying and discharging the goods to which the freight relates. It does not embrace passage money, nor does it include money payable by a charterer to a shipowner, manager, etc., but, as a charterer's interest, the term would extend to embrace freight to be earned by a charterer in the operation of the chartered vessel. The shipowner, manager, shipping company or charterer, as the case may be, has no insurable interest in freight which has been paid in advance by a shipper on a non-returnable basis. Where "bulk" cargoes (eg grain, oil, coal, ores, etc.) are involved it is customary for the carrier to undertake to load, care for, carry and discharge the goods safely, against payment of the freight relating thereto on delivery of the goods at the agreed destination. If the goods, or any part thereof, are not so delivered the freight due on the undelivered goods becomes forfeit. This type of freight is termed "freight at risk". The carrier has an insurable interest in the freight at risk during the voyage. Insurances on freight at risk are restricted by the "disbursements" clause in the H & M policy conditions

(5) *Anticipated freight* - When planning for the operation of a ship during the period covered by a 12 months H & M policy the assured takes into account the freight he will expect to earn during that period. During the year he will probably enter into various contracts of carriage and will probably effect freight at risk policies in this respect. Whilst this practice takes care to protect the ship operator from loss of freight at risk none of these policies nor the H & M policy will reimburse him for the anticipated freight he will lose if his ship is lost during the year and for which he has not effected freight at risk insurance protection at the time of the ship is lost. It is difficult to predict, with any certainty, the amount of this anticipated freight so it is customary to insure it for an agreed sum insured, by an unvalued policy, on a TLO, PPI (see Part 7, below) basis. Hull underwriters accept this nebulous type of insurance but the conditions of the H & M policy restrict the sum insured in the policy covering anticipated freight. Effecting an anticipated freight policy for more than the permitted amount would constitute a breach of warranty in the H & M policy and would discharge underwriters from all liability thereunder.

6. *Charterhire* - Under the terms of a charterparty the charterer will be liable for payment of hire money to the owner, manager or shipping company who has hired

the vessel to him. Subject to the terms of the charterparty he will still be liable for the hire money if the ship is out of commission during the period covered by the charterparty; even where the lay up is caused by an accident. The charterer has an insurable interest in the amount he has to pay under the charterparty for the period during which the ship is out of commission as a result of an accident to the ship and may effect a policy for a an agreed sum insured to cover this.

The owner, manager or shipping company, as the case may be, also has an insurable interest in charterhire that may not be paid due to loss of the vessel. A policy effected to cover this interest is termed a "loss of hire" policy and, usually, pays an agreed amount per day for a maximum number of days; often with an excess of so many days before a claim becomes payable.

7. *Disbursements* - By way of definition the term "disbursements" refers to money paid out by the master for the continuance of the voyage (eg purchase of fuel, water, victuals, stores, etc.). At one time the money to cover these costs was carried on board the vessel and was insured as "disbursements" under a policy which paid the full sum insured in the event that the ship was totally lost by an insured peril; irrespective of the fact that some of the cash might have been spent by the time the loss occurred. To avoid complications underwriters, customarily, waived proof of interest (ie a PPI policy was used) and admitted a full interest in the sum insured.

With the passage of time it was appreciated by brokers, shipowners, etc. that the nebulous nature of this insurable interest could be used to provide extra total loss cover, at a very low premium rate, as a supplement to the cover provided by the full terms H & M policy. So it became common practice for the proposer of an H & M time policy to propose, also, a disbursements TLO PPI policy for a fairly large amount to run concurrently with the H & M policy and to pay in full in event of a total loss of the ship from an insured peril. At first underwriters went along with this practice; allowing the hull assured to effect the disbursements policy for any amount agreed between underwriter and proposer. But, eventually, the hull market recognised that premium income from the underlying H & M policies, required to meet the cost of ship repairs, was diminishing in favour of ever increasing cover in disbursements insurances. Rather than combat this trend by increasing the premium rates for H & M policies (a practice to be avoided, if possible, in a competitive market) hull underwriters introduced the "disbursements" clause in the insurance conditions (eg the ITC) used for H & M policies. An express warranty in this clause discharges the underwriters covering the **H & M** policy from all liability thereunder if the assured effects a TLO PPI policy on disbursements in excess of the amount permitted by the clause.

(8) *Mortgagees interest (MIA, 1906, sect. 14)* - When a ship is mortgaged the mortgagee (the one who lends the money on the security of the ship) has an insurable interest in the ship for the sum due, or to become due, in respect of the mortgage (ie the amount of the loan and any interest accruing thereto). Nevertheless, the mortgagor (ie the shipowner, shipping company or manager, as the case may be) retains a full insurable interest in the ship, notwithstanding that another party may have agreed to reimburse him for his loss, and he may effect his own H & M policy to cover the mortgaged vessel. In a case such as this, where both mortgagee and mortgagor have an insurable interest in the same subject matter insured at the same time, this is referred to as a "quantum of interest".

Although one often sees a mortgagees interest expressed in the ship operator`s H & M policy, in addition to the named assured therein, a mortgagee is entitled to insure his interest separately; either in his own name or on behalf of, or for the benefit of, other parties. In practice, it is customary for a mortgagee, who regularly enters into mortgage contracts, to effect a form of open cover contract which covers his insurable interest in a number of vessels which are to be declared as they attach to the cover. Trainees and practitioners might care to note that the ILU publishes a standard set of hull insurance conditions for use in mortgagees interest policies.

(9) *Hull liabilities (MIA, 1906, sect. 5-2)* - Ownership and operation of a ship can expose the shipowner, manager, shipping company or charterer, as the case may be, to potential legal liabilities both contractual and third party. Contractual liabilities can be incurred only where a contract exists between the ship operator and the party claiming damages. A third party liability is a legal liability which is incurred in circumstances where no contract exists between the ship operator and the party claiming damages; the latter basing the claim on breach of a statutory requirement or a precedent existing in common law.

The following examples illustrate some of the liabilities to which a ship operator might be exposed:

(1) *Contractual liabilities in connection with -*
- (a) Carriage of goods (eg to cargo owners, freight forwarders, container operators, etc.)
- (b) Loading, stowing and discharging (eg to cargo handlers - stevedores, longshoremen, etc.)
- (c) Use of harbours, ports, port installations and waterways
- (d) Salvage operations and services in the nature of salvage
- (e) Ship construction and/or repair
- (f) Towage services (customary or otherwise)

(2) *Third party liabilities in connection with -*
- (a) Collision of the insured ship with another ship or vessel
- (b) Contact of the insured ship with objects other than another ship or vessel (eg buoys, wharfs, piers, bridges, etc.)
- (c) Loss of or damage to property of others, not already embraced by *a* and *b* above (eg caused by an explosion on the insured vessel)
- (d) Removal of obstructions (eg removal of wreck from a waterway)
- (e) Pollution and/or contamination of the seas or environment

The standard H & M policy extends to cover some of these liabilities (eg limited collision liability, liability for salvage charges, etc.) but the majority of the contractual liability and third party liability interests listed above are insured with protection and indemnity clubs. P & I clubs are mutual insurance societies set up by groups of shipowners to reimburse members for losses (mostly in respect of liabilities) incurred by members where such loss is not insurable in the open hull insurance market. Trainees and practitioners are advised to consult "Marine Insurance - Vol. 3 - Hull Practice" by Brown (Witherby - 2nd edition 1993) for detailed information on the above listed insurable interests and insurance contracts effected, in practice, to cover these interests.

(Text continues on Page 12)

5. Insurer`s Right to Reinsure

Section 5 of the MIA, 1906, provides that any person may insure a liability which could arise from the operation of a maritime peril. The underwriter who writes a marine risk has such potential liability in claims he might be called upon to pay under the marine insurance contract and section 10 of the MIA, 1906, provides that a marine insurer may reinsure in respect of his risk under the original insurance contract.

Reinsurance is limited to the underwriter`s written line in the first instance and he may effect a reinsurance contract for this amount or for part of the written line, at his option. However, if the underwriter`s written line in the original contract is reduced in policy signing, the amount covered by the reinsurance contract must be equally reduced to the signed line.

Examples

	Sum insured by Original written line	Reinsured	Sum insured by Original signed line	Reinsured
(1)	£100,000	100%	£80,000	£80,000
(2)	£100,000	50%	£80,000	£40,000

This is termed "proportional" reinsurance but there are other types of marine proportional reinsurance and several types of marine non-proportional reinsurance. These introductory notes are not intended to extend to detail in respect of reinsurance practice. Trainees and practictioners seeking such information are advised to consult "Marine Reinsurance" by Brown & Reed (Witherby).

The original underwriter may reinsure on the same conditions as the original insurance or he may reinsure on more restricted conditions. For example, where an original H & M insurance is subject to the ITC (1983) the underwriter may reinsure "as original" in which case any valid claim for partial loss that is paid on the original policy is recoverable from the reinsurer; as would be, also, a claim for actual or constructive total loss. Alternatively, where an original H & M insurance is subject to the ITC (1983) and the underwriter reinsures "as original but TLO" he would be reimbursed by the reinsurer only when the original policy pays an actual or constructive total loss; no partial loss claim being recoverable under the reinsurance contract. It must be remembered, however, that the principle of insurable interest prohibits an underwriter from effecting a reinsurance contract on wider conditions than those on the original insurance contract or for an amount in excess of the sum insured by the original policy.

In practice, it is customary for a marine insurance underwriter to arrange reinsurance contracts to protect his portfolio as part of his underwriting philosophy. This practice has the effect of increasing his capacity and his acceptances are often influenced by the reinsurance security established by his treaty and other regular reinsurance contracts.

It may happen that a broker obtains a large lead line by arranging a substantial facultative reinsurance contract to protect that line. There is nothing wrong in this practice but the broker is obliged to disclose the existence of the reinsurance contract to following underwriters before concluding the contract with them. Failure to make such disclosure could be construed as a breach of good faith (See notes in Section 7).

It should be noted that no claim is recoverable under a reinsurance contract where the relevant loss has not been already settled under the original policy. Accordingly, where an insurance company becomes insolvent and is unable to meet its liabilities no action can been successfully pursued against the reinsurer in rega . unsettled losses. Exceptions might occur in the laws of other countries but it is important to appreciate that, under English law (ref. MIA, 1906, sect. 10), the original assured has no rights in a reinsurance contract. Thus, an assured who has been unable to recover a valid loss from an insolvent insurance company cannot pursue his claim against an underwriter who has reinsured the original insurance company for that loss.

6. Marine Insurance Contracts that are Invalid in Relation to Insurable Interest

A contract of marine insurance is deemed to be invalid if it is *void* in a court of law. Such contracts are unenforceable but this does not mean that the contract is necessarily illegal. Where a contract is legal but is still void in law it is termed an "honour" policy. That is to say the insurer is only morally bound to honour the contract. In London market practice underwriters scrupulously abide by their moral responsiblities in such contracts. Nevertheless, one must not forget that an official receiver or other officer given the task of winding up the affairs of an insolvent insurance company has no powers to commit the company`s assets to honour such policies.

Earlier comments have considered various types of policy that come within this category and comment on the use of PPI policies appears in Part 7, below. However it should be appreciated that there may be other factors which can influence the validity of a marine insurance policy and, in this respect, one might find the following summary useful. A marine insurance contract is void if:

(a) It does not comply with the legal requirements regarding the existence of an insurable interest;
(b) The law of the country in which it is issued demands that the policy shall be subject to stamp duty and the policy is not so stamped or is stamped for an amount less than is required by law;
(c) The law of the country whose jurisdiction shall apply demands that the policy shall be subject to stamp duty and the policy is not so stamped or is stamped for an amount less than is required by law;
(d) The law of the country in which the contract is concluded or from which the business emanates, as the case may be, demands that IPT (insurance premium tax) be paid and such tax has not been paid or less than the required IPT has been paid;
(e) The underwriter has agreed, in the contract, to waive the requirement for the assured to prove the existence of, or the extent of, insurable interest at the time of loss;
(f) The underwriter has agreed, in the contract, to waive his salvage rights, subrogation rights or any other rights to which he is entitled on settlement of a claim.

Note - Stamp duty on marine insurance policies issued in the UK, or which were subject to UK jurisdiction, was abolished in August 1970. Reference should be made to the notes in Section 4 regarding IPT on English insurance contracts.

(Text continues on Page 14)

O^x ·

olicies in Marine Insurance Principles and Practice

.aw requires the assured to prove he has an insurable interest, and the ., at the time of a loss that is the subject of a claim under a marine ,olicy. An underwriter is at liberty to waive his rights in this respect and, w so agrees during negotiations to conclude the contract, he issues a PPI (policy proo. of interest) policy to cover the risk.

Section 4(2b) of the MIA, 1906, declares such a contract as void; so a PPI policy is not recognised by a court of law. At one time it was thought practitioners could get round this legal position by omitting reference to the PPI agreement in the policy form and by pinning a PPI clause to the policy form; it being understood that the clause could be removed from the document in event of dispute and the policy submitted as evidence in court. This theory was dispelled in the case of "Edwards, John & Co. -v- The Motor Union Insurance Co. (1922)" when it was held that a policy issued <u>without</u> the term "policy proof of interest" incorporated therein is still void in law if a PPI agreement appears in the broker's slip or in any other document on which the contract has been concluded between underwriter and proposer. It is interesting to note that some practitioners continue to prepare PPI policies with the PPI clause pinned thereto despite the fact that no advantage has been gained from the practice since 1922.

PPI policies are used in hull practice to cover the insurance of anticipated freight, disbursements, increased value, etc. It is practical to effect such policies only on a TLO basis because, to do otherwise, would require the assured to prove insurable interest to establish the extent of a partial loss and so defeat the object of the PPI agreement. In cargo practice a PPI policy might be used to cover increased value anticipated by a dealer who has purchased the goods whilst they are still in transit.

In theory, one only has to produce a PPI policy to collect a claim thereunder but this is not sufficient in practice because, although they waive proof of insurable interest in respect of PPI contracts, underwriters do not waive proof of loss in event of a claim on the policy. Thus, when the assured presents a PPI policy to the underwriters for a total loss settlement he must also produce evidence to show that the subject matter insured has been totally lost. In practice, a PPI policy is always linked to an underlying policy. For example, a PPI policy covering anticipated freight would be linked to an underlying H & M policy covering loss of and/or damage to the ship; the latter being the subject matter insured for the purpose of the PPI policy. To prove that a total loss has occurred the assured produces the PPI policy accompanied by the underlying H & M policy with evidence that a total loss has been settled on the latter. The same procedure is followed for a claim on a cargo PPI policy. It follows that, in practice, unless a total loss has been settled on the underlying H & M or cargo policy, as the case may be, no claim can be made on a PPI policy.

Further, it will be recalled that, upon settlement of a total loss, the underlying hull and machinery policy lapses, whether it be for a period of time or for a voyage; the same applying where a total loss claim is settled on an underlying cargo policy. Accordingly, a linked PPI policy would also lapse upon settlement of a claim thereon; so the PPI policy pays only once.

(Text continues on Page 15)

8. Co-insurance, Underinsurance and Overinsurance

These subjects may not be directly concerned with insurable interest but they are related thereto in that the principles of insurable interest apply as much to co-insurance, etc. as to any other contract of marine insurance.

Co-insurance - A co-insurance exists where the insured risk is shared between several underwriters; each being responsible for the loss to the extent that his written line (subsequently his signed line) bears to the whole amount insured. Co-insurance can be illustrated by a single policy document evidencing the subscriptions of a number of insurers, as in the case of a company combined policy (see notes in Section 4), or by separate policy documents which jointly cover the same risk.

In most cases the premium rate and insurance conditions are the same for each contract and the gross premium and each claim is allocated proportionately between the co-insurers. Where claims for sue & labour charges and/or salvage charges are concerned (see notes in Section 13) these are borne proportionately by each of the co-insurers and, generally, each shares equally in recoveries made by the exercise of subrogation rights (see notes in Section 13).

It sometimes happens that a broker places part of the risk with one market and part with another market with, perhaps, different conditions and/or a different premium rate. In such cases the rules regarding allocation of claims continue to apply, insofar as each co-insurer is liable for the loss, but where (due to a difference in conditions) part of the loss is not recoverable under a co-insurance policy the *assured* becomes a co-insurer for that part of the loss. The assured, also, remains as a co-insurer where part of the risk is not placed; but the assured is not deemed to be a co-insurer nor entitled to any recovery rights, in English law and practice, in respect of any franchise, deductible or excess (see notes in Section 4) in the contract whereby he bears part of a loss. See, also, comments below regarding the deductible in H & M policies.

Further, the broker could encounter problems with premium allocation where different premium rates are applied to co-insurances so it is preferable that insurance contracts with varying conditions and/or varying premium rates are treated as separate insurances. Nevertheless, it must be borne in mind that where the subject matter insured is covered by separate policies each policy must show the relationship of the sum insured thereby to the sum insured of the whole.

Deductible in H & M policies - It is customary for a hull & machinery policy to incorporate a deductible which is applied to most partial loss claims. English law holds that, although the assured is self insured where the deductible is concerned, he is *not* a co-insurer in this respect. Accordingly, the assured is not entitled to any part of a recovery under subrogation rights so far as the deductible is concerned. Trainees and practitioners should bear in mind that this may not be the case where a policy is subject to foreign law and practice except where the policy conditions apply the English rule of law in this respect; the ITC (1983) incorporate a clause which follows English law on the apportionment of recoveries.

Underinsurance - An assured who effects an unvalued policy (see notes on unvalued policies in Section 4) for less than the insurable value of the property at risk becomes a co-insurer with the underwriter for the uninsured balance of the insurable (market) value. Similarly, an assured who effects a valued policy (see notes on valued policies in Section 4) for a sum insured that is less than the insured value becomes a co-insurer with the underwriter for the uninsured balance of the insured value. The following two examples illustrate:

Example 1 (Unvalued policy) - The proposer expects his goods to have a sound value, on arrival, of £10,000 and he effects an insurance contract on an unvalued policy for that amount. On arrival the goods are found to have a sound value (estimated in the case of a total loss) of £12,000 so they are deemed to be underinsured. Claims in respect of a total loss, partial loss and/or insured expenses would be allocated to the policy as follows, with the balance being for the assured`s account. Further, the underwriter would receive only an apportionable part of any amounts recovered by the exercise of subrogation rights.

	Underwriter	**Assured**
Total loss £12,000	£10,000	£2,000
Partial loss (50%) £6,000	£ 5,000	£1,000
Insured expenses £1,200	£ 1,000	£ 200
Recoveries (£6,000)	(£5,000)	(£1,000)

Example 2 (Valued policy) - A merchant estimates that the value of his goods at destination will be £14,000 but, for an undisclosed reason, he insures them for only £12,000 by a valued policy which expresses the insured value as £14,000. Following the example above, claims in respect of a total loss/partial loss and insured expenses would be allocated to the policy as follows, with the balance being for the assured`s account. Further, the underwriter would receive only an apportionable part of any amounts recovered by the exercise of subrogation rights.

	Underwriter	**Assured**
Total loss	£12,000	£2,000
Partial loss (50%)	£ 6,000	£1,000
Insured expenses £1,200	£ 1,028	£ 172
Recoveries (£6,000)	(£5,143)	(£ 857)

Undervaluation - Example 2, above, relates only to cargo insurance because, where a cargo insurance contract is effected by a valued policy for less than the market value of the goods both a total loss claim and partial loss claims would be affected by the undervaluation. Such is not the case where a *ship* is covered for loss or damage by a valued policy wherein the insured value is less than the market value of the ship. For example, consider a ship with a market value of £4,200,000. The assured effects a policy with an insured value of £4,000,000. The measure of indemnity for total loss would be £4,000,000; the assured bearing the balance of £200,000. But, where insured damage to the ship is concerned, the measure of indemnity is "the reasonable cost of repairing the damage with a limit of the insured value in any one accident" (MIA, 1906, sect.69). It follows that claims for ship repairs are influenced by undervaluation only when the cost of repairs exceeds the insured value in any one accident; otherwise they are paid in full (subject to the policy deductible) without regard for the undervaluation. Nevertheless, it should be noted that sue & labour charges, salvage charges and collision liability claims recoverable under a hull policy may be affected by undervaluation in the policy.

Overinsurance - A proposer is not permitted to effect an insurance contract covering maritime property at risk by an *unvalued* policy for more than the insurable value of the subject matter insured. If the proposer wishes to be covered for more than the insurable value he must agree an insured value with the underwriter when negotiating the contract and this value must be expressed as the insured value in a *valued* policy. It is customary for cargo underwriters to agree an insured value which reflects the insurable value of goods plus a reasonable percentage anticipated profit. There is no set pattern established regarding overinsurance in the hull market. The insured value agreed in a hull & machi... is conclusive, even when the ship is overinsured (MIA, 1906, sect. 27). See the no... in Section 4 for further information on valued policies.

9. Effect of Assignment of Rights in a Marine Insurance Policy

Assignment of interest occurs when a party with beneficial rights in that interest (ie the assignor) passes such rights to another party (ie the assignee). For example, when a cargo owner sells his goods to another party he automatically assigns any interest he has in the goods upon passage of title to the goods to the purchaser. Where there has been no express or implied agreement to assign the policy prior to the passage of title the insurance contract lapses as soon as the assured loses his insurable interest in the subject matter insured (MIA, 1906, sect. 51). In other words, assignment of a marine insurance policy does not automatically follow assignment of interest in the subject matter insured. The following comments regarding assignment of a marine insurance policy apply equally to assignment of a cargo certificate issued off an open cover.

Section 50 of the MIA, 1906, provides that a marine insurance contract is freely assignable except where it incorporates a condition prohibiting assignment. It is not customary for a cargo insurance contract to incorporate such prohibition so there are no restrictions on the assignment of a cargo policy; provided the assignment takes place before the assured`s insurable interest lapses. Once the policy lapses due to lack of insurable interest the assured has no beneficial rights to assign; this applying to both hull and cargo insurance contracts. Where a seller effects an insurance policy to cover goods that have been sold on CIF (cost, insurance and freight) terms, or on any like terms by which the buyer has paid for the insurance in the purchase price for the goods, there is an implied agreement that the policy shall be assigned to the buyer. In such case the assignor can assign the policy before or after the passage of title.

Hull underwriters do not permit assignment of the H & M policy without their prior agreement thereto. The H & M policy provides that this agreement must be obtained in writing from the underwriter otherwise the policy lapses automatically upon the passage of title to the ship to the buyer. It makes no difference that the contract of sale or any other agreement contained an implied condition whereby the policy would be assigned; without the underwriter`s written approval to the assignment such agreement is not effective.

A policy can be assigned by indorsement thereon or by any other customary means (MIA, 1906, sect. 50-3). Cargo policies are normally assigned by "blank" endorsement (ie the assignor endorses the document in much the same way as a cheque is endorsed to pass its benefits to another party) and passes it to the assignee with the documents of title. Where the hull underwriters agree to assignment of the policy practice demands that a signed and dated notice of assignment must be endorsed on the document.

By assigning the policy the assignee gives up all his rights in the insurance policy in favour of the assignee who may claim on the document in his own name. Whilst the assignee gains all the rights of the assignor he cannot enjoy any benefits to which the assignor was not entitled. For example, the underwriter is entitled to raise any defence in the contract which he would have been entitled to raise in defending the claim against the assignor (MIA, 1906, sect. 50-2). This latter point is particularly important because it allows the underwriter to avoid the contract if he discovers a breach of good faith on the part of the assignor, even though the assignee was unaware of the breach. Further, where the underwriter discovers, after the policy has been assigned, that the assignor had commited a breach of warranty (eg breach of the disbursements warranty in a hull contract) he can exercise his right to be discharged from liability under the policy as from the date of the breach, even though the assignee was innocent of the breach of warranty. In practice, hull underwriters waive their rights in regard to breach of the disbursements warranty when the policy is assigned to an innocent mortgagee who has accepted the policy in good faith.

SELF STUDY QUESTIONS

Before moving on to the next Section satisfy yourself that you have absorbed the subject matter in the previous Sections. The following questions should be answered without reference to the text.

1. Can you define the term "insurable interest"? What is its relationship to the term "subject matter insured"?

2. In what circumstances can one propose a marine insurance contract without having an insurable interest at the time of the proposal?

3. When is a marine insurance contract deemed to be "void"?

4. Can you list three examples of (a) cargo interests and (b) hull interests?

5. In regard to marine insurance, what is the difference between a contractual liability and a third party liability? Can you give an example of each?

6. To what extent can a marine insurer reinsure his line?

7. What is a PPI policy and in what circumstances are such policies used in the marine insurance market?

8. What is a co-insurance? Can you give practical examples of co-insurance contracts?

9. Are claims under a hull and machinery policy prejudiced if the shipowner insures his ship on full terms but for an insured value which is less than the market value of the ship?

10. Can an innocent assignee be prejudiced by a breach of good faith committed by the assignor during negotiations to conclude the contract with the underwriter?

SECTION SEVEN

PRINCIPLE OF UTMOST GOOD FAITH

1. Introduction
2. Material Circumstances
3. Disclosures to the Underwriter
4. Excuses for Non-disclosure to the Underwriter
5. Representations and Mis-representations
6. Innocent Mis-representations
7. Effect of Breach of Good Faith by the Assured or Broker
8. Negligence of Broker in Regard to Good Faith

SECTION SEVEN

1. Introduction

When a marine insurance contract is proposed the proposer has, or should have, all the information concerning the subject matter insured and the insurable interest to be insured necesary for a reasonable assessment of the risk. The underwriter, on the other hand, has no information; other than such circumstances as have come to his knowledge in the ordinary course of his business. Therefore, the underwriter is dependent on the information which is disclosed and represented to him by the proposer. The underwriter is free, of course, to ask questions before he commits himself but he might not have sufficient knowledge of the risk to ask relevant questions on matters of which the proposer is aware and of which the underwriter is unlikely to be aware in the ordinary course of his business. This puts the underwriter at a disadvantage; particularly because a proper assessment of the contract and the risks to which the subject matter insured may be exposed is possible only when it is based on a meeting of minds with equal knowledge of the risks to be insured.

Withholding material information which is prejudicial to the risk can be advantageous to the proposer; for it causes the underwriter to see the risk in a better light than might, otherwise, have been the case; thereby encouraging him to accept the proposed contract more readily and, perhaps, at a lower premium rate. To preserve equity, section 17 of the MIA, 1906, provides that a contract of marine insurance is *uberrimae fidei* (ie bound by the utmost good faith). This section of the Act incorporates an implied condition in every contract of marine insurance whereby the parties to the contract, and agents representing them, must exercise good faith in concluding the contract. This makes it essential for the proposer to disclose every material circumstance, and to properly represent each disclosed circumstance, before the contract is concluded. It will be recalled that the contract is deemed to be concluded when the underwriter signifies his acceptance on the placing slip and thereby accepts the proposal of the assured (MIA, 1906, section 21).

Over the years, prior to December 1906, English courts of law determined precedents to establish the responsibilities of parties to a marine insurance contract regarding disclosure and representations, the materiality of these to maritime risks and circumstances which need not be disclosed. These precedents are embodied in sections 17 to 21 of Marine Insurance Act, 1906, to which trainees and practitioners should refer in connection with the following notes.

In practice, an underwriter might be inclined to leniency in circumstances where he considers the proposer to be innocent of any intentional wrongdoing and might not exercise his rights in regard to the principle of good faith. But where the underwriter discovers the assured has taken advantage of his (the underwriter`s) vulnerability and ignorance of the facts to mislead him the underwriter will, undoubtedly, exercise his right, under the principle of good faith, to avoid the contract from inception.

2. Material Circumstances *(MIA, 1906, sect.18)*

The proposer and his broker are required to disclose every circumstance that is material to the risk. Section 18(4) of the MIA, 1906, provides that whether or not any particular circumstance, which is not disclosed, be material or not is, in each case, a question of fact. On the face of it, this would appear to be conclusive but the provision in the Act is qualified, to some extent, by section 18(2) which provides that a circumstance is material if it would influence the judgement of a prudent insurer in fixing the premium or determining whether he will take the risk. It will be noted that the Act refers to a *prudent* insurer in this respect and gives no guidance to define this term. In cases of doubt the court would decide, on the facts presented, whether or not the defendant should be considered a prudent insurer in contemplating the proposal; probably taking evidence from other marine insurers, where deemed necessary, in making its determinations.

As matters stand at present, and in the absence of litigation, it is left to underwriters to decide what is material to the risk; no regard being given to the proposer's views on whether or not he thinks a particular circumstance need not be disclosed because he considers it will not influence the judgement of the underwriter. It has been suggested, in legal circles, that current law, in this respect, is unfair to the proposer and should be changed to allow greater freedom to the honest proposer in deciding what he should disclose to the underwriter.

These introductory notes are concerned only with English law as it stands today, the comments herein on materiality being based on the provisions of the MIA, 1906. Nevertheless, trainees and practitioners are advised to watch out for possible legal directives which might change law and practice regarding the extent of disclosures and the materiality of circumstances to the risk.

Pedantic students should note that, when he commits a breach of good faith, the guilty party is technically the "proposer" but, by the time the insurer (underwriter) exercises his rights in regard to the breach of good faith in practice, the risk has already attached and the guilty party has become the "assured". Accepting this, a court of law will refer to the plaintiff as the "assured"; the MIA, 1906, also referring to the proposer as the "assured". The text of these notes follows the Act, in this respect, referring to the "assured", instead of the proposer, on the understanding that, where appropriate, the term "assured" means the proposer. Further, although the MIA, 1906, uses the term "insurer" to describe the underwriter, it is more common for the latter term to be used in practice; so these notes follow practice, in this respect.

3. Disclosures to the Underwriter *(MIA, 1906, sects. 18* & 19)

By way of definition a "disclosure" is an advice by the assured and/or his servants and/or his broker to the underwriter. A disclosure may be made verbally or in writing but must be in such terms that its meaning is clear to the underwriter. Failure to disclose a material circumstance (referred to, in practice, as a "non-disclosure"), prior to conclusion of contract, constitutes a breach of good faith.

Before the contract is concluded the proposer must disclose to the underwriter every material circumstance which is known to the assured. The term "circumstance" includes any communication made to, or information received by, the assured. The assured is deemed to know every circumstance which, in the ordinary course of business, ought to be known to him. Where a material circumstance did not come to the knowledge of the assured until *after* he concluded the contract non-disclosure of such circumstance would not be accepted by a court as a breach of good faith unless the underwriter can show that the assured should have been aware of the circumstance, at the time he concluded the contract, in the ordinary course of his business. Any servant of the assured who proposes the insurance contract on behalf of his employer is equally bound by the rules of disclosure and it is no defence of the breach of good faith for the assured to allege he was innocent of the breach of good faith committed by his servant.

Where a broker (or other agent) represents the assured in proposing the contract the broker is equally bound by the rules of disclosure (ref. MIA, 1906, sect.19). The broker must dislose every material circumstance that is known to him (the broker) or which should be known to him in the ordinary course of his business or which ought to have been communicated to him. Further, the broker must disclose every material circumstance that is known to the assured, or which should be known to the assured in the ordinary course of his business. There is, however, one exception which appears in section 19(b) of the MIA, 1906. The Act provides that the assured and his broker are **not** bound to disclose a material circumstance which comes to the assured's knowledge too late to communicate it to the broker before the contract is concluded. Nevertheless, from a practical point of view, practitioners would do well to disclose such late advices to the underwriter, even after the contract is concluded, because, by so doing, an atmosphere of trust between the parties is maintained and, apart from this, there is always the chance it might be held, in cases of dispute, that the assured and/or his broker should have been aware of the material circumstance in the ordinary course of their business. It is no defence against a breach of good faith based on non-dislosure for the assured to allege that the fault lay with the broker for the non-disclosure, whilst he (the assured) was innocent of the breach; as, for example, where the assured had disclosed a circumstance to the broker but the broker did not pass on the disclosure to the underwriter. For remedies open to the assured in such case see the notes in part 8, below.

The MIA, 1906, imposes the conditions regarding disclosure of material circumstances on the assured and his broker only during negotiations to conclude the contract. So the Act does not take into account material circumstances which come to light after the underwriter has written the risk. Nevertheless, brokers should be aware that any material circumstance which comes to light during the placing procedure (ie after the leader and others have concluded the contract but the broker has not completed the placing) must be disclosed to those underwriters who have not yet concluded the contract. In practice, a broker, placed in this position, would also advise the leader and other underwriters who have already signified their acceptances on the placing slip of the newly disclosed circumstance. Although an underwriter is not legally bound to honour his line on a broker's slip it would be contrary to market practice for an underwriter, who has already concluded the contract, to withdraw from the contract on advice of a late disclosure; although some adjustment of the premium might be agreed between the parties where the risk is enhanced by the change in circumstances.

Where a contract is renewed the renewal is deemed to be a new contract in the eyes of the law, even when the terms in the new contract are the same as in the expiring contract. Accordingly, the principle of good faith applies during negotiations to renew the contract and the assured and/or his broker must disclose every material circumstance which affects the renewal before the renewal contract is concluded.

If the underwriter asks a question, regarding the proposed contract, before concluding the contract the answer to that question is deemed to be material to the risk. The assured and/or his broker must answer the question truthfully. If the question is not answered or is answered untruthfully there is a breach of good faith and the underwriter is entitled, upon discovery of the breach, to avoid the contract.

4. Excuses for Non-Disclosure to the Underwriter *(MIA, 1906, sect. 18-3)*

In the absence of inquiry by the underwriter the following circumstances need not be disclosed to the underwriter:

(a) Any circumstance that diminishes the risk -

It would obviously be advantageous for the assured and/or his broker to disclose a circumstance which would find favour with the underwriter because, by so doing, the assured and/or broker would encourage the underwriter, more readily, to accept the risk and possibly at a lower premium rate. This section of the Act allows an assured to defend an apparent breach of good faith, based on non-disclosure, if he can show that the circumstance, whilst material to the risk, has put the risk in a better light from the underwriter`s point of view.

(b) Any circumstance that is known or may be presumed to be known to the underwriter -

The underwriter should know everything which, in the ordinary course of his business, he ought to know. For example, when he is asked to insure a ship of standard construction one would expect a hull underwriter to be experienced in the customary insurance contract used to insure the type of ship offered for insurance and, amongst other things, to have a reasonable knowledge of that type of ship and the usual operation pattern for that type of ship; including a general knowledge of its construction, the customary procedures for operating that type of ship, the hazards to which the ship is likely to be exposed during a normal voyage and the potential liabilities the assured could incur; insofar as these are to be covered by the insurance contract.

Further, the underwriter may be presumed to know matters of common notoriety or knowledge, including:

(1) Matters that are common knowledge in the insurance market in which he operates and/or have been the subject of notices generally circulated or posted on notice boards in his marketplace (eg An active underwriter at Lloyd`s is expected to have regard for notices posted in the "Room");

(2) Matters published in the national newspapers of his country of domicile and/or in Lloyd`s List;

(3) Matters brought to the attention of the general public by the media in his country of domicile (eg Television news, etc.)

(c) Information waived by the underwriter -

Where the underwriter waives information concerning a material circumstance he gives up any rights he might otherwise have, at a later date, to allege a breach of good faith based on non-disclosure of that circumstance.

(d) Information which is superfluous to disclose due to the existence of a warranty in the contract -

Where there is a warranty, express or implied, in a marine insurance contract the assured need not disclose, during negotiations to conclude the contract, any circumstance which would constitute a breach of warranty; the underwriter being protected by the warranty during the currency of the contract. For example, if it is intended that the ship covered by a hull policy will trade in waters that are particularly hazardous this is a material circumstance which, but for the existence of a warranty, must be disclosed during negotiations to conclude the contract. However, such disclosure during negotiations to conclude the contract is not necessary where the insurance contract incorporates an express locality warranty regarding those waters in particular; even where the contract provides for the assured to be held covered in event of breach of the warranty. It should be noted that section 18 of the MIA, 1906, does not absolve the assured from his duty, where a breach of the warranty is held covered, to inform the underwriter when a breach of the warranty occurs. In any case, there is usually an express condition in the policy that breach of a locality warranty shall be advised to the underwriter without delay so that he can, at his option, charge an additional premium and/or change the policy conditions.

5. Representations and Mis-representations *(MIA, 1906, sect. 20)*

When an assured or his broker discloses a circumstance to the underwriter the way in which he does so is termed a representation. The way in which the assured and/or broker makes the representation can influence the judgement of the underwriter in deciding the premium rate or whether or not to accept the risk. Where the disclosure is represented in such a way as to mislead the underwriter this is termed a mis-representation.

Every material representation made by the assured and/or his broker during negotiations to conclude the contract must be true. If it is untrue there is deemed to be a mis-representation and the underwriter may avoid the contract (see part 7, below). The test for materiality of a representation is the same as is applied to a disclosure (see part 2, above). The MIA, 1906, provides that a representation is material if it would influence the judgement of a prudent underwriter in deciding the premium rate or whether or not he will accept the risk; qualifying this with whether or not a representation is material is a question of fact. In modern practice, however, one must have regard for the comments made earlier, in the introductory notes (pages 2 & 3), concerning the changing legal viewpoint on materiality where disclosures are concerned because the outcome of these deliberations will affect representations as well as disclosures.

Where the assured and/or broker makes a representation this may be withdrawn by the assured or broker, as the case may be, before the contract is concluded. In which case the underwriter may not avoid the contract on the grounds of the mis-representation. The Act gives no guidance on circumstances where the assured and/or broker withdraws a representation or corrects a mis-representation *after* the contract has been concluded; although, in practice, one would expect the assured and/or broker to so advise the underwriter and, provided there have been no claims relating to the particular circumstance, for the underwriter to accept the situation as though no mis-representation had been made.

6. Innocent Mis-representations *(MIA, 1906, sect. 20 - sub. 3 to 5)*

The MIA, 1906, provides that a representation can be a matter of fact or a matter of belief. So, if the assured or his broker believes he is making a true representation during negotiations to conclude the contract, and he does so in good faith, the representation is deemed to be true even where facts prove later that it was not true. The onus is on the underwriter to prove materiality and that there was a mis-representation. The onus is on the assured or broker, as the case may be, to prove his innocence in making the mis-representation.

Contrary to the position in some other forms of insurance contract, a representation made in regard to a marine insurance contract is deemed to be true if it is substantially true. That is to say, the difference between what is true and what is not true is not material to the risk as seen by the underwriter. As an example, consider a cargo insurance contract concerning goods which are normally carried in cardboard cartons of export quality; but, before the insurance contract was concluded, the director responsible for packing the goods for transit had made a decision to change the packaging to wooden boxes. The exporter`s insurance department was not advised of the change in procedure and, in answer to an enquiry from the underwriter, told the broker that the goods would be carried in export cartons of cardboard construction. The broker so advised the underwriter when negotiating the contract. Following a fire in a transit warehouse a surveyor was called to examine the goods. He reported that damage to the goods was caused by fire (an insured peril) but, although it made no difference to the cause of loss, he commented that the type of packaging was different from the customary form of packing for these goods. Technically, a mis-representation of a material circumstance had been made during negotiations to conclude the contract but, in this case, the underwriter would *not* be entitled to avoid the contract on the technicality because the difference between the truth and the untruth would not be considered sufficiently material to justify such avoidance.

7. Effect of Breach of Good Faith by the Assured or Broker (MIA, 1906, sect. 18)

Where the assured is guilty of a breach of good faith the underwriter is entitled to "avoid the contract". Where the underwriter avoids the contract *before the risk has attached* he must return the premium, if any, already paid by the assured. No return of premium is allowed where the underwriter avoids the contract *after* the risk has attached; even though the avoidance is effective from inception. Further, irrrespective of whether or not the risk has attached, no return of premium is allowed where fraud in relation to the contract has been proved.

The term "avoid the contract" means that the underwriter can step aside from the contract and treat it as though he never accepted the risk in the first place. In other words the underwriter treats the contract as void and of no effect. Thus, avoidance affects the contract from inception whether it be a contract for a specified voyage or a contract for a period of time; and irrespective of the stage in the contract when the underwriter discovers the breach of good faith and takes action to avoid the contract. The action by the underwriter, no matter how justified, does not make the marine insurance policy invalid in the eyes of the law; the assured may still take legal action to challenge the underwriter`s right to avoid the contract.

In marine insurance practice a breach of good faith is more important than a breach of warranty. In the latter case, the underwriter is discharged from liability as from the date of the breach of warranty but remains liable for all insured losses occurring prior to that date. In contrast, discovery of a breach of good faith, followed by action to avoid the contract, not only absolves the underwriter from liability for losses that occur after he discovers the breach but he is, also, not liable for losses that occurred *before* he discovered the breach of good faith. This is because the actual breach of good faith took place before the contract was accepted by the underwriter.

It follows that, strictly speaking, where claims have been paid under a term contract before he became aware of a breach of good faith the underwriter is entitled to demand refund of those claims. One can imagine the consternation of a broker and the assured if the underwriter exercised this right in regard to a long term contract that had run for many years before the breach of good faith was discovered. In practice, underwriters seldom exercise their right to refund of earlier claims paid on a long term contract. Unless the breach of good faith is of a very serious nature the underwriter is usually content that the contract no longer exists and he does not demand a refund of claims paid earlier under the contract. Nevertheless, brokers should be aware that this concession would be withdrawn in a case where the breach of good faith amounted to fraud. Similarly, an underwriter would undoubtedly exercise his right to avoid a long term contract and to recover claims paid earlier thereunder if he discovered what he considered to be a deliberate attempt at non-disclosure or misrepresentation.

Although it would appear to be unlikely, in principle, an *underwriter* could be guilty of a breach of good faith; in which case the *assured* could avoid the contract. Since, in most cases, it is the assured who has all the information during negotiations to conclude the contract, it is difficult to envisage a circumstance where one could accuse the underwriter of a breach of good faith. Nevertheless, consider, as an example, a situation where the assured asks a broker to conclude a contract to cover a ship for a specific voyage which has already commenced. Unknown to the assured and his broker the ship has already completed the voyage without incident; a fact which is known to the underwriter at the time the proposal is made. The underwriter might be tempted to accept the proposal and to insure the ship, on a "lost or not lost" basis; but, to do so, would constitute a breach of good faith on the part of the underwriter. The assured, on discovering the breach of good faith, could avoid the contract and demand a return of the full premium he paid.

8. Negligence of Broker in Regard to the Principle of Good Faith

In negotiating the contract with the underwriter the broker is acting as agent for the assured. Therefore, a breach of good faith by the broker is deemed to be a breach of good faith by the assured. Even where the assured was not guilty of the breach and had no knowledge that the broker had committed the breach it is still considered a breach of good faith by the assured who must suffer the consequences as in part 7, above. However the assured might have grounds to sue the broker for damages (see below).

Where the assured is guilty of a non-disclosure or a mis-representation in advising his broker he must suffer the consequences of the breach of good faith, if any, when the broker commits the act of non-disclosure or mis-representation, as the case may be, during negotiations to conclude the contract. In such case the assured would be unable to proceed against the broker for damages when the underwriter avoided the contract.

Where the broker fails to disclose to the underwriter, during negotiations to conclude the contract, a material circumstance that had been communicated to him by the assured the underwriter is entitled to avoid the contract on the grounds of non-disclosure, as in part 7 above, and the assured can sue the broker for damages in respect of any claim that was prejudiced by the broker`s negligence. Similarly, where the assured makes a representation to the broker who then mis-represents the facts to the underwriter during negotiations to conclude the contract the assured can sue the broker for damages in respect of any claim prejudiced by the broker`s negligence.

SELF STUDY QUESTIONS

Before moving on to the next section satisfy yourself that you have absorbed the subject matter in the previous Sections. The following questions should be answered without reference to the text:

1. Utmost good faith -
   (a) What is the principle of good faith?
   (b) Why is compliance with this principle so important when negotiating a contract of marine insurance?

2. Material circumstances -
   (a) What is a "material" circumstance?
   (b) When is a circumstance deemed to be *not* material?

3. Disclosures -
   (a) What should the proposer disclose to the underwriter during negotiations to conclude the contract?
   (b) What circumstances need not be disclosed to the underwriter during negotiations to conclude the contract?
   (c) Is a broker obliged to disclose, during negotiations to conclude the contract, a material circumstance which has *not* been advised to him by his principal; but of which he has become aware during the ordinary course of his business?
   (d) Should the assured and/or his broker disclose to the underwriter a material circumstance (of which neither of them was aware and could not have been aware in the ordinary course of their business at the time negotitations were taking place to conclude the contract) which came to their knowledge *after* the underwriter has written the risk?

4. Representations -
   (a) What is a material representation?
   (b) When is a mis-representation excused?
   (c) What is an "innocent" mis-representation?

5. Breach of good faith -
   (a) What remedy is available to the underwriter on discovery of a breach of good faith:
      (i) during negotiations to conclude the contract?
      (ii) during the currency of a short term contract (eg a hull voyage policy)?
      (iii) during the currency of a long term contract (eg a cargo open cover)?
   (b) What remedy is available to the underwriter on discovery of a breach of good faith by a broker in circumstances where the assured was not guilty of the breach?
   (c) Can an underwriter be guilty of a breach of good faith?

(Questionaire continues on Page 10)

6. Broker negligence -

(a) In what circumstances would you consider a broker to be negligent in regard to the principle of good faith?

(b) Is the assured entitled to sue the broker for damages where the underwriter avoided the contract on the grounds of breach of good faith by the broker when the assured had withheld the relevant information from the broker and such information was not available to the broker during the ordinary course of his business?

(c) Is the assured entitled to sue the broker for damages where the underwriter avoided the contract on the grounds of breach of good faith by the broker when the assured had withheld the relevant information from the broker; but the broker should have been aware of the relevant circumstance during the ordinary course of his business?

(d) What is the assured`s position when the underwriter avoids the contract on the grounds of a breach of good faith by the broker (the assured being innocent of the breach) but no claims have attached to the contract?

SECTION EIGHT

MARINE INSURANCE WARRANTIES

1. Introduction
2. Effect of Breach of Warranty by the Assured
3. Express Warranties in Policy Conditions
4. Effect of "Held Covered" Provisions Regarding Breach of Warranty
5. Introduction to Implied Warranties
6. Warranty of Legality
7. Unseaworthiness of Ship
8. Warranty of Seaworthiness - Hull Voyage Policies
9. Unseaworthiness of Insured Ship - Hull Time Policies
10. Warranty of Seaworthiness - Cargo Policies
11. Warranty of Fitness - Cargo Policies
12. Seaworthiness and/or Fitness of Craft to Carry Insured Goods (ICC)
13. Fitness of Containers to Carry Insured Goods (ICC)
14. Fitness of Overland Transport, etc. to Carry Insured Goods (ICC)

SECTION EIGHT

1. Introduction

The many dictionary definitions of the word "warranty" give it a variety of meanings. Samuel Johnson`s dictionary of 1790 gives no less than five different definitions; whilst the current Oxford dictionary is no more helpful. For the purpose of this study of the principles of marine insurance we shall confine our interest to the definition shown in section 33(1) of the Marine Insurance Act, 1906. This defines a marine insurance warranty as:

> "Sect. 33(1) - A warranty, in the following sections relating to warranties, means a promissory warranty, that is to say, a warranty by which the assured undertakes that a particular thing shall be done or shall not be done, or that some condition shall be fulfilled, or whereby he affirms or negatives the existence of a particular state of facts"

Thus, where a warranty is incorporated in a contract of marine insurance , the assured is giving an undertaking to abide by the terms of the warranty. In so doing the assured must comply *literally* with the terms of the warranty (MIA, 1906, sect. 33-3). It is not sufficient for the assured to defend his position by alleging that he complied with the spirit of the warranty. For example, section 39 (sub.1) of the MIA, 1906, requires the assured to warrant that the ship insured by a voyage policy be seaworthy at the commencement of the voyage. Non-compliance with this requirement would constitute a breach of warranty and it would not be an acceptable excuse for the assured to show that he had made every effort to make the ship seaworthy. The purpose of a warranty in a marine insurance contract is to -

(a) protect the underwriter from losses not contemplated by the policy - see "implied" warranties below; or
(b) to improve the risk in the underwriter`s favour; or
(c) to maintain the risk in relation to the premium paid.

2. Effect of Breach of Warranty by the Assured *(MIA, 1906, sect. 33-3)*

Except where the breach of warranty is excused (see below) where the assured fails to comply exactly with the terms of a warranty the underwriter is *discharged from liability* as from the *date* of the breach but remains liable for all insured losses occurring before the date of the breach. Section 33 of the Act is quite clear on this point. No action is required from the underwriter; he is automatically discharged from all liability under the contract as from the date of the breach whether or not he is aware of the breach of warranty. Effectively, this means that an assured who ignored a breach of warranty and continued trading would be uninsured as from, and including, the date of the breach; his only remedy being to advise the underwriter immediately he became aware of the breach, requesting continuance of cover (continuance being at the discretion of the underwriter unless the breach was held covered by a policy condition).

It matters not that the loss had nothing to do with the breach of warranty. To illustrate this consider the position where a ship is insured for a specified voyage. The ship becomes unseaworthy during the voyage and resorts to a port of refuge. The master decides to recommence the voyage without making the ship seaworthy. Such continuance is deemed to be a new stage in the voyage (ref. MIA, 1906, sect. 39 sub.3). The assured is, therefore, in breach of the implied warranty of seaworthiness (MIA, 1906, sect. 39 sub.1). Subsequently, during the continuance of the voyage, another ship runs into the insured vessel; the other vessel being 100% to blame for the collision. Although the accident had nothing to do with the unseaworthiness of the insured ship the underwriter would not be liable for the collision damage thereto because he was discharged from all liability under the policy as from the date the ship sailed from the port of refuge.

Further, it is no defence for the assured to argue that he remedied the breach of warranty before the loss occurred. As an example we shall take the case of a ship insured under a time policy from 1st January to 31st December, both days inclusive. The policy conditions incorporate an express warranty which restricts navigation to within specified geographical limits; breach of this warranty not being held covered by the policy conditions. During June the insured vessel sails beyond the specified limits, without the assured obtaining approval from underwriters, but returns to policy limits without incident. During September, whilst sailing within the policy limits, the ship is damaged by an insured peril. However, no claim would attach to the policy for the damage to the ship because the underwriter had been automatically discharged from all liability under the policy as from the date in June when the ship sailed beyond the policy limits which meant that, at the time of the accident, the ship had been uninsured.

Section 34 of the MIA, 1906, provides that a breach of warranty is excused where:

(a) due to a change in circumstances, the warranty is no longer applicable to the risk; or

(b) the introduction of a subsequent law makes it illegal for the assured to comply with the warranty; or

(c) the underwriter waives the breach of warranty (see notes below regarding "held covered" provisions).

3. Express Warranties in Policy Conditions *(MIA, 1906, sect. 33-2, 34 & 35)*

An express warranty is one which is included in, or written upon, the policy, or is contained in some document incorporated by reference into the policy (MIA, 1906, sect. 35 sub.2).

The warranty may be expressed in any form of words from which the intention to warrant is to be inferred (MIA, 1906, sect.35 sub.1). In practice, it is customary to commence the wording of an express warranty with "Warranted......"; thereby making its nature easily recognisable to practitioners. Until introduction of the MAR form of policy, and the Institute clauses published for use therewith, some confusion was caused by a practice whereby underwriters mis-used the term "warranted" to indicate certain policy exclusion clauses (eg "warranted free of strikes, etc."). Except in markets where the SG form of policy is still used this malpractice has been discontinued.

An express warranty does not exclude the existence of an implied warranty (MIA, 1906, sect. 35 sub.3). For example, where a voyage policy covering a ship incorporates an express warranty requiring the ship to sail by a certain date this does mean that the ship can sail in an unseaworthy condition to comply with the express warranty. On the other hand, section 35 (sub 3) of the MIA, 1906, provides that an express warranty takes precedence over an implied warranty where it is inconsistent with the demands of the implied warranty.

The use of express warranties is common in marine hull insurance practice; particularly in policies covering hull & machinery for a period of time. Examples are the towage warranty in the ITC (1983) and the Institute warranties, the latter incorporating six locality warranties which restrict navigation and one trade warranty which restricts the carriage of Indian coal as cargo. Breach of any of the warranties in the examples is held covered by the "breach of warranty" clause in the ITC (1983). The "disbursements" warranty in the various sets of Institute hull clauses is, also, an express warranty but breach of this warranty is *not* held covered by the Institute hull clauses. No express warranties appear in the ICC (1982) and, although cargo underwriters may sometimes incorporate an express warranty in a cargo insurance contract, they are not so common as in hull insurance practice.

During wartime it is customary for hull war risks underwriters to incorporate a neutrality warranty in any policy covering a peaceful merchant ship. Cargo underwriters incorporate a neutrality warranty in policies covering goods carried by the neutral vessel. In both cases this takes the form of an express warranty whereby the assured undertakes that the ship and/or goods, as the case may be, have nothing to do with the conflict. Section 36 of the MIA, 1906, requires that the insured property shall have a neutral character at the commencement of the voyage and that, so far as the assured can control the matter, this neutral character is preserved during the risk. As is the case with all express warranties, breach of this warranty discharges the relevant underwriter from all liability under the policy as from the date of the breach. Further, there is an implied condition in the hull war risks policy that the ship must carry proper documents to establish her neutrality and, if any loss occurs through breach of this condition the hull underwriter may avoid the contract.

4. Effect of "Held Covered" Provisions Regarding Breach of Warranty

Where express warranties are concerned a breach can often be resolved by immediate advice to the underwriter and payment of an additional premium. This particularly applies where the proposer has been offered a reduced premium in return for giving the undertaking incorporated in the warranty. In some cases the assured is held covered only if he accepts a change in the insurance conditions as well as paying the additional premium.

To illustrate the application of a "held covered" provision let us consider a proposal for a hull & machinery insurance contract for a period of 12 months on full terms. For illustration purposes we shall assume the premium rate to be 4% covering unrestricted navigation worldwide (note - premium rates quoted herein are for illustration purposes only and have no bearing on current market rates). The proposer agrees to give an undertaking, in the form of an express warranty in the policy, that the insured vessel shall not navigate outside limits expressed in the policy and, in return for this undertaking, the underwriter reduces the premium to 3% per annum. If the ship navigates outside the policy limits there would be a breach of warranty and, irrespective of whether or not the assured was aware that the master had broken the warranty, the underwriter would be discharged from all liability under the policy as from the date of the breach. To protect the assured from the effects of a breach of the locality warranty, particularly where the breach was outside his control, the underwriter agrees, subject to compliance of the assured with certain specified conditions, to hold the assured covered in event of such breach; thereby continuing cover under the policy despite the breach of warranty.

It is seldom necessary for a "held covered" provision, relating to breach of warranty, to specify the rate for calculating the amount of additional premium; the words "at an additional premium to be arranged" being sufficient. In practice, the AP rate will reflect the increased exposure to hazard and, where locality warranties are concerned, a scale of AP`s may be agreed by the insurance market for this purpose. For example, the ILU publishes a scale of AP`s and changes in conditions required where breach of an Institute warranty is held covered by hull underwriters in the London market.

In the absence of an agreed AP or an existing AP scale the term "premium to be arranged" is governed by section 31 of the MIA, 1906. This provides that, where no additional premium has been arranged, a *reasonable* additional premium is payable. Section 88 of the Act qualifies this by stating that "what is reasonable is a question of fact".

Underwriters recognise that an assured, who is conscious he will be charged an AP for being held covered in event of breach of a locality warranty, might be tempted to avoid the AP by waiting until the ship returns to the policy limits and only notifying the underwriter about the breach if an accident has taken place whilst the ship is outside the limits imposed by the locality warranty. To discourage this possible malpractice the policy will require the assured to notify the underwriter *immediately* he becomes aware of the breach of warranty; otherwise he is not held covered. It should not be implied from this that the assured is only held covered if he gives *prior* notice of the intention of the ship to break the warranty. If the assured does not learn that the master has sailed the ship outside the policy limits until after the breach has taken place he is still held covered provided he notifies the underwriter immediately he becomes aware of the breach.

5. Introduction to Implied Warranties *(MIA, 1906, sects. 33-2, 37, 38, 39 & 41)*

An "implied" warranty does not appear in the policy document; but its existence as part of a marine insurance contract is established by statute in the form of the MIA, 1906. The assured is required by law to give the undertaking embraced by the warranty; literal compliance with which is required in exactly the same way as for an express warranty. Ignorance of the existence of the warranty is not accepted by a court of law as a defence for non-compliance with an implied warranty.

The excuses for breach of warranty allowed by sect. 34 of the MIA, 1906, (see list in part 2, above) apply both to express warranties and to implied warranties; but it should be noted it is not customary for hull underwriters to waive or hold covered breach of an implied warranty and cargo underwriters waive breach of the warranties of seaworthiness and fitness of the ship only because they replace these warranties with specific policy conditions regarding seaworthiness and fitness of the ship to carry the insured goods.

The MIA, 1906, incorporates the following implied warranties, comments on each of which are contained in the text below:-

Sect. 41 - Warranty of legality

Sect. 39 - Warranty of seaworthiness of ship

Sect. 40 - Warranty that the ship is fit to carry the goods

6. Warranty of Legality *(MIA, 1906, sect. 41)*

The implied warranty of legality is incorporated, by law, in every policy covering a marine adventure. Amongst other things, section 3 of the MIA, 1906, defines a marine adventure as existing "where any ship or goods or other movables are exposed to maritime perils". Where the policy covers a ship for a specific voyage the warranty of legality requires the voyage to be a lawful one when it commences and, so far as the assured can control the matter, the voyage must be carried out in a lawful manner. Where the policy covers a ship for a period of time each adventure on which the ship embarks must be lawful at its commencement and, so far as the assured can control the matter, the adventure must be carried out in a lawful manner.

Where more than one interest is involved in an adventure (eg ship and the cargo carried thereon are owned by different parties) the exposure to marine perils is termed a "common maritime adventure". The implied warranty of legality is incorporated, by law, in the marine insurance policy covering each separate interest in a common maritime adventure. In each case the assured is required to ensure that the adventure, insofar as it affects his interest, is lawful at commencement and, so far as he can control the matter, is carried out in a lawful manner.

Where goods are insured on a "warehouse to warehouse" basis (ie the adventure embraces both land and sea risks) the implied warranty of legality applies throughout the period covered by the policy. The assured is required to ensure that the adventure is lawful when the risk attaches and, so far as the matter is within the assured`s control, it remains lawful until the policy terminates.

Breach of the implied warranty of legality discharges the underwriter from all liability under the policy as from the date of the breach; thereby ensuring that an underwriter does not insure interests involved in an unlawful adventure; even if he unwittingly accepts the insurance contract when it is proposed to him. It is unlikely that a marine underwriter would waive this warranty nor hold the assured covered in event of breach of the warranty of legality.

7. Unseaworthiness

It does not require technical knowledge to appreciate how important it is to hull underwriters that the ship they insure is seaworthy; nor to realise that cargo underwriters are concerned that the ship carrying insured goods be fit to carry such goods. In early marine insurance practice it was customary for the policy to cover both the ship and the goods carried thereon for a specific voyage in a single policy document (the SG form); and the term "the *good* ship....." would appear in the printed policy form. The term "good" implied that the ship was seaworthy for the insured voyage and was fit to carry the insured goods. Later, the implied warranties of seaworthiness and fitness were incorporated in all hull voyage and cargo policies (see comments in note 9, below, concerning hull time policies). This made the term "good ship" in the policy wording superfluous; although it continued to appear in marine insurance policy forms until Lloyd`s SG policy and marine insurance company policy forms based on the SG format were abrogated in 1982 (cargo) and 1983 (hull) with introduction of the MAR form of policy.

Although ship`s are classified and are subject to periodic surveys to ensure their class is maintained, classification relates only to the stuctural condition of the vessel and does not take into account other factors that might affect its seaworthiness when exposed to risk.

The requirements for a seaworthy ship vary depending on the type of vessel. Trainees and practitioners can find detailed information on seaworthiness of ships in "Marine Insurance - Volume 3 - Hull Practice" by Brown (Witherby 1993) but, for the purpose of these introductory notes, the following comments give some guidance to the marine insurance trainee and practitioner:

(1) The ship must be structurally sound in that she is capable of withstanding the ordinary action of wind and waves;

(2) The ship must be be properly trimmed in relation to her ballast and/or cargo load to ensure her stability, with particular regard to her deckload if any, and she must not be overloaded;

(3) The ship must be properly crewed. The master must be competent to handle the ship, the ship's officers must be competent to carry out the duties for which they are employed and the ship must be adequately crewed by seamen capable of carrying out the tasks allocated to them;

(4) The ship must be properly fitted and equipped to carry out the navigational tasks required of her and a cargo carrying ship must be properly equipped for the handling and care of the cargo she is designed to carry. All such equipment must be in proper working order;

(5) The ship must be adequately fuelled and provisioned for the contemplated voyage or, if applicable (see comments in note 8), for the next stage of the voyage;

(6) If the ship navigates in waters where the services of a pilot are required she must have a qualified pilot on board during such navigation.

8. Warranty of Seaworthiness - Hull Voyage Policies *(MIA, 1906, sect. 39)*

The implied warranty of seaworthiness applies only to "voyage" policies; but it applies to both hull insurance contracts and cargo insurance contracts (for comments on seaworthiness and cargo policies see note 10, below). In practice, a hull insurance contract for a voyage may attach "at & from" the place named in the policy or "from" the place named in the policy (see comments in Section 9 of these notes).

Where the insurance attaches "at & from" the place named in the policy the insurance cover commences from the time the underwriter signifies his acceptance of the risk; thereby embracing a period whilst the ship lies in the port at the place named in the policy before commencement of the voyage. In such case, the warranty of seaworthiness requires, whilst the ship is in port, that she shall be reasonably fit to encounter the ordinary perils of the port; but she need not be seaworthy for the perils she will encounter when she puts to sea (eg. a full crew is not required and she need not be fully fuelled or provisioned, etc.) Of course, when the ship commences the insured voyage she must be seaworthy to encounter the ordinary perils of the voyage.

Where the insurance attaches "from" the place named in the policy the insurance cover attaches from the time the ship gets under way to commence the insured voyage. The implied warranty of seaworthiness demands that the ship be seaworthy, when the insurance cover attaches, to meet the ordinary perils the ship would expect to encounter during the voyage.

Except where the voyage is carried out in stages (ie the ship calls at other ports or places during the insured voyage), the warranty of seaworthiness ceases to apply once the ship has commenced the insured voyage. For example, if the shipmaster fell sick during the voyage and an insured accident took place thereafter, the underwriter could not raise the defence, based on the inability of the master to run the ship properly, that the ship was unseaworthy at the time of the accident. As another example, consider the position where the insured vessel, which has been slightly damaged by an uninsured peril during the insured voyage, continues the voyage in her damaged condition. Later, during the continuation of the voyage, the ship suffers damage from an insured peril. Unless the underwriter could prove the ship was unseaworthy at the commencement of the voyage or the appropriate stage of the voyage, as the case may be, he could not raise the defence, based on the damaged condition of the ship at the time of the second loss, that there was a breach of warranty because the ship was unseaworthy from the time of the first accident. Practitioners are advised to examine the policy conditions in the latter circumstance because, although there is no breach of the warranty of seaworthiness, there might be a restriction on the vessel continuing the voyage in a damaged condition.

Where the insured voyage is carried out in stages (during which the ship requires different preparation or equipment for the next stage) the ship must be seaworthy at the commencement of each stage to meet the ordinary perils to be encountered in that stage; otherwise there is a breach of the warranty of seaworthiness.

Breach of the implied warranty of seaworthiness discharges the underwriter from all liability under the policy as from the date of the breach. To illustrate this consider the position of a ship which is insured "at & from" the place named in the policy. She is reasonably fit to meet the ordinary hazards of the port, but when she sails, she is not seaworthy for the contemplated voyage. The underwriter would be liable for insured losses occurring whilst she was in the port at the place named in the policy; but, from the date the ship sailed, all policy cover would terminate automatically and for the remainder of the voyage the ship would be uninsured.

9. Unseaworthiness of Insured ship - Hull Time Policies *(MIA, 1906, sect. 39-5)*

There is **no** implied warranty of seaworthiness in a time policy. Therefore, in a policy which incorporates the ITC (Institute Time Clauses, Hulls) or a similar set of hull time conditions, there is no implied warranty requiring the ship to be seaworthy at any time during the currency of the policy. Nevertheless, section 39, sub.5, of the MIA, 1906, provides that, where, with the privity of the assured, the ship is sent to sea in an unseaworthy condition, the underwriter shall not be liable for any loss *attributable to* unseaworthiness. The following examples illustrate:

(1) A ship, insured by a *voyage* policy, sails in an unseaworthy condition. The underwriter is discharged from *all* liability under the policy as from the date the ship sails, irrespective of the cause of the loss, and the policy lapses.

(2) A ship is insured by a *time* policy. Without the knowledge or consent of the assured the ship is sent to sea in an unseaworthy condition. Subject to the policy conditions (eg the policy deductible), the underwriter remains liable for all insured losses incurred during the voyage irrespective of the unseaworthy condition of the vessel.

(3) A ship is insured by a *time* policy. With the knowledge and consent of the assured the ship is sent to sea in an unseaworthy condition. During the voyage the ship suffers from a loss proximately caused by an insured peril but it is held that the loss

was attributable to the ship's unseaworthiness. The policy continues to remain in force but the underwriter is *not* liable for the loss.

(4) A ship is insured by a *time* policy. With the knowledge and consent of the assured the ship is sent to sea in an unseaworthy condition. During the voyage the ship suffers from a loss proximately caused by an insured peril. It is held that the unseaworthy state of the ship did *not* contribute towards the loss. The policy continues to remain in force and, subject to the policy conditions (eg the policy deductible), the underwriter is liable for the loss despite the unseaworthy condition of the ship.

10. Warranty of Seaworthiness - Cargo Policies *(MIA, 1906, sect. 39)*

Unless the policy conditions provide otherwise, the implied warranty of seaworthiness, as outlined above in note 8, applies equally to the overseas vessel which is to carry the goods insured by a cargo policy. This was practical in the days when merchants carried goods in their own vessels but, as shipping practice developed, it became clear that few cargo shippers could control the seaworthiness of the ships that were to carry their goods. Accordingly, it has become the practice for cargo underwriters to waive breach of the warranty of seaworthiness except in cases where the assured or their servants are privy to such unseaworthiness.

To protect their interests, however, cargo underwriters insuring goods by open cover usually incorporate a "classification" clause in the contract which allows them to charge an AP for goods which are carried by ships of a lower standard than is outlined in the clause. But this does not entirely protect them from circumstances where the assured, perhaps for expediency or to obtain lower freight rates, is prepared to pay the AP and choose to ship their goods on, say, a doubtful vessel. Accordingly, the standard cargo clauses incorporate a condition which provides that the underwriter shall not be liable for any loss, damage or expense arising from unseaworthiness of the overseas vessel, where the assured or their servants are privy to the unseaworthiness of the vessel at the time the cargo is loaded therein.

11. Warranty of Fitness - Cargo Policies *(MIA, 1906, sect. 40)*

In a cargo policy there is an implied warranty that the overseas vessel carrying the goods, shall, at the commencement of the voyage, be not only seaworthy but also reasonably fit to carry the insured goods to their destination.. That is to say the holds and other storage spaces in the ship shall be fit to carry the goods safely. It is unlikely that the cargo assured will have any control over the fitness of the ship to carry his goods so it has become the practice for cargo underwriters to waive breach of this warranty; except where the assured or their servants are privy to the unfitness of the vessel at the time the goods are loaded therein.

Following the current practice regarding unseaworthiness, the standard cargo clauses exclude loss, damage or expense arising from unfitness of the overseas vessel to carry the goods where the assured or their servants are privy to such unfitness at the time the goods are loaded into the vessel.

Whilst we are on the subject of seaworthiness and fitness regarding goods in transit it should be noted that there is no implied warranty or condition in the MIA, 1906, requiring insured goods to be seaworthy or fit for carriage overseas. In practice, cargo underwriter recognise their vulnerability in this respect and the standard cargo clauses incorporate an exclusion whereby underwriters shall not be liable for loss, damage or expense caused by insufficiency or unsuitability of packing (practitioners seeking more information regarding this clause are advised to consult "Marine Insurance - Volume Two - Cargo Practice" by Brown (Witherby 1985).

12. Seaworthiness and/or Fitness of Craft to Carry Insured Goods (ICC)

Although the MIA, 1906, recognises that craft may be used to transfer goods between ship and shore it does not mention seaworthiness in connection with these craft. The implied warranties of seaworthiness and fitness incorporated in the Act relate solely to the overseas vessel. For many years cargo underwriters admitted seaworthiness of the overseas vessel but made no mention in the ICC (Institute Cargo Clauses) regarding seaworthiness of craft or the fitness of such craft to carry the insured goods.

When the ICC were revised and re-published, in 1982, for use with the MAR form of policy an exclusion was incorporated therein whereby underwriters are not liable for any loss, damage or expense arising from unseaworthiness of craft or unfitness of craft to carry the goods safely. But this exclusion applies only where the assured or their servants were privy to such unseaworthiness or unfitness at the time the goods were loaded into the craft. Thus, the exclusion would not apply to circumstances where the assured handed over the goods to a freight forwarder for transit or to the carrier or port authority for handling and they were loaded into a craft the condition of which the assured or their servants had no knowledge.

13. Fitness of Containers to Carry Insured Goods (ICC)

Insurance experience since the introduction of containerisation has shown that the advantages of this type of carriage are often offset by losses arising from the poor condition of container boxes. For details trainees and practitioners are advised to consult "Marine Insurance - Volume Two - Cargo Practice" by Brown (Witherby 1985); but the following comments might be useful in a study of these introductory notes.

In addition to considering containers as a form of carriage cargo underwriters look upon stowage in containers as a form of packing and have regard for both these aspects in the ICC (1982).

The standard cargo insurance conditions exclude loss, damage or expense arising from unfitness of the container to carry the insured goods safely to their destination; but this exclusion applies only where the assured or their servants are privy to the unfitness of the container at the time the insured goods are loaded therein. Thus, the exclusion would not apply where a container operator, appointed by the assured as a forwarding agent, collects the goods from the assured or has them delivered to the container depot by the assured and the loading of the goods into the container is carried out solely by the forwarding agent or his servants in the absence of the assured or their servants.

The "insufficiency or unsuitability of packing" exclusion expressed in the standard ICC (1982) and referred to in note 11, above, embraces stowage of the insured goods in containers. If the stowage is carried out *prior to* attachment of the insurance policy or by the assured or their servants the policy excludes all loss, damage or expense caused by improper stowage in the container. If the stowage is carried out *after* attachment of the insurance policy and by persons other than the assured or their servants (eg a container operator acting for the assured as a freight forwarder) the exclusion does not apply.

The above comments apply to "lift vans" as well as to "containers". One seldom sees lift vans used in modern commercial transit. This type of container was used long before the modern "square box" design of container became commonplace. The lift van was designed to be carried on a rail flat and had a curved roof to provide maximum cargo space but with freedom to pass safely under railway bridge arches. This form of container fell out of favour because its design did not allow for the stacking of boxes upon each other.

14. Fitness of Overland Transport etc. to Carry Insured Goods (ICC)

The MIA, 1906, imposes no implied warranty regarding the fitness of any form of carriage other than that of the overseas vessel. As is the case with craft used to carry goods between ship and shore (see note 12, above) it is left to cargo underwriters to incorporate conditions in the policy to protect themselves from losses caused by unfitness of other forms of conveayance.

In considering this one must take into account all forms of conveyance used to carry the goods -

(a) from the place named in the policy for the commencement of risk to the place where the goods will be loaded onto the overseas vessel or craft; and

(b) from the place where the goods are discharged from the overseas vessel or craft to the final destination named in the policy for termination of the insurance cover.

This would include, where applicable, land transport within the port area (eg. van carriers, transtainers, fork lift trucks, etc.), rail transport, transport by road and, where incidental to a sea voyage, transport by air. In practice all these forms of transport are embraced within the generic term "conveyances".

The ICC (1982) incorporate an exclusion clause whereby the underwriter is not liable for loss, damage or expense arising from unfitness of a conveyance to carry the insured goods safely. But the exclusion applies only where the assured or their servants are privy to the unfiness of the conveyance at the time the goods are loaded therein.

SEE FOLLOWING PAGE FOR SELF STUDY QUESTIONAIRE

SELF STUDY QUESTIONS

Before moving on to the next Section satisfy yourself that you have absorbed the subject matter of the previous Section. The following questions should be answered without reference to the text.

1. Define the purpose and nature of a marine insurance warranty.

2. What is the difference between an express warranty and an implied warranty?

3. What is the effect of a breach of warranty on a marine insurance policy, where the breach of warranty is not held covered by the terms of the contract? How does this differ from the effect of a breach of good faith?

4. Subject to what conditions does a hull underwriter hold the assured covered in case of breach of a locality warranty?

5. The implied warranty of seaworthiness applies only to voyage policies. To what extent does unseaworthiness of the insured vessel affect claims in a hull time policy?

6. Breach of the implied warranty of seaworthiness is usually waived by cargo underwriters. How do cargo underwriters protect themselves, in practice, from loss, damage or expense where any of these arises from unseaworthiness of the carrying ship or craft?

7. The implied warranty of fitness applies only to cargo policies and relates solely to the fitness of the overseas carrying vessel. What condition is it customary for cargo underwriters to incorporate in the policy to protect themselves from loss, damage or expense arising from unfitness of conveyances?

8. Does the MIA, 1906, impose an implied warranty on a hull & machinery policy regarding the class or flag of the insured vessel?

9. For what purpose is the implied warranty of legality incorporated in a marine insurance policy?

10. In what circumstances is a breach of warranty excused?

SECTION NINE

DURATION OF COVER

SECTION NINE

1. Introduction

Determination of duration of cover in a marine insurance policy is very important because the policy covers only losses relating to accidents that occur within the duration of cover. In the first instance it is the proposer who establishes the duration of cover, at least in outline, when he offers the contract to the insurer. For voyage policies, whether they be in respect of hull insurance or cargo insurance, the proposer will specify the places for commencement and termination of the voyage (hull) or the transit (cargo). The agreed insurance contract will be based on this declaration; but will be, depending on the type of contract, subject to restrictions imposed by the MIA, 1906, by market understandings and by the policy conditions, as the case may be. For time policies the proposer will specify the date and time for commencement of the contract which will be, provided he has an insurable interest in the subject matter insured at that time, the date and time for attachment of cover. Termination of the contract in a time policy will be determined by the period of time for which the proposer offers the contract and to the extent the insurer is prepared to accept.

Early forms of marine insurance cover were always on a "voyage" basis and, over the years, many of these policies have been the subject of litigation which has created legal precedents concerning duration of cover for voyage policies. These precedents are codified in the MIA, 1906, and except where they are varied by policy conditions will still apply to all voyage policies, whether they relate to hull or cargo insurance. The following notes in this Section will incorporate comments on the relevant sections of the MIA, 1906, and the effect of these sections of the Act on current marine insurance policies.

One sees few hull & machinery policies effected on a voyage basis but they still exist in modern practice so the trainee and practitioner should not treat lightly the comments herein regarding such policies. It should always be remembered that errors in practice are more likely to arise when the practitioner is unfamiliar with the contract in hand because he seldom deals with that form of contract.

Practically all cargo insurance contracts are effected on a voyage basis. The fact that long term binding authorities or open covers for a periods of time are the instruments for declaring attachments to the contract makes no difference. Each declaration, and insurance certificate relating thereto, is issued on a voyage basis (warehouse to warehouse) so the contract embodied in each certificate is subject to current law and practice regarding duration of cover for a voyage policy.

Most insurance contracts effected to cover ships and shipowners` interests are effected on a "time" basis. Until 1959, when marine policy stamp duty laws were changed in the UK, the issue of marine insurance policies for periods exceeding 12 months was prohibited by the MIA, 1906; the Act declaring such policies as void in law. Today, there is no legal restriction on the period for which a marine insurance time policy can be effected but it continues to be the practice for hull underwriters to write time policies for periods not exceeding 12 months. There are many reasons for their reticence to write hull insurance contracts for a longer term but, since it is not the practice to incorporate an underwriter`s cancellation clause in a hull time policy (except where war & strikes risks are concerned), the desire to review the policy experience annually with the right not to renew the policy or to increase the premium rate if the experience has been unsatisfactory is probably the most dominant.

The MIA, 1906, has little to say on duration of cover in a time policy; but it is customary for hull underwriters to incorporate conditions in the contract whereby they can terminate the cover when a major change in exposure occurs (eg the management of the ship changes).

This introductory study is not intended for a detailed examination of the practice of marine insurance. Practitioners and trainees seeking information on duration of cover at a more advanced level are advised to consult, as applicable, the current editions of "Marine Insurance - Volume Two - Cargo Practice" and "Marine Insurance - Volume Three - Hull Practice" both by Brown (Witherby, London).

2. Attachment of Cover - Hull Voyage Policies *(MIA, 1906, sect. 42-1)*

Section 42, sub.1, of the MIA, 1906, provides that a voyage policy may commence "at & from" or "from" a particular place; the latter being the place specified in the policy for the commencement of the insured voyage.

The SG form of policy (now abrogated in the London market) was designed to cover the insured vessel for a specific voyage. The point at which cover for the insured ship should attach was printed in the policy form as "at & from". No attempt was made to qualify this in the standard hull voyage clauses so it remained the basis for attachment of cover throughout the three hundred years or more that the SG form of policy was in use in the London market. Both Lloyd`s SG policy and the insurance company hull policy based on the SG format specified that the cover commenced "at & from" the place named in the policy. So it was not necessary to specify the term in the broker`s placing slip.

The scope of the term "at & from" is defined in the Rules for Construction of the Policy which appear in the First Schedule to the MIA, 1906. Rule 3 provides as follows -

(a) Where the ship is lying in good safety at the place named in the policy for the commencement of the voyage the risk shall attach immediately the underwriter concludes the contract with the proposer (ie when he signifies his acceptance on the placing slip). This means that the ship is insured whilst she is lying in the port awaiting commencement of the voyage; including during loading of cargo, etc. In theory, there is no time limit to the period of cover in port; but where there is unreasonable delay in commencing the voyage the underwriter is entitled to avoid the contract (see Note 4, below);

(b) Where, at the time the contract is concluded, the ship has not arrived at the place named in the policy for commencement of the voyage cover does not attach until she arrives at such place in good safety. Cover attaches on arrival irrespective of the existence of an earlier voyage policy that continues to cover the ship for a period of time after she has arrived at said place. Should the cover provided by two separate voyage policies overlap in this way the underwriters subscribing each policy will be liable, by way of contribution, to settle any loss that is covered by both policies. If the loss has been settled on one policy the underwriters subscribing that policy are entitled to exercise their rights of contribution (MIA, 1906, sect. 80) to recover part of the claim from the underwriters subscribing the other policy. Once it has attached cover continues as in (a) above.

There is nothing specified in the IVC (Institute Voyage Clauses, Hulls), 1983, to indicate when the policy cover attaches; nor is there any such indication in the MAR form of policy. This makes it imperative for the broker to expressly state in his placing slip that the voyage shall commence "at & from ....". In the absence of this term in the broker`s slip it would not be embodied in the marine insurance policy and there would be no legal obligation on the underwriter to settle claims for accidents occurring before the insured ship sailed from the place named in the policy for the commencement of the voyage.

Where the broker expressly states in his placing slip that the voyage shall start "from" the place named for the commencement of the voyage this would be embodied in the policy. Rule 2 of the Rules for Construction of the Policy (MIA, 1906, First schedule) provides that, in such case, the risk does not attach until the ship starts on the voyage; that is to say when she raises her anchor or leaves her berth to commence the voyage.

Where the contract is embodied in the MAR form of policy and the broker makes no expression in his placing slip regarding attachment of risk, merely indicating the name of the place for commencement of the voyage, there will be no indication in the policy to show when the underwriter comes on risk. There is no implied condition in law or practice that the term "at & from" shall apply, so one must assume, in these circumstances, that the risk will be deemed to have commenced "from" the named place.

3. Different Voyage *(MIA, 1906, sects. 43 and 44)*

A voyage policy covers only the voyage specified therein. If the ship departs from a place other than that specified in the policy or sails for a destination other than that specified in the policy there is said to be a "different" voyage. In case of a different voyage the insurance cover does not attach and the assured is entitled to a return of the premium paid for the risk. This legal point has always been important where the insurance of ships is concerned because the standard hull voyage clauses have never held the assured covered in case of mistakes in specifying the voyage in the placing slip and/or policy.

Until the SG policy was abrogated in the London market, and the cargo clauses published by the ILU for use therewith were withdrawn, it was the practice for cargo underwriters to hold the assured covered in event of any error in description of the interest, vessel or voyage. Effectively, therefore the provisions of the MIA, 1906, in this respect did not apply to cargo policies. When the new cargo clauses were published by the ILU for use with the MAR form of policy this concession no longer appeared in the cargo clauses. So, today, both proposer and broker should be careful to ensure that information offered in this respect is accurate and that the broker`s slip correctly shows the insured voyage.

4. Delay in Commencement of Voyage *(MIA, 1906, sect. 42)*

Where a ship is insured "at & from" the place specified in the policy for the commencement of the voyage she is covered whilst at said place before she sails (see Note 2, above). However, there is an implied condition in the policy (MIA, 1906, sect. 42 sub.1) to the effect that the assured must not delay commencement of the voyage unreasonably; otherwise the underwriter can avoid the contract. In which case the ship will not be covered at all.

Where a ship is insured "from" the place specified in the policy for the commencement of the voyage she is not covered for risks which occur before she sails. Nevertheless, the implied condition in the MIA, 1906, regarding delay in commencing the voyage still applies. In practice, the underwriter might incorporate a "sailing date" warranty in the contract which specifies the date by which the voyage must commence. However, even in the absence of this warranty in the policy, the implied condition in the MIA, 1906, requires the ship to commence the voyage wthout unreasonable delay; otherwise the underwriter is entitled to avoid the contract.

Section 42 sub. 2 of the MIA, 1906, provides that the implied condition regarding delay in commencing the voyage is negatived if the assured can show that the underwriter was aware of the circumstances causing the delay when he wrote the risk. As an example, consider the position where the underwriter writes an insurance contract to cover a ship for a voyage. The contract is based on the IVC (1983) and, at the time he writes the risk, the underwriter is fully aware of the fact that the ship is strike bound in the port from which the insured voyage is to commence. Although he knows the ship cannot sail until the labour dispute has been resolved he writes the risk on an "at & from" basis. If an insured loss occurred between the time he wrote the risk and the time the ship sailed he could not avoid the contract on the grounds of unreasonable delay in commencement of the voyage and would be liable for the loss. This would apply even if the delay were to be caused by an uninsured peril as in the example; the IVC; 1983, incorporating a strikes exclusion clause.

5. Delay in Prosecution of the Voyage *(MIA, 1906, sect.* 48)

Except where a policy condition provides otherwise there is no time limit for prosecution of the voyage. The IVC (1983) do not specify any time limit for prosecution of the voyage and it is not customary for a time limit to be added to the policy. Nevertheless, the hull underwriter does not want the insured vessel to be exposed to risk any longer than is absolutely necessary and he expects the voyage to be prosecuted without unreasonable delay. The underwriter is supported in this by Section 48 of the MIA, 1906, which states that the adventure must be prosecuted throughout its course with reasonable dispatch; otherwise the underwriter is discharged from liability as from the time the delay becomes unreasonable.

Observe the difference between the effect of a breach of warranty and the effect of delay in prosecution of the voyage. A breach of warranty discharges the underwriter from liability as from the *date* of the breach; whereas unreasonable delay in prosecution of the voyage discharges the underwriter from liability as from the *time* the delay becomes unreasonable.

An example of delay in prosecution of the voyage occurred in a case where the ship, having discharged cargo at a port of call, remained in the port for a further ten days to await arrival of another cargo. The ship was insured by a voyage policy and, when a loss occurred during a later stage of the insured voyage, the underwriter was able to deny liability for the loss on the grounds that he was discharged from all liability under the policy as from the time the delay awaiting cargo became unreasonable.

It is recognised that neither the master nor the shipowner can guarantee that there will be no delays in the prosecution of the voyage. The ship is expected to call at ports en route for various reasons and to proceed only at a reasonable speed when at sea. Over the years various reasonable excuses for delay in prosecution of the voyage have been allowed by the courts of England. These are codified in Section 49 of the MIA, 1906. The following list summarises the excuses allowed by the MIA, 1906. Except in the case of (a) each excuse relies on the delay being for a reasonable purpose:

(a) Where authorised by any special term in the policy (see comments below on practice regarding hull and cargo policies);

(b) Delay beyond the control of the master and his employer (eg where caused by adverse weather conditions);

(c) To comply with a warranty (eg delay in port to make the ship seaworthy for the next stage of the voyage);

(d) For the safety of the ship and/or cargo (eg sailing from an intermediate port delayed until the weather improves);

(e) To save human life (eg delay to save someone who has fallen overboard);

(f) To go to the aid of a ship in distress where human life may be in danger (Note - this does not include delay to salvage the ship once the lives at risk have been saved);

(g) To obtain medical or surgical aid for a person on board the insured ship (Note - this does not embrace a situation where the insured ship delays to tender medical or surgical aid to a person not on board the insured vessel; although one hopes the underwriter would be sympathetic in such circumstances);

(h) Where caused by barratry, but only where barratry is covered by the policy (Note- Hull war and strikes clauses do not incorporate the peril "barratry"; nor do cargo clauses other than those covering "all risks")

Regarding (a) in the above list of excuses it is important to note that the IVC (1983) and other sets of voyage hull clauses do *not hold the assured covered* in event of delay in prosecution of the voyage. On the other hand, cargo underwriters, in the current standard cargo clauses (ICC, 1982), agree to continue cover in event of delay at any time during the adventure; provided the delay is beyond control of the assured. Thus, in practice, if delay in prosecution of the voyage occurs and it is not subject to any of the excuses listed above, the underwriter is discharged from liability as from the time the delay becomes unreasonable. This applies to hull voyage policies and to cargo policies; except, in the case of the latter, where the delay is beyond control of the cargo assured.

6. Change of Voyage *(MIA, 1906, sect.45)*

This applies only to hull voyage policies and, indirectly, to cargo policies. Where the destination of the ship is voluntarily changed after the ship has commenced the insured voyage there is said to be a change of voyage. The term is not applied to circumstances where, following an accident, there is no choice but to terminate the voyage short of destination. Nevertheless, it would apply where the shipowner or manager voluntarily terminates the contract of carriage at an intermediate port (eg due to non-payment of an outstanding freight account), discharges the cargo and abandons the voyage.

When a change of voyage occurs the underwriter is discharged from liability under the policy as from the time the decision to change the destination is manifested. As an example, consider the position of a charterer who hires a tanker to carry a cargo of oil from Kuwait to Hamburg. He insures the ship for the single voyage at & from Kuwait to Hamburg. During the voyage the charterer sells the oil to a buyer who wants it discharged at Liverpool. The assured gives instructions to the master to change the destination when the vessel is off Lisbon. In the absence of any agreement to hold change of voyage covered the underwriter would be discharged from liability as soon as the instruction is given to the master to change the ship`s destination. The ship would continue the voyage uninsured and no losses would be recoverable under the policy after the instruction to change the destination had been given; even though the loss might occur before the ship actually changes course.

In practice, the IVC (1983) hold the assured covered in event of change of voyage but only when the assured notifies underwriters as soon as he is aware of the change. This means that an assured who instructs the master to change the ship`s destination must also advise the underwriter of the change. Under the conditions in the IVC (1983) the assured must be prepared to pay an AP and to accept a change in conditions if the underwriter considers the additional exposure to risk justifies these.

The provisions of section 45 of the MIA, 1906, are not aimed at cargo policies; this section of the Act being intended to relate to hull voyage policies. Nevertheless, the provisions of the Act would apply to a cargo policy where (as in our example above) the ship operator also owned the cargo. Bearing this in mind the ICC (1982) hold the cargo assured covered in event of change of voyage; but take into account the possibility that a change in destination (under warehouse to warehouse conditions) might be construed in law as a change of voyage and hold change of destination covered as well. The held covered provision in the cargo policy is subject to the same conditions as in a hull voyage policy; requiring prompt notice, payment of an AP and change in conditions if required by the underwriter.

These notes do not extend to embrace detailed practice; but trainees and practitioners should note that cargo underwriters also terminate the contract if they are not advised when the contract of carriage is terminated short of destination. The cargo cover also terminates if the destination expressed in the policy or certificate is changed after discharge of the goods from the overseas vessel. Interested trainees and practitioners can find detail in this respect in the ICC (1982) A, B & C conditions.

7. Deviation *(MIA, 1906, sect.46)*

When insured by a voyage policy the ship, except where agreed otherwise with the underwriter, must proceed by the most direct route to the destination expressed in the policy. She may call at ports and places en route but, unless agreed otherwise with the underwriter, she must proceed to such ports or places in geographical order. Otherwise, there is deemed to be a "deviation".

The term "deviation" can be defined as applying where the ship leaves her customary or stated course with the intention of returning to that course and completing the voyage. If it is intended that the ship shall not return to her original course there is a "change of voyage" (see above) rather than a deviation.

In the absence of any lawful excuse for the deviation the underwriter is discharged from liability as from the *time* the ship changes course to deviate. Unlike change of voyage, the intention to deviate is not material (MIA, 1906, sect. 46 sub.3). Thus, if the master intends to deviate, and even so instructs the helmsman, but changes his mind before the ship changes course there is no deviation. Once the ship deviates the underwriter is off risk and this situation pertains even when the ship, without incident, regains her original course and continues on the planned voyage.

The lawful excuses for deviation are the same as those for delay in prosecution of the voyage. These appear in section 49 of the MIA, 1906, and are summarised in note 5, above. In practice, although hull underwriters do not hold the assured covered for delay in prosecution of the voyage, they do hold the assured covered in event of deviation in the same way, and subject to the same conditions, as they hold the assured covered for change of voyage. Cargo underwriters assume that deviation by the carrying vessel is beyond the assured`s control and over-ride the provisions of section 46 of the MIA, 1906, by expressly continuing the cargo insurance during deviation, without qualification.

8. Termination of Cover - Hull Voyage Policy

The MIA, 1906, does not comment on termination of cover in a hull voyage policy. The only indication in this respect appears in the sample copy of Lloyd`s SG policy form which appears in the First Schedule to the Act. This provides that the voyage terminates when the ship has "moored at anchor twenty four hours in good safety" after she has arrived at the place named in the policy as the destination for the insured voyage. Thus, there was no doubt about the time the cover terminated when the insurance was placed 100% at Lloyd`s. Unfortunately, from the broker`s point of view, whilst it tended to follow the format of the Lloyd`s SG form in most respects, the hull policy issued by insurance companies (eg the ILU hull policy form) differed in regard to termination of cover. The latter omitted the extension of 24 hours after arrival. This meant that, when the broker placed the risk with both Lloyd`s market and the insurance company market, he needed to specify "and 24 hours after arrival" in the placing slip. Otherwise, cover under the insurance company policy would terminate before the cover under the Lloyd`s policy terminated and the assured could only recover for part of any loss that occurred during the 24 hours after the ship had arrived.

It is even more important in current practice that the broker remembers to insert "and 24 hrs a.a." (24 hours after arrival) in his placing slip because the MAR policy form contains no printed conditions regarding attachment and termination of cover and there is no indication thereof in the IVC (1983).

9. Attachment and Termination of Cover - Hull Time Policies

In today`s practice, ships are usually insured on a "time" basis rather than for single voyages. The MIA, 1906, is an Act to codify the law relating to marine insurance as at 21 December, 1906. Insofar as it related to hull insurance the Act codified law in respect of voyage policies so it has little to say regarding time policies. However, it is clear that the Act recognised the existence of time policies because section 25, sub.1, defines a "time policy" as being one which relates to a contract for a definite period of time. Section 25 sub.2 refers to section eleven of the Finance Act, 1901, and states that a time policy made for a period exceeding 12 months is invalid. This section of the MIA, 1906, supported the UK stamp duty laws and ensured that the full policy stamp duty was paid every 12 months as the time policy was renewed. On 1 August, 1959, marine insurance stamp duty based on time was replaced with a single head charge of 6d per policy. Section 25 sub.2 of the MIA, 1906, was repealed by the 8th schedule of the Finance Act, 1959 and, from that date, hull insurers were not required to issue a separate policy each year for every ship they insured.

Although it is no longer necessary for hull underwriters to restrict a time policy to a period of 12 months it is market practice to continue this restriction, in principle. By so doing the underwriter ensures that the broker re-approaches him to renew the policy annually. Most hull time policies written in the London market are based on the ITC (1983). This is a comprehensive set of conditions but it contains no underwriter`s cancellation clause; so, once the risk attaches it would continue indefinitely if the policy were not restricted to a definite period of time. Therefore, annual renewal, in addition to affording the underwriter an opportunity to review the cover, allows him to consider whether or not he wishes to renew the contract. It also gives the underwriter the chance to consider whether or not the renewal should be subject to an adjustment in the annual premium rate and/or an amendment of the policy conditions.

Until recently each renewal policy prepared in the London market was a replica of the expiring policy; incorporating, of course, any changes agreed between the assured and the underwriter. However, modern streamlining in the London market has introduced a procedure whereby, renewal of a MAR form of policy can be evidenced by a simplified document, termed a MAREN form. For more detail concerning this form of policy one should refer to the comments on policies in Section 5.

The definite period of time to be covered by a hull time policy should be established at the outset by a clear entry in the broker`s slip. There should be no doubt in interpreting this entry. It should show the *time* as well as the *date* the cover is to attach and terminate; taking into account time zones in different countries and leaving no room for ambiguity. The ITC (1983) make no provision for entering the agreed time and dates for attachment and termination of cover so this detail will appear in the policy schedule.

Provided the "termination" clause in the ITC, 1983 (see comments below) does not come into effect, once the risk has attached, cover continues until the date of expiry. The restrictions outlined above, regarding a voyage policy (eg different voyage, delay in commencement of voyage, change of voyage, deviation and delay in prosecution of voyage , etc.) do not apply when the ship is insured by a time policy; the ship being covered at all times whether she be in port or at sea.

Since the time policy expires automatically at the time and date of natural expiry, it must be appreciated that this could leave the ship uninsured in the middle of a voyage unless measures are taken to renew the contract before the policy expires. It is not the practice for hull underwriters to hold covered renewal where they have not been approached by the broker to consider the renewal; so no provision is made in the policy conditions to protect an assured or a negligent broker who forgets to renew his policy before the natural expiry time and date. There is no legal obligation on the broker to remind his client that his policy renewal date is imminent but a code of practice for Lloyd`s brokers requires the broker to remind his client in good time before the policy is due for renewal.

In practice, a broker can find life difficult if too many renewals come up around the same time. This might tempt him to make an early approach to the underwriter. When considering the renewal of a hull time policy the underwriter will want to examine the claims experience during the year so he will be unlikely to consider a very early renewal when insuffient claims data is available for him to make a proper judgement. However, where a broker has not received instructions from his client and the renewal date is imminent, the underwriter might be prepared to hold covered the renewal pending receipt by the broker of instructions from his client. Nevertheless, it should be noted that such h/c agreement is valid, in the London market, for no more than 14 days.

An assured who does not want to renew his hull time policy might find himself in a difficult situation if his ship is likely to be at sea or in a port of distress or call at the time the policy is due to expire. He does not want to renew the policy and pay a full annual premium but he wants the ship covered until she reaches her planned destination. To provide for such a situation it is customary for a hull time policy to incorporate a "continuation" clause. Practitioners should remember that this clause does not automatically come into effect. It applies only when the assured has physically invoked it. To invoke the continuation clause the assured and his broker must so advise the underwriter *before* the policy expires. Provided this notice is given the assured is held covered, subject to payment of an AP, until the ship reaches her planned destination.

Although the ITC (1983) do not incorporate an underwriter's cancellation clause, they incorporate a clause which automatically terminates the policy if the ship is sold or changes management during the policy period. To avoid termination, due to change of ownership or management, the assured must obtain written approval of the transfer or change, as the case may be, from the underwriter before the transfer of title or change of management takes place; and must comply with the requirements of the policy regarding assignment. Under the ITC (1983) the policy also terminates automatically if, without the underwriter's approval, the insured vessel is hired out under a bareboat charter or there is any change in the ship's flag or any change in the ship's classification or the ship is requisitioned. These introductory notes do not embrace detail concerning the "termination" clause; so trainees and practitioners seeking further detail in this respect are advised to consult "Marine Insurance - Volume three - Hull Practice" by Brown (Witherby 1993).

10. Warehouse to Warehouse Cover - Cargo Policies

In the early days of marine insurance practice goods in transit by sea were seldom insured as a separate item from the ship. Ships tended to be owned by merchant adventurers who carried their own trade goods and, since underwriters would only insure the ship for a specific voyage, it was customary for the ship insurer to cover both ship and cargo for the specified voyage by a single SG form of policy. The SG policy insured the ship (as in notes 2 to 8, above) at & from the place named in the policy for commencement of the specified voyage; but cover for the insured goods did not attach until they were loaded onto the overseas vessel. Subject to the conditions on which comment is made in notes 3 to 7, above, regarding different voyage, delay in commencement and prosecution of the voyage, change of voyage and deviation, cover for the goods continued until they were safely landed at the destination named in the policy. The SG policy imposed no time limit so, unless the underwriter specified otherwise when concluding the contract, cover for the cargo would continue whilst the goods remained on board the ship (although, under a Lloyd's policy, the ship would cease to be insured 24 hours after arrival) and, where applicable, would embrace the time the goods were in craft, after being discharged from the overseas vessel, until they were safely landed ashore.

Experience proved that the SG policy provisions regarding cargo cover were far from satisfactory. Apart from the uninsured land risks, there was obviously a need for cargo insurance to embrace goods whilst they were in craft for the purpose of transfer from shore to ship and during loading onto the overseas vessel. So it was not long before this extension in cargo cover became commonplace; with some exceptions regarding cover for war risks (see note 11, below).

As the cargo insurance market developed to become a separate entity from the hull insurance market cargo underwriters continued to effect contracts based on the SG form of policy. Proposers and brokers, conscious of the limitations of the cargo cover in the SG form of policy, sought to extend the period of cover at both ends of the sea voyage to embrace overland transit. This was, later, to become known as "warehouse to warehouse" cover. Early cargo underwriters resisted these proposals, probably because they considered the risk to goods during land transit was much greater than during sea transit. Had "all risks" cover been available in those early days their resistance might have been stronger; but cover in the SG form of policy was very limited and related primarily to perils of the seas. So, gradually, individual cargo underwriters agreed to introduce warehouse to warehouse cover; only losses proximately caused (see notes in Section 10) by the perils expressed in the SG form of policy being covered. Although introduction of a London market wording extending the policy perils to embrace "all risks", during the 19th century, might have prejudiced cover for land risks (note - "handling" damage, a peril not covered by the SG form of policy, was and still is more prevalent during land transit and would be covered by the term "all risks") cover on a warehouse to warehouse basis soon became the norm for all cargo policies.

It is not intended, in these introductory notes, to examine the development of warehouse to warehouse cover in detail but, since it is the practice for all marine policies issued today to cover goods in transit by sea to be based on the "warehouse to warehouse" form of cover, brief comment on duration of "warehouse to warehouse" cover in a modern policy would be appropriate. Before so doing, however, it should be noted that, in practice, the term "warehouse" in this respect might be applied to other places of storage (eg on shore storage tanks for oil, freezing works and cold stores for frozen products, etc.).

Unlike the SG form of policy, the MAR policy form does not specify the perils covered by the cargo policy; nor does it specify the duration of cover where goods are insured. The insured perils are expressed in the cargo clauses attached to the policy and each set of cargo clauses incorporates a "transit" clause to specify when cover attaches and terminates. The transit clause includes the warehouse to warehouse clause.

The transit clause is standard in the ICC (1982) A, B & C but varies in some of the sets of cargo clauses designed for special trades, commodities and products (these special sets of clauses being termed "trade clauses", in practice). However, in general, the transit clause in a cargo policy covers the goods from the time they leave the warehouse at the place named in the policy for the commencement of transit. Cover continues during the ordinary course of transit until the goods are delivered at the final warehouse at the place named in the policy as the destination for the cargo.

The term "ordinary course of transit" embraces any customary form of transport incidental to the overseas shipment of the goods, including land, river and canal conveyances (eg rail transport, road transport, barge, lighter, etc.). The term, where applicable, would include carriage by air when this is incidental to a shipment by sea. For carriage by air, where no sea transit is involved, the ILU publishes separate sets of air cargo clauses; these conditions incorporating a transit clause based on that in the standard marine cargo clauses but adjusted to relate to carriage by air. The term "ordinary course of transit" also embraces customary delays and other delays that are outside control of the assured. The transit clause embraces, as applicable to the voyage covered, carriage by craft to and from the overseas vessel; plus insured risks to which the goods are exposed during loading, stowage and discharge.

No time limit is imposed between the time cover attaches and the time the goods are discharged from the overseas vessel. But, following discharge from the overseas vessel, there is a time limit during which the goods must be delivered at the final warehouse. Under the standard ICC(1982) this limit is 60 days. If the goods are delivered before expiry of the time limit cover terminates upon delivery. If the time limit expires before the goods are delivered cover terminates upon expiry of the time limit; irrespective of the position of the goods at such time. Some trade clauses have a more restricted time limit in the transit clause.

11. Restrictions in Duration of Cover - Cargo War Risks

All sets of cargo clauses published by the ILU incorporate clauses which exclude war risks and strikes risks. Where it is agreed that the contract shall embrace strikes risks the relevant set of strikes clauses is attached to the policy. This set of clauses will incorporate a transit clause providing the same duration of cover as in the marine cargo clauses attached to the policy.

When it is agreed that the policy shall cover war risks a set of cargo war clauses is attached to the policy. In the London market cargo war risks cover is subject to the "waterborne agreement". This is a market agreement whereby underwriters undertake not to insure property on land against war risks. To implement the waterborne agreement duration of cover in the cargo war clauses published by the ILU is restricted to the time whilst the goods are waterborne in craft and/or on board the overseas vessel.

Full war risks cover, as in the Institute war risks clauses, attaches as the goods are loaded onto the overseas vessel and continues until the goods are discharged overside from the overseas vessel. No time limit is applied during the sea voyage but, from the day the ship "arrives" at the port of discharge a limit of 15 days is applied. If the goods are not discharged within the time limit cover terminates on expiry of the time limit; otherwise cover terminates as the goods are discharged from the overseas vessel.

A concession is allowed when the insured goods are discharged at an intermediate port for transhipment to another overseas vessel. In such case, the 15 days time limit still applies when the ship arrives at the transhipping port but the assured is permitted to transfer the goods to the on-carrying vessel within the time limit without a break in war risks cover. The transfer can embrace a period when the goods are on land during the transfer, but applies only to goods that remain within the port area. If the goods go outside the port area cover is suspended until they return but the time limit continues to tick away during the whole period the goods are ashore. If the 15 day time limit expires cover is suspended until the goods are loaded onto the on-carrying vessel at which time it reattaches.

Limited war risks cover applies to the goods whilst they are in craft. Cover is limited to loss or damage caused by mines or derelict torpedoes. This cover continues until the goods are unloaded ashore from the craft; but is subject to a time limit of 60 days from the date of discharge if the goods have not been unloaded before expiry of the time limit.

12. Cargo Open Cover Contracts

In modern practice, an open cover becomes effective at a date agreed by the underwriter and, unless it contains a cancellation clause which is invoked by either party, it continues indefinitely. Shipments commencing transit on and after that date can be declared under the cover. The insurance of the goods covered by a declaration attaches on a "voyage" basis. Therefore, the duration of cover for the goods insured by the certificate issued for each declaration will be in accordance with the transit clause in the relevant set of clauses attaching to the certificate; the comments above regarding warehouse to warehouse cover applying.

It is customary for a cargo open cover to incorporate a cancellation clause. This entitles the underwriter to cancel the contract at any time; but subject to an agreed notice period to allow the assured an opportunity to argue a case for withdrawal of the notice or to arrange alternative cover. Suppose the notice period is 30 days. The underwriter gives notice to the assured and, unless this notice is withdrawn, the open cover facility ceases to operate on expiry of 30 days from the time the notice was given. The assured and broker can continue to declare shipments which commence transit at any time during the notice period and the underwriter is obliged to accept each declaration. Once a declaration attaches to the contract the shipment relating thereto continues to be covered within the terms of the transit clause until the goods are delivered at the final warehouse; irrespective of the fact that the open cover may have ceased to operate long before the goods have been delivered.

The notice period for marine risks may vary from the 30 days in the above example; but the notice period for cancelling war and strikes cover remains constant at 7 days (with a more limited period for certain strikes risks in some cases).

SEE OVERPAGE FOR SELF STUDY QUESTIONAIRE

SELF STUDY QUESTIONS

Before moving on to the next Section satisfy yourself that you have absorbed the subject matter of the previous Section. The following questions should be answered without reference to the text.

1. The broker's slip proposing a hull voyage contract states that the insurance shall commence "at & from" the place stated in the policy. When does the risk attach? What would be the difference if the slip stated that the insurance should attach "from" the said place?

2. Define the terms "different voyage", "change of voyage" and "deviation". What effect do any of these have on (a) a hull voyage policy (b) a hull time policy and (c) a cargo policy?

3. Define the terms "delay in commencement of voyage" and "delay in prosecution of the voyage". What effect does either of these have on (a) a hull voyage policy (b) a hull time policy and (c) a cargo policy?

4. Is there any limit applied in law to the period of time for which a hull time policy may be effected? What is the customary period of time for which such policies are effected in practice?

5. What is the purpose of the "continuation" clause in a hull time policy?

6. What effect do the following circumstances, concerning the insured ship, have, if any, on a hull time policy which is subject to the ITC (1983) -
   (a) Change of ownership?
   (b) Transfer to new management?
   (c) Chartering other than under a bareboat charter?
   (d) Change of flag?

7. What is "warehouse to warehouse" cover?

8. The "transit" clause in the ICC (1982) incorporates a time limit.
   (a) Is any time limit applied to transit prior to discharge of the goods from the overseas vessel?
   (b) For what period is the time limit expressed in the ICC (1982) A, B & C?
   (c) Does the policy continue to cover the insured goods after delivery at the final warehouse if such delivery takes place before the time limit expires?

9. Cover for war risks insurance of goods is restricted by the London market waterborne agreement. How is this agreement implemented in the Institute war risks clauses for cargo? To what extent is war risks cover for goods in craft restricted?

10. A time limit is imposed on war risks cover for goods.
    (a) What is the period of this time limit and when does it attach?
    (b) When does war risks cover terminate for goods which are discharged from the overseas vessel before the time limit expires?

SECTION TEN

PROXIMATE CAUSE AND MARINE PERILS

1. Introduction
2. The Principle of Proximate Cause
3. Introduction to Marine Insurance Perils
4. "All Risks" Insurance
5. Specified Perils Insurance - Marine Hulls
6. Specified Perils Insurance - Marine Cargo
7. Statutory Exclusions
8. An Introduction to Customary Exclusions
9. Customary Exclusions - Marine Hulls - ITC (1983)
10. War & Strikes Perils - Hulls (1983)
11. Customary Exclusions - Marine Cargo - ICC (1982)
12. War & Strikes Perils - Cargo (1982)
13. Sentimental Loss and Sympathetic Damage

SECTION TEN

1. Introduction

The subject matter insured, whether it be ship or cargo, is exposed to many perils (often termed "risks" in practice) throughout the maritime adventure. We can group these into:

(a) Insured perils
(b) Qualified perils
(c) Excluded perils
(d) Uninsured perils

Insured perils - Where these are expressed in the policy or in clauses or wording attached to the policy they are referred to as "specified" perils. In such case, unless the policy wording states otherwise, no loss is recoverable under the policy unless it is proximately caused by one of the specified perils. In cargo insurances, though not in hull insurances, it is customary for the cover to extend beyond the strict principle of proximate cause to embrace loss *reasonably attributable to* certain of the specified perils.

In cargo insurance practice the term "all risks" may be used to embrace a much wider range of perils than those expressed in other, more limited, cargo policies. In hull insurance practice the term "all risks" is often used in respect of the cover offered by the Institute hull clauses on full conditions (eg the ITC, 1983); but this must not be confused with the term when used in cargo insurance. Technically, there is no such cover as hull all risks. All hull insurance contracts covering loss of or damage to the insured ship incorporate "specified" perils.

Qualified perils - In practice it is not unusual for an insured peril to be qualified. That is to say losses caused by that peril are covered only subject to certain specified conditions. An example of this appears in clause 6 of the ITC (1983). Clause 6, the "perils" clause, is divided into two parts; being cl.6.1 and cl.6.2. The first part lists six perils (some including similar perils which are also specified). Loss of or damage to the ship proximately caused by any of these is, subject to any exclusions provided elsewhere in the policy, covered without qualification. The second part lists five perils, also embracing a number of similar perils. Loss of or damage to the ship proximately caused by any of the these perils is, subject to any exclusions provided elsewhere in the policy, covered by the policy. But, in the latter case, the cover is qualified because the clause states that the loss or damage is not recoverable under cl.6.2 if it has resulted from a want of due diligence on the part of the assured, owners or managers.

Excluded perils - This term refers to the scope of the perils covered by the policy. When writing a risk the underwriter is agreeing to make good losses suffered by the assured where such loss is proximately caused by an insured peril. But there are certain perils the scope of which could embrace losses the underwriter is not prepared to bear or losses that the premium rate agreed was not intended to contemplate. This is particularly so when the widely embracing term "all risks" appears in the policy.

The underwriter is protected by law regarding the scope of certain perils; exclusions relating to these being expressed in the MIA, 1906. These are referred to as the "statutory" exclusions (see comment in note 7, below, regarding statutory exclusions). Where the matter of concern is not embraced by a statutory exclusion the underwriter will, where he considers it necessary, incorporate in the policy express exclusions to restrict the scope of the perils covered thereby. An example can be seen in regard to the peril "explosion" which appears in hull insurance policies; the scope of this peril being restricted by a "war exclusion" clause in the policy. In this respect, the policy would continue to cover loss of or damage to the ship proximately caused by explosion; but not where the explosion was caused by a war peril.

Uninsured perils - These are perils which are not embraced by the insurance contract. Since the cover in policies varies, depending on the perils covered by each particular policy, one cannot give an example to apply to all policies. However, if one compares the perils expressed in the ICC (1982) B conditions with those expressed in the ICC (1982) C conditions one can see that, whilst the B conditions incorporate the peril "washing overboard" this peril is an uninsured peril so far as the C conditions are concerned.

It is not intended, in this introductory course, to give details of the full coverage provided by marine insurance contracts. So the comments in this section regarding insured perils are restricted to an outline of the cover in marine insurance policies; being deemed sufficient to give the trainee a general idea of marine insurance coverage. Trainees and practitioners seeking more detailed information are advised to consult the reference books recommended in earlier sections of this study.

2. The Principle of Proximate Cause *(MIA, 1906, sect. 55 sub 1)*

The principle of proximate cause (*causa proxima non remota spectatur*) is fundamental to all insurance contracts. Section 55 is the only section of the MIA, 1906, which makes reference to the principle of proximate cause despite the fact that it is an Act to codify English law on marine insurance and there must have been numerous legal disputes on the application of the principle over more than 300 years of marine insurance practice in England. Apart from comment on the principle in regard to the statutory exclusions (see note 7, below) the Act gives no definition of the principle of proximate cause; merely stating the obvious by providing as follows:

(a) Subject to the provisions of the Act, and unless the policy otherwise provides, a loss proximately caused by an insured peril is recoverable under the policy, and;

(b) Subject to the provisions of the Act, and unless the policy otherwise provides, a loss not proximately caused by an insured peril is not recoverable under the policy.

Without guidance from the MIA, 1906, claims practitioners have, from comments and decisions made in several court cases, established a number of basic rules to assist one in determining the proximate cause of a loss. These rules are summarised herein as follows:

(1) Most losses result from a chain of events; each link in the chain contributing in some way towards the loss. The last link in the chain culminates in the loss itself; so the first task is to determine when this chain commences.

(2) When considering the point at which the chain commences there must be no break in the chain of events between the link established as the proximate cause and the actual loss. If a break in the chain can be established one ignores the previous chain and a new chain commences from the time of the break. The application of this rule was illustrated in the case of the "Ikaria" ("Leyland Shipping Company Ltd - v - Norwich Union, 1918"). The ship had been torpedoed but managed to make port. While the ship was lying in the port in an unrepaired condition the threat of imminent

heavy weather caused concern to the harbourmaster who feared the ship would sink in the inner harbour. He ordered the ship to be removed to the outer harbour where she eventually sank during the heavy weather and broke her back on the harbour bed. Marine underwriters denied liability contending that the loss was not proximately caused by the peril of the seas, but by an (excluded) war peril on the grounds that there had been no break in the chain of events. Opposing opinion contended that the ship had reached safety after being damaged by the torpedo and that this constituted a break in the chain of events. The court held that the ship had never been out of danger from the time she was struck by the torpedo. So there was no break in the chain of events and the war risk underwriters were liable for the total loss.

(2) Having established the chain of events to which the loss relates the next task is to determine which of the links in the chain is the *proximate* cause of the loss. This must be the link which is most *dominant and effective* in causing the loss. It could be the first link which sets off the chain of events or it could be the last link which culminates in the loss or any link in between. An interesting case to illustrate this point was "Ionedes - v - Universal Marine (1864)", wherein it was held that the proximate cause of loss was the marine peril "stranding"; not the excluded peril "war". The court dismissed an act by a military authority, unconnected with the ship, which created the situation in which thc ship stranded as being only a contributory cause.

(3) It is possible for a court to rule that a general factor dominating the whole chain of events has sufficient force to over-ride individual links in the chain and, by so doing, to become the proximate cause of loss in itself. Practitioners might not agree with this understanding of the principle but were unable to challenge such a decision in the case of the "Coxwold" ("Yorkshire Dale Shipping Company Ltd - v - The Minister of War Transport", 1942). The vessel was carrying war stores and was in a convoy, under Admiralty instructions, when she stranded on the Isle of Skye. The court held that the proximate cause of loss was a war risk because the vessel was on a warlike engagement at the time she stranded.

Following this decision marine underwriters incorporated the, so called, "Coxwold" amendment in the war exclusion clause. This was the "F.C.&S." clause which, at that time, appeared in all marine insurance policies issued in the London market and in marine clauses published by the ILU for use with the SG form of policy. When the MAR form of policy was introduced this condition was replaced in modern practice with a reworded war exclusion clause which appears, not in the policy form, but in the new clauses published by the ILU for use with the MAR form of policy. However, practitioners might care to note that the substance of the "amendment" still appears in the war exclusion clause in the AHF (American Hull Form) and ensures that the warlike nature of the engagement of the insured vessel at the time of loss shall not prejudice a claim which is not directly caused by a hostile act.

(4) One ignores an insured peril which gives rise to a loss from an excluded or uninsured peril. As an example, take the case of "Pink - v - Fleming" (1892). The subject matter insured was a cargo of fruit carried by a ship which was in collision with another vessel. The ship put into port for repairs which necessitated discharge of the fruit into lighters whilst the repairs were carried out. When the fruit eventually arrived at its destination some of it was found to have deteriorated due to the delay. The court rejected the contention that the proximate cause of loss was a peril of the seas (ie "collision") and held that the loss was proximately caused by the inherent nature of the goods; this being an uninsured peril so far as the policy was concerned.

On the other hand, where a loss is proximately caused by an insure[illegible] the insured peril would not have come about but for the operation of an excl[illegible], the loss is not covered by the policy; the excluded peril taking precedence. This was illustrated in the case of "Cory - v - Barr" (1883). The ship was siezed and detained by Spanish authorities because the master and crew had been caught smuggling. The owner of the ship (the assured), who had no knowledge of the smuggling, sought to claim under the policy for the expenses he incurred to recover the ship; contending these to be a loss proximately caused by "barratry". The court held that, although the loss resulted from an insured peril ("barratry"), there was no claim under the policy because the excluded peril "seizure" took precedence over the insured peril.

(5) In general, one ignores remote causes in concentrating on the proximate cause of a loss but there can be situations where it is so difficult to pinpoint the proximate cause of a loss that the remoteness of other contributing causes cannot be established. Hull underwriters are strict on this point and always require the assured to show that the loss or damage was proximately caused by an insured peril; whilst reserving the right to defend the claim by proving the loss or damage was proximately caused by an excluded peril or by an uninsured peril.

Cargo underwriters, on the other hand, are more lenient where certain perils are concerned. To illustrate this consider the perils specified in the ICC (1982) B conditions. The cargo perils clause (cl.1) is in three parts. The second part (cl.1.2) specifies perils which are subject to the principle of proximate cause; but the first part (cl.1.1) specifies perils in respect of which the assured only has to show that the loss was *reasonably attributable to* the specified peril for the loss to be recoverable under the policy. As an example, consider the peril "explosion" (cl.1.1.1). The surveyor, who examines the goods in a warehouse after an explosion on the carrying vessel, might find it difficult to decide whether, say, crushing damage was caused by poor stowage, bad handling or the explosion. Cargo underwriters give the assured the benefit of the doubt and, provided the surveyor reports the loss as being reasonably attributable to the explosion, they will accept the loss as being caused by explosion.

3. Introduction to Marine Insurance Perils

Prior to the introduction of the MAR form of policy the main perils covered by the marine insurance contract, whether it be a hull or a cargo contract, were expressed in the policy form. They were the same for the SG form, the G form and the S form (see Section 4). This continues to be the case today where the same format is used in overseas markets; irrespective of the antiquity of some of the phraseology. For the benefit of trainees in those overseas markets, and for quick reference, the perils as they appeared in the Lloyd`s SG policy are shown below:

Marine Perils -

Perils of the seas, fire, thieves, jettisons and barratry.

War, etc. perils -

Men of war, enemies, pirates, rovers, letters of mart and countermart, surprisals, takings at sea, arrests, restraints, and detainments of kings, princes and people of what nation condition or quality soever.

Other perils -

All other perils, losses and misfortunes, that have or shall come to the hurt or detriment, or damage of the said goods and merchandises, and ship &c., or any part thereof.

It may appear, at first glance, that many of these perils do not relate to ships and cargoes exposed to sea hazards today. This is true in some cases but others continue to be hazards faced by ships at sea and by the goods carried aboard such vessels. References, in the comments below, to the SG form relate to the S form or G form, as appropriate to the interest insured.

Perils of the seas - The term "perils of the seas" is defined in Rule 7 of the Rules for Construction of the Policy (MIA, 1906, First schedule) as referring only to "fortuitous accidents or casualties of the seas. It does not include the ordinary action of the wind and waves". It has been emphasised that it relates to perils *of* the seas rather than to perils *on* the seas. Some examples of circumstances that come within the meaning of the term are - *heavy weather; stranding of a vessel; contact of a vessel with any external substance (other than water but including ice), including objects whether they be floating or fixed; collision of a vessel with another vessel.*

When the insurance contract is based on a MAR policy form this term is used today only in hull policies, hull interest policies and freight policies. No reference to "perils of the seas", as such, appears in the ICC (1982); although the term "all risks" in the ICC A conditions would embrace these perils. The ICC B and C conditions express some of the perils embraced by perils of the seas (eg stranding, collision, etc.) but neither of these sets of cargo clauses covers "heavy weather". Nevertheless, the ICC B conditions do cover loss or damage to the cargo caused by entry of seawater into a ship, craft, container or place of storage.

In regard to the above, the peril "stranding" refers to circumstances where the vessel accidentally runs aground and remains there for an appreciable period of time; a period of 15 minutes being considered an appreciable period. The term "collision" relates solely to physical contact of the ship or vessel with another ship or vessel. The peril "contact" refers to any contact made by the insured vessel or the vessel carrying the insured goods, other than collision, and would embrace circumstances where the carrying vessel strikes the ground. Only loss of or damage to the subject matter insured is covered by the perils collision or contact, as the case may be; neither of these, as a peril of the seas, extends the cover to embrace liability incurred by the assured to others.

Fire - No definition of this peril is required, but it should be noted that fire damage caused by excluded perils (eg war and strikes, etc. risks) is not covered by the policy. Otherwise the cause of an accidental fire is immaterial even if it arises from negligence (not amounting to wilful misconduct) of the assured or servants of the assured. The peril is covered by contracts based on the SG form of policy and on contracts based on the MAR form of policy.

Thieves - Rule 9 of the Rules for Construction of the Policy (MIA, 1906, First schedule) qualifies this term by stating that it does not cover "clandestine theft or theft committed by any one of the ship's company, whether crew or passengers". The peril was embraced by all three sets of the ICC published for use with the SG form of policy, but is not covered by the ICC (1982) B or C conditions. Nevertheless, with underwriters' agreement the modern cargo policy can be extended to embrace thieves by attaching the "theft, pilferage and non-delivery" clause to the policy. The peril was embraced by a hull policy based on the SG form of policy on the understanding that it related only to violent theft. Violent theft is a specified peril in the ITC and IVC published for use with the MAR form of policy. Practitioners considering whether or not theft falls within the category of "barratry", see below, should note that barratry is not a peril covered by a cargo policy, other than one which covers "all risks".

Jettisons - This peril refers to circumstances where the subject matter insured, or part thereof, is deliberately cast overboard in time of common peril to save the ship and goods from loss at sea. It does not embrace anything that is accidentally lost overboard nor anything that is washed overboard. Where more than one interest is at risk, at the time of loss, jettison is a general average act (see Section 15) and would be treated as such in practice; thereby being covered by all marine insurance contracts. Where only the ship is at risk, or in other circumstances where no general average act is allowed, "jettison" becomes a peril by itself and losses caused thereby are covered by a policy which specifies this peril. Since the peril appeared in the SG form of policy both hull and cargo contracts based on this form covered the peril. It is embraced within the term "all risks" in the ICC (1982) A conditions and is a specified peril (extended to embrace "washing overboard") in the ICC (1982) B conditions; but jettison is not covered by the ICC (1982) C conditions. Jettison is a peril covered by the ITC and IVC (1983).

Barratry - Rule 11 of the Rules for Construction of the Policy (MIA, 1906, First schedule) provides that this peril "includes every wrongful act committed by the master or crew to the prejudice of the owner, or, as the case may be, the charterer". In practice, this is understood to mean that barratry applies only to hull policies and does not extend to cargo policies; although it could apply to cargo owned by the overseas carrier which is probably the reason for the inclusion of this peril in "G" policies based on the SG policy format. Certainly, the ILU cargo policy based on the SG policy format incorporated the peril "barratry". Nevertheless, following the London market understanding of the meaning of this term, "barratry" is not incorporated in the ICC (1982) B or C conditions. Barratry remains a peril covered by hull policies and is specified among the perils in the ITC and IVC (1983).

War, etc. Perils - This term embraces the group of perils, quoted above, which were expressed in the SG form of policy. Many of these perils (eg letters of mart) are no longer likely hazards at sea so we shall not waste time defining every peril. Practitioners and historians seeking information and definitions of these perils should refer to the books recommended in earlier Sections of this study. It will be noted that, although practice tended to link them with war risks, the risks of strikes, riots and civil commotions (see below) were not incorporated in the perils expressed in the SG form of policy.

War, etc. perils were deleted from the SG form of policy by a war exclusion clause, known as the F.C.& S. (free of capture and seizure) clause, which appeared in Lloyd's SG policy in 1898 and remained part of the SG form of policy until its abrogation in 1982/3. The F.C. & S. clause was also incorporated, as a paramount exclusion clause, in the ITC (1970) and the IVC (1970) with other exclusions (eg malicious damage, etc.).

In the London market a separate hull insurance contract would be negotiated to cover war and strikes, etc. risks. When preparing an SG policy for this purpose the hull war & strikes, etc. clauses which were, until October, 1983, published by the ILU for use only with policies printed in the SG format would be attached to a standard policy in the SG format with the above quoted perils and an F.C.&S. clause printed therein. The wording of the war & strikes, etc. clauses would reinstate the SG policy perils excluded by the F.C. & S. clause and the malicious damage exclusion clause. The war & strikes clauses would also extend the perils expressed in the policy to embrace loss of or damage to the ship caused by the consequencies of hostilities, warlike acts, malicious damage, strikes, riots and civil commotions.

Where a hull insurance contract is based on the MAR form of policy and the assured requests cover for his ship to be insured against war and strikes risks this is negotiated in the London market by a separate contract, as was the previous practice. No perils are printed in the MAR form of policy and there is no war exclusion clause in the policy form. The ITC/IVC (1983), which relate only to marine (not war & strikes) policies, specify all the perils covered and incorporate paramount war and strikes, etc. exclusion clauses which affect the perils expressed therein (eg fire or explosion) when caused by any of the excluded perils (eg an act of war). Unlike earlier sets of hull war & strikes clauses, the hull war & strikes clauses published by the ILU for use with the MAR form of policy do not cross refer to the war etc. exclusions in the ITC/IVC (1983). They specify the war and strikes, etc. risks covered and excluded, cross-referring to the marine policy only to incorporate marine clauses that are common to both a marine policy and a policy covering war and strikes risks.

Prior to 1982 cargo underwriters also used the SG form of policy, with the war perils and an F.C. & S. clause printed therein; attaching thereto whichever set of the old (1963) cargo clauses (ie ICC - FPA, ICC - WA or ICC "All Risks") was relevant to the conditions agreed in the broker's slip. Each of the ICC (1963) incorporated an F.C. & S. clause and an F.S.R. & C.C. (Free of strikes, riots and civil commotions) clause; with the condition that should either of these clauses be deleted the relevant Institute war clauses and/or Institute strikes, etc. clauses, as the case may be, would form part of the contract.

Unlike hull underwriters, cargo underwriters did not write war and/or strikes, etc. risks by a separate policy. When agreeing to cover war risks they would add this cover to the marine policy. The slip conditions would specify that war risks were covered and the cargo war clauses published by the ILU for use in policies based on the SG format would be attached to the marine cargo policy. These were cargo clauses which covered the risks excluded by the F.C. & S. clause and added loss or damage to the insured goods caused by the consequences of hostilities and warlike acts to the cover; but they incorporated a "waterborne clause" (see notes in Section 9) which restricted the cover against war risks to the period when the goods were waterborne. If, as was customary, the underwriter agreed, in the broker's slip, to add strikes, etc. risks to the contract a separate set of cargo strikes, etc. clauses, published by the ILU for use in policies based on the SG format, was attached to the policy specifying the additional cover and incorporating malicious damage. The strikes, etc. clauses did not incorporate a waterborne clause and covered the goods throughout the period of transit on a "warehouse to warehouse" basis.

Where cargo insurances based on the MAR form of policy are concerned London market practice operates as previously with the ILU supplying a set of clauses for war risks and another set of clauses for strikes etc. risks. All three sets of the ICC (1982) incorporate war and strikes exclusion clauses but, unlike the old marine cargo clauses, there is no condition whereby war and/or strikes etc. clauses shall form part of the contract if any of these exclusion clauses is deleted. Further, in the case of the 1982 cargo war and strikes etc. clauses, neither of these sets of conditions cross-refers to the exclusions expressed in the marine clauses.

The Institute cargo war clauses (1982) and the Institute cargo strikes, etc. clauses (1982) each specify the perils covered and and excluded; no cross reference being made to the relevant set of marine clauses. It should be noted that neither set of the 1982 cargo war and strikes clauses covers "malicious damage", as did the old cargo clauses. This peril is embraced within the term "all risks" in the ICC A conditions but is not embraced by the ICC B or ICC C conditions. If the underwriters agree to extend the ICC B or the ICC C conditions to cover malicious damage it will be necessary to add the Institute malicious damage clause (ref CL.266) to the policy.

Piracy - By way of definition the peril "pirates" in the SG form of policy was intended to embrace the ordinary meaning of the word (ie thieves who plunder ships and cargoes) and was treated as a form of war risk by underwriters. Rule 8 of the Rules for construction of the Policy (MIA, 1906, First schedule) added a further definition by stating that the peril pirates "includes passengers who mutiny and rioters who attack the ship from the shore".

Despite the popular belief that "piracy" should be treated as a war risk, there must have been some doubt in underwriters' minds in 1934 because the F.C& S. clause (see note 8, below) in both hull and cargo clauses published by the ILU for use in marine insurance policies issued at that time excepted the peril "piracy". Later the F.C.& S. clause was amended to specifically incorporate "piracy" in the exclusion clause in all marine insurance policies; the risk being incorporated in policies covering war risks. This remained the position until abrogation of the SG form of policy in the London market.

With introduction of the ICC (1982) and ITC/IVC (1983) London underwriters' attitude to the treatment of "piracy" changed. It was decided that "piracy" should be treated as a form of violent theft and not as a warlike peril. So modern policies no longer categorise this peril as a war risk. Hull clauses for use with the MAR form of policy specify "piracy" among the *marine* perils and it no longer appears in the war exclusion clause; nor in the hull war & strikes clauses. Nevertheless, it should be noted that, despite the MIA, 1906, definition to include "rioters who attack the ship from the shore" as pirates, the strikes, etc. exclusion clause in the ITC and IVC would exclude this form of piracy.

Where cargo insurances are concerned, since theft is not covered by the ICC (1982) B or C conditions, these do not cover "piracy"; nor do the cargo war risks conditions cover "piracy". The cargo strikes etc. clauses cover piracy only where it involves rioters who attack the ship from the shore. The ICC (1982) A conditions embrace the peril piracy within the term "all risks"; and specifically except the peril from the effects of the war exclusion clause therein.

Other perils - Rule 12 of the Rules for Construction of the Policy (MIA, 1906, First Schedule) restricted the term "all other perils ...", which appeared in the SG form of policy, to embrace "only perils similar in kind to the perils specifically mentioned in the policy". The legal dictum *ejusdem generis* (of a like kind) was applied to claims made under this section of the SG form of policy. Despite its apparently all embracing phraseology the term had the effect of only reducing the, otherwise rigid, application of the principle of proximate cause (see note 2, above).

The term "all other perils" became effective in circumstances where the cause of loss was not actually specified in the SG form of policy but was something so closely related to a specified peril that the loss could be recovered as being caused by the specified peril to which it related. For example, consider a circumstance where the insured goods were temporarily stored in a warehouse during the ordinary course of transit. The goods suffered damage caused by "heating". If the heating arose from a change in climate no claim would be recoverable under an SG form of policy but, if the heating was caused by fire (an insured peril specified in the policy form), the loss would be recoverable as a loss by fire.

The ICC (1963) WA and FPA made it easier for practitioners to apply this rule by extending the policy perils to cover loss or damage *reasonably attributable to* fire, explosion and some other perils; thereby complementing the term "all other perils...." in regard to these specific perils; but no such concession was given by hull underwriters in the ITC (1970) or IVC (1970).

It is important to note that the term "all other perils" does not appear in policy conditions used with the MAR form of policy; but the ICC (1982) still incorporate a "reasonably attributable to" provision where appropriate to the perils covered.

Practitioners seeking more detailed information on the perils expressed in the SG policy form are advised to consult "Marine Insurance - Vol. 1 - Principles and Basic Practice" (Fifth edition) by Brown (Witherby 1986).

4. "All Risks" Insurance

The term "risk" is not defined by the MIA, 1906, and English dictionary definitions provide little guidance to the use of the term in insurance practice. It is intended to refer only to "fortuities" (ie misfortunes encountered by the subject matter insured). The term is used only in policies which cover loss of or damage to the subject matter insured and is not intended to embrace third party liabilities the assured might incur in connection with the subject matter insured. Further, the term does not embrace inevitable loss, such as the inherent nature in foodstuffs which causes them to deteriorate or oxidisation (eg rust) in metal products or ordinary wear and tear. One might argue that customary loss (eg loss in weight or quantity due to evaporation and customary breakage in the case of fragile goods, etc.) is not embraced by the term "risk" but, in some instances, this contention might be difficult to fully substantiate (see notes later regarding exclusion clauses in the ICC A conditions). Nevertheless, one can say, in general, that the term "all risks" embraces only accidental losses suffered by the subject matter insured.

Contrary to popular marine insurance jargon hull insurance policies have never been effected on "all risks" conditions. Prior to abrogation of the SG form of policy claims were recoverable under a hull & machinery policy only where the accident was proximately caused by a peril expressed in the policy form or, as appropriate, in the, so called, "Inchmaree" (additional perils) clause which was incorporated in the policy conditions. This practice did not change with introduction of the MAR form of policy; claims under this form of contract being recoverable only where the loss is proximately caused by a peril specified in the clauses attached to the policy form.

Until 1757, when the "memorandum" first appeared in the SG form of policy, cargo insurances were effected on "WA" (with average) terms. That is to say the policy covered, in addition to total loss (see Section 11), "average" losses (ie partial losses); these being "particular average" and "general average sacrifice" (see Section 15 regarding the latter). But no loss was recoverable where it was not proximately caused by a peril expressed in the SG form of policy. Introduction of the memorandum brought a new approach which reduced the cover for particular average with an "FPA" (free of particular average) condition for some cargo policies and introduced a franchise which was applicable to particular average claims in all cargo and hull policies (see Section 4). The "FPA" type of cover found favour with many underwriters and was extended beyond the scope of the memorandum to became commonplace for certain types of policy. Until the 19th century restricted to WA cover and FPA cover in various forms. During more extended form of cargo cover termed "all risks" was int radical change which was not welcomed by the more co underwriters; most of whom preferred to stay with WA ter insurances and, the more limited form of cover, (FPA) for use in policies covering certain cargoes (eg corn, fish, salt, fruit, flour and seed) and for deckload cargoes such as timber.

There was still a limited use of "all risks" insurance in the cargo market in 1912 when the Institute cargo clauses were first published. So limited that the ILU published standard clauses (the ICC) for use only in WA contracts and FPA contracts. Gradually the demand for "all risks" cargo insurance grew but it was not until after the 1939/45 war that the acceptance of these wide conditions was sufficient to justify publication of cargo "all risks" clauses by the ILU.

The relevant clause in the ICC "All Risks" took precedence over the perils expressed in the SG form of policy to which these conditions were attached. It also incorporated the term "irrespective of percentage". This took precedence over the "memorandum" which was printed in the policy form so that the FPA provision and the franchise provision therein were not taken into account when calculating particular average claims. Even so the "all risks" clause was not all embracing. The cover excluded losses proximately caused by delay and from inherent vice or nature in the subject matter insured.

With introduction of the MAR form of policy the ILU withdrew the old ICC and published new sets of ICC in a different format; for use only with the MAR form of policy. The MAR policy form does not specify any perils so the perils covered are expressed in the relevant set of ICC attached thereto. The new format for "all risks" conditions is expressed in the ICC (1982) A conditions. These follow the previous pattern by incorporating an "all risks" clause which covers the same perils as the earlier versions; but with a formidable list of exclusions (see note 11, below). The overall effect is to clarify "all risks" cover and to reduce the scope of former sets of "all risks" conditions. For details one should refer to a set of these clauses.

5. Specified Perils Insurance - Hulls

As commented earlier, the hull clauses published by the ILU (both ITC and IVC), for use with policies based on the SG format, were subject to the perils specified in the SG form plus the additional perils in the, so called, "Inchmaree" clause. The memorandum did not affect this cover because an "average" clause in the ITC/IVC replaced its provisions, first, with a qualified franchise and, later, with a qualified deductible (see Section 4). Further, it will be recalled that all hull insurance contracts are embodied in a specified perils policy.

Both the ITC (1983) and the IVC (1983), which are published for use only with the MAR form of policy, incorporate a "perils" clause which, apart from the reference number (cl.6 in the ITC and cl.4 in the IVC), is identical in both sets of clauses. It is not intended, in these introductory notes, to comment in detail on each peril. Trainees and practitioners seeking more detail can refer to the ITC, 1983 (CL.280) to see the perils and consult "Marine Insurance - Volume 3 - Hull Practice" by Brown (Witherby 1993) for detailed comment on each peril. The following brief comments refer to the perils clause in the ITC (1983) but apply equally to the perils in the IVC (1983) and, where appropriate thereto, to other sets of hull and hull erest clauses based on these two main sets of conditions.

The perils clause covers *loss of or damage* to the insured ship *proximately caused* by any of the listed perils. It should be noted that no reference is made in the perils clause to expenses incurred in consequence of the operation of any of these perils. Nevertheless, sue & labour charges (see Section 13) incurred in connection with the specified perils are covered by cl.13. Nor do the perils refer to liabilities incurred by the assured in consequence of any of these perils. The extent of collision liability cover is expressed elsewhere in the policy conditions (see the RDC, cl.8).

The perils clause is in three parts; being cl.6.1, cl.6.2 and cl.6.3. The perils listed in cl.6.1 (Perils of the seas, etc.) relate to circumstances where it is considered neither the assured nor their servants (eg master, officers and crew) have any control over the situation; thus cover in respect of these perils is not qualified. The perils listed in cl.6.2 (accidents in loading, etc.) relate to circumstances where the underwriter feels that, with more care, the accident might not have happened. Loss or damage caused by any of these perils is not covered if it results from a want of due dilligence on the part of the assured, owners or managers of the ship. By cl.6.3 any master, officer or crew member is exempted from the qualification to cl.6.2 should they hold shares in the insured ship.

In hull practice an "additional perils" clause might be attached to a hull & machinery policy. Where hull clauses attached to the SG form of policy the term "additional perils" referred to perils such as "negligence of master, officers or crew" and other perils not embraced by those expressed in the SG form of policy. A clause, termed the "Inchmaree" clause, the "negligence" clause or the "additional perils" clause in practice, was incorporated in the ITC and IVC for this purpose. With the underwriter's agreement a further condition, the "liner negligence" clause (not an Institute clause), might have been attached to the policy to extend the scope of certain of the additional perils (eg negligence, etc.) expressed in the policy conditions. When the new hull clauses were drafted for use with the MAR form of policy the substance of the earlier "additional perils" clause was incorporated in the standard "perils" clause so use of the term "additional perils", for the earlier purpose, does not apply to any of the perils expressed in cl.6 of the ITC (1983). Today, in hull insurance practice, the term "additional perils" is applied to a version of the liner negligence clause which is, now, published by the ILU as a separate clause (CL.294) for use with the ITC (1983). Hull underwriters are very selective in agreeing to the attachment of this Institute clause to hull policies.

6. Specified Perils Insurance - Cargo

Prior to abrogation of policies in the SG format all sets of cargo insurance conditions, other than those covering "all risks", covered only specified perils. The two basic sets of cargo clauses, published by the ILU for use with the SG form of policy were the "WA" clauses and the "FPA" clauses. Unlike the standard clauses published by the ILU for the insurance of ships, these cargo clauses did not incorporate an "additional perils" clause (see note 5, above). In both cases the only perils covered were those printed in the SG policy form (see note 1, above). The principle of proximate cause was relaxed in regard to some of these perils but, otherwise, the ICC merely qualified the cover in the SG policy form so far as policy perils were concerned;

the only difference between the two sets of clauses being in the treatment of particular average claims.

With abrogation of the SG form of policy the London cargo insurance market agreed to discontinue the practice of insuring on FPA terms. Further, since the WA clauses were originally designed to complement the SG policy form, they now have no place in modern practice. Accordingly, when the MAR form of policy was introduced in the cargo market (1982) the ILU withdrew all sets of cargo clauses previously published for use with policies in the SG format. The ICC "All Risks" were redesigned and published in a new format (see note 4, above) but the WA and FPA clauses were **not** replaced. This radical change gave cargo underwriters the opportunity to re-assess the cover they are prepared to offer today so far as specified perils are concerned. To give effect to this the ILU, following withdrawal of the old ICC, published two completely new sets of cargo clauses. These are the ICC (1982) B conditions and the ICC (1982) C conditions. At first, some uninformed practitioners caused confusion by assuming that the B conditions replaced the ICC (WA) and the C conditions replaced the ICC (FPA). This was not true! So far as cargo insurance is concerned, in the London market, the SG form of policy and the WA and FPA conditions are gone forever. It is not intended, in these introductory notes, to examine in detail each peril specified in the 1982 cargo clauses. Trainees and practitioners seeking more detail can refer to the ICC (1982) B & C conditions, as appropriate, to see the perils and consult "Marine Insurance - Volume 2 - Cargo Practice" by Brown (Witherby 1985) for detailed comment on each peril.

As commented earlier, no perils are printed in the MAR form of policy. All the perils covered, when the ICC (1982) B or the ICC (1982) C conditions are used, are specified in cl.1 of the relevant set of clauses. The perils clause in the ICC B conditions is in three parts; cl.1.1, cl.1.2 and cl.1.3. Before we consider the first two parts let us dispose of cl.1.3. This is not so much a specified peril but an extension of the cover to embrace total loss of any package lost overboard during loading, transhipment or discharge; this extension not appearing in the C conditions. Apart from this provision, claims attaching to the perils clause relate solely to loss of or damage to the insured goods either proximately caused by a specified peril or, where so stated, reasonably attributable to a specified peril. No provision is made in cl.1 to reimburse the assured for expenses incurred in connection with these perils; but provision is made elsewhere in the clauses regarding sue & labour charges. Further, the cargo policy does not extend to embrace liabilities incurred by the assured in connection with these perils; with the exception of the peril "collision"; reimbursement for liability in this respect being covered under the "both to blame collision" clause (cl.3).

Most of the specified perils appear in cl.1.1 and, in respect of these, underwriters do not require the assured to prove that the loss was proximately caused by one of the specified perils. The assured only has to show that the loss was *reasonably attributable to* the specified peril for the loss to be recoverable under the policy. As an example, consider the peril "explosion" (cl.1.1.1). The surveyor, who examines the goods in a warehouse after an explosion on the carrying vessel, might find it difficult to decide whether damage to, apparently crushed, packages was caused by poor stowage, bad handling or the explosion. Damage from poor stowage or bad handling is not covered by the B conditions but cargo underwriters would give the assured the benefit of the doubt in this case and, provided the surveyor reports the loss as being reasonably attributable to the explosion, they would accept the loss as being caused by explosion.

Cargo underwriters take a firmer stand where the perils specified in cl.1.2 are concerned. The most important of these, in practice, is "entry of sea, river or lake water" (cl.1.2.3); which is not covered by the C clauses. In regard to this peril the assured is required to prove that water damage to the insured goods was proximately caused by the entry of water (as specified) into the ship, craft, hold, conveyance, container, lifvan or place of storage. Other forms of water (eg rainwater, condensation, etc.) are not embraced by the cover; nor does this peril embrace water damage to goods which were not in a hold, etc. (eg goods on deck) when the loss or damage occurred. One finds an important difference, in this respect, when comparing the ICC (1982) B conditions with the cover in the old WA conditions. Neither the old nor the new sets of Institute clauses would cover rainwater or condensation; but the term "perils of the seas" in the SG policy form, which term does not appear in the new conditions, embraced perils relating to "heavy weather" which are not specified in the ICC (1982) B conditions. Cl.1.2.2 covers "jettison", as did the SG form of policy, but extends this peril to embrace "washing overboard"; thereby embracing, at least, one of the perils relating to "heavy weather" not covered elsewhere in the absence of cover for "perils of the seas". Finally, cl.1.2.1 covers loss or damage to the insured goods proximately caused by general average sacrifice; thereby confirming the assured's right under section 66(4) of the MIA, 1906, to claim directly from the cargo underwriter for loss of or damage to the insured goods proximately caused by a GA sacrifice, without waiting for completion of the GA adjustment (for more detail see notes in Section 15).

On the face of it, there would appear to be very little difference between the cover provided by the B clauses and the cover in the C clauses. Differences appear only in the "perils" clause. With the exception of cl.1.3 (loss of goods overboard during loading, etc.), which is absent from the C conditions, the format of cl.1 in both sets of conditions is the same. As in the B clauses, the principle of proximate cause is applied only to the perils expressed in cl.1.2. The specified perils are also the same; except that the certain perils specified in the B conditions are omitted from the C conditions; these being cl.1.1.6 ("earthquake", etc.) and cl.1.2.3 ("entry of seawater", etc.).

7. Statutory Exclusions *(MIA, 1906, sect. 55 sub.2)*

Irrespective of the comments above concerning perils covered by an SG form of policy and/or perils covered by clauses attached to a MAR form of policy all loss or damage to ship or cargo is subject to the "statutory exclusions" that appear in Section 55 (2) of the the MIA, 1906. These may be summarised as follows:

(1) Wilful misconduct of the assured
(2) Loss proximately caused by delay
(3) Ordinary wear and tear
(4) Ordinary leakage
(5) Ordinary breakage
(6) Inherent vice or nature in the subject matter insured
(7) Loss proximately caused by rats or vermin
(8) Machinery damage not caused by maritime perils

The first of these, wilful misconduct, applies to all marine insurance contracts irrespective of anything expressed in the policy to the contrary. The remainder apply to all marine hull and cargo insurance contracts, as relevant to the subject matter insured, unless contrary wording appears in the contract.

Wilful misconduct - Irrespective of the proximate cause of the loss no claim is allowed if the loss was *attributable to* the wilful misconduct of the assured. The master or crew of a ship are not deemed to be the assured for this purpose, so where a master commits an act of misconduct, or is guilty of negligence, which results in loss proximately caused by an insured peril the claim is recoverable. But where the contract was based on the SG form of policy no loss proximately caused by negligence of master or crew was recoverable unless the policy perils were extended to embrace negligence as an insured peril. It was customary, from 1887, for the perils expressed in a hull and machinery SG form of policy to be extended to add this peril; but no such extension was applied to cargo insurances. Today, negligence of master, officers or crew is still a peril covered by the hull policy but is not a specified peril in the ICC B and C conditions.

Loss proximately caused by delay - This should not be confused with the effect of delay in the prosecution of a voyage (see Section 9). It refers to loss actually caused to the insured goods by the transit of such goods being delayed. An example would be loss caused by deterioration of perishable goods which would not have occurred but for the delay. The exclusion still applies even if the delay is caused by an insured peril.

Ordinary wear and tear - This refers to the normal wear and tear that occurs to material over a period of time. It is, therefore, a form of inevitable loss and, as such, is outside the ambit of the term "all risks". Most cargoes in transit by sea are either raw materials, commodities or new products sold or for sale in the commercial market; so loss from ordinary wear and tear is not likely to be a factor in most cases. Nevertheless, in case a cargo might be susceptible to wear and tear, all three sets of the ICC (1982) incorporate a specific exclusion regarding wear and tear; thereby making it clear that no claims in this respect will be paid.

Where the insurance of a ship is concerned depreciation of market value does not affect a claim for actual or constructive total loss; the insured value being the basis for the claim (see "valued policies" in Section 4, above). The measure of indemnity (see Section 12, below) for damage to the insured ship is governed by section 69 of the MIA, 1906. Amongst other things, this section of the Act allows the claims adjuster to reduce the amount recoverable under the policy to allow for wear and tear in parts and material being replaced with new parts and material in repairing the damage to the ship. In practice, however, it is customary for the policy to incorporate a "new for old" clause; whereby the underwriter waives his right to apply the deduction for wear and tear.

Ordinary leakage - Ordinary leakage is a form of "trade loss"; that is an inevitable loss which a trader must expect during transit whether or not an accident occurs. In this instance the trade loss is evaporation experienced by liquid cargoes (eg oil) and shrinkage in some solid cargoes (eg grain) resulting from evaporation of moisture content in the cargo. The term may be also applied to contraction experienced by some liquid cargoes (eg oil) when the cargo is loaded in a hot climate and is discharged in a place with a cooler climate; although claims assessors must be aware that cargoes which contract can, depending on the circumstances, expand instead of contracting and must allow for this possibility in their calculations.

Where cargoes affected by this type of trade loss are concerned it is customary for the claims assessor to obtain the volume or weight (whichever is relevant to the cargo concerned) of the cargo on arrival at the destination named in the policy and to compare this with the volume or weight, as relevant, recorded at the time transit commenced. In theory the difference so established should indicate the loss to the assured. To reduce misunderstandings in this respect the exclusion clause in all three sets of the ICC (1983) incorporates the exclusion "ordinary leakage".

Ordinary breakage - This is another form of trade loss. It relates to fragile cargoes which experience has shown suffer from breakage during transit even when no accident has occurred. Examples would be glass, plywood, earthenware, etc. The perils clause in the ICC (1982) B and C conditions does not specify "breakage" as an insured peril so breakage would be covered only where the accident was caused by (or attributable to, in some cases) a peril expressed in the perils clause. On the other hand, since the ICC (1982) A conditions do not exclude breakage, one could recover a claim for accidental breakage under a policy with the A conditions therein. Nevertheless, unless the policy specifies otherwise, the claims assessor would be entitled to reduce the amount recoverable to take into account any trade loss from breakage.

Inherent vice or nature in the subject matter insured - The inherent vice exclusion refers to the insurance of certain types of cargo which are prone to suffer from infestation (eg bole weevil in cotton, weevils in flour, etc.), and/or from damage caused by something inherent therein which can give rise to an insured peril in certain circumstances. A cargo of soft coal could serve as an example of the latter. When the coal is stowed in a hold in a wet condition it needs adequate ventilation to prevent it from heating. If, in heavy weather, the ventilation is restricted it is possible the coal will heat to a degree whereby spontaneous combustion takes place. Fire is a peril covered by all cargo policies so the assured would, naturally, attempt to claim for a fire loss. The underwiter could defend the claim by contending that, although the proximate cause of the loss was fire, the fire was caused by inherent vice, an excluded peril. In support of the underwriter's contention all cargo policies incorporate a clause which excludes loss or damage caused by inherent vice in the subject matter insured.

However, if one carefully reads the exclusion, in both the MIA, 1906, and in the cargo policy, it will be noted that it applies *only when the inherent vice is in the subject matter insured.* To illustrate this consider a situation where bales of jute (another cargo that is subject to spontaneous combustion when carried in a wet condition) are stowed in the same hold as a cargo of Indian carpets. During the voyage spontaneous combustion in the jute develops into a fire which, in addition to damaging the jute, damages the cargo of carpets. Whilst the exclusion in the cargo policy allows defence of a claim for fire loss on the jute, the underwriters covering the Indian carpets could not use the exclusion to defend a claim for fire damage because the inherent vice was not in their cargo.

The term "inherent nature" relates to a quality in a cargo which causes a loss without any assistance from outside. In other words, the loss is inevitable whatever happens. This can be illustrated by considering a cargo of plums. Unless something happens to destroy a plum before nature takes its course the fruit will eventually rot. Modern storage and stowage can retard but it cannot prevent the inevitable. One might argue that such loss is usually caused by delay but it must be remembered that the deterioration will take place if a voyage takes long enough even without delay in prosecution of the voyage. It is to this type of deterioration that the exclusion is intended to apply; but, as with inherent vice, it applies only to the cargo with the inherent nature therein.

Inherent vice or nature in the subject matter insured is excluded in all three sets of the standard ICC (1982) and in cargo trade clauses. However, trainees and practitioners might care to note that the exclusion in some frozen meat clauses exempts loss caused by variation in temperature attributable to breakdown of machinery or certain other specified perils.

One sometimes hears hull insurance practitioners referring to latent defect in the hull or machinery of the insured ship as a form of inherent vice and subject to the exclusion in the MIA, 1906. Whether or not this contention is upheld in law it is interesting to note that, in practice, hull policies cover loss or damage *caused by* latent defects but underwriters (except where the policy has been extended to embrace the part with the latent defect) do not replace the part with the latent defect therein.

Rats and vermin - This exclusion is mainly concerned with the insurance of goods in transit; particularly foodstuffs. It would exclude loss caused by contamination resulting from the presence of rats in, say, a cargo of rice in bags. But it must be appreciated that the exclusion relates only to loss *proximately caused* by rats. In the case "Hamilton Fraser - v - Pandorf & Co." (1887) rats gnawed through a leaden discharge pipe making a hole through which seawater entered and damaged the insured cargo. It was held that the loss was recoverable under an SG form of policy because it was proximately caused by seawater (a "peril of the sea"); the predilection of rats for lead piping being only a contributory cause.

One might consider "vermin" to be already embraced by the "inherent vice" exclusion, above. In fact, the separate exclusion expressed in the Act embraces such vermin as cockroaches which, whilst not being inherent vice in any particular cargo, can cause considerable contamination to foodstuffs. It is interesting to note that, whilst the exclusions clause in the ICC (1982) A, B & C conditions incorporates most of the statutory exclusions there is no mention therein of the exclusion "rats and vermin"; although one cannot suggest an explanation for these omissions. In any case these perils would not be covered by the B or C conditions because they are not among the specified perils. However, it would be interesting to see an underwriter defending a claim under the ICC (1982) A conditions (these covering "all risks") relying solely on the exclusion in section 55 of the MIA, 1906.

Machinery damage not caused by maritime perils - In practice one should read the latter term as "insured" perils because the intention is to absolve the underwriter insuring a ship from paying for repairs where the ship's machinery simply breaks down. In the case of relatively new machinery the assured might be able to claim on the grounds that the breakdown was caused by latent defect. Nevertheless, it will be recalled that, whilst, hull underwriters cover loss proximately caused to the ship by the manifestation of a latent defect they do not normally cover replacement or repair to the part with the latent defect. The policy would certainly not cover the mere discovery of a latent defect during an ordinary inspection by a surveyor.

8. An Introduction to Customary Exclusions

Underwriters are always at liberty to incorporate an exclusion in a hull policy when negotiating the contract with the broker. It is then for the assured to approve the exclusion when ratifying the contract (ref. MIA, 1906, sect. 86) or to withdraw the proposal. The term "customary exclusions" is applied to those exclusions that have become so commonplace in marine insurance practice that both parties expect them to form part of the contract whether or not they are mentioned during negotiations to conclude the contract. In this respect, one tends to think of the exclusions expressed in the Institute clauses and other sets of standard clauses used in practice.

Apart from some comment on the development of customary exclusions in marine insurance policies we shall, for the purposes of these introductory notes, restrict the following comments to the customary exclusions printed in the ITC (1983) and the ICC (1982) A, B & C conditions. The exclusions expressed in the ITC (1983) are common to all sets of Institute hull clauses. The exclusions in the ICC (1982) are, for the most part, common to all sets of Institute cargo clauses; but vary in some cases depending on the perils covered. The exclusions expressed in Institute trade clauses follow the pattern of the basic ICC but some of the wording varies a little in favour of the assured. For detail concerning these variations trainees and practitioners should study the relevant clauses and/or consult the reference books recommended earlier.

Without delving too deeply into marine insurance history it can be said that, probably, the first "customary" exclusion clause began to appear in marine insurance policies following the "Smyrna fleet" disaster in 1693. Some 100 ships out of a convoy of 400 merchantmen were captured or destroyed in this single action; resulting in ruin for many of the private marine insurers accepting proposals at Edward Lloyd`s coffee house and elsewhere in the City of London. There was no syndication at that time and the individual private underwriters who survived, in spite of heavy losses, were apprehensive of continuing to offer insurance against war risks. Almost to a man they agreed not to write marine insurance policies without incorporating a war exclusion clause in the SG form of policy. It will be recalled that, in the absence of this exclusion, the SG policy cover would include loss or damage to the insured ship and cargo proximately caused by warlike acts.

This exclusion was called the "F.C.& S." (free of capture and seizure) clause which, in its early format, was printed in the SG policy revised and adopted by Lloyd`s in 1779. Records do not show how long this survived as the only form of the SG policy in use at Lloyd`s. Certainly, by the time the MIA, 1906, was being drafted there were two formats for the SG form in use at Lloyd`s; these being the A policy form and the B policy form. Subject to any conditions to the contrary attached to contract, the policy in the A format covered loss of or damage to the subject matter insured proximately caused by any of the perils (including warlike perils) expressed in the policy form. The B policy was in the same format but incorporated the F.C.& S. clause; thereby excluding war perils and leaving the assured to effect insurance for the excluded risks elsewhere.

Those interested in the historic development of the SG policy might care to note that the recommended policy printed in the First schedule to the MIA, 1906, is in the A policy format (ie it does not incorporate the F.C.& S. clause). The SG policy in the B format gradually disappeared at Lloyd`s but the A policy format continued to be used at Lloyd`s, with the F.C.& S. clause incorporated in clauses attached to the policy document, until abrogation of the SG form of policy in the London market. Insurance companies, on the other hand, appear to have adopted the B format because the hull and cargo policies in the SG format used in the company market all had the exclusion actually printed in the policy form. In practice, this difference proved immaterial when, eventually, the F.C.& S. clause was incorporated in the Institute hull clauses and in the Institute cargo clauses; these being used with both Lloyd`s policies and company policies..

The F.C.& S.clause was amended following the "Coxwold" case (see note 2, above) to ensure that it applied only to hostile acts and did not take into account a warlike engagement of the insured ship or, as the case may be, the carrying vessel for cargo insurances. The amended exclusion continued to appear in hull and cargo clauses until abrogation of the SG form of policy by London market underwriters in 1982 for cargo and 1983 for hulls. The Technical & Clauses Committee drafted a new format for the war exclusion clause to be used in the new hull and cargo clauses. The new format for the ITC (1982) and other, relevant, sets of Institute hull and hull interest clauses excepts the perils "barratry" and "piracy" from the exclusion. The new format for cargo insurances is common to all sets of the ICC (1982) and similar sets of Institute cargo clauses; apart from those which cover "all risks" (eg ICC, 1982, A conditions) wherein the war exclusion clause excepts the peril "piracy" from the exclusion.

Today, when considering war risks insurance, one tends to think also of insurance against the risks of strikes, riots and civil commotions. Early marine insurance underwriters seemed content with the limitations of the perils expressed in the SG form of policy; no doubt deeming these not to embrace the risks of strikes, riots and civil commotions as a proximate cause of loss. Nevertheless, some concern was expressed regarding loss or damage to the subject matter insured, proximately caused by SG policy perils, which would not have arisen but for the existence of a riot or civil commotion. It is not clear when the F.R.C.C. (free of riots and civil commotions) clause began to appear in company policies and in marine clauses attached to Lloyd's SG policy form. Nevertheless, early formats of this exclusion clause incorporated the risk of "strikes" as well as the risks of "riots and civil commotions"; so that it became more familiarly known as the F.S.R& C.C. (free of strikes, riots and civil commotions) clause, in practice. Certainly, early in the 20th century it was the practice for the F.S.R.& C.C. clause, to appear in both hull and cargo insurance conditions; this clause continuing to be incorporated in marine insurance clauses until it was replaced by a similar exclusion, but in a different format, in the ITC (1983), the ICC (1982) and other relevant sets of Institute hull and cargo clauses.

When war broke out, in 1914, it became illegal for British ships to trade with Germany. This law prevented two British ships from delivering their cargoes of linseed to a German importer. The cargo policy was in the SG format and included coverage for war risks. A claim was made against the cargo underwriters based on frustration of the adventure by "restraint of princes" (a war peril incorporated in the SG form of policy). The underwriters contended that there had been a breach of the warranty of legality (see Section 8) and denied liability. In the subsequent court case, "Sanday -v- British & Foreign" (1914), the underwriters' defence regarding breach of warranty failed because the assured had abandoned the voyage; thereby avoiding breach of the warranty. It was held that the adventure had been frustrated by an insured peril and the claim was recoverable under the policy. No further action, regarding frustration of adventure, was taken until after the cessation of hostilities when, in 1919, underwriters introduced the "frustration" clause as a customary exclusion for use in all cargo policies. This clause, which still appears in all cargo clauses covering war risks, excludes any claim based on frustration of the voyage or adventure. The clause also appears in cargo clauses covering strikes risks.

9. Customary Exclusions - Marine Hulls (ITC 1983)

For the purpose of this introductory study comments are confined to an outline of the exclusion clauses found in the ITC (1983). Trainees and practitioners seeking detailed information on the perils that are subject to the customary exclusions are advised to consult "Marine Insurance - Volume 3 - Hull Practice" by Brown (Witherby 1993).

The exclusions, which are embraced by cl.23 to cl.26, are *paramount* clauses. That is to say, they take precedence over any condition or peril in the policy with which they are inconsistent. As an example, consider the peril "piracy" which is specified in the perils clause (cl.6) in the ITC (1983). The term "pirate" includes "rioters who attack the ship from the shore" (see note 3, above). The "strikes exclusion" clause in the ITC (1983) is cl.24. Amongst other things cl.24 excludes the peril "riots"; thereby over-riding the marine peril "piracy" where the act of piracy is committed by a rioter attacking the insured ship from the shore.

The preamble to both the "war exclusion" clause and the "strikes exclusion" clause provides that no claim will be paid for "loss, damage, *liability or expense* caused by any of the perils specified in the exclusion. By this preamble underwriters emphasise that the exclusions apply also to claims under the "collision" clause and the "duty of assured" clause (the latter being concerned with sue & labour charges); although for marine risks the cover in both cases is deemed to be supplementary to the main contract. These exclusions also embrace claims for general average sacrifice, general average contributions and salvage charges.

There are no war perils expressed in the marine clauses so the purpose of the war exclusion clause is to protect the underwriter from loss, damage, liability or expense proximately caused by any of the marine perils where such proximate cause was itself caused by a warlike peril. The exclusion embraces all forms of war peril and civil strife, including capture or seizure or attempts thereat. It also embraces circumstances where the insured vessel is in contact with a derelict mine, torpedo or any other derelict weapon of war; these "grey" areas being treated as war perils in modern practice.

The perils "strikes, riots and civil commotions" are not expressed in the marine clauses so the purpose of the strikes, etc. exclusion clause is to protect the underwriter from loss, damage, liability or expense proximately caused by any of the marine perils where such proximate cause is itself caused by a person or persons engaged in a strike, a labour dispute, or a civil commotion. The strikes, etc. exclusion clause also embraces the actions of terrorists or other persons acting from a political motive. It should be noted that, whereas an act of barratry or piracy is not excluded by the war exclusion clause, no such exception is made where strikers, etc. are concerned (see comments above regarding rioters as pirates). Thus, if a striking crew member set fire to the ship (an act of barratry) no claim for the fire damage would be recoverable under the policy.

The preamble to the "malicious acts exclusion" clause (cl.25 in the ITC, 1983) is much wider in its scope than that which precedes the war and strikes, etc. exclusion clauses. By this clause the underwriter is protected from loss, damage, liability or expense *arising from* (not just "caused by" as in the war and strikes, etc. exclusion clauses) the excluded peril. Nevertheless, it is more limited in its effect because it only excludes malicious acts where the person concerned detonates an explosive or uses a weapon of war. The clause treats an act by a person with a political motive as being malicious and within the ambit of the exclusion.

The final exclusion clause in the ITC (1983) and similar sets of hull and hull interest clauses is the "nuclear weapons" exclusion clause. This clause (cl.26 in the ITC, 1983) protects the underwriter from loss, damage, liability or expense when it *arises from* any nuclear or similar weapon of war. In practice, insurers writing hull war and strikes risks tend to embrace the perils specified in the earlier exclusions but they **never** embrace nuclear or similar weapons in the war & strikes risks cover.

10. War and Strikes Perils - Hulls (1983)

Underwriters in the cargo market, when writing war, etc. risks do so on a set of conditions which apply exclusively to war risks cover. When writing strikes etc. risks they do so under a separate sets of conditions. The reason for this is the need to comply with the "waterborne" agreement; whereby London cargo underwriters have agreed not to cover goods on land against war risks. Except in the case of shipbuilding insurance, to which the waterborne agreement applies, (separate hull and strikes conditions being published by the ILU for this purpose) hull underwriters do not write war and strikes risks separately from each other; the conditions for both war and strikes cover being incorporated in a single set of clauses.

Although this might not be the practice in other markets it is customary, in the London market, for hull war and strikes risks to be placed separately from marine risks. The ILU publishes clauses for both time policies and voyage policies. For the purposes of this introductory study an outline of the perils covered by, and excluded from, the "Institute War & Strikes Clauses - Hulls Time" (CL.281 1983) is deemed sufficient to give the trainee an introduction to hull war & strikes risks cover. More detailed information is available in the hull practice book recommended in note 9, above.

The policy covers loss of or damage to the insured vessel *caused by* a list of perils which embraces those specified in the war and strikes exclusions in the marine clauses, on which comment appears in note 9, above, plus confiscation and expropriation. The cover extends to embrace "malicious acts" by *any* person where these are not covered by the marine policy. It does **not** embrace nuclear weapons; in fact the war & strikes policy specifically excludes loss, damage, liability or expense arising from the detonation of a nuclear weapon. The policy excludes "piracy" except where a rioter attacks the ship from the shore. Trainees and practitioners should examine CL.281 for more detail concerning the excluded perils.

Whilst we are on the subject of hull war & strikes cover it would be useful to note that the policy is cancelled automatically upon the hostile detonation of a nuclear weapon anywhere in the world. The policy is also cancelled automatically on the outbreak of a major war; losses arising therefrom not being covered. Further, underwriters reserve the right to give 7 days notice to cancel the war & strikes policy at any time during its currency; although, in this case, it is customary for cover to be reinstated subject to an agreed adjustment to the rate and conditions.

11. Customary Exclusions - Marine Cargo - ICC (1982)

The war and strikes exclusion clauses that appear in the ITC (1983) appear, also, in the ICC (1982). Apart from the fact that they are not printed as *paramount* clauses the effect of these exclusions on a marine cargo policy is the same as the effect of the war and strikes exclusions in the hull policy; so the comments in note 10, above, regarding these exclusions apply equally to a cargo policy. There is no "malicious acts" exclusion clause in the cargo policy; but one must not assume from this that malicious acts are covered by a cargo policy. Neither the ICC (1982) B conditions nor the ICC (1982) C conditions covers malicious damage; nor is it covered by the cargo strikes

The perils specified in the war and strikes exclusion clauses that appear in the ITC (1983) are, also, specified in the ICC (1982). Apart from the fact that they are not printed as *paramount* clauses the effect of these exclusions on a marine cargo policy is the same as the effect of the war and strikes exclusions in the hull policy; so the comments in note 10, above, regarding these exclusions apply equally to a cargo policy. It should be noted, however, that there is no "malicious acts" exclusion clause in the cargo policy; but one must not assume from this that malicious acts are covered by a cargo policy. Neither the ICC (1982) B conditions nor the ICC (1982) C conditions covers malicious damage; nor is it covered by the cargo strikes clauses. The ILU publishes a "malicious damage" clause for use in marine cargo policies where the underwriter agrees to extend the cover in this respect. Another important difference to note is that the strikes exclusion clause in a cargo policy not only excludes loss, damage liability or expense caused by the specified strikers, terrorists, etc. but, also, excludes loss, damage, liability or expense *resulting from* strikes, etc. risks. For example, no claim would attach to the cargo policy for warehousing costs incurred by the assured because a strike had delayed the goods during transit.

12. War & Strikes Perils - Cargo (1982)

All sets of marine cargo insurance conditions incorporate both a war exclusion clause and a strikes exclusion clause (see note 11, above). A cargo assured is not obliged to have cover for the risks excluded by these two clauses and the cargo underwriter is not obliged to provide such cover. However, in practice, it is common for the assured to request an extension of the cargo policy conditions to cover both war and strikes risks and, to implement this, the broker incorporates the words "incl. war, etc. at scale" in the placing slip conditions. Sometimes, though rarely, one sees a cargo policy extended to cover only strikes risks; particularly where the transit includes a known war zone. The "scale" rates are minimum premium rates for cargo insurance war and strikes risks which are determined by a war risks rating committee which sits, as circumstances demand, to represent the interests of the London market in this respect. Although these rates are primarily intended for business written in the London market they are usually followed by other markets.

Unlike hull war and strikes insurance practice it is not the practice for cargo insurance contracts to be placed with a different group of underwriters from those who write the marine risks contract. In the cargo market, with the underwriter`s agreement, it is the practice for the marine policy to be extended to embrace war and strikes risks. Further, whereas the war & strikes risks cover is embraced in one set of clauses for use in the hull policy, the conditions published by the ILU for use in cargo policies are in one set of clauses for war risks and in a completely separate set of clauses for strikes risks.

Cover under the war clauses is subject to the waterborne agreement (see Section 9, above). The conditions for duration of cover for war risks are, in the main, common to all cargo policies. The exceptions relating to such interests as postal sendings and air sendings where some concessions are made regarding the strict application of the waterborne agreement. Where strikes, etc. risks are concerned duration of cover follows that expressed in the "transit" clause in the marine clauses attached to the policy; thus where this varies from the norm (eg in some cargo trade clauses) a separate set of cargo strikes clauses is published by the ILU for use in such policies. Practitioners might care to note that the only cargo war clauses published by the ILU for use with trade clauses are those issued for "commodity" trades; it being intended that this set of cargo war clauses be used for any policy that is subject to any set of the Institute trade clauses.

Following the pattern set earlier in this introductory study it is intended to give only an outline of the perils covered and excluded from the cargo war and strikes clauses; this being deemed sufficient to give the trainee a general understanding of the cover. Trainees and practitioners seeking more detailed information on the individual perils and exclusions are advised to consult "Marine Insurance - Volume 2 - Cargo Practice" by Brown (Witherby 1985).

War risks - perils and exclusions - The policy covers only those perils specified in the exclusion clause printed in the marine cargo clauses. On the face of it, one might be forgiven for assuming that the war risks clauses simply reinstate the perils expressed in the relevant cargo policy as though the war exclusion clause had not appeared therein and that a policy with the ICC (1982) C conditions attached thereto would provide narrower cover than one with the ICC (1982) A conditions. But this is not so! The war risk perils, while specifying practically the same risks as the exclusions expressed in the marine clauses, stand by themselves so *any* loss of or damage to the insured goods proximately caused by, say, a hostile act would be covered. As an example, consider a circumstance where the goods are insured by a policy with the ICC (1982) C conditions attached thereto, plus the standard cargo war clauses. Seawater enters the hold and damages the insured goods. In the absence of a warlike act the damage would not be covered. But, if the seawater entered the hold through a hole caused by a shell being fired at the ship the damage would be covered by the war clauses.

It should be noted that the cargo war clauses cover only loss of or damage to the insured goods *caused by* the specified perils. There is no cover for expenses incurred by the assured as a consequence of the warlike act.

The exclusions expressed in the cargo war clauses are the same as those in the basic marine clauses (eg ICC, 1982, A conditions). These include a repetition of the "statutory" exclusions and exclusions regarding inadequate packing, insolvency or financial default of carriers and unseaworthiness and/or unfitness of carrying vessels, etc. There is, of course, no war exclusion clause. One might be surprised at the absence of a strikes exclusion clause; although it is unlikely that a policy covering war risks will not also cover strikes risks so the absence of this exclusion is not likely to cause problems in practice. One exclusion in the cargo war clauses which is peculiar to this type of cover is the "frustration" clause (see Note 8, above).

Strikes, etc. risks - perils and exclusions - The strikes clauses do not cover losses which *result from* a strike. Earlier it was mentioned that the assured could not recover, under the ICC (1982), warehousing expenses he incurred as a result of the insured goods being delayed during transit by a strike. It should be noted that these expenses would not be recoverable either under the strikes risks clauses; for the cover in these clauses is limited to "loss of or damage to" the insured goods *caused by* the actions of strikers, terorists, etc. or by persons taking part in labour disturbances, riots or civil commotions.

The exclusions expressed in the strikes, etc. clauses are the same as those in the cargo war clauses (including a "frustration" clause). But in this case a "war exclusion" clause is incorporated. This being necessary because there may be an occasion when the cargo policy covers strikes, etc. risks but not war risks.

13. Sentimental Loss and Sympathetic Damage

Before we leave the subject of policy perils and losses relating thereto some comment could be useful on two types of loss which the trainee might encounter in practice and which are not mentioned in policies. These concern goods in transit and are "sentimental loss" and "sympathetic damage".

Sentimental loss - In non-marine insurance practice one might equate this with "emotional" value rather than "intrinsic" value. For example, a wedding ring may have a sentimental value far in excess of its intrinsic value. In marine insurance terms, however, the term is applied to circumstances where the goods diminish in financial value due to fear of damage rather than because they have actually suffered from damage. As an example, consider a cargo of tea in cases. The cargo is covered by the ICC (1982) B conditions. During transit seawater enters the carrying vessel`s hold. It damages some of the tea and also stains a number of the other cases; the tea in the latter showing no sign of water damage. The tea which is damaged is the subject of a claim under the cargo policy and is destroyed as being unfit for human consumption. The cases with the undamaged tea are offered for sale but those with stained cases fetch a lower price because buyers contend the tea in these cases might be damaged. The differencc bctween the price paid and the price the tea should have fetched is a "sentimental" loss and is not recoverable under the cargo policy.

For certain types of cargo (eg chemicals which could change their nature if exposed to, say, heat) special policy conditions are usually agreed to cover the assured where the cargo has to be destroyed in circumstances which might, otherwise, have been considered a "sentimental loss" and so debar a claim on the policy.

Sympathetic loss - This is damage to insured goods caused by the proximity of other goods in the same hold, warehouse, etc. Usually, it takes the form of contamination and often relates to foodstuffs. As an example, consider a cargo of hides in bundles which become wet from condensation in a ship`s hold and give off an odour. This odour contaminates a cargo of butter, in cases, which is stowed in the same hold. The butter is insured by the ICC (1982) B conditions so no claim would attach to the policy since the damage to the hides was not caused by a peril insured by the policy covering the butter. However, what if the hides were damaged by *seawater* entering the ship`s hold? In the latter circumstances the assured might be able to recover under his policy for the damage to the butter because the damage to the hides was caused by an insured peril. The underwriter might, in these circumstances, be able to exercise subrogation rights (see Section 13) to recover his loss from the carrier if he can show the butter should not have been stowed in the vicinity of the hides and was, therefore, improperly stowed

---

SEE OVERPAGE FOR SELF STUDY QUESTIONAIRE

SELF STUDY QUESTIONS

Before moving on to the next Section satisfy yourself that you have absorbed the subject matter of the previous Section. The following questions should be answered without reference to the text.

1. Do you understand the principle of proximate cause? In what circumstances is this principle not applied to a claim under a marine insurance policy?

2. Define the term "all risks". In which type of marine insurance contract would you expect to find "all risks" cover?

3. The perils covered by a policy based on the SG format were expressed in the policy form. Where in a policy document, based on the MAR form of policy, would you expect to see the perils covered specified?

4. In which of the following sets of Institute cargo clauses are the perils not specified?
   ICC (1982) A, ICC (1982) B, ICC (1982) C

5. What are the "statutory" exclusions? In the absence of anything in the contract to the contrary, do these apply to all marine insurance contracts as applicable thereto?

6. The exclusions expressed in a hull policy, based on the ITC (1983) are said to be "paramount" clauses. How does this restriction affect claims proximately caused by perils expressed in the "perils" clause. Can you illustrate your answer with an example?

7. The peril "piracy" was at one time treated as a war peril. Today it is treated as a marine peril.
   (a) What form of piracy is still excluded by the paramount clauses in the ITC (1982)?
   (b) Which peril expressed in the hull war & strikes clauses covers loss or damage caused by a form of "piracy"?
   (c) Is "piracy" covered by any of the following?
      (1) ICC (1982) A conditions
      (2) ICC (1982) B conditions
      (3) ICC (1982) C conditions
      (4) Institute cargo war clauses?
      (5) Institute cargo strikes, etc. clauses?

8. The ILU publishes one set of hull clauses to cover both war & strikes, etc. risks? Why does the ILU publish separate sets of clauses for cargo war cover and cargo strikes, etc. cover?

9. What is a "frustration" clause and in which type of insurance contract would you expect to see this clause?

10. What is a "sentimental" loss in marine insurance terms?

This page has been left blank for trainees` notes

SECTION ELEVEN

TOTAL LOSS

1. Introduction
2. Actual Total Loss
3. Claims in Connection with Missing Ship
4. Total Loss of Part - Cargo
5. Constructive Total Loss
6. Notice of Abandonment
7. Compromised and Arranged Total Loss
8. Underwriters' Rights and Obligations Regarding Disposal of Wreck
9. Waiver Clause
10. Freight Waiver Clause

SECTION ELEVEN

1. Introduction

Having established that the proximate cause of a loss was an insured peril or, in certain circumstances (see comments on perils expressed in the ICC, 1982, B & C conditions in note 10, above), that the the loss was reasonably attributable to an insured peril one must determine the *type* of loss. This is important because section 56 sub.1 of the Marine Insurance Act, 1906, provides that a loss can be total or partial; and, in some cases, a partial loss is not recoverable under the policy (eg a hull & machinery policy covering total loss only). Further, the policy might incorporate a provision whereby partial losses, but not a total loss, are subject to a deductible or franchise (see Section 4).

To determine which type of loss relates to a claim one must first test the circumstances for a total loss; because the MIA, 1906, sect. 56 sub.1 provides that any loss other than a total loss must be treated as a "partial" loss The comments in this section of the study are concerned only with the various types of marine total loss as established by the MIA, 1906, and as qualified in modern marine insurance practice; plus comment on "compromised or arranged total loss" which is not recognised by the MIA, 1906, but which sometimes provides the basis for a settlement under a hull & machinery policy. Comments on ATL (actual total loss) as defined by the Act and as applied in practice appear in note 2, below. Comments on CTL (constructive total loss) as defined by the Act and as qualified in practice appear in notes 5 and 6, below. Comments on Comp.TL (compromised or arranged total loss) appear in note 7, below.

Section 56 sub.3 of the MIA, 1906, provides that, except where the policy specifically states otherwise, a marine insurance policy which covers total loss covers both actual total loss and constructive total loss. In practice all marine policies cover total loss but some exclude partial loss; an example of the latter would be a hull TLO policy.

Determining the type of loss does not necessarily mean a claim is recoverable under the policy; one must also prove that the loss was proximately caused by an insured peril or, where applicable (see section 10 regarding perils expressed in the ICC, 1982, B & C conditions), the loss was reasonably attributable to a particular peril expressed in a cargo policy. There is no obligation on the assured to claim a total loss. If the circumstances indicate that it would be to the assured's advantage to claim a partial loss (even a 100% partial loss) he may take this course. If the assured decides to claim an ATL or a CTL the type of loss must, unless the policy provides otherwise, fall within the scope of the relevant definition expressed in the MIA, 1906. Where the assured claims a total loss, but the circumstances dictate that the loss is partial rather than total, the assured may (provided no policy condition debars a claim for partial loss - eg the policy is not a TLO contract) withdraw his TL claim and, instead, claim for a partial loss (MIA, 1906, sect. 56 sub.4). Thus, failure to prove a CTL does not necessarily mean no claim attaches to the policy.

Sometimes goods of mixed varieties are identifiable only by labels attached to the packets, cans, etc., or by other means of identification (eg marks stencilled on boxes). Should such goods arrive at the destination specified in the policy without the labels or with the other means of identification obliterated, as the case may, it is often impossible to identify the varieties. Where the loss of labels or obliteration of marks has been caused by an insured peril the assured might wish to submit a claim under the policy for a total loss. But, section 56 sub.5 of the MIA, 1906, provides that such a loss must be treated as a "partial loss" not as a "total loss". Unfortunately, whilst making this stipulation, the Act gives no guidance to claims assessors on how to calculate the claim for partial loss. In practice, it is customary for a cargo policy covering goods in cans, where identifying labels might be washed off, to incorporate a "labels" clause in the wording of the policy with the intention of clarifying the underwriter`s intention and the treatment of claims resulting solely from loss of labels.

Except where the policy provides otherwise (eg as in the "break-up voyage" clause in the ITC, 1983) the measure of indemnity for actual total loss and constructive total loss is, subject to the adequacy of the sum insured, the insured value expressed in the policy. Where the sum insured is less than the insured value (eg where the policy underwriters are co-insurers with underwriters appearing in another policy) the measure of indemnity is the sum insured by the policy. In all cases, the policy lapses automatically following a total loss of the subject matter insured; the assured not being entitled to a return of premium in respect of the unexpired period of the policy; even where the total loss was not covered by the policy. In practice, any lay-up return earned by a hull assured, during the currency of a time policy, becomes forfeit when the ship is totally lost before the time the policy is due to expire; whether or not the total loss is covered by the policy.

2. Actual Total Loss *(MIA, 1906, sect.57)*

The MIA, 1906, gives four definitions for actual total loss; each applying depending on the circumstances of the loss and the subject matter insured. No other circumstance than these will be recognised in English law as constituting an actual total loss. There is an actual total loss where -

(1) the subject matter insured is destroyed; or
(2) the subject matter insured is so damaged as to cease to be the thing insured [this is termed *loss of specie* in practice]; or
(3) the assured is irretrievably deprived of the subject matter insured; or
(4) the subject matter insured is a "missing" ship or cargo carried in a "missing" ship.

The following comments will help the trainee to understand the scope of these definitions.

Totally destroyed - This would appear to be self explanatory. However, one must use commonsense in circumstances where the subject matter insured is not completely destroyed but, for all practical purposes, it might just as well have been. Consider the following examples -

(a) The insured ship runs aground on rocks and is pounded by heavy seas until she is nothing more than a wreck. If one takes the term "destroyed" too literally it could be said that the definition in the Act would not apply. Nevertheless, it is unlikely that an underwriter would argue that these circumstances justify a claim for an ATL.

(b) Insured goods, though not completely destroyed, are so badly damaged by fire that the surveyor considers what is left is unusable. In practice the underwriter would accept the surveyor`s recommendation and the assured`s claim for the loss to be treated as an ATL.

Loss of specie - Although it has been suggested the term could apply to a ship, one tends to think of this type of ATL as relating to cargo. An example, often suggested by insurance teachers to illustrate this, concerns multi-ply paper sacks, each containing cement, which are carried by a ship that runs aground. Seawater enters the hold via a hole made when the ship grounded on rocks. Eventually the ship is refloated but when the cement is discharged the whole cargo has solidified in consequence of the immersion in seawater. The cement is no longer the thing insured so an ATL can be claimed on the grounds of loss of specie. A further dimension for this type of loss can be applied where the subject matter insured is so damaged as to be unusable for the purpose for which it was intended. As an example, consider a cargo of potatoes in sacks which were also immersed in seawater for a long time. On discharge they were found to be soggy in consequence of the immersion in seawater and, because of this, they could not be used for human consumption. The assured was able to, successfully, claim for an ATL based on loss of specie.

Irretrievably deprived - When considering this aspect of ATL one must have regard for section 60(2i) of the MIA, 1906, which provides that where the assured is *unlikely* to recover the subject matter insured there is a case for a CTL rather than an ATL. However, where the circumstances are such as to make the difficulties involved in recovering the subject matter insured insurmountable there is a case for an ATL claim on the grounds that the subject matter insured is irretrievable. One normally associates this type of ATL with capture or seizure and attaching to a war risks policy. But, as a "marine" example, consider the case of a ship which was sailing in the Andaman Sea, off the coast of Burma. She was caught in a monsoon near the delta which forms the several mouths of the Irrawaddy river and, the master having lost all control, the ship was carried inland by a huge wave which dumped her in swamps some three miles from any navigable waters. There was no possibility of recovery so she was deemed to be an ATL.

3. Claims in Connection with Missing Ship

When a ship has been reported "overdue" and, after fruitless enquiries, no news of her fate can be established she is posted as "missing". In the London market it is customary for the name of the ship to be entered in the "missing ship" record at Lloyd`s and for its new status to be posted on notice boards. At this stage the assured may institute a claim for an ATL; this applying to both the assured in the hull policy and any assured in a cargo policy where it can be reasonably established that the goods were on board the ship when she commenced the voyage during which she disappeared.

As commented earlier, establishment of the *type* of loss (ie that it is an ATL) does not necessarily mean a claim is payable under the policy. Therefore, in addition to showing the ship has been posted as "missing" there is, technically, a responsibility on the assured to show the loss was caused by an insured peril. Hull underwriters recognise the impracticality of insisting on compliance by the assured with this obligation and tend to treat the loss as having been proximately caused by a peril covered by the "marine" policy; making an exception only where the "balance of probability" indicates a war loss.

Where cargo is concerned it is not usually necessary for underwriters to worry about the difference between marine and war risks cover because both are commonly combined in the same contract. However, there could be a problem where the cargo policy covers limited perils. Take, for example, a policy which is subject to the ICC (1982) C conditions; the cover thereunder not embracing any form of loss from heavy weather. It should be remembered that waiving the assured's obligation to prove the cause of loss is a peril covered by the policy, when considering missing ship claims, is entirely at the discretion of the underwriter and trainees will need to learn from experience the trend in their particular cargo markets.

In cases of mysterious disappearance one's suspicions turn to the seaworthiness of the ship. By reference to the notes in Section 8, it will be recalled that, under a time policy, a hull underwriter is not liable for any loss attributable to unseaworthiness where, with the knowledge and privity of the assured, the ship was sent to sea in an unseaworthy condition. Therefore, if the hull underwriter can show the ship was unseaworthy when she sailed from her last port he could decline the claim for missing ship on the grounds of unseaworthiness; leaving the assured to prove, if he can, that the loss was proximately caused by an insured peril unconnected with the seaworthiness of the ship. It is not so easy for cargo underwriters to deny liability on these grounds because, although there is technically an implied warranty of seaworthiness in the cargo policy (see Section 8), the effect of breach of this warranty is waived, in practice, except where the underwriter can prove the assured or their servants were aware of the unseaworthiness of the ship.

In all cases (hull or cargo) should the "missing" ship be found after a total loss claim has been settled the underwriters are entitled to demand title to the ship or cargo, as the case may be, in respect of which they settled the claim. Under English law the respective underwriters can dispose of the ship or cargo, as the case may be, at their discretion; retaining the whole proceeds even if these exceed the claim paid.

4. Total Loss of Part - Cargo (MIA, 1906, sect. 71 sub.2 & 3)

Section 71 (sub.1) of the MIA, 1906, provides that where "apportionable" goods (eg goods in packages rather than in bulk) are insured by a valued policy and part of the goods is totally lost the claim shall be assessed as a total loss of part; rather than a partial loss of the whole.

To apply this procedure in its simplest form, provided all packages can be said to have an equal value, one would divide the insured value in the policy by the number of packages insured; thereby determining the insured value of one package. The claim for loss of one package would be the insured value of that package. Where claims under the ICC (1963) WA & FPA conditions were concerned claims assessors treated each craftload as being an apportionable part and often found it convenient to settle a claim for a lost craftload as a total loss of part. Today, in the absence of a franchise in cargo policies or FPA type of cover, there is seldom need to treat craftloads as separate insurances; but, where practical, the procedure is still applied to a claim under cl.1.3 in the ICC (1982) B conditions when a package is dropped overboard during loading, transhipment or discharge.

In the unlikely event that cargo is insured by an *unvalued* policy a claim for total loss of part will be based on the insurable value of the goods (MIA, 1906, sect. 71 sub.2).

(Text continues on Page 6)

5. Constructive Total Loss *(MIA, 1906, sects.60 to 63)*

The purpose of the CTL (constructive total loss) procedure is to allow an assured, whose property is not an ATL but is so badly damaged or inaccessible that it is of little economic use to him, to abandon what is left of the insured property to the underwriter and claim a total loss. This right is granted to the marine assured in English law but he is not obliged to take this course of action even though the circumstances entitle him to claim a CTL. The assured can, if he wishes, retain what is left of the insured property and claim a "partial" loss; even 100% partial loss. For example, consider a ship that is built for a special job; requiring special building skills and special building equipment, the latter being disposed of after completion of building. The rebuilding cost of such a vessel could be much higher than her insured value so, if the ship suffered damage from an accident where her damaged condition would justify a CTL, the assured might prefer to have her repaired (himself bearing costs in excess of the insured value) rather than abandon her to underwriters and claim a CTL.

There might be occasions when an assured, finding himself in difficult economic circumstances, would find it advantageous to claim a total loss under his marine insurance policy. In such case he would, no doubt, welcome a fortuitous accident to his property which gave him the opportunity to turn an economic liability into hard cash. It is for this reason that strict compliance with the rules to establish a total loss is important. The rules applying to claims based on ATL (actual total loss) can be found in Part 2, above. The rules for determining a CTL are even more strict and literal compliance with these is, particularly, required in practice.

Cargo underwriters are prepared, on the face of it, to accept a CTL based on the procedure laid down in the MIA, 1906; emphasising this with a CTL clause in the ICC (1982). Hull underwriters, on the other hand, whilst accepting the principles established by the MIA, 1906, qualify these principles by insisting that a claim calculated with the value of the ship in mind shall take into account the *insured value* expressed in the policy. However, before considering this aspect of hull practice one must clearly understand the rules established by the MIA, 1906, regarding determination of a CTL; for there are factors besides valuation which could establish a CTL.

Section 60 of the MIA, 1906 specifies the circumstances in which a marine assured can claim a CTL. It is important to remember that the Act only defines the *type* of loss. It does not say the loss is recoverable under the marine insurance policy. A CTL is recoverable under a hull insurance policy only when the loss was proximately caused by a peril specified in the policy. A CTL is recoverable under a cargo policy only when the loss was proximately caused by a peril specified in the policy, or embraced within the term "all risks", if applicable to the policy conditions. Further, in the case of the ICC (1982) B and C conditions a CTL would be recoverable under the policy if it was reasoably attributable to any of the particular perils expressed therein for this purpose (see comment on cargo insurance perils in Section 10).

A summary of the provision in section 60 of the MIA, 1906, shows that the assured can claim a CTL where he reasonably abandons (See comments in Part 6, below) the insured property because -

(a) An actual total loss appears to be inevitable; or

(b) The assured has been deprived of his ship or goods, as the case may be, and recovery is <u>unlikely</u>; or

(c) Recovery is possible but the estimated costs involved in the recovery would exceed the value of the property when saved; or

(d) The estimated cost of recovering and/or repairing the insured ship would exceed the repaired value of the ship; or

(e) The estimated cost of recovering and/or reconditioning and/or forwarding the insured goods to their intended destination would exceed the market value of the goods on arrival at the destination.

Some comment on the provisions of this section of the MIA, 1906, would be appropriate at this point.

(a) *ATL unavoidable (MIA, 1906, sect. 60 sub.1)* - This can be illustrated with a situation where a ship has run aground on rocks and is being consistently pounded by wind and waves in circumstances where nothing can be done to save the ship. It is the opinion of competent authorities (eg the "Salvage Association") that, unless the situation changes soon, the ship will break up under the assault of wind and waves and become a complete wreck; thereby qualifying for an ATL claim under the hull policy. The assured need not wait for the ATL to occur. He can abandon the wreck to the underwriter and claim a CTL under the hull policy (MIA, 1906, sect. 60 sub.1).

(b) *Unlikely to recover (MIA, 1906, sect. 60 sub.2)* - It will be recalled that where the subject matter insured is irretrievable the loss can be treated as an ATL. On the other hand, where the subject matter insured is retrievable, but the assured is *unlikely* to recover it the loss should be treated as a CTL. One tends to think of this circumstance occurring where insured property is captured, seized or detained by belligerents in a war situation. The property may be recovered but experience has shown this to be unlikely in most cases.

It is peculiar that cargo underwriters do not seem to recognise this form of CTL. The CTL clause in the ICC (1982) categorically states that *no* claim for CTL will be entertained except as provided by the clause; this not incorporating circumstances where the assured is *unlikely* to recover the cargo. The cargo war clauses do not incorporate a CTL clause; therefore, in the absence of anything to the contrary in the policy wording, a loss caused by one of the war perils should be subject to the ruling in the MIA, 1906 to determine whether or not it could be a CTL. Bearing in mind that it is customary for cargo war risks to be incorporated in the same policy document as cover for marine perils, any anticipated problems arising out of this situation could be resolved by incorporating some form of "detainment" clause (see below) in a cargo policy covering war risks; thereby allowing the assured to claim a CTL if the cargo has been detained by a war peril for, say, 12 months.

Marine hull clauses (eg ITC, 1983) refer only to claims for CTL based on comparison between costs and values but do not restrict CTL claims to those so based. For example, the hull assured could claim under his war & strikes policy for a CTL, caused by an insured peril, based on any of the circumstances specified as a CTL in (a) to (d) in the above list. In any event, where hull war and strikes risks are concerned the Institute clauses incorporate a "detainment" clause which allows the assured who has been deprived from free use and disposal of his ship by capture, seizure, etc. for a continuous period of 12 months to abandon it and claim a CTL. In practice this may be extended by an additional clause to embrace blocking or trapping of the ship, in consequence of insured perils, for a continuous period of 12 months.

(c) *Recovery costs exceed saved value (MIA, 1906, sect. 60 sub.2i)* - As an example consider insured goods carried by a vessel that is cast aground on a barren rocky coastline by a violent storm. The vessel is badly holed and cannot be refloated.

Sufficient of the cargo has survived the initial accident for consideration to be given to salvaging the sound cargo and carrying it ashore. However, estimates indicate that the costs of salvage would exceed the value of the cargo when saved. Here would be grounds for the assured to abandon the cargo and claim a CTL based on a comparison between the estimated costs of recovery and the saved value of the cargo.

This section of the Act could apply also to a ship where the estimated costs of recovery would exceed the saved (market) value of the ship. See notes below regarding replacement of the market value with the insured value, in practice.

(d) *Costs of recovery and repair exceed repaired value (MIA, 1906, sect. 60 sub.2i & 2ii)* - This applies to ship insurance and relates to circumstances where the insured ship is damaged and in a situation where she has to be salvaged or moved to a place of safety before a repair procedure can be implemented. It should be noted that, whilst anticipated GA contributions and salvage costs can be included in the estimated costs, the Act does not allow a deduction from the cost of repairs in respect of recoveries in general average to be taken into account. Incidentally, although this is not mentioned in the Act, hull underwriters do not reduce the cost of repairs by any recoveries they might make for disposal of wreck.

The following example (based on the MIA, 1906; **not** on the ITC) illustrates where the estimated costs of recovery and repairs compared with the market (repaired) value of the ship indicate that it would be uneconomical for an uninsured person to save the vessel; thereby providing grounds for a CTL claim on the policy:

Estimated cost of temporary repairs necessary to effect removal		£ 150,000
Estimated cost towage to safety		50,000
Estimated costs to be incurred at port of refuge		25,000
Estimated cost of towage to repair port		60,000
Estimated cost of permanent repairs		5,800,000
	Total	£6,085,000

Market (repaired) value of ship £6,000,000

These sections of the MIA, 1906, apply also to circumstances where no salvage costs are involved but the estimated cost of repairs, etc. would exceed the repaired value of the ship; using the above calculation, with the salvage items removed, one can see that a CTL claim on this basis would fail.

In practice hull underwriters will not accept a comparison based on the *market (repaired)* value of the ship in CTL calculations. Ships are frequently insured for values which are in excess of their market values; particularly when ship values are diminishing whilst repair costs remain high or are increasing. Underwriters fear that, in the absence of a protective clause in the hull policy, an assured might, if it is to his advantage, claim a CTL based on the market (repaired) value and recover the full insured value. Hull underwriters do not try to restrict the assured's right to claim the full insured value but they do restrict his right to base a CTL claim on the ship's market (repaired) value. The CTL clause in the ITC (1983) replaces the market (repaired) value with the *insured* value in the above calculation; thereby denying a CTL claim if the insured value is more than the total estimated costs; even though these costs exceed the market (repaired) value of the ship. Where a CTL claim fails the assured can, in theory, claim only for a partial loss (ie subject to the policy deductible, the cost of recovering and repairing the ship up to the insured value in any one accident). In practice, consideration might be given to a compromised total loss settlement (see below).

Further, in practice, the assured is not permitted to include, in the CTL calculation, the cost of repairing damage that has remained unrepaired from a previous accident; nor may the assured include, in the calculation, the cost of repairing damage incurred in more than one accident.

To ameliorate the effects of the CTL clause the underwriter might agree to incorporate a "dual valuation" clause (or other form of multi-valuation clause) in the hull policy. These introductory notes do not embrace detail concerning the use of multi-valuation clauses in hull practice; suffice to say that a dual valuation clause allows the assured to use one agreed value for CTL purposes and the other agreed value for all other purposes. For detail on these clauses trainees and practitioners are advised to consult "Marine Insurance - Volume 3 - Hull Practice" by Brown (Witherby 1993).

(e) *Cargo - Costs of recovery, etc. (MIA, 1906, sect. 60 sub.2iii)* - Cargo underwriters confirm, rather than qualify, the provisions of this section of the Act by the CTL clause incorporated in the policy conditions. The clause in the ICC (1982) allows the assured to claim a CTL (where such was caused by or was reasonably attributable to, as applicable to the policy conditions, a peril covered by the policy) when the estimated costs of saving, etc. the property would exceed its estimated value on arrival at the intended destination for the goods. In the case of cargo it is assumed that, whilst some reconditioning (eg repackaging, etc.) might be necessary, no repair costs are likely to arise. The estimated arrival value of the cargo is based on its market value, in whatever condition it is on arrival (ie sound, damaged or short delivered); not taking into account its insured value. Further, unlike underwriters in hull practice, cargo underwriters do not require a comparison between the estimated costs and the *insured* value. Cargo underwriters accept the *arrived* value of the goods as a basis for the calculation; but pay the full insured value (subject to the adequacy of the sum insured) if the CTL is proved. The following examples illustrate comparisons between costs and arrived values:

Example 1 - The goods are insured for £5,000, so valued. The carrying vessel is driven ashore during heavy weather. Pending salvage operations on the ship, it is suggested that the insured cargo be discharged into lighters and taken ashore with the intention of transferring the goods to another vessel to complete the planned transit. However, upon examination on board, it is found that considerable damage to the goods has occurred and some repackaging of sound goods will be necessary. In view of the low value of the goods doubts are raised regarding the practicality of salvaging the goods and forwarding them. The estimated costs are as follows:

Estimated costs of lighterage (including handling)	£ 600
Estimated cost of reconditioning the goods	300
Estimated cost of warehousing at POR	250
Estimated cost of forwarding to planned destination	600
Total	£1,750

Estimated *damaged* value on arrival £1,500

There are clearly grounds for claiming a CTL in these circumstances and one would expect the assured to abandon the goods on board the stricken vessel and claim a CTL for the full insured value of £5,000. It would be for the underwriter to decide whether to accept abandonment (see Part 6, below) and whether or not to salvage the goods and sell them locally.

Example 2 - The goods have an insured value of £420,000. During extreme heavy weather the carrying vessel is involved in a collision with another ship; neither vessel being at fault. The carrying vessel is badly damaged and puts into a port of refuge. The carrier, exercising a liberty granted to him under the contract of carriage, discharges the cargo at the intermediate port and terminates the contract of carriage. The cargo underwriters are advised of the situation so termination of the contract of carriage does not prejudice a claim under the policy; which might otherwise have been the case. The cargo was apparently damaged by the collision and a surveyor is appointed to examine the damage and to report on the situation. The surveyor reports that the goods are badly damaged and that it would be impractical as well as uneconomical for them to be forwarded to the planned destination. Using the surveyor's estimated figures, below, the assured claims a CTL:

Estimated costs of reconditioning the goods	£1,000
Estimated cost of warehousing at POR	800
Estimated cost of forwarding to planned destination	1,200
Total	£3,000

Estimated *damaged* value on arrival £2,800

For a CTL the amount of the claim under the policy would be £420,000, being the insured value. But, where a local market can be found, underwriters might propose a "salvage loss" settlement; whereby the goods are sold locally by the assured and the claim under the policy would be settled for the difference between the insured value and the proceeds (less sale costs) from the sale.

6. Notice of Abandonment *(MIA, 1906, sect. 62)*

The assured cannot expect to claim a CTL and retain title to the insured property. He **must** abandon the insured property to the underwriter as a condition precedent to a CTL. It is also a condition precedent that the assured must give *notice* of his intention to abandon the property and claim a CTL. The following should be noted:

(a) *Failure to give notice* - Failure to give notice of abandonment means that the loss can be treated only as a partial loss (MIA, 1906, sect. 62 sub.1).

(b) *When notice is not necessary* - The purpose of notice is to give the underwriter an opportunity to prevent or minimise the loss; therefore notice of abandonment is not necessary when, at the time the assured receives the information, the notice can be of no benefit to the underwriter (MIA, 1906, sect. 62 sub.7). Notice of abandonment is not necessary when claiming an ATL (MIA, 1906, sect. 57 sub.2). It is not necessary for a direct insurer to give notice of abandonment when claiming a CTL under a reinsurance contract (MIA, 1906, sect. 62 sub.9). The underwriter may waive notice of abandonment (MIA, 1906, sect. 62 sub.8).

(c) *No delay in giving notice* - Notice of abandonment must be given with reasonable diligence after the assured becomes aware of the circumstances of the loss; but, where reliability of the information is doubtful, the assured is allowed reasonable time to make enquiries (MIA, 1906, sect. 62 sub.3).

(d) *Method of giving notice* - Notice may be given by word of mouth or in writing or partly by both methods. It must clearly indicate the intention of the assured to unconditionally abandon his interest in the insured property to the underwriter (MIA,

1906, sect. 62 sub.2). In practice it is customary for notice of abandonment to be given in writing (see below for London market notice procedure).

(e) *Underwriter may reject the notice* - The underwriter may, at his option, accept the notice or reject the notice. Acceptance of the notice may be either express or implied by the contact of the underwriter; but mere silence is not an acceptance of notice (MIA, 1906, sect. 62 sub.5). It is customary for the underwriter to reject the notice.

(f) *Acceptance is admission of liability* - When an underwriter accepts a properly given notice of abandonment it is a conclusive admission of liability for the loss (even if it transpires the loss was caused by an uninsured peril) and an irrevocable aknowledgement of the sufficiency of the notice (MIA, 1906, sect. 62 sub.6). Acceptance of the notice is also an acceptance of abandonment; including title to the insured property and responsibility for any liabilities attaching thereto.

(g) *Rejection does not prejudice the assured's right to claim* - When the underwriter rejects the notice of abandonment this does not prejudice the rights of the assured. He can issue a writ against the underwriter and take legal action to enforce the claim under the policy (MIA, 1906, sect. 62 sub.4). If this action fails the assured can still pursue a claim for a partial loss.

In London market practice it is customary for notice of abandonment to be tendered to the underwriter by a written letter. It is to be expected that the underwriter will formally reject the notice to preserve his position until all the facts are known. Upon rejection it is necessary for a *writ* to be issued against the underwriter. A writ is defined in the English dictionary as a "mandatory precept issued by a court of law requiring the attendance of a defendant in a criminal or civil action". It is important that the writ be issued without delay because it is the circumstances pertaining at the time the writ is issued which will be taken into account in the subsequent court case, if any.

In anticipation that the underwriter will formally reject the notice it is customary for the broker to incorporate a, so called, "writ clause" in the document by which notice is given. The purpose of the writ clause is to obtain the underwriter's acceptance of a position as though a formal writ had been issued against him without involving the broker and his client in unnecessary effort and expense in acquiring a formal writ from a court of law.

There are various methods used to achieve this end, in practice. One such method is for the broker to prepare a notice of abandonment with the "writ clause" incorporated therein. He tenders two copies of the letter to the underwriter, one for the underwriter and the other as a "broker's copy". The underwriter writes on both copies that he rejects the notice and signs the broker's copy as acknowledgement of the writ clause; thereby indicating that he accepts the position as though a writ has been issued against him. Trainees must learn, from experience, the method used in their market.

7. Compromised Total Loss

In practice this may be termed a "compromised and/or arranged total loss" but, for the purpose of this introductory course we shall refer to it, simply, as a "compromised total loss". The MIA, 1906, does not recognise this type of total loss; nor is there any precedent whereby the assured can enforce a settlement on this basis in a court of law. Nevertheless, one sees reference made to this type of loss, where appropriate to the circumstances, in hull insurance conditions (eg in the Institute "increased value" hull TLO clauses). There appears to be no equivalent in the cargo market; perhaps the nearest one comes to such a settlement in cargo insurance is where a "salvage loss" settlement (see Part 5, above) is agreed.

A compromised total loss can arise in circumstances where an insured ship is so badly damaged that a prudent uninsured owner would abandon the wreck rather than spend more than the ship's repaired value to recover and repair the ship. Of course, where the ship is insured the assured would claim a CTL. In the absence of the CTL clause in the hull policy the claim would be based on the provisions of section 60 of the MIA, 1906. However, where the policy incorporates a CTL clause, the total loss claim would fail if the estimated costs did not exceed the *insured* value. In these circumstances, the assured, unable to claim a CTL, would be entitled to recover the ship and have her repaired; pursuing a claim for a 100% partial loss.

In such circumstances a partial loss settlement, based on repair costs, is unreasonable for both assured and underwriter. To claim under his policy the assured must have the ship repaired and bear any costs in excess of the sum insured by the policy. The underwriter would have to pay the full sum insured by the policy but would be denied any recovery rights he might have enjoyed from disposal of the wreck had it been a total loss settlement.

A compromised settlement is probably the best solution. Because it is a compromise the basis of the settlement is a matter between the parties and no rules can be laid down for practitioners to follow. As a suggestion, trainees might consider it reasonable to base the settlement on a payment by the underwriter of a sum equal to the current market value of the ship less an agreed amount in respect of the value of the wreck; leaving the assured to dispose of the wreck at his discretion.

It must be appreciated that an underwriter who settles on this basis cannot recover his loss from a TLO reinsurance contract unless special provision is made therein for this purpose. Further, except where a hull interest policy so provides, no claim is allowed on a hull interest policy based on a total loss settlement on the underlying hull & machinery policy. In practice, the only exception regarding the latter relates to hull "increased value" TLO policies. The Institute TLO clauses published for use in "Disbursements and Increased Value" insurance contracts incorporate a "compromised total loss" clause; whereby the policy will pay a claim in the same proportion that the claim on the underlying policy bears to the insured value therein. For example, if the underlying H & M policy has an insured value of £4,000,000, and compromised settlement of £3,000,000 is made thereon, an ancillary policy with the Institute I/V clauses therein and with a sum insured of £1,000,000 would pay a claim for £750,000.

8. Underwriters' Rights and Obligations Regarding Disposal of Wreck

(MIA, 1906, sects. 63 and 79)

When the underwriter accepts a notice of abandonment he, also, accepts "abandonment" of the insured property. The underwriter is not obliged to accept the notice and, in practice, he always rejects it. Nevertheless, on settlement of a total loss, whether it be an ATL or a CTL, in respect of which he has rejected notice of abandonment, the underwriter has the option to take title to the property (MIA, 1906, sect. 79).

An underwriter who accepts a valid abandonment accepts proprietary rights in the subject matter insured and becomes the legal owner of the insured property (MIA, 1906, sect. 63). He can dispose of the property as he thinks fit and retain all proceeds from such disposal; even where the proceeds exceed the claim paid (MIA, 1906, sect. 79). However, as owner of the property he also assumes any liabilities attaching to the property; which is one of the factors has in mind when rejecting a notice of abandonment. If, for example, the insured ship was sunk in the fairway of a harbour, the underwriter would not be happy to accept abandonment where he might incur high costs in respect of liability for removal of wreck. Similarly, an underwriter who has settled a total loss claim for fruit that has been discharged in a damaged condition would not be happy to be held reponsible for removal of the useless fruit from the port warehouse and for its disposal.

As commented earlier, the right to take over the insured property, following a total loss settlement, is optional to the underwriter. Provided he has not already accepted abandonment the underwriter can settle a total loss and "walk away", so to speak, leaving whatever remains of the insured property to the assured; with its attendant liabilities, if any. Or he can take over the property; thereby accepting responsiblity for disposal of, and liabilities incurred in connection with, the property.

9. Waiver Clause

It will be recalled that acceptance of abandonment can be *implied* by the conduct of the underwriter (MIA, 1906, sect. 62 sub.5). It follows that measures taken by the underwriter, or on his behalf, to preserve insured property from loss can be construed as an acceptance of abandonment. The purpose of the "waiver" clause in a marine insurance policy is to protect the underwriter in such circumstances. The clause appears in all sets of clauses where the underwriter might be prejudiced in this way (eg ITC, 1983; ICC, 1982; Institute freight at risk clauses, etc.).

The clause allows the underwriter and/or his representatives to take such measures as are necessary without this action being considered an acceptance of abandonment or prejudicing the underwriter`s rights in any way. The clause also allows the assured the same freedom without prejudicing *his* rights under the policy.

This clause appears in all sets of marine insurance conditions covering ship or cargo; and also in policies covering freight at risk.

10. Freight Waiver Clause *(MIA, 1906, sect. 63 sub.2)*

An interesting situation could arise where a ship is badly damaged in a collision whilst carrying a cargo (say, a "bulk" cargo) in respect which freight is payable upon discharge of the cargo. The ship puts into a port of refuge and the assured successfully claims a CTL. The underwriter, having settled the total loss, accepts abandonment. The underwriter now becomes the owner of the ship which still has the cargo on board. When the cargo is, eventually, discharged the consignee is liable for the freight earned by the ship for carrying the cargo and this is due to the owner of the ship who is, now, the underwriter (MIA, 1906, sect. 63 sub.2). In hull practice underwriters recognise the inequity of this situation and it is customary for the hull policy conditions to incorporate a clause whereby underwriters waive their rights in this respect (see "freight waiver" clause in the ITC, 1983).

SELF STUDY QUESTIONS

Before moving on to the next Section satisfy yourself that you have absorbed the subject matter of the previous Section. The following questions should be answered without reference to the text.

1. The MIA, 1906, indicates four circumstances in which the assured can claim an ATL. What are these?

2. Does proving a total loss obviate the assured`s obligation to prove the cause of loss?

3. Where the assured fails to prove a total loss can he still pursue a claim for a partial loss?

4. Do all marine insurance policies covering property at risk cover total loss?

5. When a "missing" ship turns up, after the hull underwriter has settled a total loss thereon, who has title to the ship?

6. What is the basis for calculating a CTL of ship as provided by the MIA, 1906? How is this qualified in hull insurance practice?

7. What is the basis for calculating a CTL of goods?

8. What is the purpose of a notice of abandonment. In what circumstances is such notice not necessary?

9. What is the purpose of the "waiver" clause in a marine insurance policy and how does it operate?

10. What is a "compromised" total loss?

SECTION TWELVE

MEASURE OF INDEMNITY FOR PARTIAL LOSS

1. Introduction
2. Partial Loss of Goods
3. Percentage of Depreciation - Cargo
4. Partial Loss of Ship
5. Measure of Indemnity for Damage to Ship
6. Principle of Successive Losses
7. Application of Hull Policy Deductible
8. Deferred Repairs to Ship
9. Treatment of Unrepaired Damage to Ship
10. New for old deductions
11. Partial loss and underinsurance
12. Measure of Indemnity for Partial Loss of Freight at Risk

SECTION TWELVE

1. Introduction

The term "measure of indemnity" is defined in section 67 of the MIA, 1906, as the "extent of liability of the insurer for loss"; in other words it is the amount that can be claimed under the policy where the loss is covered by the policy.

The intention of the principle of indemnity is to place the assured, as far as is practical, in the position he enjoyed before the loss occurred. The nearest one gets to this ideal, in marine insurance practice, occurs where damage to an insured ship is concerned. For ship damage the measure of indemnity is so designed that the underwriter pays, subject to any limitation expressed in the terms of the policy, for the cost of repairing the damage and returning the ship to the condition in which she was before the accident. Nevertheless, even hull insurance practice does not achieve the ideal; in fact the assured often finds himself better off by reason of new materials and parts replacing old worn material and parts (see comment in Part 10, below).

Where a partial loss of goods takes place the underwriter does not usually attempt to restore the goods to their original condition. In this case the system is designed to provide the assured with equitable financial compensation for his loss; but, unlike the position where a ship is repaired, the cargo system is so designed that the assured should not make a profit from the loss.

The measure of indemnity expressed in the MIA, 1906, allows for a policy to be "unvalued" or "valued" (see Section 4 to understand the difference). In practice, insurance contracts covering either ship or cargo are, customarily embodied in "valued" policies. However, in the unlikely event that an unvalued policy is effected to cover a ship the measure of indemnity will always treat the *insurable value* of the ship as the maximum amount recoverable in respect of the loss. Thus, even where the sum insured is more than the insurable value, the assured can recover only up to the insurable value in respect of any one accident. Where an unvalued cargo policy, with a sum insured that is more than the insurable value, is concerned the measure of indemnity for a total loss would be limited to the insurable value of the goods and a partial loss claim would be based on the insurable value rather than the sum insured.

By reference to the comments in Section 4 trainees will recall that, where the insurance of ships and cargoes are concerned, it is customary for these, always, to be effected with an insured value; this being expressed as such in the hull & machinery policy or, where cargo is concerned, in the policy or certificate, as the case may be. Therefore, apart from the above brief comments on unvalued policies, the comments and examples in this Section are confined to contracts based on valued policies.

As commented in the previous Section, the measure of indemnity for a total loss is, subject to the adequacy of the sum insured, the insured value expressed in the policy. Comments on the measure of indemnity for total loss of part (cargo insurance) can also be found in the previous Section.

There is a tendency, in practice, to think of the term "partial loss" as relating, solely, to *damage* to property. Technically, however, the term refers to *any loss* that is not a total loss (MIA, 1906, sect. 56 sub.1). An understanding of this is particularly important when dealing with claims under a hull policy on full terms. The hull policy covers both total and partial loss and incorporates a deductible which is applied to all partial loss claims. Therefore, except where the policy conditions provide otherwise, the deductible will apply to particular average, general average sacrifice, general average contributions, sue & labour charges, salvage charges and contributions, and claims under the collision clause; all these types of loss being termed partial losses.

2. Partial Loss of Goods *(MIA, 1906, sect. 71)*

One comes across many ways in which cargo claims adjustments are carried out in practice in various parts of the world; presumably the relevant underwriters and local practitioners being happy with these procedures. Be that as it may, in these introductory notes we are concerned only with the procedure established by English statutory law; that is, in accordance with section 71 of the MIA, 1906. It is this procedure which will be followed by English courts of law in disputes where no other procedure has been agreed and specified in the policy wording.

Where part of the insured goods is lost and it is possible to apportion the loss in relation to the whole (eg the consignment comprises a number of packages of equal value and the loss relates to entire packages) it is customary to settle the claim as a "total loss of part" (MIA, 1906, sect. 71 sub.1). The procedure for this form of settlement can be found in Section 11. Where part of the goods is lost and it is not possible to apportion the loss in relation to the whole (eg the consignment comprises packages of unequal value or the consignment has been shipped in bulk) the measure of indemnity is calculated in the same way as for damaged goods.

In circumstances where partial loss claims are based on loss of weight, and the weight of packaging (eg drums, etc.) is a significant constant factor, allowance must be made for the weight of the packaging (termed the *tare* in practice) so that the true loss is shown by comparing the net weight at the time transit commenced with the net weight at the time transit terminated. The comments in these introductory notes do not extend to embrace illustrations in this respect. For information on this and other more advanced cargo claims procedures trainees and practitioners are advised to consult "Marine Insurance Claims" by Goodacre (Witherby - new edition in preparation) or "Marine Insurance - Volume 2 - Cargo Practice" Brown (Witherby 1985).

Although the MIA, 1906, deals only with damage discovered when the goods are delivered at the cargo`s intended destination, in practice, damage may be assessed prior to delivery of the goods at the final warehouse. When goods are discharged from the overseas vessel in a damaged condition it is customary for a survey to be carried out to ascertain the extent of the damage and, as far as is possible, the cause of the damage. Ideally, this will be a joint survey on behalf of the consignee and the carrier so that, in event of a claim being made against the carrier, there will be no dispute regarding the extent and cause of the damage. This procedure could take place at the final place of discharge or at an intermediate port or place where the contract of carriage is terminated early.

The cargo surveyor will make out a report which, amongst other things, gives an opinion as to the cause of the loss and, where practical, an estimate of the extent of the loss. If transit is abandoned at this point any claim under the policy will be calculated by using the surveyor`s estimated percentage of depreciation (see Part 3, below). If transit is not abandoned following discharge from the overseas vessel the figures calculated at the place of discharge will be used only for any claim to be made against the carrier.

Section 71 (sub. 3 & 4) of the MIA, 1906, is concerned with claims in respect of goods that are delivered to the final warehouse in a damaged condition. If the goods are sold at the destination the measure of indemnity is based on a percentage of depreciation determined by a comparison between the sound and damaged market values of the goods at the destination. If no sound goods are available for sale an estimate of the sound market value is used. If the goods are not sold the same basis is used but with the percentage of depreciation calculated by comparing estimated values for both sound and damaged goods. The measure of indemnity is calculated by comparing the estimated gross arrived sound value with the actual gross arrived damaged value. The difference between these two figures represents the loss to the assured but is not taken as the claim on the policy. Examples to illustrate these calculations can be found in Part 3, below.

To calculate the claim the loss suffered by the assured is assessed as a percentage of the gross arrived sound value. This is termed the *percentage of depreciation*. The claim under the policy is determined by applying the percentage of depreciation to the insured value expressed in the policy (see Part 3, below).

Where it is intended that the goods are to be sold at the destination to which they are consigned they are said to be shipped "on consignment". In case of a claim for damage to goods shipped on consignment the assured cannot include in the claim the sale costs, even though the claim is based on the values determined by the sale. However, where there was no intention to sell the goods on arrival but they are sold, solely, because they arrive in a damaged condition (termed a "forced sale") the assured can add the sale costs to the claim arrived at by applying the percentage of depreciation to the insured value.

Where the sum insured by the policy is less than the insured value the claim under the policy is reduced in proportion to the underinsurance.

3. Percentage of Depreciation *(MIA, 1906, sect 71 sub.3)*

Where the insured goods are sold at destination the percentage of depreciation is assessed by applying the formula laid down in section 71(3) of the MIA, 1906. In assessing the percentage of depreciation the Act requires that *gross* values be used. Before considering the reasons why gross values are to be used it is advisable that one clearly understands how to arrive at a percentage of depreciation. The following example illustrates:

Gross arrived sound value (estimated)	£100,000
Gross proceeds from sale	75,000
Loss suffered by assured	£ 25,000 or 25% depreciation

It will be noted that these figures do not take into account the insured value or the sum insured expressed in the policy. Their purpose is, solely, to find the percentage of loss suffered by the assured. Where some of the goods have arrived in a sound condition it is usually possible to use the sound of value of such goods to arrive at an estimate for the whole. For example, if in the above illustration half the goods arrived sound with a sound value of £50,000, one can asume the whole, if in a sound condition, would have had a sound value of £100,000.

When adjusting the claim under the policy one simply applies the percentage of depreciation to the insured value and the amount of the claim is reflected in the amount of the insured value; so that if the goods are undervalued in the policy the assured gets less than his loss and if the goods are overvalued in the policy the assured gets more than his loss (the insured value being a conclusive value - see MIA, 1906, sect. 27 sub.4). The following examples illustrate:

(1) Sum insured by the policy £80,000 so valued.	Claim 25% x £80,000 = £20,000
(2) Sum insured by the policy £100,000 so valued	Claim 25% x £100,000 = £25,000
(3) Sum insured by the policy £120,000 so valued.	Claim 25% x £120,000 = £30,000

The MIA, 1906, requires that, where sound and damaged values are used in claim calculations, only *gross* values are to be used. The "gross" value is the wholesale price of the goods or, if there is no wholesale price, the estimated value of the goods; including, in either case, freight (remuneration paid to the overseas carrier), landing charges and duty paid beforehand (MIA, 1906, sect. 71 sub.4).

At one time cargo underwriters might have agreed to a "net values" clause in policies covering certain types of cargo carried in bulk; by this clause they agreed to settle cargo partial loss claims on a net value basis in place of the gross value basis required by the Act.. The term "net" value means the gross value less landing charges. The net value clause works against underwriters` interests and one is unlikely to see it in modern cargo policy conditions. The following example illustrates:

	Gross values			Net values
Sound value	£50,000	Sound value	£50,000	
		less charges	5,000	£45,000
Damaged value	40,000	Damaged value	£40,000	
		less charges	5,000	35,000
Loss	£10,000	Loss		£10,000
Depreciation	20% of £50,000	Depreciation	22.2% of £45,000	

If the insured value expressed in the policy was £50,000 the goods would be covered for their full value. By calculating the claim using the percentage of depreciation assessed by using gross values (ie 20% x £50,000 = £10,000) the assured recovers the full amount of his loss. If net values were used the assured would be paid 22.2% x £50,000 = £11,100; thereby making a profit out of the loss. In maritime practice one often finds handling charges increase when goods are discharged in a damaged condition; this aggravating the position further to underwriters` disadvantage. Further, the claim is not influenced by market trends when gross values are used; which might otherwise be the case where net values are used.

The claim under the policy is assessed by applying the percentage of depreciation to the insured value or, if the sum insured be less than the insured value, to the sum insured by the policy. The simple examples which follow are based on the percentage of depreciation shown under the gross values column above:

(a) Sum insured £60,000 Insured value £60,000 Claim £60,000 x 20% = £12,000
(b) Sum insured £50,000 Insured value £60,000 Claim £50,000 x 20% = £10,000

This method of calculation applies both to a particular average loss and to a claim in respect of general average sacrifice of the insured goods.

Where "bonded" goods (ie goods held in bond pending payment of import duty) are concerned the bonded value is deemed to be the gross value in claim calculations (MIA, 1906, sect. 71 sub.4).

4. Partial Loss of Ship

As commented earlier, section 56 (1) of the MIA, 1906, provides that "any loss other than a total loss" is a *partial* loss. A full terms H&M policy (eg one based on the ITC, 1983) covers the following types of loss:

(1) Total loss (actual and constructive)
(2) Particular average (damage to ship)
(3) General average sacrifice to ship
(4) Sue & labour charges
(5) Salvage charges
(6) General average and salvage contributions
(7) Collision liability (3/4ths)

Accordingly, when reference is made, in practice, to the term "partial loss covered by the policy" it means any loss embraced by items (2) to (7) in the above list. On the other hand, when section 69 of the MIA, 1906, refers to "partial loss" in defining the extent of the measure of indemnity it confines the definition to *damage* to the insured vessel. This embraces both particular average damage and damage caused by a general average sacrifice; but this section of the Act does not define the measure of indemnity for any partial loss suffered by the assured in connection with items (4) to (7) in the above list. It will be noted that the policy deductible, to which reference is made in the ITC (1983), applies to *all* partial losses, as defined above.

5. Measure of Indemnity for Damage to Ship *(MIA, 1906, sect. 69)*

Section 66 (4) of the MIA, 1906, provides, amongst other things, that an assured who has suffered loss from a general average sacrifice incurred in consequence of an insured peril may recover his loss directly from the underwriter without waiting for the GA adjustment to be completed; the underwriter recovering the GA loss from the GA fund by exercising his subrogation rights when the GA adjustment has been completed. The measure of indemnity defined by section 69 of the Act is applied to all insured damage to ship; whether it relates to particular average or to general average sacrifice.

Subject to the principle of "successive losses" (see Part 6, below) the maximum amount recoverable for cost of repairs is the insured value, expressed in the H&M policy, in respect of any one accident. Of course, where the sum insured is less than the insured value, the maximum amount recoverable in respect of any one accident is the sum insured by the policy. In either case, the claim is subject to reduction by application of the policy deductible (see Section 4, above). Should it be estimated that the cost of repairs is likely to exceed the insured value the assured should bear in mind the he is uninsured for the excess amount of repair costs and should seriously consider whether it would be more practical to abandon the ship to the underwriter and claim a CTL (see Section 11, above).

The measure of indemnity for damage to ship is the *reasonable cost* of repairing that damage. What is reasonable depends on the facts, but underwriters incorporate a "tender" clause in the H&M policy conditions to ensure they have a right of veto in decisions made regarding acceptance of repair tenders, the repair firm instructed to do the job and the place where the repairs shall be carried out. The following list (which is not exhaustive) gives the trainee some guidance regarding the sort of costs one would expect to be included in the term "reasonable cost of repairs":

(a) cost of temporary repairs necessary to enable the ship to be moved to the place where permanent repairs can be carried out;
(b) cost of removing the damaged ship to the place for permanent repairs;
(c) wages and maintenance of master, officers and crew who move the ship to the place for permanent repairs (but only those incurred whilst the ship is "under way");
(d) cost of entering dry dock, lay days in dry dock and leaving dry dock, but only insofar as these costs relate to repairs for underwriters' account;
(e) actual cost of removing damaged material (less proceeds, if any, from sale of scrap);
(f) actual cost of supplying replacement parts and material and completing the repairs

(Trainees and practitioners seeking more detailed information are advised to consult "Marine Insurance Claims" by Goodacre (Witherby) and/or "Marine Insurance - Volume 3 - Hull Practice" by Brown (Witherby 1993)

One should be aware of the fact that repairs which do not affect the seaworthiness of the ship might be deferred until a time when it is more convenient for the ship to be taken out of service. If another accident occurs whereby repairs relating to two or more separate accidents are carried out at the same time claims adjusters must apportion the costs relating to the repairs over each separate casualty, as appropriate thereto. Further, all heavy weather damage occurring during a single passage between two ports is aggregated and treated as having taken place in a single casualty.

Where partial repairs are carried out to allow the ship to proceed or to continue trading the assured is entitled to the reasonable cost of the partial repairs (MIA, 1906, sect. 69 sub.2). In practice, costs relating to the partial repairs are added to the costs relating to the permanent repairs and the policy limit is applied to aggregate thereof.

Where the ship has been partially repaired and the policy expires before the permanent repairs have been carried out the assured is entitled to the reasonable cost of the partial repairs plus a reasonable allowance for depreciation in the ship's value due to the unrepaired damage (MIA, 1906, sect. 69 sub.2). Where the ship has been partially repaired, and she becomes a total loss before the permanent repairs are carried out, the assured forfeits his right to a depreciation allowance but can still claim for the cost of the partial repairs which were completed before the total loss occurred; this being in addition to a claim for the total loss if such is caused by an insured peril. See, also, comments on treatment of unrepaired damage in Part 9, below.

6. Principle of Successive Losses *(MIA, 1906, sect. 77)*

When defining the principle of successive losses the MIA, 1906, makes no distinction between the insurance of ship and the insurance of goods. In practice, however, it is difficult to envisage a circumstance where a claim for damage to goods could exceed the insured value since damaged goods are not replaced or repaired during transit. In theory, one could apply the principle of successive losses to a hull voyage policy; but in reality the principle is aimed at hull time policies.

Section 69 of the MIA, 1906, provides that each casualty shall be treated separately; the insured value (subject to the adequacy of the sum insured) being the limit of indemnity in respect of each separate casualty. Section 77 of the Act takes this principle a stage further by automatically reinstating the sum insured by the policy after each casualty and allowing the assured to claim up to the full sum insured in respect of each casualty even though, in the aggregate, the policy could pay considerably more than the full sum insured during the currency of the policy. In other words, apart from the sum insured as the limit of recovery in respect of any one casualty, the underwriter`s liability for repair costs, etc. is unlimited during the policy period.

The following example illustrates the application of the principle of successive losses (for simplicity the example ignores application of the policy deductible):

Estimated repaired value £5,000,000
Insured value & sum insured £4,500,000 Cover - MAR policy ITC (1983)

Period of cover - 12 months at noon GMT 1 January 1994

Casualties	*Cause of loss*	*Repair costs*
15 Feb 1994	Stranding damage to bottom	£2,600,000
6 June 1994	Fire damage to superstructure	£1,900,000
20 October 1994	Collision damage to stern	£ 850,000
	Total cost of repairs	£5,350,000

It should be noted that the apparent underinsurance arising from the difference between the insured value and the repaired value of the ship does not affect claims for damage repairs to the ship. Therefore, since none of the casualties give rise to repair costs exceeding the sum insured by the policy, the underwriter would be liable for all these repair costs. No additional premium is required to reinstate the full sum insured after each casualty.

7. Application of Hull Policy Deductible

A policy deductible may be defined as an amount expressed in a policy which is deducted from a loss before the claim for the amount in excess of the deductible is settled. Obviously, where the loss is less than the amount of the deductible, the assured bears the whole loss and no claim attaches to the policy.

An introduction to the use of policy deductibles appears in Section 4. The MIA, 1906, makes no reference to policy deductibles in either cargo insurance contracts or hull insurance contracts; hence the application of a deductible depends on agreement between the parties to the contract as expressed in the insurance conditions attached to the marine insurance policy. No explanation should be necessary for application of a deductible incorporated in a cargo insurance contract; this being self evident by the definition of the term. The application of a hull policy deductible is more complicated and requires explanation. The following comments, and examples, are based on London market practice and the standard deductible provisions appearing in clauses (eg ITC, 1983) attached to a policy covering loss of or damage to a ship.

Whilst hull insurance clauses incorporate conditions for application of the deductible no standard deductible is printed in the clauses. Instead, a space is left for the insertion of a deductible the amount of which is agreed during negotiations to conclude the contract with the underwriter; or, if there be more than one insurer subscribing the contract, the leading underwriter with whom the terms of the contract are negotiated.

The deductible is applied to each accident or series of accidents arising out of one occurrence. The following examples relate to a ship which is insured by the ITC (1983) with a deductible of £20,000.

Example 1 - The ship runs aground during a storm. The next day the ship is towed off the strand. A survey reveals that bottom damage (amounting to £100,000 in repair costs) was caused by the stranding; but further damage (amounting to £50,000 repair costs) was caused during the towage operation. Although the two lots of damage occurred at different times they both relate to the same occurrence so only one deductible is applied to the cost of repairs:

eg	Repairs to bottom	£150,000
	Policy deductible	20,000
	Claim	£130,000

Example 2 - The ship suffers heavy weather damage (amounting to £15,000 repair costs) during a single passage. The damage does not affect the ship's seaworthiness so she continues the voyage. Subsequently, during the same voyage, the ship is involved in a collision with another vessel (no fault attaching to the insured ship) and suffers damage to her stern (amounting to £100,000 repair costs). Although all repairs were carried out at the same time, to apply the policy deductible, the two casualties must be shown separately in the adjustment.

eg	*Casualty 1*	*Casualty 2*	*Assured*
Heavy weather repairs	£15,000		£15,000*
Collision damage repairs		£100,000	
Total repair costs	£15,000	£100,000	£15,000
Policy deductible	- 20,000	- 20,000	+20,000*
Claim	nil	£ 80,000	£35,000

*Transferred to assured's account -
(a) £15,000 (casualty 1) not recoverable under policy following application of deductible
(b) £20,000 (casualty 2) deductible

Policy pays in respect of casualty 2	£ 80,000
Assured bears repairs for casualty 1	15,000
Assured bears deductible applied to casualty 2	20,000
Total cost of repairs	£115,000

The deductible is applied to all claims, other than a claim for total loss (actual or constructive). It is also ignored, in practice, where a compromised total loss is agreed. In general, the deductible applies to all damage claims and to GA and salvage contributions, etc. It also applies to claims for sue & labour charges but an exception is made where the sue & labour charge is incurred in connection with a total loss. Further, the deductible is not applied to a survey charge incurred specifically for sighting the bottom of the ship to see if any damage has been caused by a stranding. It should be noted that this exception does not apply to sighting the bottom for any purpose other than to check for "stranding" damage. For example, the exception does not apply to circumstances where the ship has struck rocks below the surface but has not actually stranded.

Where partial losses falling into different categories (eg sue & labour charges, collision liability, etc.) are incurred in the same accident or occurrence all such partial losses are aggregated and the deductible is applied only once to the total.

Claims practitioners are advised to check the hull policy conditions to see if there are any other deductibles which might affect the claim (eg the "machinery damage additional deductible" which sometimes appears in policies that are subject to the ITC, 1983)

8. Deferred Repairs to Ship

Where the ship is insured by a time policy and repairs of a minor nature do not affect the seaworthiness of the ship the assured may request that the repairs be deferred until a more convenient time for the ship to be taken out of commission. Ordinarily, where the deferment will not enhance the repair costs and/or the ship is a liner (ie she has to maintain a regular schedule), the underwriter will concede to the assured`s request.

Under a time policy the underwriter is not liable for loss or damage attributable to unseaworthiness where, with the privity of the assured, the ship is sent to sea in an unseaworthy condition (see Section 8, above). Nevertheless, in no case will the underwriter allow deferment of repairs necessary for seaworthiness of the vessel. Exceptionally, where the damage is covered by the policy and has caused the vessel to be unseaworthy such unseaworthiness does not affect a claim under either a time or a voyage policy, and the underwriter might agree to temporary repairs being carried out to make the ship seaworthy to enable a liner to maintain her schedule or, perhaps, to allow completion of a charterhire contract or, in the case of a voyage policy where the ship is lying at an intermediate port, to allow the ship to complete the insured voyage. Provided the underwriter has agreed to deferment of the permanent repairs the cost of the temporary repairs can be added to the cost of permanent repairs and included in the claim for damage to ship; the whole being subject to a limit of the insured value and to the policy deductible.

Where permanent repairs cost more by being deferred the average adjuster, usually, makes an allowance in the underwriter`s favour so that he shall not be prejudiced by his leniency in allowing deferment of permanent repairs.

9 Treatment of Unrepaired Damage to Ship *(MIA, 1906, sect. 69 sub.2 & 3)*

Where the insured ship has been damaged by an insured peril and has not been repaired or has been only partially repaired the assured may claim a depreciation allowance in lieu of the cost of repairs. However, payment of the allowance is subject to the following:

(a) The allowance shall be calculated by comparing the sound value of the ship at the time the policy expires with the value of the ship in her unrepaired condition at the time the policy expires;

(b) The amount of the allowance shall not exceed the reasonable cost of repairing the damage;

(c) The depreciation allowance shall not exceed the insured value of the ship at the time the policy expires;

(d) The assured is not entitled to a depreciation allowance until the policy expires. Where policy is terminated before the natural expiry date (eg the ship is sold in her damaged condition) the assured can claim a depreciation allowance in respect of unrepaired damage;
(e) No depreciation allowance can be claimed under the policy if the insured ship is totally lost during the currency of the policy; irrespective of whether or not the total loss is covered by the policy.

Regarding the last item, in the above list, a total loss occurring during the currency of a *succeeding* policy does not prejudice the assured`s right to claim a depreciation allowance under the expired policy; even where the same underwriters have written lines on both policies.

10. New for Old Deductions *(MIA, 1906, sect. 69 sub.1)*

The principle of "indemnity" is intended to place the assured in the same position he enjoyed before the loss occurred. Further, section 55 sub.2(c) of the MIA, 1906, states that, unless the policy provides otherwise, the underwriter shall not be liable for ordinary wear and tear. In support of the principle of indemnity and the exclusion in the MIA, 1906, the Rules of Practice of the Association of Average Adjusters provide that, where a claim attaches to the policy for the cost of repairing damage to ship, a deduction shall be made from the cost of repairs to compensate the underwriter for the "betterment" enjoyed by the assured where a new part replaces an old part and/or where new material replaces old material. Section 69 of the MIA, 1906, refers to these deductions as the "customary" deductions but, for many years they were termed "thirds" (because the most common form of deduction was one third of the claim). In later years they were referred to as "new for old" deductions.

Over the years, there has been considerable controversy over whether or not these deductions should be made and, for a long time, it has been the practice for hull underwriters to waive customary deductions when settling claims for repair costs to ship (see "new for old" clause in the ITC, 1983). Average adjusters continue to apply customary deductions to ship repair costs in general average adjustments; but only where the insured ship is more than 15 years old. So, whilst no new for old deductions are made in hull policy claims practice (whether the claim be for particular average damage or for general average sacrifice), underwriters must appreciate that a "new for old" deduction might cause a recovery from a GA fund to be less than the claim paid under the policy.

Before we leave the subject of new for old deductions it should be noted that the "new for old" clause in a hull policy does not *entitle* the assured to replacement of old with new. Hull underwriters waive the deduction but do not guarantee they will replace an old part with a new part. Thus, if it is expedient to replace, say, a shaft with one of the same age and in the same condition as the shaft that was drawn the underwriter has fulfilled his duty to indemnify the assured for his loss. Accordingly, any plea by the assured for compensation because he did not receive a new shaft would not succeed in a court of law.

(Text continues on Page 12)

11. Partial Loss and Underinsurance

Underinsurance, in this context, means where the ship is insured for less than a, so called, "proper" value. From comments made in Section 4 regarding valued policies it will be recalled that accurate ship valuation is very difficult to determine. This is appreciated by hull underwriters who usually accept the assured`s valuation on the assumption that the assured would not wish to be underinsured in event of a total loss. Hull underwriters accept that the insured value expressed in the hull policy is conclusive as the insurable value of the ship for a total loss and as the limit of indemnity for any one casualty where the cost of repairs is concerned; but a claim for cost of repairs is not reduced by any underinsurance displayed by comparing the insured value of the ship with the ship`s insurable value at the time of the accident.

Nevertheless, where other partial losses (ie S & L charges, salvage charges, GA contributions and claims under the RDC) are concerned, the policy provides that, whilst the insured value remains the basic limit of liability for each casualty, each partial loss claim shall be reduced by any underinsurance demonstrated by comparing the insured value with a "proper" value. A "proper" value is one which truly reflects that the ship is fully insured. In some cases it will be the market value of the ship. In others it could be the contributory value or, where collision liability is concerned, a value commensurate with the basis for calculating limitation of liability. More information on this subject can be found in Sections 13 and 14, below.

12. Measure of Indemnity for Partial Loss of Freight at Risk *(MIA, 1906, sect. 70)*

This section of the Act is not concerned with policies effected on "anticipated freight", to which reference was made in Section 6. Nor is it concerned with "freight" paid in advance by a cargo owner; the latter being incorporated in the insurable value of the goods to which it relates. Section 70 of the Act is concerned, solely, with policies effected to cover freight at risk of the overseas carrier; that is freight payable at destination on outturn of the goods (usually a bulk cargo). Apart from the provisions of the MIA, 1906, the measure of indemnity for partial loss of freight is specified in the standard freight clauses, both time and voyage, published by the ILU for use with the MAR form of policy.

The measure of indemnity for partial loss of freight is based on the amount of loss suffered by the goods to which the freight relates. Where part of the goods has been lost, and such loss has been proximately caused by a peril expressed in the freight policy, a partial loss can be claimed under the freight policy. To calculate the claim on the freight policy one finds the percentage of depreciation applied to the loss of goods and applies this to the sum insured by the freight policy:

Example - The cargo loss is 20% of the whole cargo carried by the ship. The freight policy has a sum insured of £20,000. The freight policy pays 20% x £20,000 = £5,000.

Where several policies exist to cover the freight at risk each policy pays its proportional part of the partial loss in the proportion that the sum insured by the policy bears to the total of the sums insured by all the policies. Further, it should be noted that a partial loss, other than a GA loss, is subject to a franchise of 3% in practice. For details regarding implementation of a franchise one should refer to the notes in Section 4, above. The franchise in the Institute freight clauses does not operate where the cargo loss was caused by fire, sinking, stranding or collision of the carrying vessel with another ship or vessel. For the purpose of the franchise freight attaching to each craftload of goods is treated as a separate insurance.

It needs to be emphasised that a partial loss paid under a cargo policy is not automatically followed by a claim for partial loss under the freight policy. Take, for example, a cargo of bulk oil which is insured by the Bulk Oil Clauses published by the ILU for use with the MAR form of policy. The perils include a section whereby the proof of the proximate cause of loss is not required for a loss that is reasonably attributable to fire. The perils expressed in the freight clauses are the same as those in the ITC (1983) and claims are subject to the principle of proximate cause. So, for a loss to be recoverable under the Institute freight clauses, the assured must show that the loss was proximately caused by an insured peril. Both sets of clauses incorporate "fire" as an insured peril but, whereas a loss "reasonably attributable to" fire would be recoverable under the oil clauses a corresponding loss would not be recoverable under the freight clauses without proof that the loss of the cargo was "proximately caused" by fire.

SEE OVERPAGE FOR SELF STUDY QUESTIONAIRE

SELF STUDY QUESTIONS

Before moving on to the next section satisfy yourself that you have absorbed the subject matter in the previous Sections. The following questions should be answered without reference to the text:

1. Define the term "measure of indemnity".

2. In the absence of anything to the contrary expressed in the policy the MIA, 1906, defines the measure of indemnity for partial loss of goods. What is the measure of indemnity where -
(a) part of the goods, insured by a valued policy, has been totally lost?
(b) the whole of the goods, insured by a valued policy, have been delivered but in a damaged condition?

3. Why are cargo claims calculated by using "gross" values rather than "net" values? In what circumstances are "gross" values *not* used in the calculation?

4. What is a "percentage of depreciation"? How is it determined and how is it applied to a claim on a "valued" cargo policy?

5. Define the term "partial loss of ship".

6. What is the measure of indemnity under a "valued" H&M policy for -
(a) particular average damage to ship?
(b) general average sacrifice of part of the ship?

7. Do you understand the principle of successive losses and how it affects claim for partial loss of ship?

8. In what circumstances would you expect hull underwriters to agree to deferred repairs? What is underwriters` liability where the policy expires whilst insured damage has remained unrepaired?

9. What are "new for old" deductions and how are these treated in practice?

10. What is the measure of indemnity for partial loss of freight at risk?

SECTION THIRTEEN

MINIMISING LOSS AND SUBROGATION

1. Introduction
2. The Sue & Labour Clause in the SG Form of Policy
3. Sue & Labour Charges
4. Duty of Assured Clause in Cargo Policies
5. Duty of Assured Clause in Hull Policies
6. Salvage and Salvage Charges
7. Underinsurance - S & L and Salvage Charges
8. Underwriters` Subrogation Rights
9. Double Insurance, Contribution and Underinsurance

SECTION THIRTEEN

1. Introduction

Except in cases of public notoriety or special advice through, say, Lloyd`s intelligence service, the marine underwriter remains unaware of an accident which befalls the subject matter insured until he is advised thereof by the assured or the assured`s representative (eg the broker).

There is no condition in the ICC (1982) which specifically requires the assured to give immediate notice of an accident to the underwriter; although there is a "reasonable despatch" clause which demands that the assured must act with reasonable despatch in all cases. On the other hand, the ITC (1983) incorporate a "tender" clause, the first part of which demands immediate notice to the underwriter of any accident whereby a claim might arise under the policy.

The fact remains that an underwriter can do nothing to avert a loss or to minimise a loss until he becomes aware of the loss. Nevertheless, there is a probability that the assured or an agent of the assured might be in a position to, at least, take measures to prevent further loss and to minimise the effects of the accident on the subject matter insured. To protect underwriters where such action can benefit their situation section 78 (1) of the MIA, 1906, provides "It is the duty of the assured and his agents, in all cases, to take such measures as are reasonable for the purpose of averting or minimising loss".

Basically, one can place efforts to avert or minimise loss into three categories:

(1) Action taken to save insured property at risk, termed "salvage". The costs incurred being termed "salvage charges";

(2) Action taken to save a common adventure in which the subject matter insured is at risk, termed "general average". The costs incurred being termed "general average expenditure";

(3) Action taken in circumstances where "salvage" does not apply and "general average" does not apply, termed "sue & labour". The costs incurred being termed "sue & labour charges".

The comments in this Section are confined to items (1) and (3); general average being the subject of a Sections 15 and 16, later in these notes. However, before comment is made on salvage and sue & labour, it must be emphasised that the underwriter is not liable in respect of, nor indeed interested in, salvage or other (apparently S & L) charges incurred in connection with uninsured losses or losses which are the subject of policy exclusions.

2. The Sue & Labour Clause in the SG Form of Policy *(MIA, 1906, sect.78)*

This clause appeared in early Italian policies which the Lombards brought to England during the 12th century. It was in a much abbreviated form compared with the S & L clause printed in Lloyd`s SG form shown in the MIA, 1906. The early format merely gave the assured the right to sue and labour in and about the defence of the insured ship and goods without prejudicing his right to claim under the policy. In other words, the underwriter could not use the assured`s action, where it proved unsuccessful, as a defence aganst a valid claim under the policy. It was not until many years later that the S & L clause was extended to allow the assured to claim under the policy for reimbursement of expenses incurred in his efforts to avert or minimise loss.

The contract entered into by the underwriter by incorporating the S & L clause in the SG form of policy was considered to be supplementary to the main contract of insurance. Effectively, therefore, the assured could claim a total loss under the main contract and still claim for reasonable expenses properly incurred under the S & L clause; these being recoverable in addition to the total loss. S & L charges are still treated in the same way today.

The MAR policy form does not incorporate a sue & labour clause nor is this clause incorporated in the standard hull or cargo clauses published by the ILU for use with the MAR form of policy. Nevertheless, the spirit of the S & L clause is maintained in modern practice and the right to claim S & L charges, where properly incurred, is incorporated in the "duty of assured" clause which appears, albeit in different formats, in clauses published by the ILU for both hull insurance contracts and cargo insurance contracts.

3. Sue & Labour Charges *(MIA, 1906, sect. 78)*

A "sue & labour charge" is defned in the MIA, 1906, as an expense properly incurred by the assured pursuant to the sue & labour clause in the policy. The sue & labour clause, as such, no longer appears in marine insurance policies but, in practice, one still refers to expenses incurred by the assured in complying with the "duty of assured" clause (see Parts 4 and 5, below) as sue & labour charges.

Taking into account the provisions of section 78 of the MIA, 1906, and customary practice, when considering to what extent an expense can be considered a sue & labour charge and, as such, recoverable under the policy one must bear the following rules in mind -

(a) The principle of sue & labour is intended to apply to circumstances where a misfortune has occurred and, by taking early remedial measures, further loss can be avoided. Therefore, trade expenses incurred by the assured in the ordinary course of events, even though they preserve the subject matter insured from exposure to risk, cannot be claimed as sue & labour charges. For example, warehousing costs incurred to protect insured goods from the weather, theft, etc. the during the ordinary course of transit at a transhipping port would not be allowed as sue & labour; except, possibly, in the case of forced discharge at an intermediate port due to operation of an insured peril.

(b) The expense must be incurred by the assured, his servants or agents (ie not by a third party);

(c) The expense must be incurred for the sole benefit of the insured property;

(d) In a hull voyage policy the expense must be incurred short of destination;

(e) In a cargo policy the expense must be incurred short of delivery of the goods at the place named named in the policy for termination of transit;

(f) The assured must be able to demonstrate that, without the expense being incurred, the underwriter would almost certainly have suffered a loss under the policy;

(g) A salvage charge cannot be claimed as a sue & labour charge;

(h) An expense incurred in connection with a general average act cannot be claimed as a sue & labour charge;

(i) Expenses incurred in defending a claim under the RDC in a hull policy are not sue & labour charges. Such defence costs are covered by the hull policy only where the underwriter has approved the defence;

(j) Only a *reasonable* expense may be recovered as a sue & labour charge. That is to say the action must be such as a prudent uninsured person would carry out to preserve his own property from loss and the amount must be reasonable in the light of the circumstances. Should the assured incur an expense properly but for an unreasonable amount the underwriter`s liability is only for the proportion thereof that is reasonable;

(k) A sue & labour charge is not recoverable under a policy if it is incurred in connection with an uninsured peril or an excluded peril;

(l) Where a sue & labour charge is properly incurred it can be claimed under the policy even though it be unsuccessful;

(m) A sue & labour charge can be claimed in addition to any other loss recoverable under the policy, even a total loss;

(n) In hull insurance practice a sue & labour charge must be added to any other partial losses incurred in the same casualty and the policy deductible be applied to the whole;

(o) A sue & labour charge incurred in connection with a hull total loss is not subject to the policy deductible;

(p) Although a sue & labour charge can be recovered under the policy separately from any other claim it is still subject to the insured value expressed in the policy as a limit of indemnity;

(q) In hull practice a claim for a sue & labour charge may be reduced in proportion to any underinsurance demonstrated by comparing the market value of the ship with its insured value. For more detail in this respect see Part 7, below.

4. Duty of Assured Clause in Cargo Policies

This clause has a dual function. First it is concerned with sue & labour charges and second it is concerned with preservation of the underwriter`s rights of recovery against carriers, other bailees of the insured goods and third parties. The title is taken from section 78 (4) of the MIA, 1906, from which it quotes the duty of the assured and their agents to take such measures as are reasonable for the purpose of averting or minimising loss.

The clause amplifies the duty expressed in the Act by adding "servants of the assured" to those required to carry out this duty, otherwise one can say that the clause does nothing to qualify the rules for sue & labour charges listed in Part 3, above; the latter continuing to apply.

International rules concerning carriage of goods require a consignee to make a claim in writing against the carrier within a time limit. Failure to comply with which requirement could prejudice the consignee`s right of recovery from a carrier or other party who is responsible for the loss or damage; thereby prejudicing the underwriter`s rights under the principle of subrogation (see Part 8, below). A cargo assured, claiming under his policy, might consider it unnecessary to claim also against a carrier and, by the time the underwriter is made aware of the loss, the claim against the carrier could become time barred. Accordingly, further to confirming the duty of the assured, etc. regarding sue & labour, the cargo "duty of assured" clause imposes a duty on the assured, his servants and agents to properly preserve the assured`s rights against carriers, bailees and other third parties when goods are not delivered or are delivered in a damaged condition.

5. Duty of Assured Clause in Hull Policies

As we know, the modern hull policy does not incorporate a "sue & labour" clause, as such, but the spirit of sue & labour is maintained by the "duty of assured" clause. In fact the clause in the ITC (1983) incorporates the words "Sue & Labour" in its title so that there shall be no misunderstanding regarding its main purpose.

The hull clause complements the provisions of section 78 of the MIA, 1906, by pointing out that the assured, his servants and agents have a duty to take reasonable measures to avert or minimise a loss that would be recoverable under the policy; underwriters agreeing to pay, subject to the policy deductible, reasonable sue & labour charges properly incurred in compliance with this duty. The clause does not go into great detail but the rules listed in Part 3 above will apply, where appropriate to a hull interest, equally to sue & labour charges attaching to a hull policy.

Part of the clause is concerned with the treatment of sue and labour charges where the ship is underinsured (see Part 7, below). Incidentally, although it has no connection with sue & labour, the hull "duty of assured" clause incorporates the "waiver" clause to which reference was made in Section 11.

6. Salvage and Salvage Charges

Technically, the term "salvage" refers to the remuneration paid to a salvor who, independent of any contract with the owner of the saved property, renders successful services to save maritime property in peril at sea. Taken in a marine context it should not be confused with the non-marine term "salvage" which might be applied to the property saved or recovered following an insured accident.

An act of "pure salvage" is one where, in the absence of a salvage contract, the salvor renders his services on a "no cure - no pay" basis. In other words the salvor takes a chance on whether or not he can recover the maritime property, expending his own efforts and money in the operation, with no hope of recovering his expenses or receiving a salvage award if his efforts are unsuccessful.

A salvor may exercise a maritime lien on the saved property. This entitles the salvor to prevent the owner of the property from having the free use thereof until a salvage award has been paid. In the absence of any other arrangement, the award for pure salvage is determined by an admiralty court and is based on the value of the saved property and the expense incurred by the salvor. Other factors taken into account by the court are the circumstances of the operation (eg difficulties encountered, hazards involved, etc.) plus the skill and experience required for a successful outcome. To encourage salvage of maritime property, court awards tend to be generous; particularly where human life is also saved. Otherwise, where life salvage by itself is concerned, the law does not allow the salvor to exercise a maritime lien nor is the salvor entitled to demand a salvage award for saving life. Further, the law does not allow a salvor to exercise a maritime lien on saved personal effects nor is the salvor entitled to an award for saving personal effects.

Details concerning the rules governing maritime salvage operations and remunerations relating thereto are outside the scope of these introductory notes but trainees might bear in mind that international conventions on salvage operations have agreed to an amelioration of the strict interpretation of pure salvage where professional salvage services are undertaken and the laws of ratifying countries allow some concessions not contemplated by the principle of pure salvage; for example a professional salvor, today, may be able to recover at least some of the expenses involved in unsuccessful salvage operations.

Although the principle of pure salvage demands the absence of any form of salvage contract few professional salvors will undertake a major salvage operation without some form of agreeement. In practice, underwriters recognise the operation as an act of salvage where the agreement is effected on a "no cure - no pay" basis. Lloyd`s open form of salvage agreement is such an acceptable form of salvage contract; the award relating thereto being settled by arbitration; except where the parties agree to a fixed award.

A "salvage charge" is a claim under the marine insurance policy to reimburse the assured for the salvage award he has paid to discharge the maritime lien on his ship or goods, as the case may be. When considering a salvage award the following basic rules should be borne in mind -

(a) In practice, maritime salvage awards are frequently merged in a general average adjustment; in which case a separate claim for a salvage charge is unlikely to attach to the policy; the underwriter`s liability for the salvage charge being embraced within his liability for the GA contribution (see Section 15);

(b) In hull insurance practice, the ITC (1983) provide that a salvage charge is covered *only* where it was incurred in consequence of an insured peril;

(c) In cargo insurance practice, the ICC (1982) provide that a salvage charge is covered irrespective of whether or not it was incurred in consequence of an insured peril (this applying to A, B and C conditions); but *not* if it was incurred in consequence of an excluded peril;

(d) Salvage charges recoverable under a hull policy are subject to the policy deductible;

(e) Salvage charges recoverable under a hull policy are reduced in proportion to any underinsurance. See Part 7, below;

(f) Where the salvage operation involves the saving of other interests besides the subject matter insured, but in circumstances where no general average act can apply, the salvage award will be apportioned over the saved interests; each interest making a contribution in the same manner as for a general average contribution (see Section 15). Except where the policy provides otherwise the underwriter`s liability for the salvage charge is the amount of the assured`s contribution. Where hull insurance is concerned the underwriter`s liability for the salvage contribution is subject to reduction in proportion to any underinsurance and is subject to the policy deductible.

Where a salvage operation is carried out under an agreement between the owner of the property at risk and the salvor, whereby the owner will pay an agreed amount to the salvor whether or not the salvage operation is successful, this is termed "contractual salvage". An example of contractual salvage could be where a ship in ballast is stranded and a tug is engaged to tow her off the strand and to a place of safety. Except where the contract so provides, the salvor does not have a right to detain the property pending payment of the agreed amount. Depending on the circumstances, the underwriter may treat the claim, if any, under the policy as a salvage charge or as an expense incurred for "services in the nature of salvage"; the latter often being settled as a sue & labour charge.

7. Underinsurance - S & L and Salvage Charges

Sue & Labour Charges - In dealing with the measure of indemnity for sue & labour charges section 78(1) of the MIA, 1906, provides that the underwriter is liable for expenses properly incurred pursuant to a sue & labour clause; making no reference to underinsurance. In cargo insurance practice the ICC (1982) accept liability for sue & labour charges, as in Part 3 above, and make no reference to the effect of underinsurance.

On the other hand, whilst hull underwriters also accept liability for sue & labour charges as in Part 3 above, the ITC (1983) demand that any underinsurance indicated by comparing the sound (market) value of the insured vessel at the time of loss with the insured value expressed in the policy shall be taken into account when settling a claim for sue & labour charges. This rule is strictly applied in all circumstances other than where the underwriter enjoys proceeds from disposal of wreck after settling a total loss; it being qualified in the latter case. The following examples illustrate:

Example 1 - No total loss:

	Insured value	Sound value	S&L charge	Claim*
(a)	£4,000,000	£3,800,000	£4,500	£4,500
(b)	£4,000,000	£4,000,000	£4,500	£4,500
(c)	£4,000,000	£4,500,000	£4,500	£4,000

(*The claim is subject to the policy deductible)

Example 2 - A CTL claim attaches to the policy. The underwriter accepts the abandonment and disposes of the wreck, enjoying proceeds amounting to £4,000 net. The underwriter pays the full sum insured in respect of the CTL (ie £4,000,000) plus the £4,000 (ie the amount of the proceeds from disposal of the wreck) in respect of part of the sue & labour charge. The balance of the sue & labour charge (£500) is reduced by the underinsurance rule:

	Insured value	Sound value	S&L charge		Claim*
(a)	£4,000,000	£3,800,000	£4,500		£4,500
(b)	£4,000,000	£4,000,000	£4,500		£4,500
(c)	£4,000,000	£4,500,000	£4,000	£4,000	
			500	444	£4,444

(*The claim is **not** subject to the policy deductible)

Salvage Charges - In dealing with the measure of indemnity for salvage charges section 73(2) of the MIA, 1906, provides that the claim shall be treated in the same manner as a claim for a GA contribution. Where a contributory value is used to determine a salvage contribution this value shall be compared with the insured value expressed in the policy to determine any underinsurance. The Act gives no guidance for determining underinsurance where no contributory values are available.

In cargo insurance practice one frequently sees a "GA in full" clause in the insurance contract. Subject to the wording of this clause (eg it refers to both general average and salvage charges) the underwriter does not apply the rule of underinsurance to the claim. In the absence of this special market clause the underwriter is entitled to reduce the claim in proportion to the underinsurance. For salvage charges, where no contributory value is available, it is customary to use the invoice value in the comparison and, since one seldom sees a cargo policy with an insured value that is less than the invoice value, the point is probably academic.

In hull insurance practice there is no market "GA in full" clause and the ITC (1983) expressly provide that the claim shall be reduced to reflect underinsurance. Where contributory values are used to determine the assured's liability for a salvage charge underinsurance is determined by comparing the contributory value with the insured value. Where no contributory values are available underinsurance is determined by comparing the sound (market) value of the ship with the insured value. The following illustrates the latter:

	Insured value	Sound value	Salvage charge	Claim*
(a)	£4,000,000	£3,800,000	£4,500	£4,500
(b)	£4,000,000	£4,000,000	£4,500	£4,500
(c)	£4,000,000	£4,500,000	£4,500	£4,000

(*The claim is subject to the policy deductible)

Excess Liabilities - Where a claim for a sue & labour charge or a salvage charge recoverable under a hull policy is reduced by reason of underinsurance the amount not recoverable under the marine insurance policy is termed an "excess liability". If the hull assured's P & I club considers the insured value expressed in the marine insurance policy to be a "proper" value the club will probably bear the whole of the excess liability. Otherwise, except where the assured has effected adequate excess liabilities cover elsewhere, the assured must bear the excess liability himself.

8. Underwriters' Subrogation Rights *(MIA, 1906, sect. 79)*

Subrogation is one of the fundamental principles of insurance. It is a corollary of the principle of indemnity; strict application of the latter ensuring that the assured shall not make a profit from his loss. There is no compulsion on underwriters to exercise their rights in subrogation but, although marine insurance practice does not always adhere to the strict application of the principle of indemnity, underwriters usually exercise their subrogation rights where, by so doing, they realise a substantial benefit.

Section 79 of the MIA, 1906, which deals with the matter of subrogation, is in two parts. The first part is concerned with circumstances where a claim for total loss is settled under the policy. The second part is concerned with circumstances where the insured property has suffered a partial loss.

Where the underwriter has settled a total loss under the policy he is entitled to take title to whatever may remain of the property and to dispose of it at his discretion. The underwriter may retain the *whole* proceeds; even where these exceed the claim paid under the policy. It must be emphasised that the underwriter is not **obliged** to exercise subrogation rights. For example, where the exercise of a subrogation right will not benefit the underwriter he may not bother to exercise the right; in fact he would most certainly refrain from exercising his right to title of the property where by so doing he could incur liabilities to third parties. Reference to the notes in Section 11 will give more detail in this respect where total loss is concerned.

In addition to proprietary subrogation rights, following a total loss settlement, the underwriter acquires subrogation rights in respect of any recoveries the assured may make from other parties responsible for the loss. This form of subrogation right is separate from the underwriter's right to take over whatever may remain of the property and, he can exercise this right even if he rejects title to the property. This form of subrogation right is the same as for partial loss; comment on which appears below.

An assured who has suffered a partial loss from an accident caused by another party has, in most cases where the loss is covered by an insurance policy, a right to recover his loss from two sources. One source is the underwriter subscribing the policy that covers the loss and the other is the party responsible for the loss. It would be unfair if the assured could recover his loss from both sources; thereby making a profit from the loss. In any event, he usually finds it more convenient to claim under the policy and, on the face of it, to forgo his recovery from the party responsible for the loss. Recognising this practice, section 79 of the MIA, 1906, allows the underwriter who settles the loss to take over the assured`s legal right to recover the amount of the claim from the third party responsible for the loss. This applies to both total loss and partial loss; but, in the case of the latter, the underwriter is **not** entited to take over what remains of the property; his subrogation rights being restricted to recoveries from third parties.

In other branches of insurance the underwriter might be able to exercise subrogation rights before he pays the claim to the assured; but section 79 of the MIA, 1906, restricts the marine underwriter`s subrogation rights to circumstances where the underwriter has actually settled the claim under the policy. Further, although the marine underwriter who has settled a claim is automatically entitled to subrogation rights to pursue an action against a third party, it is customary for the assured to sign a letter of subrogation formally passing on his rights against the third party to the underwriter. This practice smooths the procedure by making it clear that any legal action taken by the underwriter, in this respect, shall be deemed to be that of the original claimant. Although section 79 of the Act restricts the underwriter`s right of recovery to the amount of the claim paid under the policy (this applying both to total loss and partial loss claims where recoveries from third parties are concerned) the letter of subrogation allows the underwriter to press for full settlement. Where the recovery exceeds the amount paid as a claim under the policy the underwriter is deemed to hold the excess in trust for the original claimant (the assured).

One example of the exercise of subrogation rights against a third party occurs where the insured goods (or part of them) have not been delivered or the goods have been delivered but in a damaged condition. In such case the consignee has a right to claim against the carrier. The right to claim against the carrier could be prejudiced if the consignee (usually the assured`s assignee in practice) does not comply with legal requirements to prevent the claim against the carrier becoming time barred. Cargo underwriters are conscious of this disadvantage and incorporate a clause in the cargo policy or certificate requiring the cargo assured to preserve all rights against carriers and other third parties so that the underwriter`s subrogation rights shall not be prejudiced. It should be noted that the contract of carriage usually incorporates provisions which exempt the carrier from responsibility in certain circumstances (eg loss or damage caused by Act of God) and, in most cases, allow him to limit his liability in accordance with the terms of the contract of carriage and based on a maximum amount per package or kilo. Trainees and practitioners seeking further information are advised to consult "Marine Insurance - Volume 2 - Cargo Practice" by Brown (Witherby 1985).

Where a ship, carrying goods, is involved in a collision, in respect of which the other ship is wholly or partly at fault, the owners of both ship and cargo can claim against the other vessel for loss suffered as a consequence of the collision. Where the ship and/or goods are insured the underwriter settling the claim on the cargo or hull policy, as they case may be, can exercise subrogation rights to recover the amount of the claim paid; the recovery being restricted, as above, in both cases. Shipowners can claim limitation of liability in collision cases; this being based on the tonnage of the vessel. Trainees seeking further information are advised to consult "Marine Insurance - Volume 3 - Hull Practice" by Brown (Witherby 1993) and/or "Marine Insurance Claims" by Goodacre (Witherby).

It is important to note that, although underwriters are not obliged to exercise subrogation rights when they arise, any clause incorporated in a marine insurance policy expressly waiving subrogation rights could make the contract void in the eyes of the law (MIA, 1906, sect. 4 sub.2b).

English law provides that, where a deductible appears in a policy, the assured shall not be treated as a co-insured in regard to the deductible. Thus, the deductible does not prejudice the right of the underwriter to recover the full amount of his claim from a third party. Further, where interest is added to a recovery to compensate for time lost between the date of the accident and the date of the recovery, the underwriter is entitled to such proportion of the interest as relates to the period between the date the claim was settled and the date the recovery was made. This interest is in addition to the recovery, even where the latter is for the full amount of the claim paid under the policy. To avoid dispute where foreign law does not equate with English law, in this respect, the ITC (1983) incorporate a clause giving effect to the above position regarding interest on recoveries.

9. Double Insurance, Contribution and Underinsurance

(MIA, 1906, sects. 80 & 81)

Double insurance occurs when two or more policies are effected to cover the same insurable interest in the same subject matter insured for an amount that, in the aggregate, exceeds the insurable value, in the case of unvalued policies, or the insured value, in the case of valued policies. Where fraudulent double insurance is effected the party or parties involved in the fraud are liable to criminal prosecution and all policies concerned are declared void; any monies derived from the existence of the policies is forfeit to the Crown.

Innocent double insurance can take place where more than one party effects an insurance contract covering the same interest in the subject matter insured in ignorance of the existence of the other insurance contract. An example could be where a seller assigns a policy, which he has effected to cover goods on a warehouse to warehouse basis, to the buyer who has also effected his own insurance policy to cover the goods on a warehouse to warehouse basis. Where the assured is overinsured by innocent double insurance he can claim proportionately from both policies; provided he does not receive more than a proper indemnity overall. Alternatively, the assured can claim from one of the policies; leaving the underwriters to sort out their position under the right of contribution established by section 80 of the MIA, 1906. In which case the underwriter settling the claim is entitled to recover any overpayment from the other policy. The recovery being for such proportion of the claim as the sum insured by the other policy bears to the aggregate of the sums insured by both policies.

In principle, section 81 of the MIA, 1906, provides that where the assured is insured for an amount less than the insured value (or less than the insurable value in the case of an unvalued policy) he is deemed to be self insured for the difference by which he is underinsured. This principle is applied in all cases where the sum insured by the policy (or, where there be more than one policy, the total of the sums insured by all policies) is less than the insured value, or the insurable value, as the case may be.

Examples -

	Insured value	Sum insured	Loss	Policy	Assured
(1)	£4,000,000	£3,800,000	£4,000	£3,800	£200

(2)	Insured value	Sum insured	Loss	Policy
Policy A	£4,000,000	£2,000,000	£4,000	£2,000
Policy B	£4,000,000	£1,500,000	£4,000	£1,500

Assured bears amount not covered by policies = £500

These examples relate to circumstances where the sum insured is less than the insured value in a cargo policy or a hull policy and apply to both total loss and partial losses. The examples apply, equally, to unvalued policies (eg policies covering shipowners' liabilities) where the sum insured is inadequate to meet the full liability incurred by the assured.

Undervaluation is another form of underinsurance. That is to say where the assured has effected a policy with an insured value which is less than the insurable value of that property. In cargo insurance practice such underinsurance affects claims for both total loss and partial loss; total loss being restricted to the amount insured by the policy and partial loss (ie damage to the goods, etc.) being restricted by application of the percentage of depreciation to the amount insured by the policy (see notes in Section 12). Whilst a total loss under a hull policy is, of course, similarly restricted, an exception occurs in the case of hull insurance claims for damage to ship. Apart from a limit of the sum insured by the policy in respect of each casualty, claims for damage to ship are based on the reasonable cost of repairs and are not affected by undervaluation (see notes in Section 12); although they would be affected by underinsurance in regard to the sum insured compared with the insured value. Other partial loss claims attaching to a hull policy *are* affected by undervaluation (see notes in Part 7, above, and in Section 16).

Where the same risk is covered by two separate policies (eg goods are insured against fire by a marine policy and also by a policy covering warehouse risks only) the assured can, in theory, recover his loss from either policy but not from both. Where experience has shown confusion could arise in such cases it is customary for one policy (or maybe both policies) to incorporate a "non-contribution" clause; which provides that the loss is not recoverable under the policy if it is insured by another policy.

SEE OVERPAGE FOR SELF STUDY QUESTIONAIRE

SELF STUDY QUESTIONS

Before moving on to the next section satisfy yourself that you have absorbed the subject matter in the previous Sections. The following questions should be answered without reference to the text:

1. Why was the "sue & labour" clause introduced to the SG form of policy? This clause does not appear in the MAR form of policy. What is the title of the clause in the ITC (1983) and the ICC (1982) which upholds the spirit of applying sue & labour charges to a modern marine insurance policy?

2. What are the rules governing the application of sue & labour charges to a marine insurance policy?

3. When are sue & labour charges -
(a) not recoverable in addition to a total loss?
(b) not subject to a hull policy deductible?
(c) the subject to an underinsurance reduction?

4. The "duty of assured" clause in a cargo policy is not confined to the treatment of sue & labour charges. What other duties are imposed on the assured, their servants or agents by the clause?

5. Define the term "salvage" in regard to a maritime adventure.

6. What is the difference between "pure" salvage and "contractual" salvage?

7. A salvor can exercise a maritime lien to enforce a salvage award. What is a maritime lien? Can the salvor exercise this lien in respect of salvaged personal effects? What is the position of a salvor who saves life at sea?

8. When is a salvage charge not recoverable under a marine insurance policy?

9. How does underinsurance affect claims for sue & labour charges and salvage charges under a hull policy? What are "excess liabilities"?

10. What is the extent of underwriters` subrogation rights in respect of -
(a) a cargo total loss ?
(b) a claim for damage to goods?
(c) a hull total loss?
(d) a claim for damage to ship?

SECTION FOURTEEN

MARINE LIABILITY INSURANCE

1. Introduction
2. Statutory Powers
3. Contractual Liability
4. Third Party Liability
5. Ship Operator`s Liability and Shipowners` Mutual Clubs
6. Collision Liability and the Marine Hull Policy
7. Both to Blame Collision Liability - Hull
8. Cargo Owner`s Legal Liabilities and Marine Insurance
9. Carrier`s Liability to Cargo Owners
10. Both to Blame Collision Liability - Cargo
11. Limitation of Liability
12. Direct Underwriter`s Policy Liability and Reinsurance

SECTION 14

1. Introduction

The term "liability" refers to the responsibility everyone has to avoid inflicting loss or damage to the property, life or person of another. The context of these notes relates solely to *legal* liabilities; that is to say liabilities incurred by the defendant which can be substantiated in a court of law. The notes are not concerned with *moral* liabilities; that is self-imposed liablities generated by one`s conscience but which have no basis in law. To illustrate the latter, consider the position where a yacht owner, whilst working on his own yacht, carelessly sprays paint on a friend`s yacht. The paint sprayer may feel a moral obligation to repair the damage but, unless he can show a legal liability for the damage, no claim for the liability would attach to his yacht policy.

Legal liabilities embrace a wide scope of activity and laws vary in different countries. These introductory notes are confined to legal liabilities as determined by English law (much of which is based on international agreements) and, apart from appropriate comment on matters outside marine insurance but which can relate thereto, only to the extent that liabilities affect a marine insurance contract.

In practice, legal liabilities fall into three main categories; these being "statutory powers", "contractual liabilities" and "third party liabilities". In some cases these overlap. For example, a statutory liability may qualify a contractual liability; as in the case of the Carriage of Goods by Sea Act which qualifies contracts of carriage agreed between shippers and carriers.

Whilst, in general, English law does not impose compulsory insurance on the owners of property and on the life, etc. of persons (leaving the public to decide whether or not they need insurance protection) in some branches of insurance one encounters circumstances where there is a legal compulsion to effect *liability* insurance. Examples are third party liability insurance in respect of the operation of motor vehicles on English roads and employers` liability insurance regarding contracts of employment. However, where maritime property is concerned and apart from employers` liability insurance regarding crew etc., English law does not make it compulsory for any person to effect insurance to cover legal liabilities the owner of goods in transit or a ship operator might incur. Nevertheless, section 5(2) of the MIA, 1906, provides, amongst other things, that a person has an insurable interest "in any legal or equitable relation to the adventure or to any insurable property at risk therein in consequence of which he may incur liability in respect thereof". Accordingly, such person has an insurable interest in potential liabilities and, provided he can find an insurer who is prepared to accept the risk, he may insure his liabilities for any amount acceptable to the insurer.

Prudent underwriting demands a capacity for recognising risks and anticipating potential losses. Liability claims experience in other branches of insurance show the sagacity of early marine insurers in not embracing liabilities within the SG policy cover. In fact, it was not until considerable pressure was exercised in the demand for collision liability cover that marine hull underwriters relented and allowed a limited extension of the SG policy cover, during the 19th century, to embrace collision liability. Even in today`s commercial world, where proposals for liability insurance cover proliferate, insurers writing hull and cargo policies resist demands for liability cover and leave these risks, particularly where there is an enormous potential for loss, to mutual insurance societies (see notes in Part 5, below).

The notes in this Section are not concerned with liabilities incurred by the assured in connection with sue & labour charges, salvage charges, salvage contributions or general average contributions. Reference to these forms of liability and "excess liabilities" relating thereto can be found in Section 13.

2. Statutory Powers

This category relates to a liability arising from a breach of condition imposed by a Statute enacted by a Government authority. Since the middle of the 19th century various British Acts of Parliament have come into force giving statutory powers to the courts to enforce liabilities against ship operators and others coming within the scope of the Acts. In some cases, the relevant Act applies to contracts entered into by those referred to by the Act; whilst others relate to obligations and liabilities incurred in common law (eg third party liabilities). It is not proposed, in these introductory notes, to go into detail regarding the contents of these Statutes, but trainees might care to note the introduction and existence of Acts of Parliament in respect of the following (bearing in mind that any of these might have a scope beyond maritime practice and might be the subject of international conventions which could introduce amendments or addenda to an Act in succeeding years):

(1) Fatal accidents (1896)
(2) Harbours, docks and piers (1847 and 1865)
(3) Merchant shipping (1884, 1898, 1900, 1906, 1921, 1958, 1979)
(4) Maritime conventions (1911)
(5) Carriage of goods by sea (1971, 1992)
(6) Prevention of oil pollution (1971)
(7) Unfair contract terms (1977)

3. Contractual Liability

This category relates to liabilities incurred by parties to a contract. When entering into the contract each party undertakes to perform the contract as agreed therein. If one party fails in his performance he may be held liable to the other party for damages as specified within the terms of the contract, or, where the contract is subject to statutory legislation, to liabilities for damages or penalties imposed by such legislation. For example, a contract of carriage relating to the transit of goods by sea from any port in the UK must embody the rules laid down by the UK Carriage of Goods by Sea Act. Similarly, a contract of employment agreed between a ship operator and a crew member is subject to the terms and conditions laid down by the Merchant Shipping Act and relevant subsequent Acts relating thereto.

Where two or more parties enter into a contract they agree the terms of the contract before its performance and, subject to any statutory restrictions, they are free to agree any terms and conditions. In the past, this freedom has led to abuse of the system whereby the more powerful party (ie the party that has power to dictate the terms of the contract) has taken advantage of the other party. In 1977 the British Government introduced the "Unfair Contract Terms Act" which can be invoked in defence of a court action brought against a party to a contract in respect of which the defendant feels his liability to the other party for non-compliance with the contract has been based on an unfair term or condition in the contract. It should be noted that insurers have given an undertaking to abide by certain rules in the construction of marine insurance contracts and have, thereby, obtained exemption from this Act.

4. Third Party Liability

Although contractual liability, as defined above, can involve more than two parties in practice, in principle, a contract is deemed to be between two parties; being the first party and the second party. Accordingly, when considering a liability incurred outside a contract, one refers to it as a "third party" liability. In law one uses the term *tort* in regard to legal measures taken to recover damages in the case of third party liability. The dictionary definition of this term is "a private injury to person or property for which damages may be claimed in a court of law". Except where the circumstances are subject to a Statute the outcome of an action in tort will be determined by arguments raised by counsel, often based on legal precedents, and the judgement of the court. Thus, one cannot lay down any hard and fast rules regarding third party liability; each case being judged on its merits. However, in general, it can be said that a degree of negligence must usually be established for a third party liability to be determined.

Negligence can be unintentional or it can be culpable. The difference is not material where liability is concerned; provided there is a degree of fault on the part of the defendant (and the court takes into account the actions of servants of the defendant in this respect) the defendant can be found to be liable for damages. Culpable negligence may be defined as circumstances where the person responsible carried out the act of negligence deliberately and in full knowledge that his negligence might result in loss or damage. Where culpable negligence is proved the negligent person may have to face criminal charges if his negligence has resulted in, say, loss of life and/or personal injury. For example, if the master of a ship commits an act of culpable negligence whereby there is loss of life, the master could face criminal charges and his employer, though personally innocent, could be required to pay damages. It should be noted that, where culpable negligence results in punitive damages being awarded against an assured it is unlikely that an insurance contract will cover such liability; even where the act of negligence was carried out by an employee and not by the assured himself.

Since third party liability is not governed by any contractual terms neither party involved can contract out of liability; nor can a defendant, on the face of it, limit his liability. Thus, in theory, the owner of a small fishing vessel which collided with and sank a giant tanker could be held to be liable for damages way beyond his means. Fortunately, for such defendants, international conventions have agreed to allow limitation of liabilities incurred by maritime defendants; particularly where collision is concerned. English law has ratified such agreements and the limitations are embodied in the Merchant Shipping Acts to which reference is made in Part 2. Further comment on these limits can be found in Part 11, below.

5. Ship Operator`s Liability and Shipowners` Mutual Clubs

The range of liabilities a ship operator can incur is vast enough to fill a book by itself. These introductory notes are confined to an outline of these liabilitities and the way in which insurance can offer the shipowner some protection against financial loss. Most ships are commercial vessels; that is to say each ship is operated as a business engaged in trade of some form or other. The majority of commercial vessels are carriers but one must not forget the numerous service vessels (eg tugs, dredgers, floating cranes, supply vessels, etc.) as well as working vessels (eg cable layers, fishing vessels, etc.) any of which can be exposed to the same third party liabilities as carriers. A commercial vessel may be operated by its owner, a manager representing the owner, a shipping company or a charterer. The exposure to legal liability is much the same whatever the category of the operator.

By reference to Part 1 of this Section it will be recalled that early 19th century underwriters writing hull risks were reluctant to extend the cover in the SG policy to embrace liabilities; even liabilities incurred in consequence of an accident involving an insured peril. When it became clear that persons suffering losses caused by others were not prepared to let the loss lie where it fell shipowners became concerned about the potential liabilities they could incur in everyday ship operations. Approaches to hull underwriters still fell on deaf ears, so to speak, and ship operators decided they must form their own mutual protection societies to cover potential liabilities. The formation of mutual insurance clubs was not new! Various mutual protection societies had been formed in the 18th century to cover war risks during a period when shipowners lost faith in the ability of the London marine insurance market to compensate them for war losses. Some of these societies had closed down when faith in the London market was restored; but most were resurrected to join those that still operated in offering insurance protection for liabilities incurred by ship operators. At first this cover was restricted to third party liabilities and contractual liabilities relating to the running of the ship; but, later, it was extended to embrace carriers' liabilities to cargo owners. So were born the P&I (Protection and Indemnity) clubs of today.

A P&I club is a mutual insurance society. The term "mutual" means the members are self insured; that is to say, each policy holder contributes to maintain a fund from which losses suffered by himself and fellow members are made good. In principle, no profits are made by either the club or the members thereof. Reserves remaining at the end of each financial year are carried forward to support claims in succeeding years. Each member contributes an initial premium, based on the tonnage of his entered vessels, at the start of each financial year. The amount so collected covers management costs and creates a reserve from which demands for the year are met. Should the reserves so created prove to be insufficient to meet the demands on the club, members must pay "calls" to make up the shortfall. Club rules vary but it is customary, in all cases, for the financial year to commence on February, 28th and for entered ships to remain with the club year after year; unless the ship operator gives notice, as required by the club rules, to withdraw the ship from the club.

Until fairly recently P&I clubs did not impose limits on claims made by members; relying on international limitation of liability, and well planned reinsurance contracts, to protect them from catastrophic loss. The raising of limitation amounts, in regard to clean-up costs following pollution and/or contamination of the seas in some areas, to astronomic figures has caused the clubs to reconsider their position and limits are being imposed on claims for such categories of loss. Today, one sees special clubs providing supplementary cover for pollution liability (eg TOVALOP - Tanker Owners' Voluntary Agreement Regarding Liability for Oil Pollution). Further, in recent years, one has seen P & I claims subject to deductibles; requiring the member to bear part of the loss. This move, together with careful selection in the acceptance of club members, encourages ship operators to take more care in maintaining their ships and in appointing officers, crew and others who are to care for and navigate their ships.

6. Collision Liability and the Marine Hull Policy

"Collision" is a "peril of the seas" so loss of or damage to the insured ship proximately caused thereby would be covered by the SG form of policy. This was commented upon in the case of "De Vaux -v- Salvador" (1836) when a claim was made against the underwriters for liabilities incurred by the shipowner in consequence of collision. Whilst admitting the above concerning loss of or damage to the insured vessel, the court did not uphold the contention of the plaintiff that collision liability should be covered and found in favour of the defendant. From the findings in this case stemmed a long dispute on whether or not the cover in the SG form of policy should be extended to embrace collision liability. The arguments for and against ranged over some 18 years during which time some London market underwriters agreed to incorporate a, so called, "running down" clause (later to become known by its initials as the RDC) in policies covering hull & machinery; whilst the majority refused to extend the SG cover in this way.

Eventually, in 1854, the dissidents withdrew their objections in favour of a limited form of collision liability clause; whereby the assured bore one quarter of each loss. Thus, was born the 3/4ths RDC. At first the RDC was introduced as a separate supplementary clause which was attached to the policy at the option of the underwriter. However, by the time the standard hull clauses were published by the ILU in the latter part of the 19th century, use of the RDC had become so commonplace that the clause, in a standard 3/4ths format, was incorporated in the ITC and in other relevant sets of Institute hull clauses. P & I clubs agreed to pick up collision liability claims not covered by the marine hull policy; including the 1/4th collision liability not embraced by the London market RDC. Foreign sets of hull clauses based on the SG policy format (eg the AHF - American Hull Form) also incorporated an RDC in the hull policy conditions; but, probably because P & I cover was not always available outside the UK in those days, such sets of foreign hull & machinery insurance conditions usually incorporated a 4/4ths RDC.

Since its introduction the RDC has been the subject of many changes; some to clarify the intention of the cover and others to make it clear that certain liabilities, irrespective of the fact that they were incurred in consequence of collision, were not embraced by the RDC. Prominent amongst the latter were the exclusion of liability for loss of life or personal injury and exclusion of liability for loss of or damage to anything other than another ship or vessel and/or property carried thereon.

The RDC incorporated in the current ITC, and other relevant sets of Institute hull clauses, is a *supplementary* contract; that is to say one can collect a collision liability claim in addition to any other claim under the policy; even a total loss claim. Nevertheless, claims are still subject to the policy deductible and to the *paramount* war, etc. exclusion clauses expressed in the policy. The RDC continues to maintain a 3/4ths limit and restricts cover solely to *legal* liabilities consequent upon collision between the insured vessel and any other ship or vessel. The RDC cover is for 3/4ths of the assured`s legal liability with a limit of 3/4ths of the insured value expressed in the policy. The other 1/4th liability, not covered by the RDC, is borne by the assured`s P&I club.

Claims under the RDC are subject to reduction arising from any underinsurance (see Section 13). Although the P&I club does *not* reimburse the assured in regard to the policy deductible, provided the club considers the H&M policy to be effected for a *proper* value, it will usually pick up any excess liability (see Section 13) arising from underinsurance, or, where excess liabilities are insured elsewhere, 1/4th of the RDC excess liability not borne by the excess liabilities policy. In recent years several clubs have offered full collision liability cover to members and one begins to see H&M policies with the RDC deleted from the clauses attached thereto.

7. Both to Blame Collision Liability - Hull

The term "collision liability" (see Part 6, above) refers to physical contact between two vessels; it does not embrace contact between a ship and anything other than another vessel. Collision liability can be the fault of one of the vessels or both vessels could be partly at fault. Where only one vessel is at fault all liabilities will, naturally, fall on the owner, manager, charterer or other operator of such vessel. Where both vessels at at fault a proportionate degree of blame will be determined and the liabilities apportioned over each vessel accordingly.

Example -

Ship A is held to be 60% at fault in collision with ship B.

Damage suffered		*60%*	*40%*
(1) Hull A	£200,000	£120,000	£80,000*
(2) Hull B	£100,000	£ 60,000*	£40,000
(3) Cargo A	£100,000	£ 60,000	£40,000*
(4) Cargo B	£160,000	£ 96,000*	£64,000

*A is liable to B for items (2) and (4) = £156,000
*B is liable to A for items (1) and (3) = £120,000

Assuming each carrier is not liable for loss of or damage to cargo carried on board his own vessel (see Part 8, below) the other losses would be borne by the hull and cargo owners or their underwriters, as the case may be.

A court of law would settle this on a "single" liability basis; whereby the owner of vessel A would be required to pay the difference between the two liabilities (ie £36,000) to B. In hull insurance practice this causes problems for the assured which, except where one of the parties limits his liability (see Part 11, below), are resolved by the hull underwriter basing the collision liability claim attaching to A`s policy on the full amount of liability (ie £156,000); the underwriters covering collision liability under B`s policy doing likewise. This is termed a "cross liabilities" settlement.

Where the two vessels involved in the collision are owned by the same person no liability for damage to either ship will be entertained by the courts. Hull underwriters, however, incorporate a "sistership" clause in the H&M policy by which they agree to treat the ships as though they are separately owned. In such case the degree of fault is determined by arbitration and the assured`s collision liability claims are settled in the normal manner.

8. Cargo Owner`s Legal Liabilities and Marine Insurance

It is not the intention of these introductory notes to go into detail but, in general, it can be said that the shipper (eg the cargo owner) must take care, amongst other things, to properly pack and mark the goods to ensure that, as far as is reasonably possible, the goods will not cause loss of or damage to the ship or other conveyances or to other goods carried thereon or impair the lives or persons of those who will handle the goods. Failure to take such care could involve the cargo owner in legal liabilities, contractual or third party as the case may be, to parties who suffer from such carelessness.

Once the carrier takes delivery of the goods from the shipper any third party liability arising in connection with carriage of the goods will normally devolve on the carrier. However, there remain areas of both contractual and third party liability which might fall directly on the cargo owner. Take, for example, a cargo which causes loss or damage to other cargoes (eg by contamination). The carrier could suffer a contractual liability where improper stowage caused the loss; but the cargo owner could be held liable, under his contract of carriage, to make good the liability loss suffered by the carrier if improper marking of packages had not warned the carrier of the hazardous nature of the goods. Further, where the carrier was not at fault, a third part liability action could be pursued directly against the cargo owner by the injured party if the loss or damage resulted from, say, improper packaging of the goods or failure to declare their hazardous nature.

Where hazardous goods are shipped, without knowledge of their hazardous nature being conveyed to the carrier, the carrier, upon discovery of their hazardous nature, can, without incurring any liability to the owner of the hazardous goods, land them short of destination or destroy them or render them innocuous. The owner of the hazardous goods is liable to compensate the carrier for expenses, etc. arising or resulting from such action. Further, the owner of the goods is liable to the carrier for any loss or damage caused to the ship by the hazardous goods and, as stated above, for loss or damage caused to other cargo.

Where hazardous goods are shipped with the knowledge and consent of the carrier and become a danger to the ship or cargo, the carrier may still treat the goods, as above (eg render them innocuous, etc.), without liability to the owner of the hazardous goods; but the carrier remains liable for general average contributions, if any.

Although the cargo owner has an insurable interest in the above potential liabilities one sees no evidence of these being insured in the marine market. If one discounts sue & labour charges, salvage charges and general average contributions (these sometimes being referred to as "liabilities", in practice), the only form of liability cover embraced by marine cargo policy appears in the "both to blame collision" clause which one finds in all sets of the ICC. This clause seeks to recompense the assured for losses suffered in consequence of the implementation of a "both to blame collision clause" which might be incorporated in a contract of carriage. To understand the operation of this clause one needs to have some knowledge regarding carriers` liabilities; so we shall leave notes on this subject to appear in Part 10, below.

9. Carrier`s Liability to Cargo Owners

Carriers` liability to cargo owners is governed by the terms of the contract of carriage (sometimes referred to as the "contract of affreightment"). To maintain a worldwide standard for the terms of contracts of carriage the law in relation to these has been the subject of a series of international conferences over many years. For much of the 20th century the law relating to the carriage of goods was based on a 1924 set of international rules termed the "Hague Rules". These rules were ratified in the UK and embodied in the Carriage of Goods by Sea Act, 1924. Other ratifying countries embodied the rules in their own Statutes. The Hague Rules were amended in 1968 and replaced by the "Hague/Visby Rules"; which, in turn, were embodied in the UK Carriage of Goods by Sea Act, 1971; this Act repealing the 1924 Act and some other Statutes (eg sections of the Merchant Shipping Act) which affected contracts of carriage. Other ratifying countries, similarly, changed their statutory law. Further international conferences resulted in a new set of rules being agreed in 1978; these being styled the "Hamburg Rules"; but, although other countries ratified the Hamburg Rules and changed their laws accordingly, apart from a change in the basis for calculating limitation of liability (see Part 11, below) and a 1992 Act regarding bills of lading, no new UK Statute has been enacted, at the time of this revision, to complement the Hamburg Rules. These introductory notes do not extend to embrace detail regarding the international Rules nor the Statutes complementing the Rules; but attention of trainees is directed to the existence of the Rules as background information; also for the benefit of those outside the UK who may wish to relate the comments herein to the Rules followed by their own legislation. More detailed information can be obtained from the comments in, and appendices to, "Marine Insurance - Volume 3 - Hull Practice" by Brown (Witherby 1993).

By reference to the notes in Section 4 it will be recalled that legal disputes relating to marine insurance contracts that are subject to clauses published by the ILU must be determined in accordance with English law & practice, as specified in each set of Institute clauses. Nevertheless, one must appreciate that liabilities of carriers to cargo owners are insured, mainly, by P&I clubs and, as such, are not subject to insurance conditions published by the ILU.

The carrier's liability is based on the terms of the contract of carriage which is unlikely to incorporate a provision that court disputes must be settled, within the jurisdiction of or, in accordance with the law & practice of any particular country. Further, whereas contracts in respect of goods exported from the UK are, by English statutory law, subject to the English Carriage of Goods by Sea Act current at the time of issue, contracts of carriage relating to goods shipped from other countries may be subject to a different legislation. Nevertheless, it is reasonable to assume the latter contracts of carriage will be based on the Hague/Visby Rules; albeit amended, in some cases, by the Hamburg Rules.

English law imposes very little responsibility on the carrier regarding the safety of the goods he carries; granting him immunity from liability in all matters where the cause of the loss of or damage to the goods is outside his control. Even the carrier's responsibility to provide a seaworthy ship fit to carry the goods, and to properly man, equip and supply such ship, is tempered by a provision whereby the cargo owner must show there was a lack of *due diligence* on the part of the carrier in this respect for a claim against the carrier to succeed. For example, there is no an <u>absolute</u> condition that the ship must be seaworthy. Provided the carrier has exercised due diligence to make the ship seaworthy he cannot be held liable for loss of or damage to the goods caused by perils of the seas even though such loss or damage resulted from unseaworthiness of the ship.

Further to its apparent leniency, regarding the carrier's responsibility for seaworthiness and fitness of the ship, the law grants immunity to the carrier for a list of casualties which might befall the ship without the actual fault or privity of the carrier. For example, loss of or damage to the goods caused by fire generated by negligence of a member of the crew (an employee of the carrier) would not give rise to a legal claim against the carrier unless it could be proved that the carrier was at fault by, say, failing to provide proper fire fighting equipment. In fact, the carrier could probably avoid liability, even in the latter circumstance, if he could show he exercised due diligence to provide such equipment.

The Carriage of Goods by Sea Act, 1971, absolves the carrier from liability for loss of or damage to the goods if the consignee does not claim in writing within a prescribed time from when the goods should have been delivered (in the case of missing goods) or within a limited number of days from delivery in the case of damaged goods. At this introductory stage one would not expect marine insurance trainees to absorb details in this respect so further comment is not necessary here. Those seeking more detailed information should consult the Act itself; bearing in mind that this Act is based on the Hague/Visby Rules and different provisions might apply where a contract is based on the Hamburg Rules.

Where the marine cargo policy covers the loss or damage to the goods the assured may claim directly from his underwriter to recover his loss; leaving the underwriter to pursue an action against the carrier for any recovery to which the assured would be entitled (see "subrogation rights" in Section 13). Cargo underwriters, anxious to protect their subrogation rights in regard to claims against carriers, require the cargo assured to properly preserve his rights against carriers and other bailees (see "Duty of assured" clause in the ICC, 1982).

10. Both to Blame Collision Liability - Cargo

The title of the clause in the ICC (1982), to which this subject relates, is somewhat of a mis-nomer because it has nothing to do with third party collision liability incurred by the assured. The title is taken from the "both to blame collision" clause in a contract of carriage. However, before considering this one should look at the position of the carrier in regard to collision damage to the goods carried on board.

As we have seen in Part 9, above, the carrier is absolved from liability for damage to cargo on board his own vessel where the collision is without his actual fault or privity. But this does not stop the cargo owner from claiming against the other vessel.

Under American law, and possibly the law of some other countries, the cargo owner can claim 100% of his loss from the non-carrying vessel; irrespective of the degree of fault attaching to such other vessel. Because this is a third party liability claim the non-carrying vessel cannot contract out of the liability; nor is the non-carrying vessel protected by any international law which might otherwise absolve him from liability to the cargo owner.

American law recognises the inequity of this situation, when the non-carrying vessel is only partly to blame for the collision, and allows the non-carrying vessel to include the relevant proportionate part of the cargo owner`s claim in his third party claim against the carrying vessel. This is also a third party liability and there is no way the carrying vessel can avoid the liability. Recognising that this situation could arise the carrier incorporates the "both to blame collision" clause in his contract of carriage. By agreeing to this contract the cargo owner finds himself having to reimburse his carrier for the third pary liability the latter has incurred in respect of his own cargo. The following example illustrates the relative positions of both ship operators in regard to the cargo owner`s claim.

Ship A is 60% responsible for a collision with ship B. The cargo in A suffers damage amounting to £100,000. Unable to recover this from ship A the cargo owner claims £100,000 from B. Figures shown in ( ) represent debits:

	Cargo Owner	*Ship A*	*Ship B*
Cargo damage	£100,000		(£100,000)
B's T/P claim		(£60,000)	£ 60,000
A's claim on cargo	(£ 60,000)	£60,000	
	£ 40,000		(£ 40,000)

From these figures one can see that the cargo owner recovers only 40% of his loss. In practice he would in fact recover the full £100,000 from his underwriter; relinquishing his claim against the non-carrying vessel to the underwriter. By exercising his subrogation rights the underwriter would recover £100,000 from the non-carrying vessel. Accordingly, on the face of it, the above figures would present a loss of £60,000 to the cargo assured. Cargo underwriters recognise the inequity of the asssured's position and, by incorporating the "both to blame collision" clause in the ICC (1982), agree to reimburse the assured for the £60,000 he has paid to his carrier.

11. Limitation of Liability

It is not humanly possible to forsee when and where an accident will take place nor what losses will be involved. Shrewd judgement, based on experience and perhaps the law of averages, enables underwriters to assess a risk and to accept proposals for the insurance of maritime property but only within certain limits; these being related to the insured value and sum insured in the policy. Such judgement is of little use when it comes to the insurance of third party liabilities because it is impossible to anticipate the extent of a third party liability. It is mainly for this reason that hull underwriters have, for over 100 years, avoided the acceptance of proposals to insure third party liabilities; other than the limited cover provided by the RDC. Nevertheless, lack of insurance protection does not make the risk go away so ship operators continue to be faced with the unknown quantity of third party liabilities; albeit that these liabilities might be covered (sometimes to a limited extent) by a P&I club.

As an example, consider the position of the owner of a small coastal vessel which collides with a supertanker and causes a fire which results in a total loss of the tanker. On the face of it, without protection from a P&I club, the owner of the coastal vessel, even if only partly at fault for the collision, could face bankruptcy. Faced with such a situation the owner of the small vessel might seek to limit his liability.

The British Merchant Shipping Acts, and similar Statutes in other countries, allow ship operators to apply for limitation of third party liabilities in circumstances where the liability has been incurred without the actual fault or privity of the ship operator. Although the example, above, relates to collision a ship operator can apply for limitation of *any* large third party liability (eg liability for clean up costs in regard to oil pollution; liability to a waterways authority for removal of wreck, etc.). Further, as can be seen in the notes below, a ship operator (as a carrier) may limit his liability in regard to goods that are lost or damaged whilst in his care. It is even possible to apply for a single (lower) limit in circumstances where the aggregate of all limits incurred in consequence of a single casualty exceed a fixed amount.

Where a ship operator applies for, and is granted, limitation of a third party liability he pays a fixed amount per ton of the ship involved to create a limitation fund.

The basic amount per ton will vary depending on the form of liability. In the absence of international agreement regarding the limit for certain types of liability (eg oil pollution clean up costs) it remains for each country to determine a proper limit which, in some cases, can be very high. Conversely, by international agreement, a standard limit is applied to collision liability for loss of or damage to other ships and property thereon; this increasing where loss of life or personal injury result from the collision.

For many years limitation funds were based on the "gold franc". This was an imaginary unit of exchange which related to the gold value of each international currency. Each country issued an annual statutory instrument declaring a fixed amount in their currency to be used as the gold franc equivalent for the next 12 months. This was satisfactory whilst currency rates remained stable. It may seem unbelievable to the modern trainee that there was stability in currency rates at one time; but this was so when inflation was very low for the so called hard currencies. After world war II worldwide inflation became a major factor in creating instability in currency exchange rates to such an extent that several major variations in exchange rates could take place during a 12 month period. This, eventually, made it impractical to base liabilities on a fixed annual rate of exchange. So, in 1984, the gold franc, as a unit of exchange was abandoned; to be replaced with the SDR (special drawing right). The value of an SDR is established on a daily basis so it more accurately reflects current rates of exchange. When a court determines a liability it does so in SDRs. When the liabilities are settled the amount paid is the equivalent on settlement day, in the relevant currency, to the number of SDRs awarded.

For ships under 500 registered tons the limit for collision liability is SDR330,000 where loss of life and personal injury is involved or SDR167,000 where only liability for loss of or damage to property is involved. Where a larger vessel is concerned the basic limits, above, apply to the first 500 tons; but, thereafter, each extra ton attracts an additional limit based on a standard scale. These introductory notes do not embrace details regarding the formula for creating a collision liability limitation fund; nor the apportionment of the fund over the various claimants against the ship operator. However, the trainee might care to note that loss of life and personal injury claims are given precedence in the apportionment of the limitation fund. Interested trainees and practitioners can find detailed illustrations in "Marine Insurance - Volume 3 - Hull Practice" by Brown (Witherby 1993).

It will be recalled that the terms of a contract of carriage impose obligations on the carrier to properly care for the goods; but the laws relating to carriage of goods absolve him from liability for loss of or damage to the goods caused by circumstances outside his control. In law, the carrier may increase his responsibilities but he may not incorporate a condition in the contract of carriage whereby he reduces his reponsibilities as provided by law. For example, the Carriage of Goods by Sea Act, 1971, forbids the carrier to incorporate a "benefit of insurance" clause in the contract of carriage; a common practice indulged by warehousemen who care for the goods during the ordinary course of transit.

Despite the apparent leniency of the laws, regarding carriers` liability, there can be occasions when the carrier is held to be responsible for loss of or damage to the goods in his care. In such case, provided the loss or damage did not result from any act or omission on the part of the carrier with intent to cause loss or damage, or recklessly with knowledge that loss or damage might result (and except where a higher limit has been agreed in the contract of carriage), the carrier is permitted to limit his liability as provided by the Statute governing the issue of the bill of lading (the latter embodying the contract of carriage). The limits agreed in the Hague/Visby Rules and embodied in the Carriage of Goods by Sea Act, 1971, and its amendments are SDR666.67 per package or unit or SDR2.00 per kilo of the gross weight of the goods lost or damaged; whichever of these is the higher. Practitioners concerned with bills of lading issued in conformity with laws based on the Hamburg Rules should note that these replace the above quoted limits with SDR835 per package or unit and SDR2.50 per kilo.

12. Direct Underwriter`s Policy Liability and Reinsurance

Before we leave the subject of liabilities one must not forget the liabilities incurred by underwriters when meeting claims attaching to the policy. The underwriter has an insurable interest in such liabilities and is entitled to effect a reinsurance contract to cover his potential liability under the direct insurance contract. It is important to appreciate that an underwriter has an insurable interest only in respect of potential liabilities under the direct insurance contract he has written. Therefore, he may reinsure his line, either wholly or partly, but he may not effect a reinsurance contract for more than his written line. If the written line is reduced for signing purposes (see Section 5) the relevant reinsurance line must be reduced, also, in the same proportion. Further, where (as is customary) the reinsurance contract is made "valued as original policy or policies", any reduction in the insured value expressed in the original policy is deemed to be reflected in the reinsurance contract.

The direct insurer can reinsure for less than the direct line he has written; in which case the reinsurance contract covers only part of the claim paid on the original policy; such part being determined by the wording of the reinsurance contract. Where reinsurance contracts are effected for amounts that, in the aggregate, exceed the potential liability of the direct insurer the rules of "contribution" (see Section 13) apply to claims attaching to such reinsurance contracts.

The direct insurer can reinsure on the same terms as the original direct insurance contract or on more limited terms. Where the reinsurance is on more limited terms the direct insurer can recover by way of reinsurance only such claims as he has paid that are embraced by the reinsurance contract. For example, consider the position of a direct insurer who has written a line on a "full terms" H&M policy but has reinsured for TLO (total loss only). The word *only* is particularly important in the reinsurance contract. The direct insurer can recover under his reinsurance contract once only; this being for an ATL or a CTL settlement paid under the original policy. Unless the reinsurance conditions so provide he cannot recover from his reinsurer S&L charges, salvage charges or general average contributions settled on the original policy; even where he can show such liabilities were incurred to prevent a total loss.

A reinsurer is responsible only to the direct insurer who is the other party to the reinsurance contract. He is liable only for losses the direct insurer has actually paid under the direct insurance policy. Where the direct insurer fails to settle a claim through insolvency no liability falls on the reinsurer and, except where a "direct action Statute" is in force, a direct assured cannot pursue his unpaid claim against the reinsurer.

SEE OVERPAGE FOR SELF STUDY QUESTIONAIRE

SELF STUDY QUESTIONS

Before moving on to the next section satisfy yourself that you have absorbed the subject matter in the previous Sections. The following questions should be answered without reference to the text:

1. What is the difference between each of the following categories -
   (a) Statutory powers liability?
   (b) Contractual liability?
   (c) Third party liability?

2. Is it compulsory, in English law, for the owner of a ship to maintain a third party liability insurance contract?

3. What is the structure and purpose of a P&I club?

4. What is an RDC? To what extent does it extend the cover in the ITC (1983)?

5. What is "single liability" in connection with both to blame collision liability? What is a "cross liability" settlement?

6. What are the following -
   (a) The Hague /Visby Rules?
   (b) The Hamburg Rules?

7. What are the obligations of the carrier under a contract of carriage?

8. To what extent is a carrier responsible to provide a ship that is seaworthy and fit to carry the goods?

9. The "duty of assured" clause in a cargo policy requires the assured to "properly preserve" his rights against the carrier and other bailees. What is the purpose of this clause?

10. What does the abbreviation SDR mean. Why was this unit introduced and how is it used in procedures for calculating third party liability settlements?

11. In what circumstances is a cargo carrier *not* allowed to limit his liability to the consignee in regard to goods that have been lost or damaged whilst in his care?

12. Does a reinsurer have any liability to settle a claim made by an original assured where the original assured has been unable to collect his claim from the direct insurer?

SECTION FIFTEEN

GENERAL AVERAGE PRINCIPLES & PRACTICE

1. Introduction

2. Carrier`s Responsibility for Sacrificed Goods

3. General Average Procedure at Port of Discharge

4. Discharging the Carrier`s Lien on Goods

5. Introduction to the York/Antwerp Rules

6. Rules for Calculating General Average Contributions

7. Underwriters` Liability for GA Sacrifice

8. Underwriters` Liability for GA Disbursements

9. Underwriters` Liability for GA Contributions

SECTION 15

1. Introduction

General average is a principle which is designed to ensure that a loss, deliberately incurred for the benefit of the whole in circumstances where all those at risk would suffer if it were not incurred, shall not lie where it falls but shall be borne proportionately by all those who benefit from it.

The term "average" when used in maritime matters means *partial loss.* In this context there are two categories of "average"; these being "particular average" and "general average".

Particular average is peculiar to marine insurance terminology and is defined in section 64(1) of the MIA, 1906, as "..... a partial loss of the subject matter insured, caused by a peril insured against, and which is not a general average loss". Particular average does not include expenses incurred, or financial loss, as such, suffered in consequence of an insured peril; it relates only to *total loss of part* of, or *damage* to, the insured property; but, in the case of insurance of freight at risk the term is applied also to freight lost as a consequence of a particular average loss of goods. Further, to come within the ambit of particular average the loss or damage must have been *accidently* caused by an insured peril or, in the case of some cargo perils, have been reasonably attributable to such specified peril in consequence of an accident. Deliberate loss or damage is not embraced within particular average; but, in the right circumstances, can fall within the ambit of general average sacrifice (see below).

Contrary to the belief of less informed practitioners, the term "general average" is *not* peculiar to marine insurance. It is, in fact, an accepted rule of the sea and applies, when the relevant circumstances permit, irrespective of whether or not any interest in the adventure is insured.

The term "general average" still refers to a partial loss; but, in this case, it means a partial loss of the whole adventure. One could have a total loss of, say, a particular consignment of cargo as a general average sacrifice; but this would still come within the definition of general average because it would be a partial loss of the whole adventure. Marine insurance students often quote section 66(2) of the MIA, 1906, when defining the term general average viz. "there is a general average act where any extraordinary sacrifice or expenditure is voluntarily and reasonably made or incurred in time of peril for the purpose of preserving the property imperilled in a common maritime adventure". This definition has some value in considering marine insurance law but it has little use in defining general average for maritime adventures where no insured interests are involved. Better, perhaps, to be guided by a definition which relates to contracts of carriage. Most contracts of carriage embody the York/Antwerp Rules (see Part 5, below) in which general average is defined as -

> **There is a general average act when, and only when, any extraordinary sacrifice or expenditure is intentionally and reasonably made or incurred for the common safety for the purpose of preserving from peril the property involved in a common maritime adventure**

One can summarise the above as comprising the following components -

(a)	Common maritime adventure	(e)	Reasonable (and prudent)
(b)	Sacrifice or expenditure	(f)	In time of peril
(c)	Extraordinary circumstance	(g)	To preserve from peril
(d)	Intentional (ie voluntary) act		

It is not for the marine insurer to test the existence of general average. This is done by an "average adjuster" who is appointed by the ship operator. The average adjuster acts impartially in determining the existence or not of a general average act; but any of the parties involved can dispute his decision and, if necessary, the matter may be resolved in a court of law. The average adjuster tests the circumstances with regard to the essentials listed above. If any one of these essentials is missing there can be no general average act. The subject is involved and is embraced by a wide range of rules and court decisions over many years so it would be impractical for these introductory notes to cover the whole range of general average. Nevertheless, the following comments will help the trainee to grasp an outline of the subject.

Common adventure - A "maritime adventure" is the exposure of property to peril at sea. General average is a rule of the sea so is not concerned with non-marine adventures. Accordingly, although goods in transit may be covered by a marine insurance policy on a warehouse to warehouse basis, only that part of the adventure which involves sea transit can be subject to general average.

The adjective "common" refers to an adventure in which more than one interest is at risk. An obvious example would be a ship carrying cargo for another; ship and cargo being two separate interests. Where the cargo comprises several consignments owned by different parties, each consignment becomes a separate interest. Where freight has not been paid in advance and, being due on discharge, is at risk of the carrier at the time of the GA act such freight becomes a separate interest in the common adventure. In general, one cannot consider, in general average, a ship sailing in ballast (ie with no cargo on board); but where more than one interest stands to suffer if the ship were lost (eg she is under charter, etc.) a case for general average might be substantiated.

Sacrifice - A general average sacrifice is the deliberate destruction of property exposed to peril in a common maritime adventure; such action being taken to to save the adventure. Except where the carrier can prove the GA act he must take responsibility for the sacrifice of goods in his care and make good the loss thereof to the cargo owner. The following examples of GA sacrifice will illustrate:

Example 1 - A ship has run aground in a storm. Where a ship runs aground at low tide, and in the absence of serious damage to her bottom, she can usually wait for the tide to rise and refloat her. In this case, however, the ship has run aground when the tide is fairly high and the master calculates that she will not refloat without losing some of her weight. It is impractical to unload cargo into lighters; so the master takes a decision to jettison some of his deckload to lighten the vessel. The jettisoned cargo would constitute a GA sacrifice.

Example 2 - A fire breaks out on a ship at sea. Water is used to extinguish the fire. The water damages other cargo which is not on fire. Assuming the goods are insured by a policy covering fire risks loss and damage would be treated as follows:

(a) Each package destroyed by the fire is, except where a total loss of the insured goods applies, a particular average loss;
(b) Fire damage to a package is a particular average loss;
(c) Water damage to a package that is already on fire is a particular average loss;
(d) Water damage to packages not on fire is general average sacrifice.

It should be noted that the cargo assured would claim directly from his underwriter for both the PA loss and the GA sacrifice, together, leaving the underwriter to recover the GA loss from the GA fund in due course.

Example 3 - A serious fire has developed in a hold of a ship at sea. To reach the seat of the fire it becomes necessary to cut a hole in a transverse bulkhead forming one wall of the hold. The fire is extinguished. The cost of repairing the bulkhead is GA sacrifice of ship.

Example 4 - During a voyage sea water is found to be entering a ship between sprung bottom plates. The master calculates that he cannot reach the nearest safe port so he deliberately runs the vessel aground in shallow water to avoid losing her in deep water. Following some temporary repairwork to her bottom the ship is eventually refloated and taken into dry dock for permanent repairs. Replacement of plates not caused by the stranding (ie those that had sprung) would not be allowed in general average but repair of damage caused to the ship`s bottom by the process of stranding would be allowed as GA sacrifice.

Expenditure - General average expenditure relates to costs incurred by a ship operator pursuant to a general average act. The term does not embrace expenses incurred by average adjusters nor fees paid to the average adjuster for his services; these being incorporated in the GA fund but not as GA expenditure. Two of the above examples, regarding GA sacrifice, will serve to illustrate.

Example 1 - A ship has run aground in a storm. Where a ship runs aground at low tide, and in the absence of serious damage to her bottom, she can usually wait for the tide to rise and refloat her. In this case, however, the ship has run aground when the tide is fairly high and the master calculates that she will not refloat without losing some of her weight. Rather than sacrifice cargo the carrier finds it expedient to discharge some of his deckload into lighters and to store the discharged goods ashore during the refloating process. The costs incurred to hire the lighters plus lighter towage and labour costs, together with the costs of warehousing the goods would all be allowed as GA expenditure. Incidentally, any accidental loss of or damage to the goods caused during the unloading and reloading operations would be treated as GA sacrifice, in practice.

Example 2 - During a voyage sea water is found to be entering a ship between sprung bottom plates. The master calculates that he cannot reach the nearest safe port so he deliberately runs the vessel aground in shallow water to avoid losing her in deep water. Following some temporary repairwork to her bottom the ship is eventually refloated. She is taken in tow to a place of safety. These towage costs would be treated as GA expenditure. Should further towage be necessary for permanent repairs to be carried out, such towage cost becomes part of the cost of repairs, and is not embraced within GA expenditure.

Average adjusters advise that an insurance contract be effected by the ship operator to cover GA expenditure because, although it has been incurred by the master with GA in mind, if it transpires that the ship operator is unable to substantiate a GA loss (eg the adventure is not saved despite the master`s efforts) there will be no GA fund from which the expenditure can be recovered. Further, whilst the ship operator`s H&M policy covers expenditure embraced within a GA contribution, there is no direct claim under the policy for the expenditure in the absence of a GA contribution.

Extraordinary circumstance - A ship operator cannot claim, as a GA loss, for any loss he incurs in the ordinary course of his business. In the case of "Wilson -v- Bank of Victoria" (1867) the master of an auxiliary schooner (ie a sailing vessel fitted with an auxiliary engine) was forced to use coal fuel to reach safety after his sails had been blown away in a storm. The shipowner attempted to recover part of the cost of the fuel from the cargo owners; alleging that it was GA sacrifice. The court held that there was no GA sacrifice because this was the ordinary use of the fuel and burning it was not an extraordinary circumstance. The same rule would be applied to modern circumstances where, in time of peril, the master used fuel from reserve tanks because he had exhausted his main fuel tanks. Obviously, where the master uses cargo as fuel this could constitute a GA sacrifice. Similarly, expenses incurred during the ordinary course of the ship`s business cannot be claimed as GA expenditure. For example, whereas the cost of towage to safety might be allowed as GA expenditure one could not, normally, include towage costs within the port area to move the ship from one berth to another to discharge cargo not concerned with the GA act.

Intentional (voluntary) - On the face of it the ship operator must be able to display that the sacrifice was made deliberately for GA to be allowed. Consider a situation where, during heavy weather, deck cargo is being jettisoned to save the ship from capsizing and sinking. Any cargo that fell overboard accidentally due to the listing of the vessel could not be treated as GA sacrifice; even though its loss contributed to the efforts to save the adventure. In marine insurance practice this distinction could be important because no claim for cargo "lost" overboard at sea is recoverable under the ICC (1982) B or C conditions; except were it is embraced in a GA contribution. Further, property that is already virtually lost cannot be claimed as GA sacrifice. An example of this can be seen above where water damage to packages already on fire was not allowed as GA sacrifice.

Exceptions to this rule have been allowed. It will be noted that, in an example above, cargo accidentally damaged during the operation of a GA act was allowed as a GA sacrifice. The same would apply to accidental damage caused to a ship whilst carrying out a GA act. For example, where a ship entered a port of safety as part of a GA act, and accidentally struck the pier on the way in, the damage to the ship so caused was allowed as a GA sacrifice.

Reasonable - The basis for determining this essential is "would a reasonable uninsured person sacrifice his own property in the circumstances or, in the case of expenditure, consider such costs as economic to incur?". Actually, Rule A of the York/Antwerp Rules makes no reference to *prudence* but commonsense tells us that a critic of a GA act would demand prudence on the part of the master in deciding whether or not to sacrifice property and, given the choice, which property to sacrifice. Similarly prudence would come into a decision whether to incur an expenditure or not. If incurring an expense was imprudent it would not be allowed in GA. If incurring the expense was prudent but the amount unreasonable it would be allowed in GA but only up to the amount that was reasonable in the circumstances.

Time of peril - The adventure must be imperilled at the time of the GA act and the sacrifice must be made or the expense incurred for the purpose of avoiding loss from the peril. The type of peril is immaterial because unlike claims under an insurance policy, when determining general average, one is not concerned with whether or not the interests in the adventure are insured. The peril need not be present at the time of the GA act but it must be imminent. For example, a shipowner could claim as GA an extraordinary expense incurred to avoid being exposed to, say, a hurricane wind that is bearing down on the ship. However, the peril must be factual. This was illustrated in the case of "Watson -v- Fireman`s Fund Ins Co of San Francisco" (1922). The ship was a coal burning vessel. She had a cracked smokestack from which smoke from the furnace leaked, seeping through the cargo and issuing from a deck hatchway. The master, seeing the smoke, thought the ship was on fire and ordered water to be poured into the hold. The court held that there could be no GA act because there was no peril in fact. No account was taken of the good intentions of the master because fear of a peril does not constitute a peril.

To preserve from peril - The purpose of the GA act is to save the adventure. Therefore, no matter how well intentioned, any sacrifice made or expenditure incurred which does not achieve this end cannot be general average. In principle, the adventure is saved when the ship reaches a place of safety but, in practice, many factors have to be taken into consideration in applying this principle. For example, suppose a ship was in peril and the master sacrificed 100 packages from a cargo consignment of 500 packages as a GA act. The ship reached safety but became a total loss later with the remaining 400 packages still on board. The sacrificed 100 packages would be disallowed in a GA adjustment because they were already destined for loss with the rest of the cargo before completion of the adventure (ie before final delivery at the end of the voyage). Similarly, if the total loss had not occurred but 150 of the saved packages failed to arrive at the final destination only the 250 packages left would contribute towards any GA fund.

In this respect, it is interesting to contrast the rules for general average with the rules for salvage. In the latter case, once the property is brought to a place of safety the salvage act is deemed to have been completed and the saved interests must contribute on the saved values at such place. Where GA is concerned the matter is not resolved until the ship completes the voyage and discharges the cargo at its intended destination port. An exception occurs when the voyage is abandoned (eg because the ship is too badly damaged to continue) when the place of abandonment is deemed to be the final port for GA purposes.

2. Carrier`s Responsibility for Sacrificed Goods

Comment has been made earlier in Section 14 regarding the carrier`s liability under the contract of carriage so we shall not dwell further on that subject in this Section. Suffice to say that the carrier of goods has a responsibility to maintain, so far as it is within his control, the safety of the adventure. In practice, of course, this responsibility is delegated to the master, officers and crew of the ship and international maritime law, based on the Hague/Visby Rules and/or the Hamburg Rules, protects the carrier from liability where loss or damage to cargo in his care is caused by circumstances outside his control or by the master, officers or crew without the carrier`s actual fault or privity.

However, the protections afforded by the laws relating to the carriage of goods do not necessarily apply to circumstances where cargo is deliberately sacrificed. Nor is limitation of liability allowed where loss or damage results from "an act or omission of the carrier done with intent to cause damage, or recklessly with knowledge that damage would probably result". It follows that, where the carrier cannot avail himself of any of the immunities allowed in law, he remains responsible to make good the value of the sacrificed goods to the owner thereof; and, further, he would probably be unable to limit his liability. In such case, his only recourse is to prove a GA loss; whereby he reduces his liability to the amount of his GA contribution.

Where the carrier incurs costs to pursue the voyage he must bear these expenses himself. If he can prove the costs to be GA expenditure he can have them included in the GA fund from which he will be reimbursed when the adjustment is finally completed. Having contributed himself to the GA fund he will be, in effect, bearing his proportion of the expenditure.

3. General Average Procedure at Port of Discharge

The onus is on the carrier to prove general average and to institute proceedings to recover contributions, from those who benefit from the GA loss, to make good the loss to the owner of the sacrificed property and/or to reimburse himself for GA expenditure. To this end the carrier declares the ship as "under average" when she enters port to discharge to goods belonging to the contributing interests. The carrier is entitled to exercise a maritime lien on the goods discharged and to place these in store pending discharge of the lien. The storage (warehouse) costs, so incurred, will be added to the GA fund to be made good by the contributing parties.

The carrier appoints an average adjuster to administer the details of the GA adjustment; the adjusters fees also being added to the GA fund. A general average agreement is drawn up (in English practice this is termed a GA bond; although the term "GA bond" when used in the USA can refer to a GA guarantee - see below). Except where he is disputing the circumstances of the GA loss, in which case the matter may go to court, the consignee signs the agreement as one of the conditions for release of his goods. By signing the GA agreement the consignee undertakes to abide by the decisions of the average adjuster and to pay the GA contribution which will become due from him when the GA adjustment has been completed. Where the carrier has incurred GA expenditure the agreement might permit him to draw on the GA fund before completion of the adjustment; although, in practice, this can be implemented only where adequate GA deposits, if any, have been made to support the withdrawal.

4. Discharging the Carrier's Lien on Goods

In theory, the carrier's lien is not discharged until the GA adjustment has been completed and the consignee has paid the GA contribution. At one time the adjustment of general average could take many years (some involved cases have been known to take as long as 10 years); but modern communications and streamlined practices have improved the procedure so that one sees adjustments settled much earlier these days. Nevertheless, there is still a period of time during which the consignee is deprived of free access to and disposal of his goods and, whilst such period might not affect the condition of some goods, the delay could seriously affect the condition of others. In any event the consignee, usually, wants to take delivery as soon as possible to avoid, perhaps costly, delays in his trading pattern.

Subject to acceptance by the carrier, the consignee can obtain early discharge of the carrier's lien by any of the following procedures -

(a) *Cash deposit* - A cash deposit will be acceptable to the average adjuster; who determines the amount of the deposit. The deposit will need to be sufficient to cover the eventual GA contribution. Deposits are placed in a special joint account in the names of the carrier and average adjuster; any interest accruing being credited to the GA fund and the depositor receiving interest at an agreed rate when the final adjustment is made. The depositor is given a GA deposit receipt which (except where an underwriter or bank demands the receipt in return for funding the deposit) is kept with the documents of title to the goods and passed on with any transfer of title to the goods. On completion of the GA adjustment the holder of the receipt is entitled to draw on the GA fund for any balance of the deposit not absorbed by the GA contribution.

(b) *General average guarantee* - Rather than pay a GA deposit it is more customary for the consignee to offer the carrier a GA guarantee to discharge the lien and obtain release of his goods. The carrier is unlikely to accept a guarantee from the consignee himself. One would, however, expect a carrier to accept a GA guarantee from any of the following -

(1) A well known merchant bank;
(2) A bonding insurance company;
(3) The underwriter who insured the goods during the voyage.

A merchant bank will usually be prepared to guarantee a good client`s liability for a general average contribution. This is probably the most acceptable form of guarantee because it is not likely to be qualified in any way. The consignee is still liable to pay the contribution when it falls due; but, should he fail to meet this obligation (eg through insolvency), the average adjuster will turn to the bank for settlement.

A bonding company is an insurance company which specialises in selling bonds (or guarantees). The consignee pays a premium to buy the guarantee. The consignee is still liable to pay the contribution when it falls due; but, should he fail to meet this obligation (eg through insolvency), the average adjuster will turn to the bonding company for settlement.

A guarantee from the underwriter who insured the goods is acceptable only if it is unqualified. An underwriter might not be happy to give an unqualified guarantee; preferring to limit the guarantee to only the amount of the contribution that is recoverable under the policy. By reference to the notes in Section 16 it will be seen that, unless the policy otherwise provides, the underwriter is not liable for a GA contribution when the GA loss was incurred in connection with an uninsured peril or an excluded peril. Further, the underwriter`s liability can be reduced if the goods are not insured for their full contributory value. At one time it was common for cargo underwriters to give a full guarantee in exchange for a counter guarantee; whereby the assured agreed to reimburse the underwriter for any amount of the contribution not covered by the policy. This practice might still exist in other markets but it fell into disuse in the London market when it became apparent that the long tail nature of GA settlements made it difficult to enforce counter guarantees. The problem is resolved, to some extent, in modern practice by use of the "GA in full" clause (see Part 9, below) in cargo insurance contracts. Where an underwriter`s guarantee is accepted by the carrier the average adjuster by passes the consignee and goes straight to the underwriter for settlement.

5. Introduction to the York/Antwerp Rules

General average is a maritime practice which is subject to Rules. Where nothing appears in the contract of carriage, regarding the adjustment of general average, the adjustment will be based on the law & practice of the country in which the adventure terminates. English law and practice, in this respect, is embodied in the average, in those early days. Apart from this voluntary code there was little to guide practitioners in the implementation and adjustment of general average and each country established its own laws and practice in this respect.

Even today, if nothing appears in the contract of carriage regarding the adjustment of general average, the adjustment will be based on the law & practice of the country in which the adventure terminates. English law and practice, in this respect, is embodied in the Rules of Practice of the Association of Average Adjusters. These Rules cover many aspects of an average adjuster's function; embracing Rules for, in addition to the treatment of general average, the treatment of damage and repairs to ship and particular average on goods. The Rules of Practice are subject to amendment from time to time; the latest amendment being in 1992. Interested trainees and practitioners can find the 1992 Rules in "Marine Insurance - Volume 3 - Hull Practice" by Brown (Witherby 1993).

Following international conferences to reach agreement between carriers and cargo owners on uniformity in the treatment of general average, a set of Rules was drafted during the latter part of the 19th century. These, known as the "York/Antwerp Rules (1890)", were not intended for embodiment in Statutes so were not subject to ratification by any State. The Rules were made available for embodiment in contracts of carriage if the parties to the contract so agreed. They found favour with most carriers and it became a, more or less, general practice for contracts of carriage to incorporate the Y/A Rules.

Over the years various amendments have been made to the Y/A Rules with new sets of Rules being issued when the amendments so justified. The last set of Rules to be issued is the York/Antwerp Rules 1974; but even these are subject to a 1990 amendment. Where these Rules are implemented it is an accepted practice to apply the *current* set of Rules to an adjustment; even where the bill of lading (or other contract of carriage) refers to earlier sets of Rules. Marine insurance underwriters, also, accept that the current Y/A rules will apply to adjustments affecting claims under the policy. Further, in some cases, hull underwriters also apply the Y/A rules to settlements relating to services in the nature of salvage where no GA applies.

At this introductory stage of study it is not necessary for trainees to be familiar with the content of the Y/A Rules but an outline of their structure could be useful. The Y/A Rules (1974) comprise:

(1) A rule of interpretation
(2) Lettered rules A to G
(3) Numbered rules 1 to 22

The rule of interpretation provides that, in determining a case of general average, one shall first have regard for the numbered rules. The numbered rules are concerned, amongst other things, with defining general average in relation to specific circumstances. If the circumstances being considered are not embraced within the numbered rules, regard shall be had for the principles of a general average loss as set out in the lettered rules.

It will be recalled that Rule A defines general average and sets out the essentials therefor; comment on these being shown in Part 1, above.

6. Rules for Calculating General Average Contributions

General average adjustments take a long time to prepare. The average adjuster must accumulate an enormous amount of information; with the result that the file containing the adjustment is a complicated and involved document in most cases. No attempt will be made in these introductory notes to explain the details of a GA adjustment but the trainee should understand the basics of a GA adjustment as a background to practical marine insurance knowledge. Trainees and practitioners seeking more detailed information are advised to consult "Marine Insurance Claims" by Goodacre (Witherby).

The average adjuster operates on a principle which intends to ensure that each party who has derived benefit from a GA loss shall contribute in relation to such benefit to make good the loss suffered by the aggrieved party. Once it has been established that the circumstances justify a GA adjustment the average adjuster follows a basic procedure.

The first stage is to establish the amount to be made good. If it is cargo that has been sacrificed the adjuster must obtain documentation to show the value of the cargo sacrificed. In principle, one assesses the value sacrificed cargo would have had at the place where the adventure would have terminated for those goods; but, in practice, where it is sacrifice of a whole consignment, complications can be avoided by using invoice values where it is practical so to do. If the GA sacrifice relates to the ship, that is, a part of the ship (eg an anchor and chain) has been sacrificed or the hull and/or machinery has been deliberately damaged in the GA act, the average adjuster must obtain documentation covering the reasonable cost of replacing the sacrificed part or repairing the damage caused by the GA act. Where freight at risk is involved in the adventure the average adjuster must determine the amount of freight attaching to the sacrificed cargo to which the freight relates. Where the ship operator has incurred expenditure the average adjuster must determine how much shall be allowed as general average expenditure and/or GA disbursements. When all this information is to hand the amount of the GA fund can be established:

Example:

Cargo sacrificed	£100,000
GA damage to ship	80,000
GA expenditure/disbursements	20,000
Amount to be made good	£200,000

The second stage is to establish the values that must contribute to make good the amount of the fund. These are termed *contributory values*. There are various rules applied in establishing contributory values; but they all have the object of making sure that everyone who benefits from the GA act shall contribute and that the apportionment shall be fair. For example, when calculating the contributory value of saved goods based on the damaged "arrived" value one must not forget that any amount made good in respect of the goods constitutes a "benefit" to the party with the interest therein; so the "made good" must also contribute. Similarly, where the a whole consignment has been sacrificed the value of that consignment, being "made good", must contribute. Where the contributory value of the ship is based on the saved (unrepaired) value of the ship, the cost of repairing damage to be made good in general average must also contribute.

The illustrations below show the the calculations necessary to arrive at the contributory value of each interest and the apportionment thereto of the GA fund above. For illustration purposes a further consignment of cargo, not affected by the GA losses, has been incorporated in the illustrations. Consignment 1 suffered a partial loss caused by the GA sacrifice, shown above, and had a damaged "arrived" value of

£1,400,000. To this must be added the "made good" of £100,000; to arrive at the contributory value of £1,500,000. Consignment 2 was undamaged and had a sound "arrived" value of £4,000,000. The ship had a saved (unrepaired) value of £4,420,000, having suffered damage which cost £580,000 to repair; including the GA damage (£80,000) as shown above. In principle, the "made good" must be added to the unrepaired value to arrive at a fair contributory value of £4,500,000; but the illustration (whilst arriving at the same contributory value) takes into account the sound value of the ship and the cost of repairing PA damage. It should be noted that, although PA (particular average) is a marine insurance term, in this context it embraces *all* damage, other than GA damage, some of which might not be insured. Further, it should be noted that, although the GA expenditure was incurred by the shipowner this has nothing to do with the "value" of the ship so is not to be taken into account in calculating the ship's contributory value. Nor does GA expenditure contribute towards the GA fund.

The following illustration shows the contributory value of each saved interest and the apportionment of the above GA fund thereto:

Interest					*Contribution*
Ship					
Sound value		£5,000,000			
Less repairs PA	£500,000				
GA	80,000	580,000			
		£4,420,000			
Add "made good"		80,000			
Contributory value			£ 4,500,000	pays 2%	£ 90,000
Consignment 1					
Arrived value		£1,400,000			
Add "made good"		100,000			
Contributory value			£ 1,500,000	pays 2%	£ 30,000
Consignment 2					
Arrived value		£4,000,000			
Contributory value			£ 4,000,000	pays 2%	£ 80,000
		Totals	£10,000,000	pays 2%	£200,000

7. Underwriters' Liability for GA Sacrifice

Whilst neither the SG form nor the MIA, 1906, actually state that general average sacrifice is covered by a marine insurance policy it has always been the practice to embrace general average sacrifice in the cover where the GA act has been incurred in consequence of the operation of an insured peril. In modern practice cargo policies specifically state that GA sacrifice is covered (ref. ICC, 1982, B and C conditions) and the ITC (1983) refer to cover for GA sacrifice, as do both sets of the ITC (1994). However, it should be noted that limited terms hull policies do not cover GA sacrifice; even where the policy conditions extend the cover to embrace GA contributions; nor do hull interest disbursements and increased value policies incorporate cover for GA sacrifice.

Where the policy covers GA sacrifice section 64(4) of the MIA, 1906, allows the assured to claim directly on the underwriter for an insured loss caused by GA sacrifice. The assured does not need to wait for the GA adjustment to be completed to claim from the GA fund to make good his loss. He can pursue a claim under his policy and leave the underwriter to exercise his subrogation rights to recover the amount of the claim paid under the policy from the GA fund. Except where the policy provides otherwise this rule applies to both sacrifice of ship and sacrifice of goods.

The measure of indemnity for GA sacrifice is the same as for PA loss or damage. Where cargo claims are concerned one calculates a percentage of depreciation and applies this to the sum insured (see Section 12). Where hull insurance is concerned the measure of indemnity is the reasonable cost of replacing the sacrificed part or repairing the damage (see Section 12). Section 69 of the MIA, 1906, applies the, so called, customary deductions to hull claims for GA sacrifice, but underwriters waive these deductions by the "new for old" clause in hull policy conditions (see Section 12); nevertheless, hull claims for GA sacrifice are still subject to the policy deductible (see section 4).

8. Underwriters` Liability for GA Disbursements

The term "GA disbursements" refers to expenditure incurred by a ship operator in connection with a general average act. There is no direct liability on the hull underwriter to reimburse the assured for GA disbursements but section 66(4) of the MIA, 1906, allows the assured to recover from his underwriter that proportion of GA expenditure which falls upon him. This means that, unlike the position where GA sacrifice is concerned (see Part 7, above), an assured who has incurred expenditure pursuant to a GA act cannot claim this directly from his underwriter. Nevertheless, insofar as he is liable for a GA contribution (see Part 9, below), the underwriter is liable for that part of the contribution which represents the GA disbursements. To illustrate this consider the GA expenditure of £20,000 in Part 6, above. The ship operator`s contribution to GA, based on 2% of the ship`s contributory value, was £90,000. The GA expenditure incorporated therein was 10% = £9,000. No separate claim attaches to the policy for the £20,000 GA disbursements but this will be recovered by the ship operator when the GA fund is apportioned at the completion of the GA adjustment. The assured`s GA contribution will incorporate £9,000 of the expenditure and, subject to underinsurance and application of the policy deductible (see Part 9, below), the underwriter will, in settling his liability for GA contribution, be, effectively, bearing this part of the GA disbursements.

Where the circumstances turn out *not* to be general average, unless he can prove a separate claim for salvage charges or for sue & labour charges, the assured cannot recover his disbursements from insurance cover. It is for this reason ship operators are advised to effect separate insurance cover for GA disbursements (eg expenses relating to salvage services, towage, etc.) when operations in relation thereto are about to be undertaken.

9. Underwriters` Liability for GA Contributions

Except in the case of GA sacrifice there is no direct liability on the underwriter for GA losses. Accordingly, the underwriter is not obliged to pay a GA deposit; although, in practice, one frequently hears of cargo underwriters refunding a GA deposit paid by the assured to obtain release of his goods from the carrier. Further, there is no obligation on the cargo underwriter to give a guarantee of payment for a

GA contribution; although it is common practice for cargo underwriters to provide (perhaps qualified) guarantees so that the assured can obtain release of his goods from the carrier. Strictly speaking the underwriter`s liability is, subject to the comments below, for the contribution eventually levied against the assured on completion of the GA adjustment.

Section 66(6) of the MIA, 1906, provides that, except where the policy specifies otherwise, the insurer is not liable for a GA contribution where the loss was not incurred for the purpose of, or in connection with, the avoidance of a peril insured against. Hull policy conditions uphold this rule but cargo underwriters partly waive it, in that they apply the rule only where the peril is specifically excluded by the policy. For example, where a cargo policy is effected on ICC (1982) C conditions and the GA loss is incurred in connection with the avoidance of the entry of seawater into a hold the claim for GA contribution would be allowed; even though entry of seawater is not a peril covered by the C conditions. On the other hand, if the entry of seawater was caused by an excluded peril (eg a torpedo striking the carrying vessel; this being subject to the war exclusion clause) no claim for GA contribution would attach to the policy.

Section 73(1) of the MIA, 1906, provides that a claim for a GA contribution shall be liable to reduction in proportion to any underinsurance illustrated by comparing the insured value with the contributory value.

This is upheld by the standard cargo clauses (eg ICC, 1982), except where the contract incorporates a "GA in full" clause. Using the figures in the apportionment for consignment 1 in Part 6, above, the following illustrates the position where no such clause appears in the cargo insurance contract:

Consignment 1 -	Contributory value £1,500,000 pays 2%	£30,000
	Insured value £1,300,000 pays 2%	£26,000

Where the cargo insurance contract incorporates a "GA in full" clause the underinsurance is ignored and the underwriter`s liability is for the full contribution. It should be noted that, whereas a "GA in full" clause waives underinsurance, it does not take precedence over the condition that a contribution towards a GA loss incurred in connection with an excluded peril is not recoverable under the cargo policy.

The provision in the MIA, 1906, regarding underinsurance is strictly upheld in hull insurance. In the following example it will be noted that PA damage is deducted from the insured value of the ship when making the comparison to determine underinsurance. This is a provision of section 73(1) of the MIA, 1906, and is confirmed in the ITC (1983) and similar sets of H & M conditions. In the following example the GA contribution illustrated earlier is applied to a hull policy with an insured value of £4,500,000 and a deductible of £50,000:

Ship Contributory value and GA contribution

Sound value		£5,000,000
Less repairs	PA £500,000	
	GA 80,000	580,000
		£4,420,000
Add "made good"		80,000
Contributory value		£4,500,000
	pays 2%	£90,000

Policy Claim

Insured value	£4,500,000	
Less PA	500,000	
	£4,000,000 pays	£80,000
Less policy deductible		50,000*
		£30,000

*In practice the deductible would not apply, having been already absorbed by the direct PA and GA sacrifice claim

SELF STUDY QUESTIONS

The following questions should be answered without reference to the text:

1. What is the purpose of a general average act?

2. What is the difference between each of the following categories -
   (a) General average sacrifice?
   (b) General average disbursements?
   (c) General average contribution?

3. What is the position of a carrier who is unable to prove general average?

4. What procedure is adopted by the carrier to implement a GA adjustment and enforce contribution by the parties who benefit thereby?

5. What is a GA deposit? Is a cargo underwriter liable for a GA deposit?

6. What is a GA guarantee? When will a ship operator *not* accept a GA guarantee?

7. What is "made good"? How does it affect contributory values?

8. Can a hull assured claim directly from his underwriter for an insured loss caused by -
   (1) a GA sacrifice? (2) GA disbursements?

9. To what extent does underinsurance affect a claim for GA contribution under
   (1) a hull policy? (2) a cargo policy?

10. What are the York/Antwerp Rules? What Rules are applied to general average when the Y/A Rules are not incorporated in the contract of carriage?

CONCLUSION

This study has been an introduction to marine insurance principles and practice. Experience has shown that a sound knowledge of technical insurance is essential to competent practice for both underwriters and brokers. Personnel who have satisfactorily completed this study are strongly advised to continue with more advanced courses and to consult the books on technical marine insurance recommended in the text.